THE SELSEY TRAMWAY

VOLUME ONE

BY
LAURIE A. COOKSEY

WILD SWAN PUBLICATIONS

© Wild Swan Publications Ltd. and Laurie A. Cooksey 2006
ISBN 1-905184-15-8

Chichester (I) *at Selsey c.1911.*

Designed by Paul Karau
Printed by Amadeus Press, Cleckheaton

**Published by
WILD SWAN PUBLICATIONS LTD.**
1-3 Hagbourne Road, Didcot, Oxon, OX11 8DP

CONTENTS

Introduction	1
Chapter One GETTING STARTED (1886-1897)	5
Chapter Two A PROMISING BEGINNING (1897-1909)	17
Chapter Three MAN MAKES PLANS & GOD LAUGHS (1910-1912)	51
Chapter Four THOUGHTS OF EXPANSION (1913-1919)	69
Chapter Five COMPLETELY OFF THE RAILS (1920-1923)	91
Chapter Six A CHANGE OF NAME (1923-1924)	113
Chapter Seven THE SLIPPERY DOWNWARD SLIDE (1925-1934)	121
Chapter Eight CLOSURE, SALE & WINDING UP (1935-1947)	155
Chapter Nine GONE BUT NOT FORGOTTEN.	175
Appendix 1 — Passenger totals and passenger receipts	179
Appendix 1A — Table of fares — 1897	179
Appendix 2 — Balance sheet for year ending 31st December 1918	180
Appendix 3 — Goods tonnages for years 1913 and 1919	180
Appendix 4 — Catalogue of surplus railway plant sold by auction	181
Appendix 5 — Goods and parcels rates	185
Appendix 6 — Pullman cars known to have travelled over the Selsey Tramway	186
Appendix 7 — Manual staff known to have worked on the Selsey Tramway	186
Bibliography	188
Acknowledgements	188

(197) AT CHICHESTER

INTRODUCTION

'SELSEY – the Island of seals – the most southerly point of the county of Sussex, familiar to every English schoolboy as Selsey Bill[1] has been called Selsey-on-Sea. It might be called Selsey 'at Sea'. For this reason, Selsey is as much 'at sea' as a yacht is anchored a mile from the shore. It is rather more 'at sea' by virtue of the fact that the sea once surrounded it, making it an island. Also, the sea is still on three sides of it, leaving its shores, sending soft and gentle, health-giving breezes across its lovely fields and commons.

'If you want to enjoy the most delightful sea air that the south coast of England can give, go to Selsey and breathe it. There you will get the ozone of the ocean, pure and unadulterated. Straight off the rippling blue waves it comes, bringing hope and joy, and a monstrous big appetite to jaded work-wearied man.'

This was the *Daily Mail*'s introduction to a long and detailed article praising the then mainly undiscovered fledgling seaside resort of Selsey in 1907, ten years after the Selsey Tramway had brought its first passengers to the village. Today, the village of Selsey lies at the foot of the Manhood[2] Peninsula that stretches south from the coastal plain close to the city of Chichester, but in the distant past it would have occupied a more central position. The peninsula is part of the Bracklesham Beds formed an estimated 50 to 42 million years ago, which are made up of sandy clays, some soft stone and loose sand. These materials offer little resistance to the constant pounding of the sea and as much as between three and eight feet are lost beneath the waves every year.

Following the Roman Conquest, Chichester was founded astride the Havant to Portslade road, after which it quickly became the local capital. Occupying an area of around 90 acres within its defensive walls, Chichester probably had a population of around 2,000 in the second century, but this would more than likely have declined over the following 200 years. It was the Romans who built the great straight way, Stane Street, to link Chichester (Roman name Noviomagus – 'Newmarket') directly with the new commercial centre of Britain, Londinium (London) 56½ miles away, or 55 miles 'as the crow flies'.

Aella, a Saxon warrior, together with his three sons, is believed to have landed at Cymenes-ora[3] (the shore of Cymen) near the southern tip of the Selsey Peninsula in the year 457, but the first exact record of a Saxon landing in Sussex is twenty years later in 477. Under Saxon rule, by the end of the 5th century Stane Street and other highways had been abandoned and the whole of Sussex had become cut off from the rest of the country by the great wealden forest known as Andredswald, (the forest of Anderida) in which wolves, wild boar and deer roamed. At 120 miles long by 30 miles wide, it stretched all the way from Kent to Hampshire.

Selsey first came to prominence as the place where Christianity came to Sussex. Having been expelled from his native Northumbria, Wilfrid (634–709), Bishop of York, headed south (probably at the invitation of Ethelwald, King of Sussex, who was already a Christian) and he arrived at the village in 681. There he found the pagan inhabitants suffering from a long drought and famine where 'bands of men would leap from the cliffs into the sea rather than face death from starvation'. Although the rivers and sea were full of fish, the people had only lines to catch eels. Having joined a number of these lines together, Wilfrid went out into the sea with them and returned with a large catch of fish. His teaching was now listened to readily and the people were converted to Christianity almost in a body. It is said that on the very day that Wilfrid baptised them, it rained and the drought was ended.[4] King Ethelwald granted 87 hides of land[5] to Wilfrid, a charter dated 683 naming Selsey, Medmerry, Wittering, Itchenor, Birdham and Sidlesham on the Selsey Peninsula, among other more distant villages. One of Bishop Wilfrid's first acts was to construct a cathedral and monastery which became the centre of the South Saxon diocese and by the end of the seventh century, and for the next two hundred years, Selsey became one of the most important places in Sussex and, culturally the most important.

In the 10th century the territorial division known as the 'Hundred' came into being, the Hundred of Manhood covering the whole of the Selsey Peninsula. Whether the term originally derived from a measurement of land, or by population is not clear, but each Hundred became important as a local court of justice. The boundaries ran (in modern terms) from the entrance of Selsey (or Pagham) Harbour, round the coast to the entrance to Chichester (now West Wittering) then up to the stream dividing Birdham from Appledram, then eastwards to 'Wayflete', then in a circuit to Jury Lane, then eastwards to Dammer-Gate and along the ditch now known as the Bremere Rife which runs south into Selsey Harbour.[6]

King William (the Conqueror) gave to his chaplain, Stigand, 'the bishopric of the South Saxons' in 1070, but he was destined to be the last of an unbroken line of 24 Bishops of Selsey as, following the Norman policy of moving sees[7] from rural areas to the towns, the See of Selsey was transferred to Chichester just five years later. Another factor in this particular case may have been the rapidly encroaching sea and Wilfrid's cathedral and monastery would eventually be lost under the waves.

The Domesday Book of 1086 described Chichester as having 160 houses and three crofts.[8] Compared to the city in Roman times there were fewer houses, but these would have been sited roughly along the lines of the four Roman streets which met where the Market Cross was later built in 1501. Selsey consisted of 10 hides of land, but the Island formed part of the larger Hundred of Manhood, whose manor house was sited just to the north of Sidlesham church. Work on constructing Chichester Cathedral began in 1088, but it was a full 57 years before it was completed, the only ancient English cathedral visible from the sea.[9] Local tradition has it that the many fine oak trees that made up the densely wooded shores of Pagham Harbour were cut down to provide timber for the construction of the cathedral.

The 1¾ mile long Chichester Canal was built as a branch off the ill-fated Portsmouth–Arun Canal that had opened to traffic in 1823. Thirty-two years later the section eastwards beyond Hunston was virtually abandoned and the Company was wound up in 1888, the section from Birdham Lock to Chichester later being acquired by the City Corporation. In this tranquil scene looking northwards towards the Canal Basin in Chichester, a young lad is seen feeding the swans close to the Old Bridge at South Bank, overlooked by the cathedral and its impressive spire in the distance.

WSCC LIBRARY SERVICE

INTRODUCTION

By the middle of the 16th century Selsey cockles had become highly regarded for their excellence, as witnessed in March 1538 when William, Earl of Southampton, wrote to Thomas Cromwell, (Henry VIII's main agent in the Dissolution of the Monasteries in 1536 and 1539) 'I have sent you by bearer certain Celsey (sic) cockles. No doubt you are daily furnished with them by my Lord of Chichester, who is lord of the soil where they be had'. The Bishop was not to be 'lord of the soil' there for much longer, and William Barlow, consecrated in 1559, was to be the last of 42 Episcopal lords of Selsey manor before Queen Elizabeth 1st passed an Act which severed it from the See of Chichester two years later. Thereafter, Selsey fell into the hands of lay proprietors.

The Isle of Selsey was connected to the mainland by two fords, the Horseway and, to the east, the Wadeway, along with a ferry close to the latter. An investigation was made in 1665 into reclaiming 900 acres of land between Selsey and the mainland by the building of a sea wall, but the scheme, like so many before it, came to nought. Between 1805 and 1809 a strong bank some 502 yards long did get constructed on the site of the old Wadeway, resulting in 312 acres of land being reclaimed from the sea, which became farmland.

Owing to a countrywide shortage of corn during the Napoleonic Wars, many of the remaining trees on the Manhood Peninsula were removed to make the maximum use of the land for the growing of crops. With the Wars over, recession set in, so to provide employment and make it cheaper and easier to transport agricultural machinery and products, a canal was built from Birdham in Chichester Harbour to join the River Arun at Ford to the south of Arundel which opened in 1823. It was then possible to travel by rivers and canals from West Sussex to London, East Anglia and the industrial north as well as to the west country. The canal was never a success and it was virtually abandoned by 1855, except for the section from Birdham Lock to near Hunston and the 1¾ mile branch from there north to the Chichester Basin which was later acquired by the City Corporation.

Over the centuries the shingle bank at the eastern end of Pagham Harbour had been gradually increasing in length from 1,445 yards in 1672 to 1,540 yards in 1774 and from 1776 yards in 1823 to 2,260 yards in 1852. A detailed survey made on the authority of the Harbour Department of the Admiralty in that year revealed that 68 vessels entered the harbour annually, carrying an average of 25 tons each, usually coal and grain for Sidlesham Tide Mill. A Reclamation Company deposited plans in 1865, but it was not until 1873 that the Pagham Harbour Reclamation Act was passed 'to Authorise the construction of Works and Reclamation of lands in Pagham Harbour' with a capital of £48,000. A Sea Bank 407 yards long was built from near the old coastguard house at Pagham to Selsey Beach which completely shut off the sea, thus reclaiming over 700 acres of land. After drainage, part of the reclaimed area was retained by the company, but 318 acres that belonged to the Crown were sold to Mr. Frederick William Grafton in 1877. A year later Mr. Grafton purchased the manor at Selsey. The rich, alluvial mud was to yield good crops of barley and corn on the eastern side, and lush grazing meadows to the west.

Then, just as today, only one winding road connected Selsey with Chichester, passing through the villages of Sidlesham and Hunston on the way. The more wealthy could travel the route by pony and trap, but the less fortunate had to either walk or hitch a ride on one of several carriers' carts (4 carriers were listed in *Pike's Directory* of 1886) or the more wealthy could travel by pony and trap. One of these carriers was Mr. William Fidler who would pick up passengers and goods at The Neptune public house in Selsey at 9am for the two hour journey to Chichester. The return trip would be made at 4.00pm.[10]

With little civil engineering work required, and keeping to the centre of the coastal plain, back on 8th June 1846 the London, Brighton & South Coast Railway's 'West Coast Line' arrived at Chichester from Brighton. It was extended westwards to Portsmouth a year later, and branches to the neighbouring growing seaside resorts of Littlehampton and Bognor were opened in August 1863 and June 1864 respectively, followed by Hayling Island in July 1867. If Selsey was to develop into a popular seaside resort, a railway was required to connect the village to the rest of the country.

Notes

1. The Island of Selsey probably got its name following the stranding of a seal there once upon a time, rather than their regular presence in the area. Selsey Bill was first named as such on Philip Overton's Map of Sussex in 1740, and it has been suggested that the headland was so called in imitation of Portland Bill further along the coast to the west.
2. Manhood comes from the Saxon 'maene wudu', which means common wood. Today there are few trees on the Selsey Peninsula.
3. Some historians suggest that it is quite likely that the Owers Rocks, now several miles south of the present coast of the Selsey Peninsula, were part of the Saxon shore in AD457, and that they were the bank on which the South Saxons first landed. To protect shipping, a light vessel has been moored near the Owers by Trinity House since 1788.
4. *The King's England – Sussex* (7th Impression) by Arthur Mee, published by Hodder & Stoughton, London 1956.
5. In the 7th century a hide was a unit of land measurement, approximately 120 acres, each hide being considered enough land to support one family.
6. These boundaries coincided exactly with those recorded almost 600 years later in a charter of Henry VIII dated 1525.
7. See = an Episcopal unit.
8. A croft was an enclosed piece of (usually arable) land.
9. *The King's England – Sussex* as above. J. R. Armstrong in *History of Sussex* published by Phillimore & Co. Ltd. in 1978 quotes Chichester Cathedral as having been built between 1076 and 1140.
10. *Chichester Observer*, 12.3.1965, 80 year old Charles Fidler reminiscing in an article in the newspaper's series entitled 'Colourful History of Selsey'.

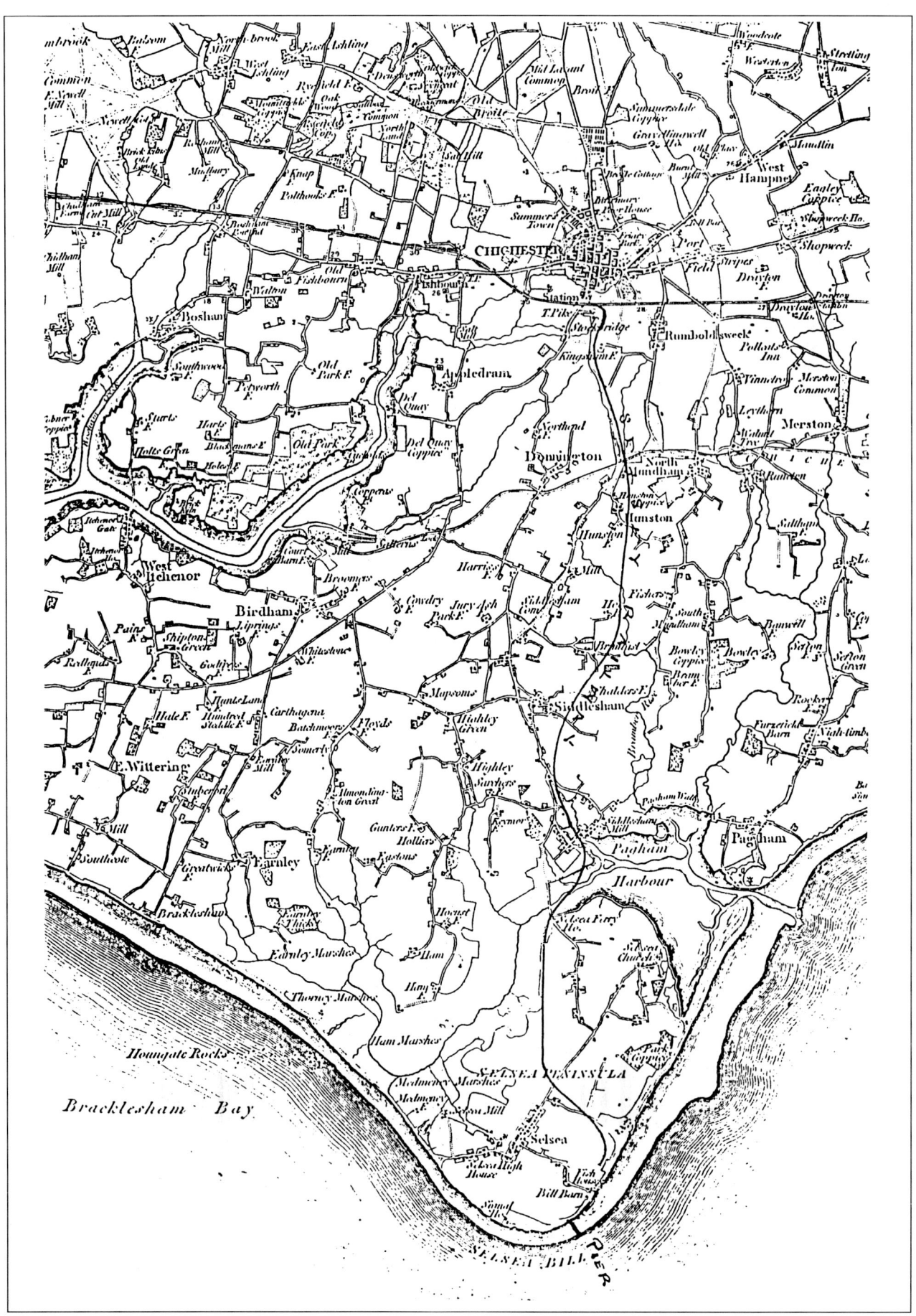

The route map of the proposed Selsey Railway & Pier Company, November 1887. Note how the route would have paralleled the eastern side of the Chichester Canal out of the City and that the Selsea (sic) terminus would have been much closer to the sea shore than the Tramway when it was built in 1897.

WEST SUSSEX RECORD OFFICE

CHAPTER ONE
GETTING STARTED (1886–1897)

IN 1887 Selsey was nothing more than a primitive fishing village consisting of a coastguard station and a ramshackle mass of tumble-down fishermen's huts set up behind a beach littered with boats of all sizes and the typical untidy paraphernalia that is all part and parcel of a busy fishing community. The population of the village was considerably less than 1,000, yet on the 15th November of that year, notice was given that application was intended to be made to Parliament in the 1888 Session for The Selsey Railway & Pier Act.

> 'To incorporate a Railway Company (hereinafter called 'The Company') and to empower the Company to make and maintain the railway and pier or landing stage, and other works hereinafter described, with all necessary stations, sidings, approaches, works and conveniences connected therewith, that is to say:–
>
> 'A railway commencing in the parish of St. Bartholemew, Chichester, in the county of Sussex, by a junction of the main line of the London, Brighton and South Coast Railway at a point 2 chains or thereabouts to the east of the signal-box on the south-east end of Chichester station platform, and terminating in the parish of Selsey, in the same county, at a point 2 chains or thereabouts north-east of the Selsey Coastguard Station, and 7 chains or thereabouts north-west of high water mark, which said intended railway will pass from and into and be situated in the several parishes of Saint Bartholemew, Hunston, North Mundham, Sidlesham and Selsey, all in the county of Sussex.
>
> 'A pier or landing stage commencing in the parish of Selsey, in the county of Sussex, on the north-east shore of the English Channel, at a point 7 chains or thereabouts northeast of Beacon House, and 2 chains or thereabouts north-west of high water mark, and extending into the channel for a distance of 100 yards or thereabouts from high water mark.'

The railway was to be 7 miles, 7 furlongs and 2 chains long with a capital of £75,000 made up of 7,500 shares at £10 each, with powers to borrow a further amount not exceeding £24,000, whilst the works were to be completed within 5 years. William Gregory, CE of Hayling was to be the engineer, with Frederick William Grafton and Sir Charles Wm. Frederick Cranfield Bart as the first directors, along with three others to be nominated by them, qualification being 25 shares each. Fares would be set at 3d per mile First Class, 2d per mile Second Class and 1d per mile Third Class, and no more than three trains were to be run in each direction on Sundays.

On or before 30th November 1887, plans and sections of the intended railway and pier, an Ordnance map with the line of the railway delineated thereon and a book of reference of such plans had to be deposited for public inspection with the Clerk of the Peace for the county of Sussex in Lewes, and according to a hand-written note on the front of the latter by the clerk, F. Merrifield, they were lodged at his office at 4.00pm that very day. Printed copies of the intended Act were then to be deposited in the Private Bill Office of the House of Commons by 21st December 1887 but, strangely, nothing more was heard of the scheme.

Around 1893 'The Selsey Brake' began operating a daily service during the summer months between Chichester and Selsey, timings being arranged for convenient connections with mainline trains at Chichester for Portsmouth, Brighton and London.

The next mention of a railway came at a meeting of Chichester City Council on Friday, 8th March 1895, when a letter was submitted from E. B. Ivatts, latterly the manager of the neighbouring Lee-on-the-Solent Railway, asking for the approval of the Council for a light railway that he was promoting between Chichester and Selsey to be routed (as was the previous scheme) via the east side of the Chichester Canal. Mr. Prior proposed that the Council should record this, being that the proposed railway would be a great public advantage and that so far as the Council was concerned, it was prepared to assist in carrying out the scheme providing that the canal banks would not be damaged, and subject to

Prior to the arrival of the Tramway, Selsey was nothing more than a fishing village with a coastguard station. This timeless scene on the East Beach shows a couple of fishermen in front of their typical ramshackle wooden huts, some of which had thatched roofs. Crab and lobster pots are seen piled up on the left, and the barrels probably contained pitch or tar. WSCC LIBRARY SERVICE

Hunston's parish church of St. Ledger was built by A. W. Blomfield in 1855 and it is picturesquely situated at the end of a lane almost half a mile from the village, opposite a duck pond and the moated Manor House.
WSCC LIBRARY SERVICE

GETTING STARTED (1886–1897)

stipulations as to level crossings, etc. He believed that Mr. Ivatts was prepared to meet any reasonable wishes on the part of the Council.

Mr. Ivatts was present, and at the invitation of the Mayor, explained the general nature of the scheme:

> It is proposed to make the railway under a Board of Trade Order, which is the least costly method of seeking powers to build. From the district of Chichester to the point where the line would terminate near Manor Farm, Selsey, it is 7 miles, whilst the estimated cost of construction is £21,000, or £3,000 per mile.
>
> Alderman Caffyn: "Does that include the purchase of land?"
>
> Mr. Ivatts: "Yes, it includes everything. The gauge would be uniform with the Brighton line, and it is expected that a good deal of the goods carried over the two systems would be in Brighton railway wagons. I do not expect any opposition from the London, Brighton & South Coast Railway Company. I am in communication on the subject with the Company, and the Engineer wishes me to point out a desirable point of junction for the Selsey line with the Brighton line – no objection has been mooted by the Company. It is hoped that any remaining difficulties with owners of land on the Selsey railway route will soon be surmounted; there have been some, but these have been got over. All things are shaping themselves in a very satisfactory way, and if the Council passes a resolution as submitted, the projectors of the line will have an increased moral force. It is, no doubt, a direct line, whereby the people of Chichester and neighbourhood will be able to get to the sea in, say 20 minutes, and for the expenditure, probably of a shilling. It will be a very desirable thing; indeed it is surprising it has not been provided before, but it is bound to be an element of advancement for both Chichester and Selsey. It has also just been proposed that a branch of the new line should go from Sidlesham to near Birdham school and that it would be practical, and it might be included in the scheme. If the consent of all the land owners concerned could be obtained in time to lodge the plans by 30th June, I could get a Board of Trade Order by August. Capital might be got without difficulty, a third of it in the Chichester district perhaps, and the remainder in London, and the construction might begin next winter. The point of junction with the Brighton line is proposed to be by going round at the back of the gas works."[1]

The Mayor thought there would be no two opinions about the possibility of having a railway to Selsey as it would be good for trade and for the whole district. He agreed with Mr. Caffyn that a general purposes committee should deal with the matter, and Mr. Ivatt's proposition was then agreed to without dissent.

The Selsey Brake may not have welcomed the idea of the proposed new railway, but on 5th May 1895 the *Chichester Observer* gave it some useful publicity when it clumsily advised

THE SELSEY BRAKE

'This is now running every day for the season as for several years past and a more enjoyable drive in this part than that which has been had by those who have one morning or other taken seats in the conveyance could not be had: for Mr. L. Gould, the livery and post master of Little London Mews, is the proprietor of the Brake – a guarantee for comfort on the drive – and appearance of the country on the journey just now is charming and the air exhilarating.'

Selsey Parish Council, however, was keen to have a rail connection with the main network, and at their meeting two days later, enthusiastically proposed that 'a committee of five members should be appointed to help forward, in any way practicable, the present scheme for building a light railway from Chichester to Selsey, and to watch the progress of the Light Railway Bill now before the House of Commons and, should it receive Royal Assent, to secure at Selsey at the earliest possible date, the advantages it may provide, and take advantage of any other opportunity that may present itself of carrying out the object in view'.

From the beginning of June, The Selsey Brake was advertised to run as follows:

Daily:
Leaving The King's Head, South Street 11.20am
Leaving The Railway Inn, near Railway Station at 11.35am
(meeting 11.25 train from London and Brighton and 11.33 train from Portsmouth)
Returning from The Crown Inn, Selsey 6.30pm

Sundays:
Leaving The Railway Inn 2.30pm
Returning from The Crown Inn, Selsey 6.30pm

The return fare was two shillings, with children half price, but with the last weekly advertisement appearing in the *Chichester Observer* on 6th November 1895, it must be assumed that the service was withdrawn soon after that date.

Mr. Gould need not have worried about railway competition as the Board of Trade Order was not applied for, so construction of the proposed railway did not commence that winter, and the subject was not discussed again until a preliminary meeting was held at the Dolphin Hotel, Chichester on 11th March 1896, followed by a private meeting in the Council Chamber, Chichester on Monday, 23rd of that month. The Mayor of the City, E. Prior, presided and, having reminded those present on the object of their assembly, called upon R. H. Powell, a land agent of Lewes, Sussex, and one of the proposed promoters of the proposed railway, to explain the scheme.

Mr. Powell stated that it was in contemplation to construct what was known as a light railway, or tramway, from Chichester to Selsey, and to form a limited liability company to be styled 'The Hundred of Manhood & Selsey Tramways Company Ltd.'[2] The gauge of the line would be the same as the London, Brighton & South Coast Railway which passed through Chichester, and the trucks of the LBSCR would be run from one line to the other to facilitate the transit of merchandise. The tramway would open up the whole agricultural district of the Manhood and the fishing district of Selsey, and anyone going into the matter would acknowledge its advisability, and the probability that Selsey would be brought within 25 minutes journey of Chichester. He explained that 'it was not intended to run trains at great speed, nor was that needed'. As to Capital, it was proposed that the nominal should be £12,000, which the promoters believed was sufficient to provide everything, including the tramway stock, etc., but there would be power to extend. It was suggested that there should be a small station at Chichester disconnected with the main one there, with a siding running on to the metals of the main line for the convenience of goods traffic, and that there would be four stations in all, the others to be situated at Hunston, Sidlesham and Selsey. He urged that if the scheme was going to be a success, it should be worked out at once, as it was a great mistake to let anything of this kind hang fire, and he would like to see the proposed company started and at work as soon as possible. In raising the capital he anticipated no trouble, nearly two-thirds might be said to be already secured, but the promoters hoped that some part of the amount would be subscribed in Chichester. In his subsequent remarks he mentioned that a light railway was more likely to pay than a heavy one, and explained that although there was to be no direct connection between the light railway and the main line, provisions would be made for through bookings, and pointed out that a scheme of this kind was scarcely contemplated in the Light Railway Bill then before Parliament, and was one for the promotion of which the aid of the Government was not necessary.

Letters were read from Lord Edmond Talbot, Member of Parliament for the division, and other persons of distinction in support of the railway and then, at the call of the Mayor, Holman Stephens, CE addressed the meeting on the scheme from the engineering point of view, expressing his opinion that the line would be economical and gave reasons why. The highest point on the Selsey Peninsula was little more than 30ft above sea level, so it would be an easy railway to construct. With questions having been invited, B. Aylwyn asked whether Mr. Ivatt's scheme had been abandoned, as many landowners had pledged to it. Alderman Smith replied that he had seen Mr. Ivatts only last Saturday, and the opinion formed from their conversation was that his proposed railway was not to be proceeded with. The chairman proposed that the scheme laid before the meeting was worthy of support and with Newton Clayton seconding, the proposition was agreed to. Newton Clayton proposed next that a limited liability company should be registered to promote the scheme and that the firm of Sir Robert Raper, and Messrs. Freeland and Tyacke should undertake the preliminary legal arrangements, etc. This was seconded by James Clayton of Sidlesham and carried, after which the Memorandum of Association was read by W. B. B. Freeland and was signed. Messrs. George Woodbridge, JP (Chairman), James Clayton (Sidlesham), Robert Lawrence Thornton, JP (High Cross, Framfield), Alderman William Smith, JP (Chichester), Reginald Henry Powell (Lewes), Alderman Sharp Garland, JP (Chichester),[3] Hubert John Powell (Lewes), and Newton Clayton (Selsey) were elected as directors, with Walter Lintott as secretary, Messrs. Millbanke, Woodbridge, Gruggen and Gauntlett of the Chichester Bank as bankers, and James L. Gauntlett as auditor.

Following a meeting held on 2nd April, the Board of Trade was approached as to whether any difficulties might arise if the railway was laid without a provisional order and they replied to the effect that they would not interfere.[4] Holman Stephens' previous post had been as engineer to the 1½ mile long 3ft gauge Rye & Camber Tramways Company (note also the plural of 'Tramways') which had opened to traffic on 13th July 1895. Although the Board of Trade had also been approached by the Rye line, after discussing 'whether the promoters needed any statutory authority to construct on land already in their possession', they came to the conclusion that they did not 'seem to have any power to authorise the use of the line'.[5] No doubt it was Stephens who suggested that the Selsey Company similarly would not require Board of Trade powers if they were able to purchase the necessary land by negotiation, and that by being a tramway, they would be free of the extensive legislation under which railway companies operated, particularly as regards the level crossing of public roads.

On 8th April the *Chichester Observer* reported:

> 'We hear through a side wind that the first meeting of the promoters of the Selsey Tramway was held at Sir Robert Raper's office on Thursday last, and that the shares allotted to the general public are very likely to be a very small proportion of the whole. This anticipated by those generally who inaugurated the scheme that the Tramway will be in working order sufficiently early to deal with the late summer traffic. Somewhen in August, we should say, it will be opened.'

The Hundred of Manhood & Selsey Tramways Company Limited was duly incorporated and registered as a Limited Company under the Companies Acts of 1862 and 1890 on Wednesday, 29th April 1896. Possibly because of the decision to have their own separate passenger station at Chichester, or perhaps owing to landowners' opposition, the route out of the City via the eastern bank of the Chichester & Birdham Canal was abandoned in favour of the west bank, and the secretary of the Tramway Company, Walter Lintott, wrote to Chichester City Council seeking their permission for the line to cross the canal at Hunston via a fixed bridge giving a 6ft headroom, and the same waterway as at existing bridges. It was hoped that, in view of the small traffic on the canal, a fixed bridge would be allowed, but if required they would erect a swing bridge, but that would necessitate a greater expense to the Company. Since 1892 the sum of £652 had been lost by the City Council on the upkeep of the canal, and with it becoming gradually choked with weeds, it was considered by several councillors to be an expensive luxury. Even so, at their meeting on 26th June the Council insisted that the Tramway Company install a swing bridge rather than a fixed one.

The Westhampnett Board of Guardians met on Friday, 10th July when a letter was read out from the Tramways Company asking for permission to cross certain roads in the district with the 'tram road' which they proposed to construct. It was resolved that as the matter was of some importance, there might be objections raised, and that the application of the Company should be referred to a committee composed of members of the Highway Committee who were not interested in the scheme. The general chamber proposed, as an amendment, that the application be acceded, subject to such regulations and restrictions as the council might find desirable. The Rev. W. F. Shaw seconded the amendment, expressing his belief that if there was any particular opposition to the application, it should have made itself heard at the meeting. On a division, the amendment was carried 7 votes to 2.

On 16th December the *Chichester Observer* printed the following letter:

> 'Sir, As the new railway to Selsey is stumped out, it occurred to me to suggest to capitalists an opportunity has arrived to open a new harbour at the east side near Park. The sea is ever breaking in on two or three marshes that lie very low, and the owners of this land are disinclined to

GETTING STARTED (1886–1897)

repair the sea bank.[6] Its advantages are deep water just outside, good anchorage the lee side of Selsey, and the fishermen tell me there is a course in there quite clear of rocks, and it will be close to the new station. Here is a chance for enterprising Cicestrians[7] to keep down rail rates, a chance more formidable than half a dozen useless canals with swaying bridges that are risking life and limb. Would a harbour here meet with Admiralty support?

Yours, ADVANCE.'

"Advance's" question was left unanswered, but the following week the same newspaper advised

'People who are sceptical as to the carrying out of the proposed scheme for a Light Railway from Chichester to Selsey can now be convinced that the promoters are in earnest. The route is stumped or pegged out and the engineer is busily engaged in taking the levels. As soon as his specifications are complete, tenders will be invited for the work. The delay has been occasioned through the negotiations with the landlords whose ground it is proposed to traverse. Satisfactory settlements have been arrived at and the course is clear for "full steam ahead".'

With all the necessary preliminaries at last being concluded, at a meeting of the directors on 15th January 1897 it was decided to proceed with the work, the various contracts being signed the following month. Holman Stephens of Tonbridge, Kent was engaged as the engineer, with Messrs. Mancktelow Brothers of Pennington's Farm, Horsmonden, Kent as the contractor, undertaking to lay the permanent way within four months of the delivery of the materials from Messrs. Thomas Ward & Co. of Sheffield. The engineer and contractor had previously worked together on the Cranbrook & Paddock Wood Railway (opened to its eventual terminus at Hawkhurst, Kent on 4th September 1893) and the aforementioned Rye & Camber Tramway.

A new 2–4–2T locomotive was ordered from Messrs. Peckett & Co. of Bristol, along with three carriages to be supplied by the Falcon Engine Co. of Loughborough. The Company also acquired an ageing 0–6–0ST and half a dozen open wagons which were immediately placed at the disposal of the contractor. Work on constructing the tramway proceeded at a rapid pace so that on 12th May the *Chichester Observer* was able to report that '…the formation of the road is practically complete and the laying down of rails is being commissioned at both ends of the line. Nearly a hundred men under the management of Mr. Staples (manager of Messrs. Mancktelow Brothers) are engaged, Mr. Stephens, the engineer, exercising constant supervision. I venture to suggest that the line will be completed considerably earlier than anticipated.'

Chichester City Council was to construct and own the bridge across the canal at Hunston, the Tramway Company's rights over it being subject to an agreement with the Council, to whom they would pay £2 per annum for its use. However, work on the bridge had not yet commenced, and the locomotive was required on the southern section of the line. The contractors had no alternative but to move their 17-ton locomotive by road, a Burrell 8hp traction engine of 1892, named *Queen of the South*, being hired to haul it over 4 miles from Chichester to most likely where the Tramway would cross Rookery Lane to the north of the site of Sidlesham station. To ease the load of the traction engine, the locomotive was in light steam and, to protect the road surface, rails placed on their sides were laid in front and under the engine, those behind being moved forward each time it had passed over them.

As the Chichester City Council's Tramway drawbridge over the canal at Hunston was not yet completed, Chichester *had to be laboriously hauled by a traction engine along the public highway, probably to where the Tramway would cross Rookery Lane, just to the north of Sidlesham, where it would help with the construction of the southern section of the line. To protect the road, rails were laid on their sides under and in front of* Chichester*, and as the locomotive was moved forward, the rails from behind were brought forward and laid in front. This picture shows labourers in the process of bringing a rail forward from behind the locomotive. The 8hp traction engine was* Queen of the South*, built by Burrell (No. 1642) in 1892.*
WSCC LIBRARY SERVICE

With about half a mile still to go, Queen of the South *and* Chichester *are seen halted outside The Anchor public house on the main Chichester to Selsey road, not far from the site of Chalder station. To ease the traction engine's load, the 17-ton locomotive was in light steam, and had been converted to an 0–4–2ST by the removal of the rear coupling rods.*

COLONEL STEPHENS RAILWAY MUSEUM & ARCHIVE

By the second week of June, with the locomotive (now named *Chichester*) working the ballast train with 50 men in attendance, the rails had been laid as far as the canal at Hunston and also at intermediate places to Selsey.[8] Whilst working on the isolated southern section of the Tramway, the locomotive overshot the rails during the construction of the timber baulk bridge over the Broad Rife to the north of the level crossing at Ferry. The unfortunate engine ended up in the water, but luckily without injury to anyone.[9]

At the second Annual General Meeting of the Hundred of Manhood & Selsey Tramways Co. Ltd., held at the Council Chamber, Chichester on Thursday afternoon, 1st July 1897, Walter Lintott was able to report that the construction of the line was proceeding in a satisfactory and efficient manner with 4½ miles of rails having been completed, and that everything pointed to its being open for traffic by the end of that month. He explained that the delay in commencing the construction of the line had been owing to the difficulties that directors, Hubert J. Powell and Reginald H. Powell (of the Lewes firm of estate agents), had met in acquiring the necessary land, a considerable portion of the track traversed belonging to various public bodies. These difficulties had been overcome, but a somewhat higher price in excess of the original estimate had been paid. It had also been found expedient to lengthen the line in order to bring Selsey station nearer the sea. (The new terminus would still be half a mile from both the village centre and the East Beach and a good mile from the West Beach.) Although the capital required had been subscribed long ago, the directors recommended that, with the consent of the shareholders, a further £7,000 should be raised in debentures. The chairman, George Woodbridge, having shown figures why it was deemed necessary for a larger sum to be raised than was originally contemplated, suggested that the Company afforded 'very excellent security' and that there would be no difficulty in raising the amount required. However, in the Company's favour he did mention that owing to the liberality of F. W. Grafton,[10] the land at the Selsey end had been purchased for £10 per acre instead of a much higher price which might reasonably have been demanded, the saving effectively being around £2,000. He expected the line to be open for passenger traffic by August Bank Holiday and did not doubt that the railway would be a great success. The resolution that not more than £7,000 be raised in debentures was agreed to and the whole of the directorate was re-elected *nem con.* for the ensuing year.

It was not until later that month that work started on building the Tramway bridge across the canal north of Hunston when the chief piles were driven and the water pumped out in readiness for laying the concrete foundations.[11] The Council's original proposal for a swing bridge had been dropped in favour of an unusual drawbridge. By the middle of July, construction of the platform at Chichester had begun and work had started at the site of

GETTING STARTED (1886–1897)

what was to have been the original terminus where the main road was now to cross over the line at Selsey. Hardly surprisingly, the railway was not completed in time for the August Bank Holiday as had been hoped, although 'Selsey had to find provisions for about 1,000 people who thronged into the place in all kinds of vehicles. Such a large number has scarcely been known in the village'.[12]

At long last, on 18th August a reporter from the *Chichester Observer* was able to advise

'I am happy to announce as a settled arrangement that the light railway to Selsey is to be formally opened on Friday of next week. Possibly an influential gentleman will take a prominent part in the inevitable congratulatory speech making and I shall possibly have obtained the name of that gentleman before next week. At any rate, I can state that the arrangements are already made to provide for the conveyance of visitors – principally the 'shareholders' – to Selsey from the Tramway station at 1 o'clock and a luncheon in a marquee at 2 o'clock. For the sake of business enterprise in this neighbourhood, I trust that the clerk of the weather will be beneficially inclined, and that the whole of the inaugural proceedings will be thoroughly successful. Whether this be so or not, it will not fail because of any want of business aptitude or assiduity on the part of the directors and more especially the able and energetic secretary, Mr. Walter Lintott.'

Eight days later, the *West Sussex Gazette* wrote

THE SELSEY TRAMWAY

'Tomorrow (Friday) will witness the opening of the Hundred of Manhood & Selsey Tramway, or as it is generally known by its short title, the Selsey railway (*sic*). The tram will leave the Chichester tramway station at one o'clock. Luncheon will be served at Selsey, the invitations of which have been issued by Mr. F. W. Grafton, the directors and officers of the Company.'

Under the unusual heading of 'Agricultural Shows', on another page in the same issue, the newspaper advised

'Though not strictly an agricultural society, we may welcome under this head the start in work of the Selsey & Hundred of Manhood Tramways Company (*sic*) which will run its first steam tram tomorrow from Chichester through a fine agricultural district to Selsey... Selsey is now setting up as a modern watering place, and we wish it success with its new tram or railway.'

So why were the directors in such a hurry to open their Tramway? Was it because they saw the summer season rapidly slipping away, and with it the chance of earning some much needed revenue from day trippers visiting the seaside? Or was it that with the delivery of the three passenger carriages from Falcons, they thought they might as well start a passenger service? Whatever the reason, by no stretch of the imagination was their railway in a fit state to open! At Chichester the station building and platform had not been completed, and cocks and hens roamed on what was to be the site of Hunston station, although a siding had been laid there. An extra station to serve the northern end of the straggling village of Sidlesham at Chalder was under construction, but not ready for use, and that at Sidlesham had not yet begun! The line terminated abruptly in the cutting where the main Selsey road was to pass over the Tramway, but the bridge had not yet been built, as was the case with Selsey station a quarter of a mile further on! Had they been obliged to invite the Board of Trade to inspect the new railway, there is no way that they would have passed it as fit to open the following day!

As requested by the reporter of the *Chichester Observer*, the clerk of the weather was 'beneficially inclined' and provided a fine, sunny Friday, 27th August 1897. Already some 32 years old, *Chichester* was intended to be the 'goods' engine, but being the only locomotive available, she was given the

Two navvies making their way along the trackbed towards the station entrance as invited guests crowded onto the short platform at Chichester on Opening Day, Friday 27th August 1897. Other well-wishers watched from the adjacent field on the right and Stockbridge Road in the background. Buffer stops were never provided at the end of the line, a pile of redundant sleepers later serving in that capacity!
COLONEL STEPHENS RAILWAY MUSEUM & ARCHIVE

This was the view from the adjacent field as Chichester stood proudly at the head of the inaugural train consisting of all three of the Tramway's new carriages in their smart crimson and cream livery.
CHICHESTER DISTRICT MUSEUM

Almost an hour later than advertised, with all the passengers on board, Chichester is seen ready to leave at last for the coast. To obtain a bird's eye view of the proceedings, some brave souls had taken their place on the curved roof of the gasworks building beyond Stockbridge Road in the background, but we can only wonder why the policeman, in traditional pose, was standing on the track.
COLLECTION LES DARBYSHIRE

GETTING STARTED (1886–1897)

honour of hauling the first train, and very smart she looked. It would appear that some principal Selsey residents had left it rather late to inform the Tramway Company that they wished to take part in the opening ceremony at Chichester, and late that morning, *Chichester*, with just one carriage, was sent down to the southern terminus to bring them up to the city. Meanwhile, at around one o'clock, the time quoted on the official invitation cards, directors, shareholders, public officials and crowds of wellwishers had gathered on the short platform at Chichester and in the meadow alongside, to witness the event, a few daring souls climbing onto the gasworks roof for a bird's eye view of the proceedings. Those that looked over into the adjacent London, Brighton & South Coast Railway's goods yard would have seen the Tramway Company's brand new 2–4–2T locomotive being unloaded from a mainline wagon for future service. On the Selsey side of the fence, all six wagons and the brakevan that comprised the whole of the Tramway's goods stock was on view, whilst the two remaining passenger carriages waited in a siding for *Chichester*'s arrival. Eventually the little train came into view, 'winding its circuitous way towards the station' with the ladies enthusiastically waving handkerchiefs from the open windows. With the late arrival of this first train from Selsey, it was later suggested that the new railway 'had caught the complaint of unpunctuality from its big neighbour, whose trains have not been keeping the best of time of late'.[13] Immediately on arrival, *Chichester* ran round the single carriage, and added the other two to the train.

It had been hoped that Lord Edmond Talbot, MP would have been present to make the opening speech, but unfortunately his lordship was unable to attend, so in his absence, the Mayor of Chichester, Alderman Ballard, consented to act. He took his position on the balcony of the carriage at the front of the train where he was greeted with 'a little cheer', and he forthwith broke into speech.

'I did not know until yesterday that a person of far more exalted position than I would have the honour of declaring this railway open,' he began. He then reminded those present of the ambitious but 'painful bashful' young lawyer who, on attempting to deliver an address at the opening of a railway bridge, got 'beautifully mixed' and said the 'spot' where they stood was a howling wilderness and he hoped would remain so! The Mayor continued: 'I would not liken the site on which the station now stands as a howling wilderness, but as a mild and peaceful meadow where lambs had frolicked and beasts had grazed. (Laughter) I do not wish it to remain so, but that the formation of the Tramway might be the means of a great deal of comfort and great prosperity both to Selsey and Chichester. (Applause) I will not take up your time any longer, as I know you are wishing to partake of the good things provided at the other end of the line. (Laughter) I cordially invite you to take your seats on the train whilst I mount the engine and set you on your first journey to Selsey, but I might mention that I remember the opening of the Chichester station of the London, Brighton & South Coast Railway in the Basin-road 45 years ago, and which was a very little wooden shanty. I hope that the present occasion is only the commencement of far more important things for the Selsey Tramway. I am now going to indulge in one of the greatest happinesses I conceived as a boy, that of driving an engine.' (Laughter)

He then duly declared the line open for traffic. Whilst the assembled company marked the close of the Mayor's speech with vociferous cheering, joined by the spectators in the meadow opposite, the Tramway Company's secretary, Walter Lintott, presented the Mayoress with a handsome bouquet. Such was the confidence that the Mayor inspired that, not withstanding that he was going to drive the engine, 'no one jumped from the cars. They felt that the Mayor could drive them to Selsey as any trained engine-driver. The Mayor, on his part, approached the task with confidence, jumped on the engine with the agility of youth, and presently an ear-piercing shriek from the whistle and the gentle motion of the train told the travellers they were off'. Almost an hour late, it was 1.57pm as *Chichester* and her train pulled out of the station to the accompaniment of exploding fog signals placed on the line, and a friendly whistle from the Midhurst railway engine standing in the main line station. The curve that takes the line round Mr. Fogden's meadow and onto the crossing of the main road was slowly negotiated,[14] the pace being such that a contingent of amateur photographers found no difficulty in getting excellent snapshots as the train passed by.

Through the big field of Mr. Humphrey's farm in a slight cutting the train gently glided along, and then after running alongside 'the anything but pellucid waters of the Chichester & Birdham Canal', the driver stopped the train on the drawbridge across the canal so that Councillor John Fielder could take a picture from the tow path before joining the train himself. The Mayor now hastily quitted his post on the locomotive and repaired to the saloon. At the site of what would become Hunston station 'the oldest inhabitant was observed looking wonderingly on as puffing billy kept on his wild career to the south. Many of the younger inhabitants also turned out; patches of bunting were observed here and there, giving colour to the scene, and the enthusiastic brothers Hodson, Kipson-bank Mill, had dressed the sweeps of their mill "rainbow fashion" as they say in the navy, and a hearty cheer was wafted from the mill as the train passed. Another pleasant greeting was given at Hoe-farm where the farmer was observed busy at harvest, but Mrs. Jupp and her daughters flew flags and waved handkerchiefs in token of their desire for good luck to attend the enterprise'. As the station at Chalder was not yet complete, the train did not stop there. It did not stop at the site of Sidlesham Mill where a station was to be built either, although, as at other points, flags were flown and a considerable number of villagers and school children had assembled to greet the passage of the train with a cheer. Among them was 86 year old Mrs. Stevens who, seated in a basket chair, appeared delighted at the novel spectacle. At the Selsey end, the railway was in a very incomplete state and 'in a meadow near the church' the company was landed on *terra firma* from the cars after having enjoyed a pleasant run of 40 minutes, including the photo-

Beacon House, Selsey, where the Tramway Company's inaugural luncheon was held on the Opening Day. The commodious building was demolished in the 1920s by local builder, Ralph Selsby, who salvaged much material from it before its remains were lost to the ever-encroaching sea.
COLLECTION J. WYNNE-TYSON

graphic stop. It was observed that 'the cars run smoothly with little or no oscillation and the working of the train was favourably commented on.' Facilities at this temporary terminus must have included a run-round loop, but it is highly unlikely that a passenger platform had been provided. Navvies were to be seen hard at work tunnelling under the main road through a natural ridge of gravel in readiness for the railway to be extended to the site where Selsey station was to be built at Manor-Farm some 400 or so yards beyond.

The village was *en fête* for the occasion with many flags fluttering in the breeze, and a large crowd had gathered to cheer the incoming train. Having alighted from the cars 'and been received with due enthusiasm', the ladies and some of the gentlemen entered vehicles; 'others of the sterner sex walked, just to stretch their legs', but all wended their way by the shortest possible route the mile or so towards the Selsey Bill and Beacon House where in a spacious marquee luncheon was spread. As it was now past three o'clock, no one required pressing to sit down to the very choice repast which the hospitality of Mr. Grafton and the Tramway directors had provided. Those specialities of Selsey, prawns and lobsters, were much in evidence on the tables, and such prawns, too! Nowhere else, but at Selsey, could prawns like these be fished; and the lobsters were in every way fit to go by the side of them. There were, of course, more substantial delicacies, prepared by Mr. and Mrs. Alfred Woodland of Beacon House close by, and Mr. G. G. Capon of Chichester supplied the sparkling 'boy' without which no great enterprise can be successfully launched.

Mr. F. F. Grafton, the representative of the Grafton Trustees, who had done much to aid the building of the Tramway, presided over the large company of mainly shareholders, which included Sir Clarence and Lady Smith, the Mayor and Mayoress of Chichester, the Hon. F. W. J. Dundas, Rev. Doctor Storrs (rector of Selsey) and Mrs. Storrs, Mr. and Mrs. Edward Arnold, Mr. F. Angel, Mr. and Mrs. Andre, Mr. B. Bean, Mr. Brockway, Mrs. Bateman, Mr. E. E. Caffin, Mr. G. Couch, Mrs. E. V. Cantbell, Mr. and Mrs. James Clayton, Mr. J. E. Clayton, Mr. G. G. Capon, Mr. G. W. Cutts, Alderman Cortis (Worthing), Mr. W. P. Cogan, Mrs. C. J. Drewitt, Rev. H. M. Davy, Mr. E. Fogden, Mr. George Fielder, Mr. and Mrs. W. B. B. Freeland, Mr. W. H. B. Fletcher, JP, Mr. H. G. Goodger, Mr. E. Hanson, Miss Gibbs, Mr. J. Gorham, Mr. Allen Hobgen, Mr. T. Cecil Hobgen, Mrs. Harvey, Mr. W. T. Haines, Mr. Vernon Inkpen, Miss Jackson, Mrs. Jones, Mr. W. Jarman, Mr. C. Knight, Mrs. Luck, Mr. Long, Mr. and Mrs. F. P. Leaf, Mr. W. Lintott (secretary), Mr. and Misses Muggridge, Miss H. Morris, Mr. J. W. McKay, Mr. G. Mancktelow, Mr. E. Mancktelow (contractors), Mr. and Mrs. Percival, Mr. E. M. Street, JP, Mr. A. Swann, Mrs. Sparkes, Mr. H. W. Stringfellow, Mr. A. Turner, Mrs. Trower, Mr. J. G. H. Wallace, Miss Woodman, Rev. Charles L. Norris, Rev. Owen and Mrs. Phillips, Miss Foster, Miss Storrs, Miss Lilian Storrs, Mr. J. Fielder, Mrs. R. H. Powell and Miss Powell, Hubert J. Powell, Mr. and Mrs. Edward Powell, Mr. Harry Scarlett, Mr. C. W. Ross, Mr. Grantham, Doctor Leonard Buckell, Doctor and Mrs. A. E.

GETTING STARTED (1886–1897)

Buckell, Mr. R. G. Halsted, Mr. W. L. Bunting, Miss Foster, Mr. Hugh Penfold, Mr. T. Mancktelow, Mrs. Newton Clayton, Miss W. Clayton, Doctor Chard, Miss G. Smith, Mr. H. Stubington, Mr. F. Griffith, Rev. J. H. Tite, Mrs. Hobgen, Mr. F. Pitts and Miss A. Pitts, Miss Massey, Major G. G. Todd, Miss Clayton, Rev. T. F. Paynter, Rev. and Mrs. Henderson, and Mr. Eugene Street. (It will be interesting to look back as the Tramway's history unfolds to see just how many of these 'mainly' shareholders will be there to support the Company in the years to come!) The directors in attendance were Messrs. James Clayton, R. L. Thornton, JP, W. Smith, JP, R. H. Powell, Sharp Garland, JP, H. J. Powell and Newton Clayton.

After the toast of 'The Queen' had been honoured, Mr. Grafton expressed the regret that the Member for the Division, Lord Edmond Talbot was absent from the chair owing to an unfortunate *contretemps*. Walter Lintott explained that letters of regret of their inability to attend had been received from 36 people, and he then read the following two:

'Derwent Hall, Sheffield August 25th 1897.
Dear Sir,
I received your wire on my return here at 7 o'clock this evening. It was the first intimation that I received of the letter you mentioned as having written to me on 14th inst., and which never reached me. I am extremely sorry that it is impossible for me to take part in the proceedings of the opening of the Chichester to Selsey Railway, a work which will, I'm sure, prove to be of the greatest advantage to the district, but it is quite out of the question for me to now alter my plans in time.
I remain, Yours faithfully, Edmund Talbot.'

'August 26th 1897.
Sir Robert Raper presents his compliments to Mr. Grafton and the directors of the Selsey Tramway Company, and regrets that he is quite unable to join the party tomorrow. Sir Robert is called to Petersfield on important business which will take him away all day. Sir Robert heartily wishes every success to the Company.'

Alderman Ballard, after expressing his disappointment at the unavoidable absence of Lord Edmond Talbot, MP, explained that the toast had fallen to him, which might have been entrusted to much abler hands, though he yielded to none in his desire for the success of the new Tramway. (Applause) He continued

'I regard this day as marking an epoch in the history of Selsey, in much the same way as the Diamond Jubilee of the Queen had marked an epoch in the history of our country. I am informed that the railway might be called a pioneer railway of its kind because, with the exception of a short line at the other end of the county[15] it is the only railway that has been constructed at so cheap a rate, having the same design and object in view. The idea of the railway is to facilitate the transit of agricultural goods between Selsey and Chichester for the benefits of the producer, and by the same means, visitors can be conveyed to the beautiful shores of Selsey to enjoy the bracing air than which none along the Sussex coast is more fruitfully laden with ozone. You have only to look at the Selsey visitors' list in the (*Chichester*) *Observer* to see the number of visitors who stayed at Selsey to realise that the want of such a railway has long been felt. (Applause) It has, at all times, been somewhat awkward to get to and from Selsey, but while disposed on the one hand to congratulate the promoters of the railway, I am not quite sure that it is a mixed blessing. (Laughter) I believe that one of the advantages of Selsey, and one of the reasons which have given rise to its popularity, is that it has been so beautifully isolated, and as you know, it is a great advantage to men engaged in business and public work to get away to holidays to a place where they are not troubled very much by letters, telegrams and such things, but where they are able to lie still and do nothing. (Laughter and applause) With respect to the new railway, I am requested to inform the public generally that it was not constructed with the idea of running trains at express speed. The idea is to convey passengers and merchandise in a slow and sure way at a cheap rate, and its locomotion – not like the railway where accidents were so frequent that a laconic reporter named Finegen sent the following telegraph to his paper recording the weekly breakdown "Down agen, up agen, on agen – Finegen". (Laughter) During the construction of the line there had been many difficulties to overcome, and I think those of you assembled here today might congratulate the directors and their officials on the pluck and perseverance which they have shown in overcoming obstacles and bringing the railway to such a satisfactory conclusion as we find today. (Applause) I believe that while the railway is not going to beat the record in the matter of time, people will be able to reach Selsey far quicker than if they drove and, perhaps, far safer. (Laughter) The directors will not probably feel it necessary to provide sleeping cars or dining cars (laughter) and I think the passengers will be able to exist from one terminus to the other without having to recourse to refreshment rooms. I hope that in the matter of punctuality the railway will be able to set an example to its big brother, the London, Brighton & South Coast Railway. (Applause) I would suggest, with all modesty to the directors that, if they find the times stated on the timetable can not be kept up, alterations should be made. Looking back on my recollections of Selsey, I can see a vast improvement in the last few years. Houses have been built and let out, and building plots, and I think there is every appearance before the lapse of many more years, that Selsey will become what it claimed to be – a rising and fashionable watering place. (Applause) I am told that, in some places, where the directors might have expected sympathy, they had met with obstruction, and in consequence of the action of some of the landowners, they have been compelled to take a circuitous route, where a straightforward road would have been more advantageous, at the same time having avoided expense and difficulty. I think we might not only congratulate the directors, but Selsey on being the possessor of such a railway, and Chichester for the opportunity of running to and from the seaside without the abominable nuisance of waiting about at Barnham Junction. I ask you to drink with all sincerity to "the success of the Hundred of Manhood and Selsey Tramway (sic) Company".' (Cheers).

F. F. Grafton eloquently responded to the toast and enlarged on the benefits which light railways must confer on the districts through which they ran.

'There is a condition that is necessary to fulfil, and that is that the work of the Company should be carried out with perfect honesty and economy in every way, no money being spent on useless promotion expenses etc., with everything done efficiently at minimum cost. These results, I believe, have been well achieved in the present case. From the course of my experience, I have never come across an undertaking which has been so admirably managed. From the beginning the Selsey line has been. (Cheers) The cost per mile has been kept lower than anything I know of in this country, in fact, somewhat on the basis of the cost of light railways and secondary railways in the north of Italy and in Belgium where they make considerable use of this class of line. There, however, they are not under the disadvantage of not being able to tap the same remunerative area of traffic as in the present case. The railway, I consider, was started under reasonable auspices, and there is every chance of making a profit for the shareholders. This being so, it should be an incentive to other districts to start similar railways. I must confess I had a momentary qualm when I heard that the Mayor of Chichester was going to drive the train. (Laughter) No doubt his Worship's intentions were admirable, but I felt a little dubious about the execution, and it was with the feelings of considerable thankfulness that I heard the engine driver would not let him anything more than blow the whistle'. (Laughter and applause)

The *West Sussex Gazette* later suggested 'tongue in cheek' that 'the whistle was never sounded more artistically'!

'The health of the solicitors' was given by W. H. B. Fletcher, JP who eulogised the invaluable and experienced services of the Company's solicitors, Messrs. Raper, Freeland & Tyacke, that negotiations with the landlords alluded to had been considerably expedited by the advice of the firm. He rejoiced that the Tramway brought the system of the London, Brighton & South Coast Railway into touch with that watering place which, for healthfulness, beauty of landscapes and, above all, its sea views, was unrivalled, in his opinion, along the south coast. (Applause)

W. B. B. Freeland made a happy response to the toast and Alderman W. Smith, JP followed to the toast of 'The engineer', whose ability and energy in the construction of the line he paid a warm tribute. Holman Stephens replied, commenting that the work of construction had been simple and cheap, and he hoped that in a short time a higher rate of speed would be attained. Hubert J. Powell proposed 'the contractor' and George Mancktelow replied. Alderman Sharp Garland, JP next proposed 'the secretary' and Walter Lintott suitably responded. The last toast, that of 'the chairman', was proposed by Edward Arnold, who referred to the vigorous spirit in which Mr. Grafton, as one of the trustees of the Grafton estate, had met the Company in regard to the concessions of land. The toast was drunk with musical honours after which Mr. Grafton responded saying 'Personally I have no direct interest in Selsey. As a trustee, however, I have a considerable interest, but that interest is divided with others who are unable to attend today. Though unable to give the land right out, we have disposed of it to the Company on as easy terms as possible, and I hope that the Tramway shall not prove false to the trust that we have reposed in it.' (Applause)

Owing to the late arrival of the train in the first place, and the speeches having gone on for so long, there was no time left in which to stroll along the "front" and enjoy the gentle breeze wafted over the waves; or to speculate on the site of the bishops' palace and cathedral of Selsey which existed long before the Norman conqueror removed the see (he couldn't remove the sea) to Chichester.' It was, however, possible to admire the view of the Isle of Wight to the south-west and of the bold sweep of coast running round to Bognor in the southeast, with the downs to the north forming a background a dozen miles inland. The journey back to Chichester was accomplished safely and pleasantly with more demonstrations from well-wishers en-route.

Notes

1. The Selsey line would have shared the LBSCR's Chichester station platforms to head eastwards on the main line company's metals over Stockbridge Road before immediately branching off to the right to cross Basin Road by its own level crossing and thence to take up a position on the eastern bank of the Chichester Canal.
2. Charles F. Klapper, in his series 'Railways in Sussex', published in *The Sussex County Magazine*, Vol. 6, 1932, suggested that the unusual title of the Company was chosen 'apparently, for free advertisement given by an interesting name'!
3. 'Sharp' was Alderman Garland's unusual Christian name.
4. 'Selsey Tramways', from *Selseyana*, Volume One by Edward Heron-Allen.
5. *The Rye & Camber Tramway – A Centenary History*, by Laurie A. Cooksey, published by Plateway Press, 1995.
6. The Park, to the east of Selsey, a home for deer in Tudor times, is now mainly under the sea, other than the marshes mentioned here.
7. A person born in Chichester.
8. *Chichester Observer*, Wednesday, 9.6.1897.
9. *The Selsey Tramways*, by Edward C. Griffith, 3rd edition published by the author 1974.
10. It will be remembered that Mr. F. W. Grafton was to be one of the directors of the ill-fated Selsey Railway & Pier scheme of 1887.
11. *Chichester Observer*, Wednesday, 14.7.1897.
12. *Chichester Observer*, Wednesday, 4.8.1897.
13. This, and all subsequent passages in parenthesis in this chapter, are taken from the *West Sussex Gazette*'s article on the Tramway's opening ceremony dated Thursday, 2.9.1897.
14. At 6 chains radius, this was the sharpest curve on the Tramway, and a 6 m.p.h. speed limit was imposed on it.
15. The Rye & Camber Tramway.

The Hundred of Manhood & Selsey Tramways Company seal. COLONEL STEPHENS RAILWAY MUSEUM & ARCHIVE

CHAPTER TWO

A PROMISING BEGINNING
(1897–1909)

With not a house in sight, Selsey station did not open to traffic until 14th November 1897 and work was still being carried out on the engine shed in this early view, with corrugated iron sheeting, guttering and drain pipes occupying the space between the main running line and the run-round loop in the foreground. Selsey is seen at the far end of the short platform with a van, an open wagon, and the Falcon brake/composite carriage bringing up the rear of what would be the next train for Chichester. LENS OF SUTTON

WHEN the Tramway was opened to the public the following day, Chichester station was more or less complete, but other than a siding into the Company's gravel pit at the temporary Selsey terminus (from whence a good deal of the line's 'ballast' had come) there was just one other siding laid, and that was at Hunston. As the only site on the Tramway where water was freely available, it was here that the locomotives *Chichester* and *Selsey* were probably serviced and stabled in the open prior to the engine shed at Selsey being in a forward enough state to accommodate them. The three passenger carriages would have been based at Chichester, and all services commenced from that end of the line. *The West Sussex Gazette* on the following Thursday thought that 'it ought to go down on the books of history that Mr. H. H. Moore of Chichester paid the first shilling' to ride on the tram, one of 96 passengers to travel that day. Hardly an encouraging start, but as well as could be expected on a railway that went via 'nowhere' to terminate 'short of somewhere' on a service advertised as being 'about' three trains on weekdays and two on Sundays!

The standard single fare was 7½d and 1s 3d return, but cheap Day Return tickets were available between Selsey and Chichester on Wednesdays by the 7.55am and 11.15am up trams and by all services on Saturdays and Sundays, with similar arrangements working in the opposite direction on the 1.00pm and 4.15pm down services on Thursdays and all services on Sundays only. Reflecting the fact that this was a Tramway and not a railway, different classes were not offered, but for a supplement of 3d per single journey, passengers could travel in the saloon compartment.

All of the many navvies busily working on the incomplete railway left their work on Tuesday, 31st August in protest of Messrs. Mancktelow Brothers having lowered their wages by a halfpenny per hour.[1] Their rightful pay must have been reinstated as they were soon back at work. Considerably more than £100 per week was being paid out in wages by the contractor at this time.[2]

On 1st September, along with a full and detailed report on the opening ceremony, the *Chichester Observer* commented

'After many years the greatly desired and needed railway from Chichester through an important agricultural district to the growing seaside resort of Selsey is a *fait accompli*. In no part of the country has a proper means of communication with the railway centre been longed for. These days, when 'time means money' something better than carrier traffic was required, not only for the needs of agriculturalists in the Sidlesham and Manhood districts, but more especially for Selsey which every year is becoming more popular to those who need a quiet holiday by the sea. The transit of goods was an expensive and laborious matter, whilst the conveyance of the rapidly increasing number of visitors and residents was an even more irksome matter... The opening ceremony inaugurative on Friday afternoon was a momentous event, not only to the shareholders, but more particularly to the inhabitants through the district which the line traverses, and at Selsey, where so much is hoped for the establishment of the Tramway...'

Unfortunately the 'agriculturalists in the Sidlesham and Manhood districts' would have to rely on carrier traffic a little longer as arrangements for the carriage of goods on the Tramway were having to be 'laid over for a month or two' until the time when Selsey station might be completed. The *West Sussex Gazette* also gave a full account of the opening celebrations and in its edition dated 2nd September under the separate heading of 'BY RAIL & STEAM' in flowery fashion wrote:

17

'The Selsey Light Railway has been opened with due rejoicing: and Sussex possesses one more link between its enchanting inland district and its salubrious seaboard. The existing link is one of iron; may the coming months forge links of solid gold. Then will Cicestrians and the good folk of Selsey wear smiling faces – and pay the income tax without a squirm.'

The Tramways Company appeared not to trust Chichester Corporation's drawbridge over the canal at Hunston, and for the first few weeks 'a barge was kept beneath it to catch the train in case it gave way'! Their mistrust of the structure may have been warranted as it tended to show 'a strong predilection for the upright position, and refused to be lowered, defying all efforts, and stopping the traffic for several days'.[3] Perhaps it was the lack of a rail service so soon after the line's opening that prompted the *Chichester Observer* to write this single sentence in the Tramway's defence on 18th September: 'Railways, even light railways, should "have a chance" before being called to account'.

What could have been a far more serious accident occurred on Saturday, 9th October when a young man, named Prior, was returning from Selsey in an open wagon drawn by one of the engines, when he attempted to alight from the train whilst it was in motion near Brinfast Farm, to the north of Chalder. In doing so, he lost his footing and fell to the ground, sustaining rather severe injuries to his face and head. It was several days before he was able to return to work.[4]

Although still incomplete, Selsey station was in a fit enough state for the first public train to terminate there on Sunday, 14th November. It might have been situated a quarter of a mile closer than originally planned, but the *Chichester Observer* the following Wednesday considered it 'to be in a very awkward position, it being so far away from the village, particularly to those passengers who are obliged to come back by the last train. There are no lights, or any prospect of any at present'. The newspaper then sarcastically added 'perhaps the Company will provide lanterns for their passengers when travelling after dark'! It is likely that goods were carried for the first time the following week and, from this date, all services originated from Selsey.

The cost of constructing the Tramway to date was calculated as follows:[5]

	£	s.	d,
To construction a/c:	14,234	12	7
To fees re engineer:	788	9	9
To purchase of land:	4,973	5	10
	19,996	8	2

After running 'about' three return trams on weekdays and two on Sundays during the first few months' operations, with the opening of Selsey station the Tramway's first published timetable came into effect on Monday, 15th November. Slower running times of some services might indicate 'mixed' trains dropping off and picking up wagons *en route*, although they weren't marked as such.

	Weekdays				Sat. only	Sundays		
Selsey	7.55	11.15	3.00	6.00	8.00	10.05	1.30	7.10
Sidlesham	8.10	11.30	3.20	6.15	8.15	10.20	1.45	7.25
Chalder	8.15	11.35	3.25	6.20	8.20	10.25	1.50	7.30
Hunston	8.20	11.40	3.30	6.25	8.25	10.30	1.55	7.35
Chichester	8.35	11.55	3.45	6.40	8.40	10.45	2.10	7.45
Chichester	10.15	12.45	4.15	7.10	10.15	10.50	2.15	8.00
Hunston	10.30	12.55	4.25	7.20	10.25	11.00	2.25	8.10
Chalder	10.35	1.00	4.30	7.25	10.30	11.05	2.30	8.15
Sidlesham	10.40	1.05	4.35	7.30	10.35	11.10	2.35	8.20
Selsey	10.55	1.20	4.50	7.45	10.50	11.25	2.50	8.35

Not long after the opening of the Tramway, an elevated water tower was provided for replenishing the locomotives' tanks at Chichester, but drivers were discouraged from using it as water rates had to be paid to Chichester Corporation! The entrance to the station was via the platform ramp to the right, alongside which the nameboard unusually faced away from the premises in an attempt to attract more custom from passengers arriving at the LBSCR station, visible between the carriage and the station building. The spire of the Cathedral can just be seen above the carriage roof.

COLLECTION LES DARBYSHIRE

A PROMISING BEGINNING (1897–1909)

The unusual lifting bridge over the Chichester Canal belonged to the City's Corporation and the Tramway Company paid £2 per year for the privilege of using it. In this early view it was in the process of being raised so that the sailing vessel could continue on its passage downstream from Chichester towards the sea at Birdham.
COLONEL STEPHENS RAILWAY MUSEUM & ARCHIVE

The Sunday service proved to be too ambitious and the afternoon trams in each direction were discontinued from 3rd January. As of that date weekday services from Selsey remained as before, but the 12.45pm and 7.10pm departures from Chichester were retimed to run a quarter of an hour and five minutes later respectively throughout, with the addition of a note concerning the Saturday only tram advising 'After the arrival of the London train'.

Early in the year the Rev. Victor L. Whitechurch made a trip over the Tramway, as he had heard so many 'jocular remarks' about it! From his account, it had already become clear that Alderman Ballard's suggestion in his speech in the opening ceremony that 'in the matter of punctuality the railway will be able to set an example to big brother, the London, Brighton & South Coast Railway' had been conveniently ignored! Rev. Whitechurch had arrived at the Chichester terminus 'situated in a field just south of the LBSC station,' and which consisted 'chiefly of a galvanised iron shed divided into "Waiting Room" and "Ticket Office". Stationmaster, clerk and porters were, however, conspicuous by their absence, and I was informed that tickets were issued "aboard the cars", from which statement I gathered that the line was being conducted on the American system.' The ticket, when issued, impressed the cleric for whereas the cardboard was white, the printing was in two colours – black for the outward journey and red for the return. It had been his intention to catch the 10.15am train to Selsey, but two minutes after the advertised departure time, *Selsey* had to undertake 'a remarkable operation in shunting when two trucks were brought in from the transhipment siding, and so manipulated with the engine and by hand that finally one was attached to the rear of the single carriage and the other in front of the locomotive!' In this manner, at 10.33 the train started, but had to stop immediately to allow the fireman, who had been working the points, to run after the train and take his place on the footplate. At Hunston, 'the coaling and watering depot', the tram backed up to take on both commodities with the carriage blocking the main road. Five minutes before they were due to arrive at Selsey, the train was on its way again at 10.50, slowing down as it passed four platelayers engaged in permanent way duties. At Chalder, the rear wagon was left

Hunston station soon after the opening of the Tramway, and just as Rev. V. L. Whitechurch described it in his article published in the Railway Magazine *in April 1898. Behind the hedge beyond the water tank is what is now the main road between Hunston and Selsey, then but a narrow track.*
LENS OF SUTTON

in the siding there and the run to Sidlesham was done 'in fine style'. Here some more 'marvellous shunting operations' were performed that occupied six minutes, resulting in the train entering the last stage of its journey with three trucks in front of the engine, and two behind the carriage – 'the very best example of a *mixed* train it has ever been my fortune to behold!' What the Board of Trade would have made of such a practice does not bear thinking about! All five wagons were left in the gravel pit siding close to Selsey, and the station was eventually reached at 11.30, forty minutes late, and a quarter of an hour after the train was advertised to return! Commenting wryly on the Tramway Company having not stated arrival times during the first few weeks' operations, Rev. Whitechurch stated 'I am rather surprised that they do so now. It is an overbold stroke of policy!'

Selsey took 'about three minutes' to run round her carriage and the train returned to Chichester immediately with a goodly number of farmers and country women as it was Chichester market day, taking 35 minutes for the 7-mile journey, an improvement of 5 minutes over the advertised time.

'About midway on the journey home, I, who was seated in the front compartment of the car, saw a red flag being violently waved a few hundred yards ahead. All sorts of misgivings rose to my mind. I had heard one weird story of the driver stopping a "Selsey Express", getting deliberately off his engine and gathering for his rabbits some green stuff,

the sight of which had proved irresistible. Was this red flag a signal to him that a turnip had been discovered growing alongside the line? Or perhaps it was some horrible danger – a donkey-cart on the road. We should shortly be crossing the canal bridge. Perhaps it had been destroyed and carried away by an unmanageable barge that had run amuck. Or, ghastly thought! There might have been a mistake at Chichester – another train had started towards us and some brave agricultural labourer working by the side of the line, and seeing what must be the inevitable result, had run on ahead of the approaching train to warn us... But all my fears proved groundless, for as the train slowed down the individual in question, a stalwart gaitered farmer, removed the danger signal from his stick, stuffed it in his pocket, and calmly came aboard the car, doubtless thanking his lucky stars for the little railway that ran within a few feet of the garden of his house. So ended my little trip on the "Hundred of Manhood & Selsey Tramway", and though in many respects it proved humorous, at the same time it afforded no small food for reflection on the introduction of light railways into our country. Already the farmers residing in the districts through which the line passes have well appreciated the new method of locomotion afforded for the transport of their produce, while the inhabitants of the villages who were wont to spend half a day in a carrier's cart on their way to market must find the new method of journeying to Chichester a great boon. Running as it does through a level country, and constructed as it has been under the Light Railways Act[6] the expenses of the line cannot have proved an exorbitant item.

'With regard to passenger traffic, it forms "the shortest route to the seaside" for Chichester and the adjacent villages and if the fares are lowered and the service is good, the Chichester people will not be slow to take advantage of these facilities. At present a journey to Bognor, a town on the coast, seven miles off as the crow flies, involves a nine and a-half miles' railway trip, with a change at Barnham Junction. This is one

A PROMISING BEGINNING (1897–1909)

To begin with, the nameboard at Sidlesham was spelt the old way with two 'D's to emphasise its pronunciation, as seen on the extreme left. The single level crossing gate, complete with its red warning diamond, was not much use to road users pushed back against the Tramway's fence and, with no protection at all, the double-ended goods siding behind the platform fence also crossed the road.

CHICHESTER DISTRICT MUSEUM

The footplate crew of Selsey *obligingly posed prior to departing bunker first to Chichester from Selsey c.1898 with the ex-LBSCR Stroudley Road Van next to the engine.* Selsey *is seen in original condition with long side tanks, curved side plates above the bunker and curved wings to the smokebox front plate.*

COLLECTION LES DARBYSHIRE

instance out of many of small towns "cutting their own throats" in the early days of railway construction. Bognor didn't want a direct connection with Chichester – it would spoil trade, etc., etc. The consequence is that this little light railway has a splendid chance of giving the Chichester people just what they have wanted for years – a short and easy route to the seaside, which will give an opportunity of enjoying a sea-dip and a breath of pure ozone to many who have only two or three hours to spare... The Company are (sic) even rising to "excursions", for I noticed a special cheap return journey advertised, by means of which the Selsey folk would be enabled to run up to Chichester and take one of the London, Brighton and South Coast excursions. Indeed, it will be no matter of wonder in the future if one sees such a bill heading as "Hundred of Manhood and Selsey Tramway. Special Excursion to London, via Chichester and the London, Brighton and South Coast Railway!" At all events, one will look forward with interest to the development of this little "tramway", especially as it is one of the first experiments of light railways in the country; and though I may have raised a laugh at its expense, I heartily wish it every success.'[7]

In Selsey, new buildings on an extensive scale were about to be commenced on land recently sold in New Road, and other existing homes in the street were being enlarged. 'This certainly looks as if Selsey is going to be prosperous since the railway has been started...' commented the *Chichester Observer* on 5th January 1898. However, 'visitors during Easter were not so numerous as last year, although 300 persons came on Bank Holiday by the new railway from Chichester',[8] but the Clapham-based Selsey Bill Club (formed in 1865 for the purpose of making excursions to the village) perhaps objected to the new mode of transport because when they visited Selsey on Saturday, 28th May, their 60/70 members travelled the old-fashioned way to and from Chichester in brakes!

A public auction of a number of freehold building plots that took place at The Crown Hotel, Selsey on Thursday, 26th May aroused considerable interest 'owing to the impetus given to the neighbourhood by the construction of the light railway connecting Selsey with Chichester'. In his opening remarks the auctioneer referred to the salubrity of Selsey air and the immense natural advantages, and pointed out that now the difficulty as to railway facilities had been solved, it was not unreasonable to anticipate that the place had an important future before it. 'The village has been growing in popularity for many years as a quiet summer resort', he continued, 'and the demand for accommodation during the season is so great that there is, no doubt, an excellent opening for building operations. Houses of the villa class for residential purposes are also required.' As an investment, the Hundred of Manhood & Selsey Tramways Company had wisely bought more land than they required for their own use, and it was some of these plots in Manor Road that

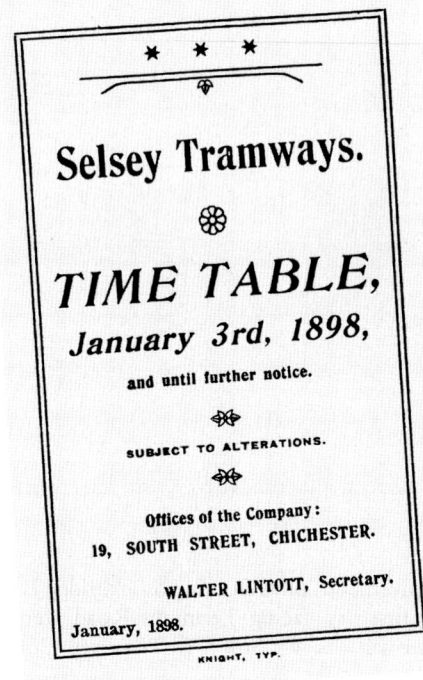

A PROMISING BEGINNING (1897–1909)

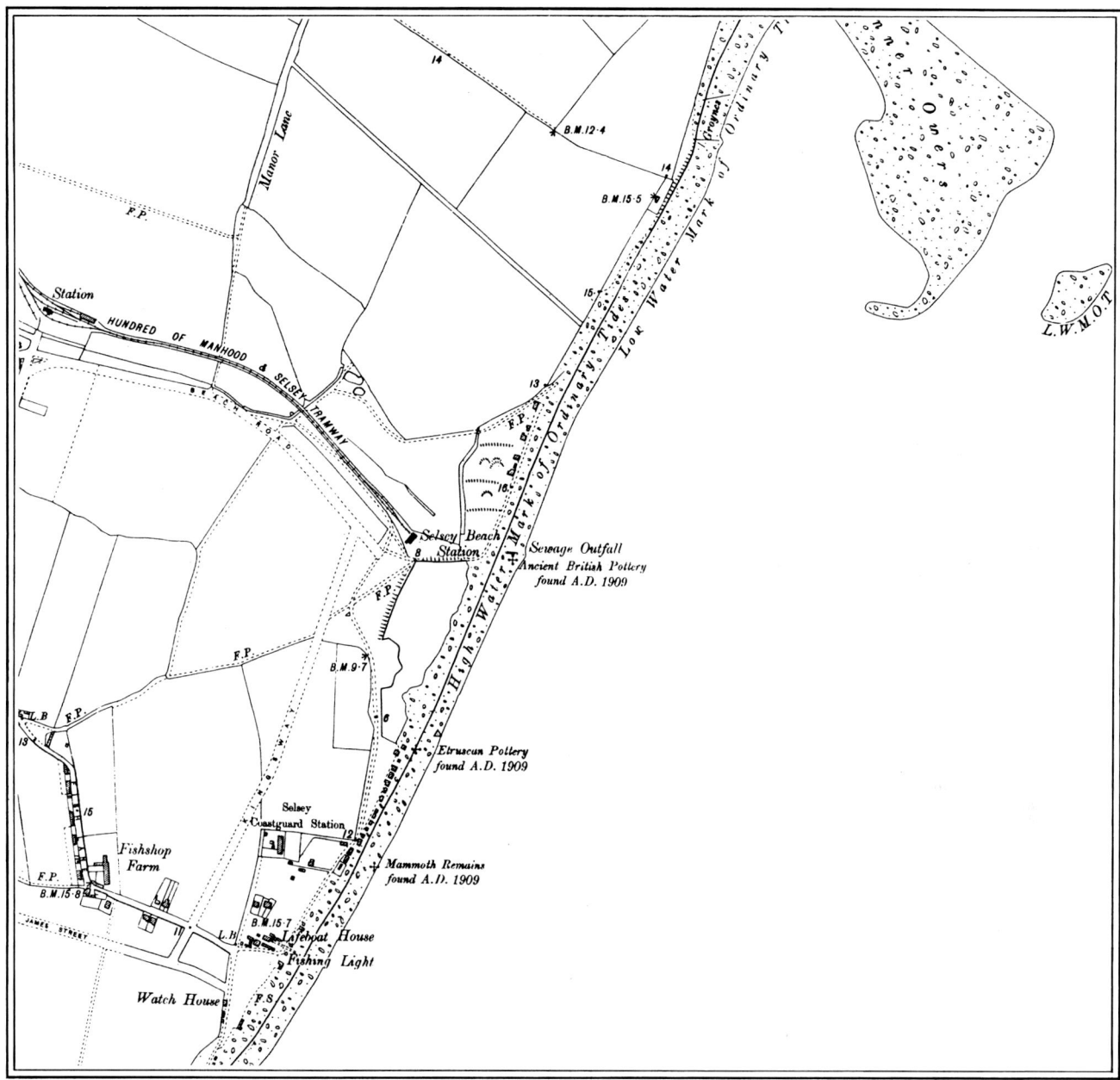

first came under the hammer. The first, with a 52ft frontage, went for £80, and the next two lots with a frontage of 80 feet each went for £105 apiece. The fourth lot, with a 50ft frontage, went for £80, and other lots of the same frontage varied in price between £75 and £82 10s 0d.[10] For the use of their staff, the Tramways Company had four houses built close to Selsey station on the north side of Church Road and these were completed by local builder, Alfred John Cutler, in July 1898.[11]

It was not only Selsey that had building land for sale, and in an auction of the late Charlie Crosbie's estate held at Dolphin Assembly Room, Chichester on Thursday, 21st July 'valuable building plots adjoining the Selsey Tramway terminus, and close to Chichester station were all sold'. Walter Lintott (the Tramway Company's secretary) took the first four most prestigious plots fronting Stockbridge Road at £35 each, the first two facing Terminus Road were purchased by Alderman W. W. Smith (a Tramway Company director) for £22 each, and the next two by a Mr. Portsmouth for a similar figure.

Monday, 1st August saw the timely opening, without ceremony, of a short extension of the Tramway across the shingle to a new terminus to be known as Selsey Beach, situated close to the sea shore. With no dwellings in the area, the extension was only to be used in the summer months. From this date, Selsey's main station became known as

Selsey Town in the timetables, but the suffix was never added to the actual name boards. Also that day, a halt with a siding was opened adjoining the main road at Ferry between Sidlesham and Selsey which, in the Company's timetables, was always shown as Ferry Siding:

	Weekdays					Thur. & Sat	Sundays		
Selsey Beach	–	9.15	1.20	3.00	6.25	–	–	2.20	7.10
Selsey	7.45	9.18	1.23	3.03	6.28	9.15	9.00	2.23	7.13
Ferry Siding	7.55	9.25	1.30	3.10	6.35	9.25	9.10	2.30	7.20
Sidlesham	8.00	9.30	1.35	3.15	6.40	9.30	9.15	2.35	7.25
Chalder	8.05	9.35	1.40	3.20	6.45	9.35	9.20	2.40	7.30
Hunston	8.10	9.40	1.45	3.25	6.50	9.40	9.25	2.45	7.35
Chichester	8.20	9.50	1.55	3.35	7.00	9.50	9.35	2.55	7.45

	Weekdays					Thur. & Sat	Sundays		
Chichester	8.30	10.30	2.15	4.30	7.25	10.20	10.55	3.15	8.00
Hunston	8.40	10.40	2.25	4.40	7.35	10.30	11.05	3.25	8.10
Chalder	8.45	10.45	2.30	4.45	7.40	10.35	11.10	3.30	8.15
Sidlesham	8.50	10.50	2.35	4.50	7.45	10.40	11.15	3.35	8.20
Ferry Siding	8.55	10.55	2.40	4.55	7.50	10.45	11.20	3.40	8.25
Selsey	9.02	11.02	2.47	5.02	8.00	10.55	11.27	3.47	8.35
Selsey Beach	9.05	11.05	2.50	5.05	–	–	11.30	3.50	–

On the afternoon of Thursday, 23rd September, the Third Annual General Meeting of the Tramways Company was held at the usual venue of the Council Chamber, Chichester, where the Directors' Report was published as follows:

'In submitting to the shareholders the audited accounts for the construction and six months' working since completion, your Directors have pleasure in reporting that after paying the interest on debentures and all charges at this date, there is an available balance on the revenue account of £277 16s 5d, which your Directors recommend being dealt with in the following manner:

'That a dividend at the rate of 3 per cent per annum be paid for the past six months, which will absorb the sum of £180.

'That £50 be placed in reserve.

'That £47 18s 5d be carried forward to the next half year.

'There has been a satisfactory increase in goods and passenger traffic since the opening of the line, and your Directors look forward with confidence to being able to recommend an increased dividend at the next yearly meeting.'

In the absence of George Woodbridge (who had been called away to attend another meeting), the chair was taken by R. L. Thornton who, referring to the Report, called attention to the fact that they had carried over 39,000 passengers, of which about 26,000 were carried during the past six months for which the dividend was proposed to be paid, and which he considered to be a very satisfactory increase, although it was felt that in this department especially, there was room for improvement. 'We hope, however,' he continued, 'that the formation of the West Sussex Brick Company, which has been decided on this morning, will materially increase the traffic and returns as every brick supplied outside the Chichester district would have to be conveyed by the Tramway before reaching the Brighton railway. It is proposed to put a siding at these brickworks near Hunston station and the shareholders of this Company could do nothing better than wish every prosperity to the Brick Company. With regard to the development of the traffic on the line, until Selsey itself is developed, it is to the Chichester end that we must look for further traffic. The people of Selsey must come to us and, of course, the Company should do everything to increase the number of "must-comes". Still it was from the Chichester end alone the temporary increase must be looked for. The shareholders should bear in mind that fact and do their utmost in the Company's interests by recommending the charms of Selsey to their friends and acquaintances.'

Turning to the expenditure side, Mr. Thornton pointed out that this was the most satisfactory part of the whole report. The expenses per train mile amounted to 9½d as against 3s 6d on many of the big railways, but as traffic increased, so must expenditure increase, and it was not to be expected that everyone who had given their services in the past would continue to do so in the future. At present the line was worked with the smallest possible staff, and that staff would have to be increased, and probably the Directors would ask for some remuneration for their time and services, although they did not think fit to do so until the prosperity of the line was assured. Alluding to the dividend proposed, he thought that possibly some might be disappointed at only 3% being paid. He admitted that it was true that a larger dividend might have been paid, but in view of the fact that increased traffic would bring the need for increased rolling stock, and that the Company had no repair or renewal fund, it was advisable that a reserve fund should be set by, and that in future an even larger sum should be placed to reserve than was at the present suggested. It was not advisable to pay a large dividend at present because the Directors and shareholders had put their money into the concern for the purpose of investment, and not for the purpose of speculation. If they had put it in for the latter purpose, they would have wanted as large a dividend as they could get in order to make shares go up in a rush and then sell out at a large profit, but what they wished to do was pay a dividend which they might well be able to increase upon in the immediate future, and so by gradual and annual advances, put the Company on a sound financial basis, and let the shares creep up to a good market value. Therefore, they did not propose to pay more than 3% at present. After the adoption of the Report and the Statement of Accounts had been carried unanimously, Newton Clayton's brother, Luther, was added to the directorate, but owing to pressure of business, James Gauntlett had to retire as auditor, and Messrs. Edmonds, Son & Clover of Portsmouth, who had acted as accountants for the Company over the past year, were elected in his place.

The directors were justly proud that their Tramway had been built and was being run extremely cheaply, but in one unenviable respect it was more akin to a main line railway in that it had to pay Passenger Duty on all passenger fares. Had the Tramway been built under the Light Railways Act of 1896 it would have been exempt from paying this duty.

When Selsey Beach station had opened to the public on 1st August, there was no cover provided for passengers, but by 29th September this had been remedied as this advertisement placed in the *West Sussex Gazette* that day advised:

'SELSEY-ON-SEA. – Beach Station. The Commodious SHELTER AND REFRESHMENT ROOMS are now open, under the management of CAPTAIN CHAS. PELHAM. Luncheons and teas provided daily.'

As noted in the above advertisement, Captain Charles Pelham was only the manager of the premises and the Refreshment Room was run and stocked by the Tramways Company. With the title of 'Successful Summer at Selsey', on 10th October the same periodical wrote:

> 'Selsey, "far from the madding crowd", has hitherto been only known as a little fishing village, famous for lobsters and prawns, but from this summer a new era of popularity dates for this charming place which, though regrettably the few who would wish to preserve the rusticity of one of the few remaining unsophisticated seaside spots of Sussex, it is hailed with delight by the many whose enjoyment of fishing, bathing and boating, has been facilitated. The light railway opened last January (sic) from Chichester to Selsey and its extension down to the beach, inaugurated in August, is the main cause of the rush of visitors this season. Several thousand guests have been received during the past months at Beacon-house, the large commodious boarding house at the point of the Bill; but as many hundreds of people have had to retrace their steps from Selsey after a vain search for rooms, arrangements have now been made for the required erection of two hotels, and red-brick villas are already beginning to spring up and line the main road leading from the straggling high street to the light-railway station. The large shelter and refreshment room at the terminus close to the sea has been an apt attraction during the season. In short, the past successful summer at Selsey promises to be the preface of a series of seasons when the salubrious and pleasant place will be widely sought.'

Convenient as it was for summer visitors, perhaps the Tramways Company may have regretted siting their Beach station quite so close to the sea as on Thursday and Friday, 12th and 13th January 1899 'a terrible storm burst over Selsey from the south-west doing considerable damage, and a great deal of wreckage has been washed ashore. The new tramway station was completely surrounded by an exceptionally high tide, and a sensation was caused by several gentlemen going about from the station to the beach in boats... Such a storm has not been experienced here for years.'[12]

Kelly's Directory for 1899 described Selsey as a village consisting of three streets, East Street, West Street and High Street, but another property auction took place at the Crown Hotel, in the village on Tuesday, 23rd May. Part of the sale comprised surplus lands of the Selsey Tramways Company, consisting of 13 plots of land at the end of the New Road, immediately overlooking the English Channel. The first plot of 60ft frontage by 148ft depth was sold for £100, Lot 5 of 100ft frontage to the sea by 293ft for £220, and Lot 6 (50ft × 171ft) for £50, the remaining lots in the section not finding bidders.[13] A month later, 70 of the Tramways Company's £5 shares were sold by the Chichester Auction Company for between £6 10s 0d and £7 0s 0d each, suggesting that some shares had been bought for the purpose of speculation after all![14]

The Tramway received some welcome extra business on Tuesday, 29th July when the scholars and friends of Sidlesham school travelled to Selsey Beach for their annual treat which had been subscribed for by the members of the school board and the principal. On what must have been a special train laid on for the occasion consisting of all the passenger stock, one carriage was filled at Chalder, and the other two at Sidlesham. The children thoroughly enjoyed the fare provided by Captain Pelham at the Refreshment Rooms at Selsey Beach station, and such was the fascination of the rippling sea that the children were reluctant to leave it for a neighbouring meadow to compete in races.[15] Twelve days later, on Thursday afternoon, 19th August, the Tramway was busy once more running extra services on the occasion of Selsey Regatta. There was a record attendance of the public and the beach on the east side of Selsey Bill 'presented and animated and picturesque scene, but the natural advantages of the spot are such that no inconvenience is caused, and every visitor was enabled to view the whole of the races from start to finish... The Selsey Steam Tramway brought down a large number of visitors in their special trams and the Selsey Regatta of 1899 must, as a social event, be considered an unqualified success...'[16]

An 'alarming accident' occurred at Selsey in August when 'a cob in a light trap', belonging to a Mr. Boniface, in which were seated Mr. Boniface's son and a friend, 'was waiting at the station for the 11.05 train when the pony, apparently irritated by flies, bolted and ran up the tramline. It had not gone far when the wheels came off, but the occupants escaped uninjured. The pony continued its mad career for nearly a mile when it was captured and found to be little the worse save for bruises.'[17]

At the Tramways Company's Annual General Meeting on Thursday afternoon, 12th October, the Chairman, George Woodbridge, read the Directors' Report:

> 'The increase of passenger traffic has been satisfactory, and that of the Goods traffic has exceeded our expectations. The extension to Selsey Beach has been completed, and the Permanent Way throughout has, during the past year, been considerably improved, the radii of the curves have been reduced in several places and heavier rails have been substituted thereupon. Additional Siding accommodation has been provided for Goods traffic, but the continual increase in this department demands still further provision. It is also necessary to procure additional Rolling Stock. These, and other requirements will involve an expenditure of about £1,000, and feeling that in the near future still further Capital Expenditure will prove necessary, your Directors have decided to recommend the raising of additional Capital, and ask you to sanction the creation of 960 New Ordinary Shares, of which they propose to issue 480 for the present, such Shares to be offered in the first instance at par to the holders of five shares and upwards pro rata to their present holdings.'

Commenting on the contents of the Report, Mr. Woodbridge expressed his satisfaction in that the goods traffic had made 'wonderful strides', the amount earned for the year being £648 11s 6d. He considered they had every reason to believe that both the goods and passenger traffic would still further increase as time went on. The alterations made in the permanent way during the year had brought about a great improvement. Some of the curves had been sharper than they would have wished, and they had been able to straighten these, and those who used the Tramway would testify to the great improvement. In order to cope with the increase in goods traffic, it was proposed to obtain additional rolling stock and provide further siding accommodation. Up to the present, the Directors had been content to do their work voluntarily, but the question of the payment of fees had again been left for the future.

The amount of accounts due to the Company appeared to H. E. Breach to be a large sum. The Managing Director,

A PROMISING BEGINNING (1897–1909)

Newton Clayton, explained that about £200 was owed to the Company by one man – a builder who was employed by the Company to erect the station at the beach. The engineer had now given his certificate and the builder had drawn his money and the Company had drawn theirs, so that the accounts outstanding were not quite as they appeared on paper. Mr. Clayton also mentioned that the amount set down for the secretary's salary was really drawn by the assistant secretary and clerk who looked after the line, while the sum of £50, set down as Managing Director's charges, had to cover petty cash and sundry other payments, a very small proportion indeed going to the Managing Director! Mr. Breach next enquired whether the laying of the curves had been credited to Revenue or Capital Account. Newton Clayton replied that the whole cost of new rails went to Capital Account, as well as a large proportion of the labour, but a certain amount went to the Revenue because the work was somewhat in the nature of substitution. He confirmed

Chichester *arriving at Selsey with a train from Chichester on 15th May 1899.* LCGB KEN NUNN COLLECTION

Taken on the same day, this companion picture shows Chichester *running back into Selsey on an afternoon train from Selsey Beach with the ex-LBSCR Stroudley Road Van and two of the Falcon carriages. Notice the platelayers' trolley leaning against the boundary fence to the left of the locomotive.* LCGB, KEN NUNN COLLECTION

that exactly the same procedure had been followed in dealing with the accounts as was practised in all railway companies. The Directors' Report was then adopted.

The Chairman next moved 'that a dividend of 4% be declared: that a further £50 be placed to Reserve Account and that £27 13s 9d be carried forward to next year'. R. L. Thornton, in seconding the motion, thought that the payment of 4% for the short time that the line had been working was very satisfactory and hoped that the shareholders were pleased in the way in which they had invested their money. He trusted that in future the Company would be able to pay a still higher dividend. Newton Clayton thanked the shareholders for their renewal of confidence and assured them that, as in the past, so in the future, he and his fellow directors who thoroughly had the interests of the shareholders at heart – would manage the affairs of the Company to the best of their ability. The Chairman also returned thanks, adding that he had always taken an interest in railways, and he was pleased that the Selsey Tramway was going on so well; he believed that 'it would make an excellent system'.

A special meeting followed, George Woodbridge, in accordance with notice, moving 'that the present Capital of the Company be increased from £12,000 to £16,800, by the creation of 960 new ordinary shares at £5 each of which 480 shares shall be placed immediately and offered in the first instance at par to existing holders of 5 shares and upwards, rateably in proportion to the present holdings, and that the remaining 480 shares be issued when and in such manner as the Directors shall consider advisable'. In seconding the motion, Newton Clayton pointed out that the Capital of the Company had already been exceeded to the extent of £325. The chief causes of that were the extensions which the Company had been obliged to make (i.e. from the intended terminus at Selsey to Selsey Town and then on to Selsey Beach) together with the relaying of curves, the deviation of the line and the acquisition of extra rolling stock. Then again, when Crosbie's estate came into the market, the Directors purchased some land at a very reasonable rate, some of it outside the city boundary, only costing £45 to £50 per acre. One piece which was acquired was for the purpose of extending the sidings at Chichester station which had been done. A three-cornered plot was also bought just outside the city boundary, the idea being that in the event of the Company's business largely developing, the Directors would be able, if necessary, to erect a goods station outside so as to avoid paying the city rates. He believed that in spending the money the Company had acted wisely. During the next year an additional car would be required at a cost of £360. More goods wagons would be wanted and a few more alterations to the line would have to be carried out. At the very least, therefore, the Company would next year require an additional £1,000. R. L. Thornton confirmed that he supported the motion on the ground that it was a great mistake to 'starve' the line, and that at the time the venture was started, the ideas of the Company were modest. He believed that there was no light railway which had been constructed at so low a cost. The motion was then carried unanimously.

The only other business before the meeting was the passing of the resolution to correct a clerical error in the articles of Association; that under the powers conferred upon public companies by section 50 of the Company's Act, 1862, regulation no. 141 of the Articles of Association of the Company shall be altered to read: '141, Capital on a poll. Every member shall have one vote for every share held by him up to 10 shares, and one vote for every 5 shares beyond 10.' A vote of thanks to the Chairman brought the proceedings to a close.

The following Wednesday, the *Chichester Observer* wrote:

'The annual meeting of the Selsey Tramways Company revealed a satisfactory state of affairs to Shareholders and Directors alike. For a 4% Dividend on the first full year's working of a not yet developed light railway is as good as could possibly be expected; the Company has the advantage of being managed by a Board of gentlemen of undoubtedly business abilities, whose knowledge of the district and personal influence cannot fail to command the confidence of those who invested money to open up Selsey and the large agricultural district around it. The Directors had received unanimous approval of the Shareholders in their proposal to raise additional capital and, as the existing holders of shares have the preference of allotment, there are not likely to be many to be divided among the public.'

Unfortunately, it would seem that the overall picture was not as rosy as the Tramway Company's Annual General Meeting had made out and on the front page of the same newspaper just two weeks later they reported under the title of 'THE SELSEY TRAMWAY'S TRAFFIC':

'The persons (whoever they may be) responsible for the proper management of the Locomotive arrangements of the Selsey Steam Tramway are alleged to have lately proved themselves capable of inflicting a serious amount of inconvenience and loss of time upon the public who use that means of communication with Chichester, and judging from complaints freely expressed among the passengers as to the utter want of punctuality in the starting and arriving of the Trams; the liability delay whence once on the road owing to some defects in the locomotive making their presence felt, and latterly the uncertainty whether Trams would start at all, the matter calls for serious notice. Ever since the opening of the line it has been the frequent mishaps to the engines and their subsequential banishment into the sheds for repair, become apparent to users of the line that one, if not both, of the locomotives are not exactly what they should be, and there is no exaggeration in saying that a great deal of anxiety exists as to the safety of travelling by the Tram under existing circumstances. It was, therefore, a matter of comment amongst many that the annual report of the Company lately published contained no information that the locomotive defects were receiving consideration, or that the Company recognise their responsibility under this head. The matter has, however, been more apparent than usual during the past week when, owing to both engines being more or less incapable of performing their work, the tram service (generally unreliable) was quite disorganised, and on some days, certain of the trams could not be run at all. The complaint against the Company seems to be that, knowing how liable the only working engine they have in use was to exhibit certain defects and, of course, dislocation of traffic and inconvenience, the Company should have made arrangements to meet the event (which happened more than once) of the engine becoming unworkable; and therefore, in not making these arrangements, they entirely overlooked what should have been their first consideration, viz. the interest, safety and convenience of the public whose custom they invite. Serious complaint also exists in the "Goods" traffic and the cleanliness of the passenger cars and the windows etc., and the general opinion seems to prevail that some traffic alterations are needed in the conduct of affairs if the Shareholders are to expect another dividend of four per cent. We have not the slightest wish to embarrass the Company, but in the interests of the public it is our duty to point out the above complaints, which we have by no means exaggerated.'

The Tramways Company was, no doubt, suitably embarrassed, but it made no public reply to the damning article. Its contents did, however, upset J. L. Belcher, the locomotive foreman, who saw fit to write the following letter (without disclosing his position) that the *Chichester Observer* printed in its edition dated 8th November:

'Sir,
'Would you kindly allow me a little space in your noted paper, for those of your readers who exist in doubt as to the safety of the Selsey Tramway Company's locomotive which you alluded to in your issue of 1st November. It will be understood that these engines are under capable supervision and are examined at regular intervals by capable inspectors. I may also mention that they are inspected by the "National Boiler Insurance Company Ltd." who also inspect the boilers etc. at regular intervals. Trusting that this will remove any existing doubt as to the safety of these engines. The defect of the engine is well known to us, the alteration of which has been in hand for some weeks past. I know that there are people in Selsey and elsewhere who venture to allude to the lubrication being common, of which this has nothing whatever to do with the defective points in the locomotive, and I may say that we use the best viz. "Vacuum Oil Company Lubricants", who supply 33 British Railway Companies.

Yours truly, J. L. Belcher.'

Two examples of The Cynicus Publishing Company's humorous postcards. These were not produced for any particular railway (or Tramway) company, and the station names were changed to suit any local line. COLLECTION J. WYNNE-TYSON

With Hurst Nelson third class carriage No. 4 being delivered in 1900, this is the only known photograph to show all four bogie carriages in a train together (see inset). Taken in front of the engine shed at Selsey, it also shows Selsey in modified condition. The Hurst Nelson carriage (third in the rake) was new.
COLLECTION PAUL LAMING

Selsey with her train at Selsey c.1901 prior to the station building being extended. The paintwork of the second (Hurst Nelson) carriage had already faded to match the two earlier arrivals. With its high rounded ends, ex-GER open wagon No. 10 can be seen on the original siding in the background.
AUTHOR'S COLLECTION

'How we arrived at Selsey' is the title of this postcard published c.1902 and, judging by the number of passengers gathered on the platform, the tram was probably already late for its return trip back to the city! Before the train had come to a standstill, the fireman was climbing down from the cab ready to uncouple so that Chichester *could quickly run round her train. The figure beside the lamp post was magistrate Edward G. Arnell and the man nearer the station building, with arms folded, was Walter Smith, the proprietor of the Fisherman's Joy Inn.*
COLLECTION PAUL LAMING

In defence of the Tramways Company it should perhaps be noted that *Chichester* was out of service receiving new cylinders at this time, but why the two-year-old *Selsey* had become so temperamental is not recorded. Just what did the newspaper expect the Tramway to do with no available locomotives? It is disturbing to note that Rev. Whitechurch's experience with late-running trams back in early 1898 was not an isolated case, but that this poor treatment of its passengers had already become 'the norm'. The Company *had* tried to redress the matter and had taken up Alderman Ballard's suggestion in his speech on opening day that 'if the times stated on the timetable could not be kept up, alterations should be made', and slight amendments had been introduced, but obviously to no avail. There was, however, no excuse for dirty windows and the lack of cleanliness in the passenger carriages.

Selsey well and truly arrived in the 20th century when, on Saturday, 21st April 1900, the directors and some shareholders of the Selsey Gas & Lighting Company Ltd. (described as mostly 'city men') visited the town 'to formerly inaugurate the use of gas as an illuminant' and that evening Selsey Town station, Station Road and the central part of the High Street 'were lit up with gas' for the first time.[18]

At a meeting of the Westhampnett Board of Guardians on Friday, 22nd June, notice was placed upon the agenda 'that the Hundred of Manhood & Selsey Tramways Company, having given notice of their intention to appeal to the ensuing quarter sessions for the county of Sussex against the poor rates of the parishes of Donnington, Hunston, North Mundham, Sidlesham and Selsey, application being made to the Board of Guardians of the Westhampnett Union for consent that the Assessment Committee may appear as respondents to such appeals in the names of the guardians in the said union'. However, the chairman announced that he had received a letter from the Tramways Company to the effect that owing to lack of time with which to complete the necessary preparations, the appeal had not been entered for the approaching Sessions, but would be proceeded with at the Sessions following. In the meantime, the Company would pay the rates under protest.

Rough weather on Whit Monday, August Bank Holiday and Selsey Sports Day resulted in disappointing numbers of people travelling to the seaside – three important days during which the Tramways Company expected to take the largest amounts in fares! Goods revenue was also being hit as the cost of building in Selsey had risen by something in the region of 30% to 40% and several people who had intended to build in the town were not doing so. It was not all doom and gloom and on the plus side a goods loop had been put in to serve the West Sussex Brick Company's premises just to the north of Hunston station.

It was announced at the Annual General Meeting on Thursday, 18th October that gross receipts for the year ending 31st August, 1900 had increased by £300 6s 10d over 1899, but that expenses had risen by £254 18s 4d to £1,715 1s 11d, resulting in a credit balance on the Revenue account of £927 5s 9d, compared with £881 7s 3d the previous year. H. E. Breach asked if the Directors were correct in adding to the capital expenditure £52 13s 10d laid out on locomotives as, in his opinion, something ought to be written off rather than added. Newton Clayton (the General Manager) pointed out that as regards locomotives, they had expended £171 on renewals and repairs which had been put on the Revenue account. Some of the expense of repairs had come into the last Statement of Account, and the £52 in question was for new cylinders, etc. William Smith then asked 'Do

This picture of Selsey station can be dated to just after the Spring of 1900 as the gas lamps (with their unusual supports on either side of the platform's backing fence) were installed in April of that year. One of the original Falcon bogie carriages can be seen outside the engine shed and a 7-plank mainline company's wagon on the goods loop. The main running line was so sharply curved that it required a check rail. Notice also the wooden coaling stage behind the oil hut beside the run-round loop. Disappearing from sight behind the engine shed, the extension to Selsey Beach ran across the shingle to the sea shore whilst in this view Selsey Town station appears to stand in splendid isolation. COLLECTION PAUL LAMING

1332

Selsey engine shed pictured when it was around 12 years old, but still in original condition with its curved roof. The 90ft x 30ft building was capable of holding up to six locomotives, and it was in here that the maintenance of all the Tramway's rolling stock was carried out. With their white warning diamonds, the doors opened inwards and a lamp holder was positioned high up on the south-east corner, although it appears never to have carried a lamp. The only natural light in the shed was provided by the three windows on either side. Behind the shed, the elevated water tank stands beside what had been the main running line to Selsey Beach.
NATIONAL RAILWAY MUSEUM

A PROMISING BEGINNING (1897–1909)

For the first few years, the Tramway Company had its offices in South Street, Chichester, but they were transferred to Selsey when the station building was extended at its eastern end in matching materials, although the join is clearly visible. Note how the station building now extended beyond the platform at this, the western end. Two extra supports were added to the lengthened awning, this time with the customary 'V' braced supports, and the gas lamp nearest the camera has had to be moved away from the building remounted on a new, but conventional post. At the far end of the platform, beyond the other lamp (still with its unusual support), there was a gap in the backing fence, where goods would regularly be unloaded down a ramp into the yard behind. Note the splendid clock on the platform just beyond the station building and the three ex-GER open wagons, still with their high curved ends, just visible on the loop siding behind the fence.
NATIONAL RAILWAY MUSEUM

Viewed from the rear we can see how the ladies' lavatories (a most unusual luxury for a Holman Stephens' station) were added to the rear of the station building, along with a stores shed to the side. Access to the gentlemen's urinal was via the outward opening shed-like door beside the shed. A gas lamp was sited above the rear entrance to the waiting room, but most passengers found it easier to make their way to the platform via its eastern ramp as there were no steps up to the door. Another of the Company's ex-GER open wagons features on the goods loop on the left. C.1909.
NATIONAL RAILWAY MUSEUM

In 1866, the parish church of St. Peter, Selsey, had been moved stone by stone from its original site some two miles away in Church Norton to bring the building closer to its congregation! In this postcard view c.1909 we look across the end of Station Road which, prior to the arrival of the Tramway, had been called Church Road, and it is renamed as such today. The main Chichester to Selsey road is seen running right to left in front of the church and the large building on the left had signs on it advertising the Selsey Hotel and Beacon House.
WSCC LIBRARY SERVICE

Judging by the position of the ex-GER covered van on the loop siding to the left of Selsey station building in the distance, this picture could possibly have been taken on the same day as the one on the facing page. Station Road turned off to the west alongside the Selsey Hotel whilst it was Manor Road which ran straight ahead to extend right into the Tramway station's yard.
COLLECTION PAUL LAMING

A PROMISING BEGINNING (1897–1909)

A fair number of passengers, including three sailors, are seen leaving Selsey station after alighting from a tram from Chichester. One of the Tramway's ex-GER covered vans features on the goods loop siding to the west of the station approach road, with open wagon No. 6 to the right of the picture, in company with a Midland Railway open and a sheeted LBSCR wagon. LENS OF SUTTON

you think the engines are worth what they stand on account?' to which Mr. Clayton replied 'More!'

Turning to the general affairs of the Company, Newton Clayton explained that, although he had hoped that it would have been larger, the increase in passenger traffic amounted to a very satisfactory £112. Expenses for traffic had gone up by £68 because instead of two boys, they now had two young men to look after the stations, and he was sure that they would all agree that they did it much better. From £21 in 1899, their rates had been increased by £43 to £64 and although the Company would pay under protest, the Directors had decided to appeal against this. There was an extra sum of £40 for the renewal of the permanent way and on coal and oil there was an increase of £55. With regard to coal and its effect on the coming year, they had a contract for the supply of smokeless fuel which would take them up to next May, the price being 30s 9d and 31/– per ton. If they had to purchase it now, it would cost them 38/– per ton! Then, referring to the *Chichester Observer's* comments the previous November and other complaints, he admitted

> 'There has been some grumbling in which the way the business of the Tramway has been conducted, but I suppose this is the case with all railway companies. Some shareholders think we should have imposing stations, and others that we should have a double line, bigger rails and double the number of trams per day; but if they would look at the accounts, they would see that we could not attempt to do these things at present. It seems to me that the first thing necessary is to look after the safety and convenience of the public, then to take care that the working plant is in good order, and that the rolling stock is kept in fair repair, and next comes the question of dividend. If we went to greater expense, we would not be able to pay the same amount of dividend as we are now paying. If Selsey continues building, as I hope it will, our revenue in the coming year should increase, and in time to come, I believe our dividend will be larger, as some of you expect.'

Notice that there was no mention (or apology) regarding the Tramway's apparent inability to keep to the published timetable!

The chairman, George Woodbridge, in suggesting that 4% was a very reasonable amount for so young a company, moved a resolution declaring that that amount, once again, be paid in accordance with the recommendations of the Directors, and with William Smith seconding, this was carried. James and Luther Clayton along with William Smith were re-elected as Directors and Sharp Garland thought that it was 'very liberal' of the Directors to take upon themselves the work without remuneration. Mr. Little also spoke of the generosity of the Directors in giving their time and ability without any fees, which was only right for businessmen to expect to receive. During the year William Payne had replaced Walter Lintott as the Company's secretary.

It had been proposed to hold a special meeting for the purpose of considering the advisability of changing the name of the Company, but the Directors having just met, had decided to postpone the matter. It was thought that the

What a contrast a London, Brighton & South Coast Railway train of the early 1900s made with those of the Selsey Tramway. Here Billinton-designed B2 Class 1896-built 4–4–0 No. 320 Rastrick (named after John Urpeth Rastrick, engineer of the LBSCR's London to Brighton line) was taking on water at Chichester while working a westbound service. The Tramways Company's station was beyond the goods yard, hidden behind the sheeted open wagons that form the background.
COLLECTION R. M. CASSERLEY

A busy South Street, Chichester, looking north towards the market cross. The London, Brighton & South Coast Railway's station was a hundred yards or so behind the photographer, with the Selsey Tramway's terminus a little further to the south beyond the main line's level crossing.
WSCC LIBRARY SERVICE

Company's name was too long (!) but upon making enquiries it was found it required some correspondence before the change could be effected!

During 1901 a general depression was affecting the country and the south coast in particular, and with no large buildings being erected in Selsey, the Company's goods receipts were considerably down as it had been the Tramway that had enjoyed the monopoly of transporting materials to the village in the past. The Tramway was also feeling the effect of the increase in the price of coal to a considerable extent, but so did other railway companies as well, this being reflected in their lower dividends paid on ordinary shares compared with previous years. A single carriage would bring up the rear of 'mixed' trains, although they weren't advertised in the timetables as such, but passengers wishing to avail themselves of the dubious 'privilege' of such a slow and uncomfortable journey, had to sign the following form:

............190

SIR,

In consideration of my being privileged to travel in the Goods Train running between Chichester and Selsey stations, I hereby agree to pay the usual Fare, and hold the Company free from any liability in respect of any injury, loss, delay, or inconvenience that may happen by accident or otherwise to my person or property whilst travelling in the said Train, and in joining or leaving the said Train.

Signed:...........................

To the Traffic Manager,

Hundred of Manhood & Selsey Tramways Company Limited.

Selsey Beach station had not been as well patronised as had been hoped for, and with many services slightly retimed and the late Thursday and Saturday trams running considerably earlier, only three weekday trams ran through to the southern terminus in the summer of 1901:

	Weekdays					*Thur. & Sat*	*Sundays*		
Selsey Beach	–	–	1.20	3.00	6.20	–	9.00	2.25	7.05
Selsey	7.55	9.25	1.25	3.05	6.25	8.30	9.05	2.30	7.10
Ferry Siding	8.00	9.30	1.30	3.10	6.30	8.35	9.10	2.35	7.15
Sidlesham	8.05	9.35	1.35	3.15	6.35	8.40	9.15	2.40	7.20
Chalder	8.10	9.40	1.40	3.20	6.40	8.45	9.20	2.45	7.25
Hunston	8.15	9.45	1.45	3.25	6.45	8.50	9.25	2.50	7.30
Chichester	8.30	9.55	1.55	3.35	6.55	9.00	9.35	3.00	7.40
	Weekdays					*Thur. & Sat*	*Sundays*		
Chichester	8.40	10.30	2.15	4.30	7.25	9.15	11.20	3.15	8.30
Hunston	8.50	10.40	2.25	4.40	7.35	9.25	11.30	3.25	8.40
Chalder	8.55	10.45	2.30	4.45	7.40	9.30	11.35	3.30	8.45
Sidlesham	9.00	10.50	2.35	4.50	7.45	9.35	11.40	3.35	8.50
Ferry Siding	9.05	10.55	2.40	4.55	7.50	9.40	11.45	3.40	8.55
Selsey	9.15	11.02	2.47	5.02	8.00	9.50	11.52	3.47	9.05
Selsey Beach	–	11.07	2.50	5.05	–	–	11.55	3.50	–

Upon receiving the Tramway's Accounts dated 17th October, the Company's auditors felt that it was their duty to make a special report pointing out the necessity, in their opinion, of there being a Reserve Account. They appreciated that it was not in their province to dictate the course to be adopted by the Company, but they felt that it was a weak point not to have a depreciation account. They also noted that nothing had been set aside to reserve in regard to any of the accounts of permanent way, etc, as in former years and there was no provision for bad debts. The Directors immediately replied, explaining that, as they saw it, the Reserve Account was one built up in good years against bad times, and that the past year had not been sufficiently good for them to provide an additional sum for it. With regard to bad debts, none of them were regarded as bad, and if any of them were found to be so, they would be written off as they came. As far as depreciation, the Company had expended no less than £90 on the locomotives from Revenue, and as far as the permanent way was concerned, they had put it in better order that year than it had been at all!

Under the heading 'CITY CHAT' on 20th November the *Chichester Observer* reported 'On Sunday evening the Selsey Tram went off and left the guard on the platform (at Chichester), who presumably had to trudge home to the little seaside resort', hardly a pleasant walk at that time of the year in the dark after a long day's work!

The Tramways Company's AGM was transferred from the Council Chamber to the Assembly Rooms in Chichester on Thursday, 21st November but, apart from the directorate, only four shareholders attended. Passenger receipts for the year ending 31st August 1901 had increased by £79 15s 4d, but gross receipts were down by £191 3s 3d to £2,451 4s 5d. Expenses had increased by £154 7s 11d to £1,869 9s 10d, this being attributed mainly to locomotive repairs, ballasting of the permanent way and the increase in the price of coal. After providing for interest on Debentures, Mortgage, etc., the Balance of Net Revenue was shown at £293 9s 10d, enabling the Directors to recommend the payment of a dividend of only 2%, leaving a balance of £20 17s 10d to be carried forward to next year's account.

Moving the adoption of the Directors' Report, George Woodbridge thought that there was some consolation in the increase on passenger receipts and, having studied them month by month, the Directors had found a very satisfactory improvement in what they had always considered to be their mainstay. With only about £300 to deal with for the shareholders, he explained that the Board felt the matter an open question for the shareholders to decide upon, the Directors simply indicating that a 2% dividend was available. As regards a Depreciation Account, it was hoped to start one, particularly for rolling stock, in the near future. One item in the accounts that required comment concerned the sale of surplus land, the Company having sold off more than they had estimated, this amount having been placed in the Capital Account.

Seconding the adoption of the Report, Newton Clayton admitted that, with regards to dividends, the Directors did not recommend anything as they hardly knew which was the best course to adopt, whether to carry the whole amount to reserve, or to declare a dividend. Personally, he should prefer there not being a dividend, but that might cause a certain amount of shareholders to be obliged to part with their shares at a sacrifice, but he had no doubt as to the ultimate success of the Company, and from all indications the undertaking would be a big success shortly. (Applause) H. E. Breach agreed that it would be best not to declare a dividend and it was ultimately resolved on his proposition, seconded by Mr. Little, that £100 should be placed to Reserve Account and the remainder carried forward.

No doubt, in no small part due to the arrival of the Tramway four years earlier, the 1901 census revealed that the population of Selsey had increased to 1,258, consisting of 312 families living in 300 inhabited houses. The 1851 census had given the population as 934 and fifty years earlier it had been 564.

For some reason in 1902, the Tramways Company found it necessary to vary the early morning trams on Mondays and Tuesdays to those of the remainder of the week. 'Up trams

The swans with their cygnets don't seem to have been at all perturbed by Selsey *and her train from Chichester approaching the lifting bridge over the canal north of Hunston.*
COLLECTION PAUL LAMING

A PROMISING BEGINNING (1897–1909)

This is the map that accompanied the Chichester Observer's article on Wednesday, 18th June 1902 promoting the proposed new road between Sidlesham Tide Mill and Pagham village that would have shortened the circuitous 14 mile journey between Selsey and Bognor by half. The Tramway's route is omitted, but it ran from the top of the plan half a mile to the right of Sidlesham Church to cross Rookery Lane close to the main road, with Sidlesham station being sited midway between Sidlesham Mill and the main road. AUTHOR'S COLLECTION

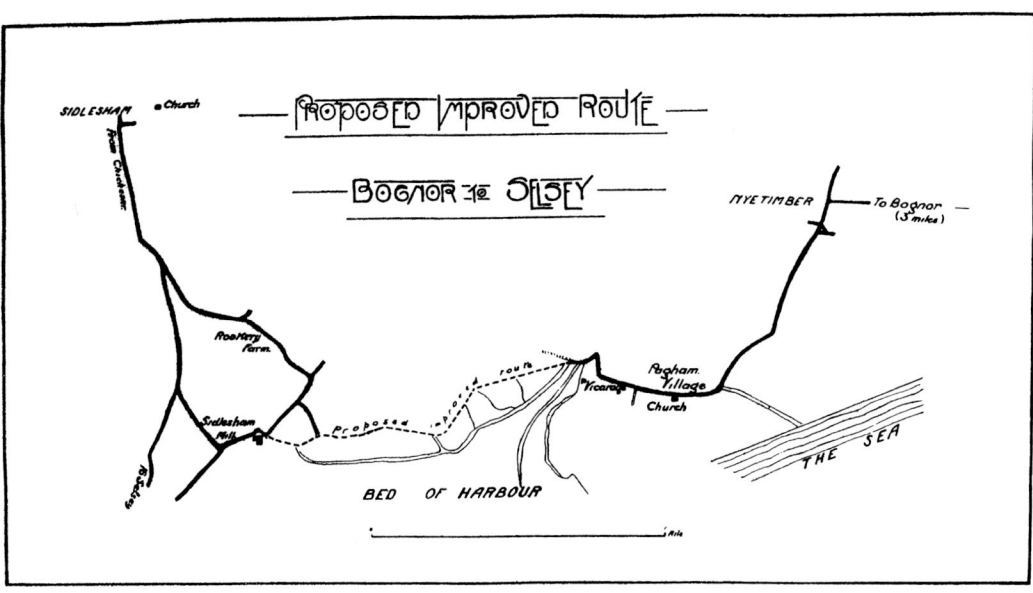

THE PROPOSED IMPROVED ROUTE TO SELSEY.

were now allowed a full 15 minutes for the two-mile run between Hunston and Chichester, although down services continued to take the more realistic 10 minutes. During the peak summer timetable only two up trams departed from Selsey Beach, in comparison with four down services which terminated there and the late Thursday and Saturday services were discontinued. However, with this timetable came the introduction of some semi-fast services omitting Ferry Siding, Chalder and Hunston on the up journey but calling at Hunston in addition on the down. The timetable was confusingly set out thus:

a great boon to Bognor, Pagham, Chichester, Sidlesham and Selsey which are cut off from all intercommunications except by the present circuitous route' via Hunston, North Mundham and Lagness. The newspaper continued: 'We believe that the public will be greatly indebted to Mr. W. H. B. Fletcher, JP, CC (Trustee of the late Mr. F. W. Grafton's estate) if the scheme is successfully carried out, for it was largely through his influence that the promoters of the Selsey Tramways agreed to give considerable support to the scheme when found practical to launch it'. It was estimated that £800 would be required to build the road, and the

	Weekdays										*Sundays*		
Selsey Beach	A	A	A	B	B	–	–	4.25	5.55	–	9.00	1.45	7.05
Selsey	7.00	8.30	9.50	7.35	9.25	11.30	1.30	4.30	6.00	7.15	9.05	1.50	7.10
Ferry Siding	7.03	8.33	9.53	7.38	9.28	11.33	1.33	4.33	–	7.18	9.08	1.53	7.13
Sidlesham	7.05	8.35	9.55	7.40	9.30	11.35	1.35	4.35	6.05	7.20	9.10	1.55	7.15
Chalder	7.10	8.40	10.00	7.45	9.35	11.40	1.40	4.40	–	7.25	9.15	2.00	7.20
Hunston	7.15	8.45	10.05	7.50	9.40	11.45	1.45	4.45	–	7.30	9.20	2.05	7.25
Chichester	7.30	9.00	10.20	8.05	9.55	12.00	2.00	5.00	6.25	7.45	9.35	2.20	7.40

	Weekdays									*Sundays*		
Chichester		7.45	9.10	8.40	10.35	12.45	2.40	5.10	6.30	8.00	11.00	2.30	8.25
Hunston		7.55	9.15	8.50	10.45	12.55	2.50	5.20	6.40	8.10	11.10	2.40	8.35
Chalder		8.00	–	8.55	10.50	1.00	2.55	5.25	–	8.15	11.15	2.45	8.40
Sidlesham		8.05	9.25	9.00	10.55	1.05	3.00	5.30	6.50	8.20	11.20	2.50	8.45
Ferry Siding		8.10	–	9.05	11.00	1.10	3.05	5.35	–	8.25	11.25	2.55	8.50
Selsey		8.20	9.40	9.15	11.07	1.20	3.12	5.42	7.05	8.35	11.32	3.02	9.00
Selsey Beach		A	A	B	11.10	–	3.15	5.45	–	–	11.35	3.05	–

Plans originally prepared fifty years earlier were revived during the summer to construct a road 1 mile 200yds long and 30ft wide from the Tide Mill at Sidlesham eastwards across the bed of the harbour to Pagham village, thus reducing the present mileage from Selsey to Bognor from 14 to 7 miles. The *Chichester Observer* on Wednesday, 18th June regarded it as 'a most desirable undertaking which will prove

Tramways Company clearly thought that it was a worthwhile cause as they subscribed £50 towards the scheme, as did W. H. B. Fletcher whilst the Grafton Estates subscribed £200. Eight weeks later the *Chichester Observer* explained '... The generosity of the Grafton Trustees and Mr. W. H. B. Fletcher to set the ball rolling with such a splendid start to the finances in addition to the land given for the purpose, should stimulate others to quickly follow so excellent a precedent. It may not be generally known that Mr. Fletcher parted with his land on special terms to the Tramway Company, that the "good turn" might be reciprocated in advancing this enterprise'. Others, however, were not to 'quickly follow so excellent a precedent' and with the necessary funds not being forthcoming, the dream of opening up 'a splendid drive from Bognor to Selsey and vice versa' remained just that – a dream.

The *Chichester Observer* reported on 6th August that 'the Selsey Tramway Company had a busy time in conveying many hundreds of Cicestrians to and from the rural attractions of Selsey-on-Sea (on Bank Holiday Monday) and these trippers, along with the large number of visitors already established there, lent a lively aspect to this rising resort'.

The first suggestion that the Tramway might not enjoy the monopoly of taking passengers from Chichester to Selsey came in a paragraph in the same periodical dated 22nd April 1903. Under the heading 'A Motor 'Bus Service' it announced 'that a Company is being promoted for the establishment of ... an omnibus service between Chichester ... and Selsey. The desirability of such facilities of communication will be readily conceded. It remains for our well to do residents to support such a venture by largely responding to the invitation to take shares in the proposed Company ... There ought to be no doubt as to this being a good opportunity for profitable investment. We understand that every arrangement has been made for speedy commencement of the undertaking, as soon as the necessary capital has been subscribed ...' Nothing more was heard of the venture, so the Tramway Company was able to breathe a sigh of relief and relax, at least for the time being.

'The increasingly popular seaside resort of Selsey was well patronised on Whit Monday, (1st June 1903) when the weather was perfect. Four or five hundred people came into the place by the Light Railway, many also arrived by bicycles and carriages ...' Sadly, the following evening, a four-year old girl (the daughter of a LBSCR goods porter) was knocked down and seriously injured by the Tram as it crossed Terminus Road on its way into Chichester station. The unfortunate child was taken to the Chichester Infirmary where she was detained.[19] Over the August Bank Holiday, Chichester was described as being 'a deserted city' with most people having gone to the seaside. Bognor was largely patronised, whilst 'not a few' were seen at Selsey, the trains being crowded.[20]

The Tramway lost a member of its staff in October when Donald Jones (known affectionately as 'Poor Don' by his colleagues) passed away following a brief illness. Aged only 32, he was described as being 'a general favourite, and his pleasant and obliging manners were often remarked by the travelling public'. His body was conveyed by tram to Chichester 'with something like funeral honours' and thence to Havant to be interred with his brother who had died only a month previously.[21]

Passengers were warned for the first time from the beginning of 1904 that the 10.35am weekday departure from Chichester (10.45am on Mondays) and the 11.30am (11.45am on Mondays) from Selsey were mixed trains, but no allowance was made for the shunting of wagons en route with a mere 30 minutes being allowed for the Up journey and 32 minutes for the Down. No wonder the Company had problems running to time. Some drivers didn't help matters by frequently waiting beyond departure time for regular passengers to turn up. On one occasion, when a young resident hadn't put in appearance at Selsey station on the day that he was due to travel to London, the driver called at his house and was heard to shout "Come on, Master John! We can't wait all day for you!"[22] Guard William Walker, who had joined the Tramways Company in the previous year, might sometimes delay the departure of the early morning school tram for stragglers, but if he was in a bad mood, he would leave on time without them![23]

The *Chichester Observer* on 6th July reported on what is believed to be the first accident at Stockbridge Road level crossing, which could have resulted in far more serious consequences:

CYCLISTS' NARROW ESCAPE AT CHICHESTER AT THE TRAMWAY CROSSING

Another revolution of the wheel of a bicycle and the Tramway crossing below Stockbridge would have been the scene of a fatal accident on Wednesday last, June 29th. On that afternoon Mr. Dawson (the master of Petworth Union) and his wife were cycling from Chichester to Selsey, and, being strangers to the road, were quite unaware of the level crossing which runs across the road at Stockbridge and as there is nothing to indicate that the level crossing exists they were not so prepared for their danger as they otherwise would be. They were proceeding along the road at an ordinary pace and as they reached the level crossing they were alarmed by seeing the engine of the tram emerging from the gate on to the road.

Mr. Dawson, who was slightly ahead of his wife just managed to jump from his machine in time to avoid being run over, and is stated by an eye witness of the occurrence that one more revolution of the wheel would have brought him underneath the engine. Mr. Dawson fell into the road and was severely grazed about the hands, and his machine received the damage which he fortunately escaped, whilst Mrs. Dawson received a severe shock.

The engine driver states that he whistled when approaching the road, but inasmuch as the approach of the Tram to Chichester from Selsey is at this point entirely obscured by the high bank of the road, a stranger cycling along the road from Chichester would, even if he heard the whistle, hardly know from whence the sound proceeded. There is a notice board obscurely placed in the hedge some couple of hundred feet from the crossing, but the greater part of it is hidden by the foliage of the hedge and nothing but the first line of the notice can be read.

Mr. Dawson complained very strongly of the want of sufficient warning of what he termed "a very dangerous crossing".

A week later, the same newspaper advised that '... while there are hundreds of holidaymakers residing in Selsey, crowds of others go down by tram or cycle and return at night. Thursday afternoons generally see the influx of "flying" visitors, many of whom bring their luncheon baskets and picnics on the sand'. Summing up the charms of the fledgling seaside resort, in November the *West Sussex Gazette* published this delightful poem extolling Selsey's unspoilt attractions:

'Where tired men and women come from busy towns awhile;
Where faces showing weariness soon brighten up and smile,

'Where children paddle, dip and dig throughout the summer's hours;
Where quaint old houses, snugly thatched, look neat with shrubs and flowers
Where all around so restful is, by sea-shore, field or lane;
Where breeze from spacious sea or land invigorates again!'

At Selsey Town station on Sunday, 5th February 1905, dairyman Walter James Ginman, aged 25, was running down the line to catch the 7.10pm departure for Chichester when he tripped over a wire and fell to the ground. Almost immediately three telephone poles broke and the tram had to be stopped as it had become entangled with the wires. Unfortunately, one of the poles fell on Mr. Ginman and, although it was at first thought that he was not badly injured, he died two hours later at his home. At the enquiry, it was revealed that death was due to a fracture at the base of the skull. The jury returned a verdict of 'accidental death', but added the rider 'that the coroner should call the attention of the Hundred of Manhood & Selsey Tramways Company to the defective condition of their telephone poles'.[24]

Alderman W. Smith presided over the well-attended Annual General Meeting of the Hundred of Manhood & Selsey Tramways Company Ltd. held at the Chichester Assembly Rooms on Thursday, 13th April, but because a number of shareholders had requested that the meeting should be conducted in private, reporters were not admitted.[25]

The threat of road competition reared its ugly head again as rumours turned to fact on 5th July when the *Chichester Observer* revealed that Mr. Claude Bishop of Norton Priory, Selsey 'being a gentleman well known in financial circles in the metropolis and a director of the Hotchkiss Gun Company', along with some of his London friends had subscribed the necessary capital for 'the running of motor buses several times a day between the cathedral town and the little seaside resort', owing to their dissatisfaction 'with the present conditions of communication with Chichester and the train service to London'. To be known as The Chichester & Selsey Motor Omnibus Company Ltd., the idea was to take the Ryde Motor Services of the Isle of Wight[26] as a pattern, with 'buses 'something of the style of "The Vanguard" now in use in the metropolis, with a "trailer" for luggage'. Three vehicles were to be provided at first, working a half-hourly service via Hunston Mill and Wyke for a 6d fare with a 'graduated scale of fares for certain distances'. The object of the service was to meet all trains at Chichester station and a Sunday service would be provided which would be popular with Chichester people 'who would be glad to have the ease of facilities of getting to the seaside'. Capital was practically subscribed, but local people would have the opportunity of taking up a few shares, although the number would be limited. It was unlikely that the service would be running that summer as it depended on the supply of the vehicles.

The following week, the newspaper added under the heading 'Selsey Shots': 'It is rumoured that, in the not very distant future, an improvement will be observed in connection with the tramway to Chichester'. Was this the Tramways Company's feeble reaction to the suggestion of a rival for its passenger traffic between Chichester and Selsey?

What the improvement might have been is not clear; it was certainly not the running of more or faster trams as the timetable remained similar to that of 1904!

The proposed 'bus service received more publicity from the same source on 19th July:

'Whatever may be the individual views of the general body of our readers as to the merits or demerits of motor cars, we think that few would deny that they are tending to render remote villages and districts as easy of access as only chief centres of commerce were but a few years ago. That the motor car has come to stay as a method of public conveyance in West Sussex is evident from the way it daily increases in public utility in the South Coast Towns. We hear that Selsey is the latest recruit to the motorist's brigade, and is following the successful example of Worthing with its up to date services to Storrington and Pulborough.[27] 'A company has been formed under the title of The Chichester to Selsey Motor Omnibus Company, (*sic*) with a view of putting a motor-omnibus of the most reliable type, upon the road between Selsey and Chichester, and further omnibuses will be provided as traffic increases. Selsey and Chichester are about nine miles apart, between them lie the villages of Donnington and Sidlesham which are, at present, considered to be indifferently served by the Hundred of Manhood & Selsey Light Railway. It is intended to connect the omnibus service with the principal trains at Chichester to and from London, and to carefully consider the suggestions of any dweller on the line of route as to how the district can best be served. No doubt a large traffic in passengers and goods will gradually be developed in accordance with the well recognised axiom of Railway lore that judicious catering for the needs of a neighbourhood quickly creates traffic…'

On 3rd August it was the *West Sussex Gazette* that announced that the motor 'bus service would not be commencing operation until the following February when it was intended to put three vehicles on the road, 'substantial conveyances costing about £850 each' of 12 horse power. They had yet to be built, but they would be equipped for carrying both passengers and luggage. A few non-stop trips would be offered, but on most journeys, stops would be made at intermediate places. If successful, it was the intention to extend services to Birdham and Wittering 'to link up this almost isolated corner of Sussex with the resources of civilisation'. Despite all this advance publicity, and no doubt much to the relief of the Tramway Company, these plans to operate a motorbus service between Chichester and Selsey once again failed to materialise.[28]

Tram departures from Selsey Beach were reduced still further throughout the summer, leaving there at 3.17pm and 5.45pm on weekdays and at 1.45pm and 7.00pm on Sundays. Weekday arrivals were at 3.15pm and 5.10pm, those on Sundays being at 12.05pm and 3.05pm. At the end of September, after having been open a mere seven years (and that only during the peak holiday season) Selsey Beach station was closed to regular passenger traffic and all trams terminated once more at Selsey Town. The track was left in situ for many years and special trams probably worked through to the Beach station on occasions.

In the summer of 1906 Edward Heron-Allen, a London barrister, was staying in Bognor with his family and, finding the air so beneficial to his two-year-old daughter, he enquired where a site might be available on which to build a house with ample grounds. Someone recommended that he went over to Selsey, so he and his wife travelled there by train. Having boarded the Tram at Chichester, they had only gone about five minutes when it stopped. 'Walker, the conductor, was passing through the train selling tickets, and I said to him "Broken down?" He replied, "No sir! There is a cow on the line!" Presently we were on again, and after about ten minutes we stopped again and I said to Walker facetiously: "Another cow on the line?" He replied "No sir, it's the same cow!" I turned to my wife and said, quoting Tennyson's *Lotus Eaters*, "This is the place for us. We will return no more...We will no longer roam".'[29] Edward Heron Allen duly bought a 5–6 acre field in Selsey laid out for sale as some 20 building plots and after his 'sporting offer' for the whole site was accepted, he built a house there known as 'Large Acres'. In time he was to become Chairman of the Directors of the Hundred of Manhood & Selsey Tramways Company. It was in 1906 that Henry Gibson Phillips succeeded William Payne as secretary.

Just as Edward Heron-Allen arrived on the scene, the Tramways Company lost one of its valued directors, Alderman Sharp Garland, JP, aged 74, who passed away on Thursday, 9th August after having suffered declining health following a serious illness 8 years previously.[30] Six months later, on Tuesday, 26th February 1907, another Tramways Company Director, Newton Clayton died suddenly, aged just 54 years, following an attack of influenza. He had moved south to work Sidlesham Tide Mill some 40 years previously, and he had been involved in the reclamation of Pagham Harbour.[31] Henry Phillips took over the post of general manager, it now being combined with that of secretary.

A. E. Parsons, writing under the heading of 'Selsey Improvements' in the *Chichester Observer* on 27th March 1907 suggested that '...The Green between Selsey Bill Coast Guard Station and the fishermen's huts should be cleared of furze and barbed wire, seats and a few ornamental trees provided, thus forming an inviting pleasure ground for schools, parties, etc. This green should thus be saved for all time...if the Tram-line were extended up to the Coast-Guard Buildings and the iron or upper part of the existing side of these buildings to provide shelter and tea, an ideal arrangement would thus be produced. Neither Bognor or Littlehampton could offer a like inducement to bring excursionists to a pleasure ground with the sea washing its edge. It should be the aim of the Selsey Syndicate to make all new streets straight, so that from the Tram station or the centre of the Village, the breakers rolling out at sea could be seen...' Mr. Parsons' suggestions were ignored and the Tramway was not extended, neither were the new roads built straight!

July 1907 saw the formation of a Company known as 'Selsey on Sea, Ltd.' (the syndicate referred to above), which purchased almost 2,500 acres of land in Selsey, Sidlesham, Pagham, North Mundham and East Wittering with the intention of developing the area as a popular seaside resort. They proposed to erect a pier on the eastern side of the estate at which pleasure steamers plying along the south coast would be able to call at any state of the tide, and the sea front was to be '...laid out so as to leave sufficient land between the building sites and the beach to allow for a Marine Drive 80 feet wide, and a grass esplanade from 120 feet to 200 feet wide, which will be over three miles in length...' There were also plans that a site to the south-east of Sidlesham station might be used 'for the construction of a Motor Track'.[32]

Perhaps it was to promote this venture that the *Daily Mail* extolled the virtues of Selsey ('an undiscovered seaside paradise') in an informative article on Saturday, 20th July. To get there it was suggested you go by train to Chichester, '...two hours from London, easy travelling, good trains, beautiful scenery. When the London train stops at Chichester, it is time to think about getting to Selsey. You can do that in one of several ways. Either you will take one of the open carriages outside the station and murmuring "Selsey" commit yourself to a drive through six (*sic*) miles of country lanes along a road which, since it follows the windings of an ancient watercourse, has twenty-six turnings in it, or you will take a ticket at a quaint little station and board one of the toy trains of the Hundred of Manhood & Selsey Tramway and rattle along at a quicker pace past farms and golf links to the same destination.' Quite where they obtained the next piece of information is unknown, (perhaps it was just wishful thinking) but they suggested that '...Before long the quaintly named light railway will be merged in the Brighton system and important trains will travel on the line bearing happy freights of parents and children to the ideal seaside place of Selsey-on-Sea...'

Bank Holiday Monday, 6th August, was the Annual Sports Day in Selsey and, with glorious weather, 'each tram which came into the growing seaside place brought more visitors'.[33] The Tramway was busy again later that month on Thursday, 23rd when 'to meet the convenience of Chichester people', a late tram was laid on to run from Selsey to the city at 10.00pm.[34]

To date the Tramway had soldiered on with only two locomotives available for traffic, but during the year a third engine was acquired, a Manning Wardle 0–6–0 saddle tank that had been built way back in 1861. Despite her age, *Sidlesham* proved to be a good investment and she put in many years of hard work on the line.

'Many Cicestrians will be pleased with the announcement in another column that the fare to Selsey on Thursday afternoons has been reduced to 9d return,' suggested the *Chichester Observer* on 6th May 1908. 'The management can be congratulated in making the reduction; for it cannot but mean "the nimble ninepence" that will result in more passenger traffic. Many a person is likely to spend three ninepences in travelling than a shilling "all at once". The finances of the Company shewed an improvement last year, and it is such concessions to the public as this that are likely to produce good dividends.'

The Tramway appeared to be getting its fair amount of custom, the same newspaper reporting a week later that '...on Thursday afternoon, the first really spring-like Thursday this year, several parties came from Chichester and neighbourhood (to Selsey) both by rail and road...' It went

A PROMISING BEGINNING (1897–1909)

Sidlesham was the train engine once more at Selsey on this postcard confusingly entitled 'Mixed Express, Selsey'. Among the staff posed for the photographer was Conductor/Guard William Walker who is seen in the shadow at the foot of the platform ramp next to Bert Morris, the Telegraph boy. The fireman in the cab was Jack Terry. The 11.30 a.m. mixed train on this occasion was made up of ex-LBSCR open wagon No. 5, the Stroudley Road Van, a mainline company's open wagon and a single carriage.
LENS OF SUTTON

With curtains being blown through the open windows, this portrait shows Chichester *awaiting departure time with the Tramway's three original Falcon carriages on a breezy summer's day at Chichester.*
COLLECTION E. C. GRIFFITH

By 1908 the nameboard at Sidlesham station had been replaced by one incorporating the modern spelling with only the one 'D'. The single crossing gate had disappeared, but now a sign warned road users to 'Beware of the Trams'. CHICHESTER DISTRICT MUSEUM

on to say '... it has been said that Selsey will never become a great residential place. Whether it will or not – and there are some charming houses there already – it is bound to become a very popular day resort. True, it is not on the main railway line, but this is, perhaps, an advantage, inasmuch as it is less likely to attract such as enjoy the noisy delights of Margate and Ramsgate... The beauty of Selsey as a holiday resort is its freedom from the noisy tripper and the less desirable of the beach attractions... No, Selsey is not so keen on your London tripper. It prefers to enjoy the patronage of those people who go there just because it is not a modernised resort. It is its "old fashioned" charm which recommends it to those whose tastes do not call for Christy Minstrels, swing boats and steam roundabouts. Selsey is satisfied with its lesser and more sober attractions. It possesses everything essential to wholesome pleasure and exercise. Amusements galore to pander to the young idea, entertainments and sports for the adults, while for those who prefer solitude for lonely contemplation by the sad sea waves, there are the miles of beautiful old rugged shore, which is the principal charm of the village.'

'The genial weather conditions of Sunday (16th May) again attracted a fair crowd to Selsey, the reduced Tramway fare being a small inducement to those desiring a change and pleasant Sunday afternoon away from home...'[35] Although bungalows were 'popping up all over the place', land sales, were not so brisk as had been hoped for, but it was thought that 'a boom was inevitable'. 'Talking of booming,' said the *Chichester Observer* on 20th May, 'one might be excused for suggesting a little better advertisement for the village and its attractions. The Tramway Company is doing its best in this direction, but a good deal more might be done by those who have everything to gain by the growth of the village.' A week later, that periodical was not so impressed with the Tramway Company's advertising and wrote:

> 'Standing at Selsey Railway Station and looking towards the village one can quite realise what a charming effect a row of smart villas on either side would have. Building plots have already been stumped out and are only awaiting purchasers who, by the way, are coming as sure as they are slowly. Meanwhile the scene which greets the eye on alighting from the train (*sic*) is not so picturesque as might be wished for. Advertisement hoarding (*sic*) at the best of times are not pretty, but scattered as they are in the vicinity of Selsey Station they, to say the least of it, give a very tawdry appearance to what otherwise might be a pleasing spot.'

Also in that edition, the newspaper also told this little tale of someone receiving their just desserts:

> 'Several crude stories are told of the Selsey Tramway, but the best is that of a man who, saying unkind things of the Tram, biked down. Arrived at Selsey, his machine gave out and having no money upon him with which to pay his fare, had to walk home – therein lies the joke!'

A Golf Club had long been the dream of many Selsey enthusiasts and on Monday, 8th June their dream became reality when everything was ready for play to begin on 'the capital nine hole course' that had been constructed a little to the north of the village. The *Chichester Observer* suggested on 10th June that 'to a place like Selsey, golf links should prove a valuable acquisition, and it is gratifying to note that the Chichester and Selsey Tramway authorities intend to afford facilities to players by making a halt at the links which are situated by the side of the track near Ferry. At this point is situated a commodious club house, and the first tee. The growth of the Hayling Golf Club is evidence of what may be effected by the willingness of the railway people to run con-

A PROMISING BEGINNING (1897–1909)

venient trains and otherwise offer facilities to players'.[36] A very basic, shelter-less wooden platform was soon constructed by the Tramways Company just 25 yards from the Club House, but being considered as a halt, it was never advertised in the published timetables, and tickets were only issued to those persons entitled to use it (Golf Club members?).

'Neptune', in his regular column entitled 'Selsey Siftings' in the *Chichester Observer* on Wednesday, 1st August, went to considerable lengths to emphasise the better class of holiday-maker that had discovered the village:

> 'We are now in the midst of Summer and Selsey is looking at its brightest. Visitors are daily pouring in and what a few weeks ago promised to be a dull season, now bids fair to being a trifle rosier.
>
> 'Apart from the usual visitors, we are being looked up by quite a large number of one-day holiday makers, and the crab and lobster teas for which the village is famous, are consequently in fair demand. These excursionists are not of the usual tripper class, but are a sane, sober sort of people who do not convert the village into Bedlam.
>
> 'The increased number of excursionists is undoubtedly due to the increased facilities for reaching the village offered by the Selsey Tramway people. Besides the cheap runs from Chichester, I note that they are now arranging for cheap return tickets from Stations both up and down the line as well as from Midhurst. There is no doubt that this will be the means of still further advertising our village.'

'Quite a substantial haystack has resulted from the cutting of the grass of the Selsey Tramway track', reported the *Chichester Observer* the following week. All railway companies regularly kept their lineside grass under control to reduce the risk of fires being started by sparks emitted from locomotives' chimneys, but it was normally burnt, under supervision, on site. However, in common with some of Holman Stephens' other railways, along with their normal duties, it was down to the platelayers to cut the grass with scythes, and after it had been turned several times to ensure that it was dry, it was forked in close to the track ready for picking up by a train made up of open wagons. Once gathered in, the hay was stacked in the small station yard at Chalder, from whence it was advertised for sale by tender, thus bringing in a little extra revenue to the resourceful Tramways Company.

On Saturday, 17th July 'special trams' were run 'to enable those who desire to visit the Franco-British Exhibition (and) to avail themselves of the cheap excursion which runs from Chichester on that day'.[37] A late tram was reintroduced on Thursdays only in August which left Selsey at 9.00pm, returning from Chichester at 10.20pm, half an hour being allowed for each journey.[38] With the inevitable slight variations of timing, this late tram was to become a regular feature of the August timetable over the next two years.

> 'Many more or less exaggerated experiences have from time to time been related concerning the Selsey Tramway, but undoubtedly, the most unique (*sic*) was that which befel (*sic*) the three or four hundred people who travelled from Selsey to Chichester by the 7.05pm train on (Bank Holiday) Monday evening (5th August). Several hundreds of people went from the City to the village during the day, and at 7 o'clock in the evening, something like four hundred passengers awaited the arrival of the tram which was to take them home. The platform and the little waiting room were filled to overflowing, while several people laid upon the grass or sat upon the fences outside the station until the train arrived. Speculation was rife as to how the crowd was to be accommodated, and jocular suggestions were made as to the probable necessity of the more fearless of the crowd adopting the methods depicted by "Cynicus" in his well-known satirical post-card entitled "The last train home from Selsey". However, as soon as the tram arrived a rush was made for seats and much jambing and hustling resulted. But there was scarcely sufficient standing room even, for half the crowd, and a cattle truck had consequently to be requisitioned as well as the guard's van thrown open. Squeezed and jumbled as they were, the passengers found the journey

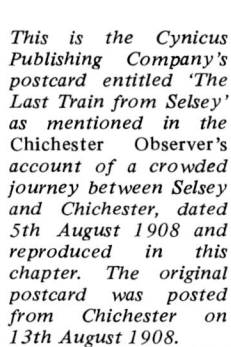

This is the Cynicus Publishing Company's postcard entitled 'The Last Train from Selsey' as mentioned in the Chichester Observer's *account of a crowded journey between Selsey and Chichester, dated 5th August 1908 and reproduced in this chapter. The original postcard was posted from Chichester on 13th August 1908.*
COLLECTION LES DARBYSHIRE

anything but comfortable, a state of things which was not improved by the continuous jolting, bumping and swaying of the train. In fact, those who had secured seats must have regretted their hastiness in entering the car, for the pressure of the standing passengers must have added much to their discomfort, and an occasional shriek told of the location of someone's pet corn or other pedal infirmity. To those who saw the passing of the train through the countryside, the sight must have been a curious one. Men, women and children, packed like sardines in a box, others hanging on by rails and sitting over buffers, everyone wonderfully good humoured despite the discomfort.

'But there was suddenly quite an amusing interlude. The train had pulled up at Sidlesham and one or two passengers had squeezed their way through and alighted with a sigh of relief, when it was noticed that something was wrong. Conductors, engine-driver and stoker were engaged in animated and mysterious conversation. Suddenly, without a word of warning, the engine was detached from the train, and shunted back.[39] "They can't pull us, so they are going to push us," suggested someone, and hundreds of necks were craned to see the operation. But instead of being connected with the train at the back, the engine sped on at Selsey express speed until it disappeared in the distance. It was returning to Selsey, and three or four hundred passengers were left stranded in an engine-less train four or five miles from home. Speculation ran high as to what was the meaning of the incident, and then it became rumoured – and rumours are often very true – that in the hurry of the moment passengers had been bundled into the guard's van to the exclusion of that most important individual himself. His presence was only missed at Sidlesham, and after an excited conversation it was thought well to return for him. Thus for something like twenty minutes the half stifled passengers were kept waiting at the little village station. But it was a good humoured crowd and even those who realised the probability of losing their connecting train at Chichester could not fail to appreciate the humour of the situation. During the wait some of the passengers took a stroll into the country-side, others sought the nearest public house, and one or two suggested that by the combined efforts of the men they might manage to push the women and children home in time for breakfast. Meanwhile some of the occupants of the cattle truck had alighted and one had an opportunity of seeing the dainty summer dresses and pretty females who were good naturedly suffering the inconvenience of a jumpy, jolty journey in such an inappropriate conveyance.

'At last a cloud of smoke was seen in the distance. The engine was returning – and at what a rate too! Surely the engine – it was the *Sidlesham* – must have eclipsed itself. As it came puffing and snorting into the station with the missing official aboard a mighty cheer went up. The driver smiled good humouredly, he too must have realised the novelty of the situation, and the engine was once again connected and the tram again bumped painfully on its interrupted journey without further incident. It was a strange experience and one which will be remembered with right good humour.'[40]

On 17th February 1909 the *Chichester Observer* printed an amusing snippet, describing Selsey as '... one of the most delightful little seaside resorts in England, and still, happily, undiscovered by the great army of trippers. Indeed, the trippers are easily kept away, because the place is not too accessible to them. A light railway runs - no, crawls - between Chichester and Selsey, and does the whole eight miles in something over half an hour. It is also the noisiest and most

Sidlesham, *now with modified safety valves and brass cover, heading for Selsey acrross the canal bridge north of Hunston with two of the original Falcon carriages early in 1909. Note the half-round sleepers. The fishplates had to be unbolted every time the bridge was raised.*
LENS OF SUTTON

rickety railway in England, and conversation is almost impossible...'

Other than the weekly publication in the *Chichester Observer* of their timetables amongst those of the neighbouring London, Brighton & South Coast Railway, the Selsey Tramway received no publicity whatsoever throughout 1909, so we can only assume that the Company continued to go about its business, providing an efficient (if noisy and slow!) transport service for the inhabitants of the Manhood peninsula. Up until 31st August passenger receipts had increased from £1,861 9s 10d in 1908 to £1,880 10s 11d, but revenue from season tickets had dropped by £9 4s 4d to £37 2s 4d and goods revenue that had peaked at £1083 6s 10d in 1908, had fallen slightly to £1,026 1s 10d.

Selsey about to leave Chichester for the coast, c.1909.   LENS OF SUTTON

Notes

1. *West Sussex Gazette*, Thursday, 2.9.1897.
2. *Chichester Observer*, Wednesday, 1.9.1897.
3. *Railway Magazine*, April 1898 'A Trip on the H of M & ST' by Rev. V. L. Whitechurch. I have been unable to find any verification of these events in the local newspapers. The Rev. Whitechurch was a regular contributor to the *Railway Magazine*, commencing with its first edition in July 1897.
4. *Chichester Observer*, Wednesday, 13.10.1897.
5. These figures have been taken from the questionnaire which Holman Stephens completed for the Light Railways (Investigation Committee) in December 1920.
6. The Rev. Whitechurch is misinformed here and the Hundred of Manhood & Selsey Tramways Company was, as we have seen, not built under the Light Railways Act of 1896.
7. *Railway Magazine*, April 1898, 'A Trip on the H of M & ST' as above.
8. *Chichester Observer*, Wednesday, 13.4.1898.
9. *Chichester Observer*, Wednesday, 1.6.1898.
10. *Chichester Observer*, Wednesday, 1.6.1898.
11. *Chichester Observer*, Wednesday, 20.7.1898.
12. *Chichester Observer*, Wednesday, 18.1.1899.
13. *West Sussex Gazette*, Thursday, 25.5.1899.
14. *West Sussex Gazette*, Thursday, 22.6.1899.
15. *Chichester Observer*, Wednesday, 2.8.1899.
16. *Chichester Observer*, Wednesday, 16.8.1899.
17. *Chichester Observer*, Wednesday, 23.8.1899.
18. *Chichester Observer*, Wednesday, 25.4.1900
19. *Chichester Observer*, Wednesday, 3.6.1903.
20. *Chichester Observer*, Wednesday, 5.8.1903.
21. *Chichester Observer*, Wednesday, 4.11.1903.
22. *The Selsey Tramways* by Edward C. Griffith, Third edition published by the author, 1974.
23. *Going off the Rails, the Country Railway in West Sussex* by Bill Gage, Michael Harris and Tony Sullivan published by West Sussex County Council, 1997.
24. *Chichester Observer*, Wednesday, 8.2.1905
25. *West Sussex Gazette*, Thursday, 20.4.1905. It may have been for a similar reason that the AGMs of the previous two years had not been reported in the local press.
26. The 'bus company, based in Ryde, was actually known as The Isle of Wight Express Motor Syndicate Ltd., and began services between Ryde and Bembridge, Newport and Shanklin on 13th April 1905 using 7 Milnes Daimler open-top double-deckers. Withdrawn after only 6 months, they were replaced by single deckers (from the same manufacturer) which were also unable to cope with the hilly terrain of the Island and the Company was wound up in 1907.
27. The Sussex Road Car Co. was formed in the summer of 1904 with two single-deck Clarkson steam 'buses. Suffering with boiler and injector problems they were replaced by two Milnes Daimler petrol vehicles in March 1905, registered BP345 and CD338. Through amalgamation with competitors, the Company became part of the newly formed Southdown Motor Services Ltd. on 2nd June 1915. Details taken from *The Southdown Story* published by Southdown Motor Services Ltd. 1965.
28. In her *A History of Selsey*, Frances Mee suggests that the Chichester & Selsey Motor Omnibus Company operated from 1906–1909, but extensive research by The Southdown Enthusiasts' Club has failed to find any reference to a 'bus service between Chichester and Selsey at this time.
29. *West Sussex Gazette*, 21.2.1935. This story had appeared in a slightly different form in the *Chichester Observer*, Wednesday, 17.1.1909.
30. Sharp Garland first arrived in Chichester c.1856 when serving as an apprentice with The Central Grocery Stores, before succeeding to the grocery and provisions business in Eastgate, Chichester that dated back to 1870. He became one of the most successful merchants in the city, and he was also a director of the West Sussex Brick Company. He had the honour to be Chichester's Mayor in 1878 and 1898.
31. *West Sussex Gazette*, Thursday, 28.2.1907.
32. *A History of Selsey* by Frances Mee, published by Phillimore & Co., 1988.
33. *Chichester Observer*, Wednesday, 8.8.1907.
34. *Chichester Observer*, Wednesday, 22.8.1907.
35. *Chichester Observer*, Wednesday 20.5.1908.
36. Unlike the new Golf Course at Selsey, the two on Hayling Island (one for ladies and the other for gentlemen) did not have their own halt, but were served by the terminus station of that branch line.
37. *Chichester Observer*, Wednesday, 15.7.1908.
38. *Chichester Observer*, Wednesday, 8.7.1908.
39. The locomotive would have run round its train via the goods loop behind the station. Presumably, no wagons occupied the siding at the time, not that this would have bothered the Tramways Company anyway!
40. *Chichester Observer*, Wednesday, 5.8.1908.

Edwardian views of Chichester LB&SCR station, level crossing and footbridge from Stockbridge Road. COLLECTION PAUL LAMING

CHAPTER THREE
MAN MAKES PLANS & GOD LAUGHS (1910–1912)

As the 11.30am mixed train from Selsey arrived at Sidlesham on Saturday, 12th February 1910 the locomotive came off the rails and it was not until shortly before 6 o'clock that the line was cleared, allowing the 6.30pm tram from Chichester to proceed as usual. During the afternoon, brakes were hired to convey passengers between Chichester and Selsey and vice versa.[1]

On 16th March the *Chichester Observer* advised

> 'The Tramway Company have arranged special Trams to and from Selsey for Easter to enable Cicestrians and others who desire to visit Selsey plenty of time in the village. Convenient trams leave Chichester at 2.30pm on Good Friday, Easter Sunday and Easter Monday, returning as late as 9.30pm on the first two days and 9 o'clock on the Bank Holiday. Selsey people wishing to witness the Band Concert can return from Chichester on Easter Monday at 1030pm. We recommend readers to see the Easter Time Sheet.'

Emphasising just how much the Tramway was a local line operating for the convenience of local people, late trams were regularly run: Wednesday, 6th April, departing Chichester at 10.40pm, 'or shortly after the performance of Poole's Myriorama;'[2] Thursday 28th April in connection with a six-a-side billiard match held at the Selsey Hotel leaving Selsey at 11.15pm, returning from Chichester at 11.50pm, (thus connecting with the Portsmouth Theatre train); Sunday, 3rd July from Selsey at 9.30pm, returning at 10.30pm (no reason given); Sunday, 17th July from Chichester at 10.30pm to connect with a LBSCR excursion to London and again for a repeat performance of Poole's Myriorama on Wednesday, 5th and Saturday, 8th October leaving the city at 11.00pm.[3] In common with the other lines in Holman Stephens' light railway empire, it is highly unlikely that the staff required to work these late services received any extra wages for their overtime! For the first time, during the summer, four trams were operated on summer Sundays, leaving Selsey at 8.50am, 1.35pm, 6.50pm and 8.00pm, returning from Chichester at 11.20am, 2.15pm, 7.25pm and 8.45pm.

Of course, it wasn't only passengers that provided revenue for the Tramway and until the advent of reliable motor transport, fishermen would be waiting at Selsey station for the Tram that was due to arrive at around 5.00pm to load as much as a ton of prawns, plus crabs and lobsters for the return trip to Chichester and onwards by rail to Brighton or Billingsgate fish market. Wet fish, though, would be sold in Selsey or sent to Chichester by horse and cart.[4] Another valued customer was Colin Pullinger, born at Ivy Cottage, Selsey in 1815. At the Great Exhibition in 1851 his self-setting mousetrap (which could hold up to twelve mice without inflicting any injury on them) went on show and it was said to have fascinated Queen Victoria. With a staff of forty employed in his factory in the High Street, 960 traps

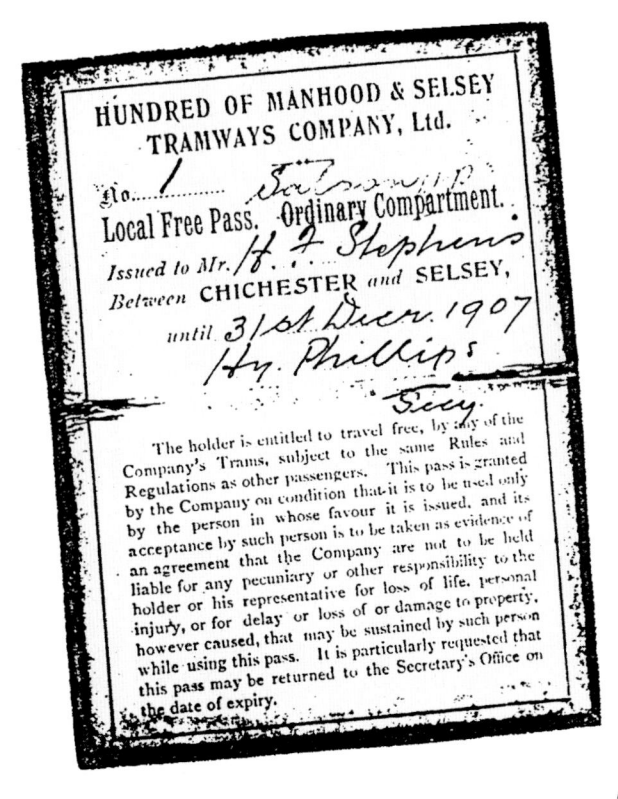

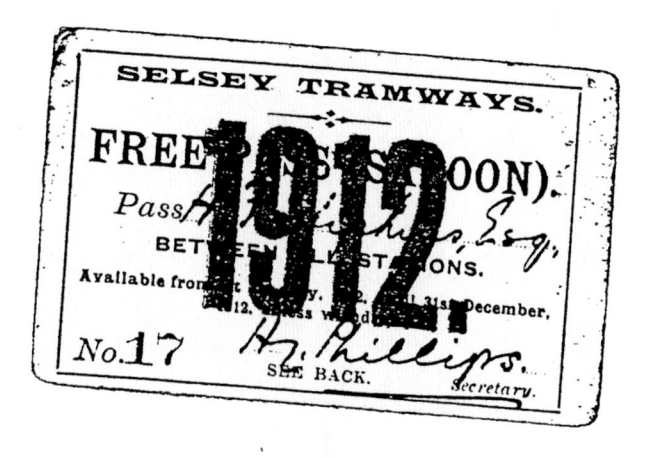

Free passes for the years 1907 and 1912 issued to Holman F. Stephens. COLONEL STEPHENS RAILWAY MUSEUM & ARCHIVE

Harry Prior's horse 'bus going about its normal business conveying passengers and their luggage from Selsey Tramway station to and from the resort's Marine Hotel which is seen on the extreme right of this photograph.

WSCC LIBRARY SERVICE

Fishermen's quarters on the East Beach, apparently in a less chaotic state with their lobster pots and nets arranged in neat straight lines. Partly owing to the ease of being able to get to the growing resort, thanks to the Tramway, chalets and bungalows were now encroaching upon the scene.

WSCC LIBRARY SERVICE

Further along the East Beach it will be seen that some of the bungalows had been constructed from redundant main-line railway carriages. What a grand edifice it is to the left!
WSCC LIBRARY SERVICE

per week were at one time turned out, the majority of these travelling outward on the Tram. By 1910, the year in which he died, the increasing popularity of the (less humane) penny mousetrap put an end to the large sale of Pullinger's 2/6d traps, and by the 1920s his grandson, Charles, was working alone in a small shed. To suggest that this industry 'was partly responsible for bringing a tramline to the village' is rather an exaggeration![5]

At the beginning of October this typically reduced winter timetable came into operation:

	Weekdays						Sundays		
Selsey	8.30	10.20	1.25	3.05	5.45	7.05	10.30	1.35	7.00
Ferry Siding	8.33		1.28	3.08	5.48	7.08	10.33	1.38	7.03
Sidlesham	8.35		1.30	3.10	5.50	7.10	10.35	1.40	7.05
Chalder	8.40	C	1.35	3.15	5.55	7.15	10.40	1.45	7.10
Hunston	8.45		1.40	3.20	6.00	7.20	10.45	1.50	7.15
Chichester	9.00	11.00	1.55	3.35	6.15	7.35	11.00	2.05	7.30
Chichester	9.20	11.40	2.20	4.25	6.32	8.00	11.20	2.15	8.15
Hunston	9.25		2.25	4.30	–	8.05	11.25	2.20	8.20
Chalder	9.30		2.30	4.35	–	8.10	11.30	2.25	8.35
Sidlesham	9.35	C	2.35	4.40	6.43	8.15	11.35	2.30	8.40
Ferry Siding	9.40		2.40	4.45	–	8.20	11.40	2.35	8.45
Selsey	9.50	12.20	2.50	4.55	7.00	8.30	11.50	2.45	8.55

C Mixed Train

The discrepancies in journey times between up and down services are extraordinary! Up trams were given just 5 minutes to travel between Selsey and Sidlesham, yet they were allowed a full 15 minutes on the homeward journey. Conversely, Hunston to Chichester still took 15 minutes, yet the two-mile return run was supposedly accomplished in 5 minutes!

To encourage more Cicestrians to travel down to Selsey the Tramway Company placed an advertisement in the *Chichester Observer* on 14th and 21st December offering a Cheap Excursion Ticket for just 9d return. Events outside the Company's control were to make this offer very short

lived! The weather during 1910 had been atrocious; strong gales that had caused considerable damage in the area at the end of January and again on 19th February were followed by violent rain storms in July which caused great damage to crops, the like of which had not been seen in the past twenty-five years. However, there was much worse to come and back in September, Mr. Alfred Rusbridge, an apiarist of Sidlesham, prophesied that the coming winter would bring some of the fiercest gales ever known in the district and that unless the sea defences at Pagham were strengthened, there would be a disaster.[6]

At a Directors' Meeting held on Thursday, 15th December the principal business considered was the electrification of the Tramway,[7] but mother nature had her own ideas for the line! Mr. Rusbridge's weather forecast proved to be all too accurate and throughout the second week of December, torrential rain and south-westerly gales battered the south coast of England. On the morning of Friday, 16th December *Selsey* had already made one return trip to Chichester, probably with just the one Falcon carriage, and had returned to the city again when, at around 10.30am,[8] with dramatic suddenness and a deafening roar, the spring tide burst through the sea defences known as 'The Narrows', 500 yards south-west of the erstwhile entrance to Pagham Harbour. Immediately a gang of around 30 men set to work, assisted by neighbouring farmers and great efforts were made to patch up the gap in the bank with bags of shingle and other materials. Simultaneously, the sea had made inroads upon the western coast of the peninsula from the southern corner of Bracklesham Bay, near Thorney, sweeping over the shingle banks and marshes, pastures and arable land until the torrent, half a mile wide, eventually joined the arm of the sea from the east via a disused sluice gate. The gas works were flooded and the retorts split, and in less than an hour, 1700 acres of land were under deep water and Selsey had

THE SELSEY TRAMWAY

On the morning of Friday, 15th December 1910, after many days of strong winds and heavy rain, the sea broke through the coastal defences, eventually flooding over 3,000 acres of land. It was the Tramway that was more affected than anyone by the floods, and its line was completely submerged between Ferry and to the north of Sidlesham. Morey Photos of Chichester were on the scene the following day and issued a set of postcards. This one shows the tide coming in, and an open wagon stranded on the goods loop at Sidlesham with flood water already all but covering the fence in the foreground.
COLLECTION PAUL LAMING

'Watching the floods — How far will they come?' Villagers Homer Richards (left), Mr. and Mrs. Simpson and Mr. Beacher looking over the floods towards Sidlesham Tide Mill. A few hours earlier the view to their right would have been of some two miles of pastures. We can now see that the stranded truck was one of the Tramway Company's ex-GER open wagons that had its curved ends cut square.
COLONEL STEPHENS RAILWAY MUSEUM & ARCHIVE

MAN MAKES PLANS & GOD LAUGHS (1910–1912)

once more become an island in the English Channel. Incredibly, no lives were lost.

Prior to the reclamation of Pagham Harbour in the 1870s, Sidlesham had been quite a prosperous fishing village, complete with a tide mill,[9] but as one old fisherman remarked, 'Man drove the fish away from Sidlesham and, you see, God has brought them back'![10] The only way to get 'dry shod' across to the new 'island' of Selsey was to scramble along the top of the bramble bank that bordered the eastern side of the submerged roadway which, although raised above the surrounding marshes, was itself under some two feet of water!

The wind that fateful day had been blowing off land, and had it continued to do so, much might have been done to mitigate the trouble, but it suddenly veered, and although the men had returned to the damaged sea defences the next morning, the gale had assumed such dimensions that the waves, lashed into a fury, carried everything before them and widened the breach from 40 to around 150 yards. It was the Hundred of Manhood & Selsey Tramways Company that was undoubtedly the most seriously affected by the inundation with at least 1¼ miles of its permanent way between Chalder and Ferry under water, and Sidlesham station plat-

'Sidlesham station and mill'. With the main running line and siding submerged under water, the station building looks like it had recently received a fresh coat of white paint.
COLONEL STEPHENS RAILWAY MUSEUM & ARCHIVE

'Selsey Tram all change. Scenes in flooded area, Dec. 1910, 1st stage.' Just short of Rookery Lane at the northern extremity of the floods, goods were being transferred from one of the pair of ex-MR low-roof vans to a horse and cart for the rest of the journey south. The Tramway Company would soon build a simple wooden platform, which it named Mill Pond Halt, on the other side of the crossing in front of Selsey and her train.
COLLECTION PAUL LAMING

Following the reclamation of Pagham Harbour in 1878, Sidlesham Tide Mill, built in 1755 by Woodruff Drinkwater, had been powered by steam.
COLLECTION PAUL LAMING

With the tide rising, the water is even deeper in this view showing children playing in the floods.
COLLECTION J. WYNNE-TYSON

This photograph is entitled 'Caravaners driven out by the sea, Pagham Harbour, Selsey', and must refer to the floods of December 1910. Two women were preparing to leave in a small cart pulled by horses, whilst six other people looked on. The small-wheeled windowless caravan seemingly made of corrugated iron to the right had a Godalming address painted on the rear. WSCC LIBRARY SERVICE

MAN MAKES PLANS & GOD LAUGHS (1910–1912)

form was completely submerged at high tides and was inches deep in the waiting room. Luckily, with *Selsey* at the Chichester end of the line and *Chichester* and *Sidlesham* at Selsey, a shuttle service was quickly arranged to either side of the inundation. A 48ft long, low, wooden platform was speedily erected at the northern end of the floods for the easier transfer of passengers and goods, and this was given the name Mill Pond Halt. With no run-round facilities here, or at Ferry, the shuttles had to be propelled in one direction. The following notice was quickly released:

NOTICE IS HEREBY GIVEN

That, owing to the flooding of the line between Sidlesham and Ferry, all Cheap Bookings are suspended. Also the Company cannot Book Passengers through from Chichester to Selsey, or vice versa. Arrangements have been made, however, to run a 'Bus Service between Mill Pond Halt and Ferry. Every reasonable effort will be made by the Company to maintain this Service, but it cannot be guaranteed, and the Company will not be responsible for same.

Through Passengers must book locally on each section of the line, viz., Chichester and Mill Pond Halt, and Ferry and Selsey.

Selsey, December, 1910.   H. G. Phillips, Manager.

An emergency timetable was hastily put together and published in the local newspapers, which carefully managed to omit any mention of a 'bus service having to be used for part of the journey, the only clue being the longer journey times allowed between Chalder and Ferry via Sidlesham and vice versa! The times shown against Sidlesham would actually have referred to Mill Pond Halt.

Just to the north of Ferry, the Tramway was submerged under the sea.
COLLECTION PAUL LAMING

	Weekdays						Sundays		
Selsey	8.10	10.20	1.15	2.50	5.30	6.50	10.10	1.25	6.45
Ferry Siding	8.13	10.23	1.18	2.53	5.33	6.53	10.13	1.28	6.48
Sidlesham	8.33	10.43	1.38	3.13	5.53	7.13	10.33	1.48	7.08
Chalder	8.35	10.45	1.40	3.15	5.55	7.15	10.35	1.50	7.10
Hunston	8.40	10.50	1.45	3.20	6.00	7.20	10.40	1.55	7.15
Chichester	8.55	11.05	2.00	3.35	6.15	7.35	10.55	2.10	7.30
Chichester	9.20	11.40	2.20	4.25	6.32	8.00	11.20	2.15	8.15
Hunston	9.25	11.45	2.25	4.30	–	8.05	11.25	2.20	8.20
Chalder	9.30	11.50	2.30	4.35	–	8.10	11.30	2.25	8.25
Sidlesham	9.32	11.52	2.32	4.37	6.40	8.12	11.32	2.27	8.17
Ferry Siding	9.52	12.12	2.54	4.57	7.00	8.32	11.52	2.47	8.47
Selsey	10.05	12.25	3.05	5.10	7.10	8.45	12.05	3.00	9.00

On 21st December the *Chichester Observer* described a Selsey-bound journey thus:

'At Mant's, midway between Chalder and Sidlesham, the passengers have to alight and board a 'bus.[11] From here they are driven through Sidlesham village a short distance beyond which the flood is encountered. It stretches right across the road, and as the horses splash through, the green water is thrown up in all directions. It reaches nearly to the box of the wheel at this point, and stretches along the road to a distance of 100 to 200 yards. The 'bus leans a little to the right, and the passengers are made aware of the serious effect the wash of the sea is having on the road. A continuation will make it quite impossible except by boat, for already a deep shelving gully has been formed there by the action of the water, which comes up level with the barbed wire fence, upon which cling weeds and other substances brought up by the sea.

'From the top of the 'bus one has a clear view of the surrounding country, for the road is high at this point. Two or three miles away, over the wide stretch of water, can be seen the long stretch of shingle which formed the defences, and in the centre the narrow breach through which the sea is rushing. A few hundred yards away the tops of the telegraph poles at regular intervals denote the spot where the Selsey tram line lay submerged in eight, ten and even twelve feet of water. Nearer still, dark spots on the surface of the water, which seem to act as breakers and cause the spray to rise as the waves meet them, resolve themselves, as the tide ebbs, into gate posts and fences, and even nearer, just over the bank which skirts the road and acts as a sea wall, logs, resembling sleepers, float on the green waters.

'At Ferry the tram is again boarded. Although the line is here clear of water there is still a large expanse stretching on either side. Away to the west, from what was once pasture and arable land, a flock of gulls, thousands in number, rise in the sunlight like a sheet of silver and sweep down again to the surface of the water as the tram moves on its way...'

In all, between 3,000 and 4,000 acres were overwhelmed, but Selsey itself remained dry, other than those cellars which regularly flooded in wet weather. Come the evening, though, with the failure of the gas supply, the village was plunged into darkness, resulting in a rush for lamps, oil and candles and a special supply was hurriedly obtained via the tram from Chichester. The Tramway was to become the only means of getting food supplies to Selsey, a horse and cart being used to bypass the flooded section. The *Chichester Observer* was worried that the 'village itself would be the greatest sufferer in the event of nothing being done to remedy the disaster. As a growing summer resort, it has much to lose by being cut off from the mainland... Whether anything will be done again to reclaim the land is to the moment an open question, but doubts are generally expressed on this score... So far as the eastern side is concerned, the reclamation would prove too big an expense... It is even suggested that, apart from reviving the fishing industry at Sidlesham, it would tend to encourage a good class of summer visitor...' On Sunday, 19th December 'the gale had gone down, and hundreds of people made the pilgrimage by motor, cycle, rail and afoot, to "Sidlesham-

'The new Selsey Tram – 2nd stage of journey.' As a pioneer of today's all too familiar 'rail replacement services', this horse 'bus met all trams to take them from Mill Pond Halt to Ferry station and vice versa via Sidlesham village. With a full complement of gentlemen on the roof and driver Harry Prior at the reins, the 'bus was posed for the photographer at the junction of Chichester Road and Rookery Lane, Sidlesham.
COLLECTION PAUL LAMING

on-Sea" to look out over the thousands of acres of salt water flowing where the green fields had been and to get photographs of the new sea coast'.[12]

The Christmas traffic on the Tramway suffered little by the unpleasant conditions, except that it was impossible to deal with any heavy goods.

> 'The inhabitants of the villages made their journeys to Chichester just the same for Christmas shopping, and they were merry groups which, laden with parcels of Christmas cheer, returned in the early evening by tram and 'bus to their homes. And it was the novelty of the 'bus journey that seemed to add to the enjoyment... The arrangement must be a serious item of expense to the Tramway Company who, considering the conditions under which they are working, are to be congratulated on the regularity of the service... The journey to Selsey by tram is still a unique experience, and many have availed themselves of it merely from the point of view of curiosity. Many visitors have been attracted to Selsey by the inundation, and the tram affords a splendid opportunity of witnessing one of the most remarkable effects of the gale throughout the whole country... An engine and ballast laden trucks were taken over the line on Friday (23rd) with satisfactory results, the test proving that the permanent way was quite undamaged. It speaks well for the line that the metals have withstood the sea's onslaught. The most dangerous spot was undoubtedly at Sidlesham where the line crosses the road, at a dip in the road, and where the action of the water had considerable effect on the road.
>
> 'Owing to the doubt which exists as to the possibilities of the Pagham Harbour again being reclaimed, much interest is evinced in the steps proposed to be taken by the Tramway Company. Many suggestions have been advanced by those not directly interested in the Company, and opinion differs as to the relative merits of raising the line to a higher level and retaining the present route, or diverting the line to the western side of the roads. So far as *Observer* enquiries have gone, the most probable course will be the erection of a bank and the elevation of the submerged portion of the line, which will continue to run over its present course across the newly formed harbour.'[13]

Christmastide in Selsey was spent in darkness and without cooking facilities for many, 'but the season was none the less merrily spent'. Many villagers had to exercise the utmost economy in the matter of artificial light as the demand for candles and oil was so great that it could not be coped with by the local shopkeepers, despite the large stock secured from Chichester. Work to repair the damaged gas works was going ahead by night and day and by 28th December 'the fires had been set going' and lighting was expected to be restored to the village 'within a day or two'.

Rumours were circulating that the Harbour Commissioners had placed a proposal before the Board of Admiralty that they should take the new Pagham Harbour over and convert it into a subsidiary Naval base for small craft, torpedo boats, destroyers and submarines. The *Chichester Observer* on 28th December thought that 'such a scheme seems quite feasible, and one that should be of great utility. It would be almost absolutely safe from attack, owing to the difficulty of an enemy's fleet finding it, and being able to get at it, and it may be assumed that it would be a welcome relief at Portsmouth. Incidentally, such a base, should the authorities entertain it and carry it out, would be a great attraction to Bognor, as it would be in easy reach, and an interesting place to visit'. Such a Naval base right on Selsey's doorstep would surely not be good for the resort's summer trade and luckily the rumours came to nothing!

Immediately addressing the unsatisfactory state of affairs that the Tramways Company now found themselves in, an Extraordinary General Meeting of the Shareholders was held in Chichester on Tuesday, 3rd January 1911 where it was announced that it had been decided to raise the line between Sidlesham and Ferry stations at an estimated cost of £2,500. A bank was to be built varying in height, but in many cases 8ft above the present rail level, from a point close to Ferry station through the bed of Pagham Harbour for about half a mile to a point some 250 yards south of Sidlesham station, continuing then for a further 200 yards opposite the station. It was not proposed to build the bank through the old mill pond at present as the arches under the old mill had been blocked, effectively preventing the water from getting through and flooding the site of the old mill pond. The Tramway embankment would be perfectly level and about a foot above high water level at the time of spring tides. Sidlesham station would have to be raised considerably as it was at present below the level of both rail and road. Work was to commence immediately and it was hoped to have the line open and running by Easter, although goods traffic was now being maintained, with trucks being run over the flooded section at low tide. Following the meeting, circulars were sent out to all Shareholders inviting them to take up Debentures in order to provide for the expense of raising the Tramway.

In February the Tramways Company amended its emergency flood service notice to read:

> SELSEY TRAMWAYS
> NOTICE IS HEREBY GIVEN, that on account of the flooding of the line between Ferry and Sidlesham Stations the Company cannot undertake to book passengers from Chichester further than Sidlesham, or from Selsey further than Ferry. The line between Sidlesham and Ferry Stations will be closed for Passenger Traffic until re-construction works are complete. Meanwhile a 'Bus Service has been arranged between Sidlesham and Ferry for passengers wishing to proceed from Chichester to Selsey, and vice versa. No extra charge will be made for this service, but the same cannot be guaranteed.
> All Cheap Bookings are suspended.
> Also, the Company cannot guarantee the delivery of Goods or Parcels without delay between Chichester and Selsey, until further notice. Every effort will be made, however, to give prompt delivery.
> The line will be re-opened for through Passenger Traffic on or before June 1st, 1911.
>
> Selsey, February, 1911.   H. G. Phillips, Manager

Harriet K. James later recalled her 'really intimate acquaintance' with the Tramway and how 'those of us who had "season tickets" on the tram knew all its vagaries and entered into many of its thrilling adventures'. Here she describes her trips to and from school in the Spring of 1911:[14]

> '...Our early morning journey to school was conducted thus. At the appointed time we travelled in the tram from Selsey. (Sometimes we could cajole the kindly omnibus driver into allowing us to ride on his 'bus from Selsey, but this was not really permissible, and ought not to be

THE SELSEY TRAMWAY

Left: *Some time later, the stranded open wagon had been recovered from the loop siding and work had started on removing the platform at Sidlesham.* Right: *Sidlesham with five open wagons and staff working busily at Sidlesham station.* COLLECTION PAUL LAMING

Left: *Incorrectly captioned 'The new embankment at Sidlesham', men are busily removing the platform and shoring up the eastern side of the original formation with redundant sleepers to prevent further damage from the sea after the Tramway was flooded in December 1910. This station was unusual in that it had a double-ended goods siding that ran behind the platform to rejoin the main running line beyond the level crossing.* COLLECTION PAUL LAMING

Right: *Work was progressing well in the Spring of 1911 with the passing loop now in position on the newly raised formation, but a point lever was still required. The new wooden 'up' platform was in situ, but work had yet to commence on the 'down' one, where chalk had been laid in readiness. Paralleling the main running line, a conventional single-ended siding facing Chichester was installed to the north of the road crossing. We can only wonder why the station building had been temporarily placed at this, the southern end of the new platform.* COLONEL STEPHENS RAILWAY MUSEUM & ARCHIVE

'Raising the permanent way at Sidlesham'. Probably taken the same day, this view shows Sidlesham *with her train on the partly raised main running line immediately to the north of Sidlesham station. Open wagons ex-GER No. 11 and ex-LBSCR No. 1 had both had their curved ends cut square. The platelayers' trolley is seen in the foreground on the remains of the severed loop siding.* LENS OF SUTTON

Pictured on a sunny winter's afternoon at Ferry, Chichester was probably working a flood shuttle service early in 1911. With no run-round loop, the engine had to propel the single ex-Lambourn Valley carriage back to Selsey.
COLLECTION PAUL LAMING

mentioned here!) At Ferry all passengers had to alight and shouldering all their burdens (if any), changed into, or on to, the waiting omnibus. With a crack of the driver's whip, we were off at a dignified pace over the road to Sidlesham and beyond to "Mill Pond Halt." I remember that certain athletic and energetic school-boys preferred to run most of the way behind the 'bus, and keeping pace with it, so that on our particular 'buses our progress was somewhat regal, for not only had we a coach-and-pair, but outriders or, more accurately, "outrunners" as well! At the "Mill Pond Halt" the "all-change" was sounded again, and out we were hustled to continue our journey once more by "tram".

Now the "Chichester engine", as we called it, was supposed always to be waiting there, so that the journey might be continued without further delay. But a devil inhabited that engine – by Satanic right, I think – and it was the most difficult thing in the world for it to get anywhere – to time, at least! Morning after morning we were left to enjoy ourselves in the quiet precincts of that diminutive Halt. On fine mornings we wandered into the lane and fields nearby, picking wild flowers and generally vegetating. As long as we kept an alert ear for its shrill whistle of triumph on arriving, or for the noisy rumble of the advancing tram, we could always rush back in time to mount it before it retreated to Chichester... When at length we had "chugged" slowly into Chichester, the morning was often well advanced and school assembled long since. However, the dear old tram always provided us with a legitimate excuse for being late, and our long-suffering mistresses accepted it with a smile.

'The return journeys were frequently brightened by the amusing things we were permitted to do which no travellers on more sophisticated trains were ever allowed even to think of! The tram guard was such a human, pleasant person, and he was ready to let us have our amusements as long as the carriage was not otherwise occupied and no other passengers were annoyed. We held concerts frequently, singing in chorus all the songs we knew, and sometimes we even forgot to hush when we stopped at a station. Some of the most exciting, loveliest games of "Blind Man's Buff" ever played were carried on by us in those carriages with their low wooden seats, whilst the tram was in motion.'

The *Chichester Observer* was able to report on 20th April that 'the work of elevating the Selsey Tramway line has so satisfactorily progressed that the Company were able to run a through tram on the evening before Good Friday, the first to make the journey being the 4.25 from Chichester which was followed by the 6.32, both passenger trams. On Saturday, several trams were run as well as on Bank Holiday, and a through service has been continued during the week. The work has been somewhat interfered with by the Spring tides, but it is hoped that the next one will be the last that would have to be considered. About eighty men are at work on the line.' Regular through traffic had commenced by the beginning of May, a full month earlier than had been anticipated back in February:

			Weekdays				Sundays		
Selsey	8.20	10.20	1.25	3.00	5.40	7.05	10.10	1.35	6.50
Ferry Siding	8.23		1.28	3.03	5.43	7.08	10.13	1.38	6.53
Sidlesham	8.30		1.35	3.10	5.50	–	10.20	1.45	7.00
Mill Pond	8.33	C	1.38	3.13	5.53	7.17	10.23	1.48	7.03
Chalder	8.35		1.40	3.15	5.55	7.19	10.25	1.50	7.05
Hunston	8.40		1.45	3.20	6.00	7.24	10.30	1.55	7.10
Chichester	8.55	11.00	2.00	3.35	6.15	7.38	10.45	2.10	7.25
Chichester	9.20	11.40	2.20	4.25	6.32	8.00	11.20	2.15	8.15
Hunston	9.25		2.25	4.30	–	8.05	11.25	2.20	8.20
Chalder	9.30		2.30	4.35	–	8.10	11.30	2.25	8.25
Mill Pond	9.32	C	2.32	4.37	6.40	8.12	11.32	2.27	8.27
Sidlesham	9.35		2.35	4.40	–	–	11.35	2.30	–
Ferry Siding	9.42		2.42	4.47	–	8.22	11.42	2.37	8.37
Selsey	9.55	12.20	2.55	5.00	7.03	8.35	11.55	2.50	8.50

C Mixed Tram

In June Cheap Excursion Tickets from Chichester to Selsey were reintroduced on Thursdays and Sundays for 9d return. Passengers had to travel on either of two specified down trams to take advantage of the cheap fare, but they were allowed to return by any service on the day of issue.[15]

The Annual General Meeting of the Hundred of Manhood & Selsey Tramways Company was held at 35 Southgate, Chichester on Saturday, 30th September when Edward Heron-Allen, in the chair, alluded to the 'apathy and want of interest' shown by the shareholders in what had

The following three photographs were taken on Friday 15th April 1911. This view shows Selsey negotiating the 6 chain radius curve as she was heading away from Chichester over Terminus Road level crossing towards Mill Pond Halt.

LCGB/KEN NUNN COLLECTION

MAN MAKES PLANS & GOD LAUGHS (1910–1912)

Sidlesham emerging from beneath the one and only overbridge on the Tramway a quarter of a mile north-west of Selsey station on an 'up' short working to Ferry. This site had been the temporary terminus until Selsey Town station opened to traffic in November 1897 and, in the late 1920s, Selsey Bridge Halt would be built on the ground immediately to the right of the locomotive.

LCGB, H. L. HOPWOOD COLLECTION

Later that afternoon, Sidlesham's train consisted of two of the ex-Lambourn Valley carriages that entered service in 1910. The ensemble was not, as it might appear, returning from Selsey Beach (this station had closed at the end of the 1905 summer season) but simply from taking water from the tank behind the engine shed. Note how the rudimentary loading gauge was positioned over the main running line, rather than over the goods loop that ran in behind it.

LCGB, KEN NUNN COLLECTION

Chichester was nearing the end of her career when photographed at Selsey with a mixed train consisting of an ex-Lambourn Valley carriage, a van and an open wagon c.1911. With the Selsey Tramway's unusual operating practices, it is quite possible that the goods vehicles would have been propelled ahead of the locomotive prior to being dropped off at a siding en route.
COLONEL STEPHENS RAILWAY MUSEUM & ARCHIVE (W. H. AUSTEN COLLECTION)

been their most critical year. Only one shareholder attended the meeting and it was stated that, in response to the appeal made by the Directors back in January, only two shareholders had assisted the Board by applying for a very small portion of the debentures offered to meet the emergency works of raising the embankment across Pagham Harbour. The chairman explained:

> 'The whole of the rest of the capital required for the work has been provided and the expenses met or guaranteed personally by the Directors, a circumstance which in itself should inspire the shareholders with confidence in the undertaking. As a result, however, of this apathy on the part of the shareholders, the Directors have decided on the highly prudent and conservative measure of charging the whole cost of the necessary works, amounting to £2,433, to revenue account, to be debited against it in coming years as the traffic profits will permit.'

Because of the disruption to the service, 8,500 fewer passengers had used the Tramway compared to 1910, but even taking into account the £167 paid out for the hire of the horse 'bus used between Mill Pond Halt and Ferry, gross receipts showed a decrease of only £73, whilst gross expenses had increased by just £150. With the raising of the line complete, the Directors felt that they had every reason to believe that they had nothing further to fear from the sea, and they were now prepared to pursue a forward and progressive policy, adding to and improving the Company's rolling stock and works and extending the line at Selsey.[16] They were, however, of the opinion that they had set a sufficient example of confidence to the shareholders, and that they looked to them to enable the Board to carry out that policy by subscribing for the debentures which had been offered to them the previous January. 'It argues well for the management of the line and for its future prosperity,' concluded Heron-Allen, 'that the balance of net revenue has increased steadily year by year from £125 in 1906 to £616 in 1910. The temporary check occasioned in 1911 by the flooding of the harbour, and the way in which it has been met, should prove to be an incident in the history of the line to which the Directors will be able to look back in future years with satisfaction, giving as it does to the shareholders, an object lesson in the manner in which their affairs are conducted.'

Heavy gales once again swept over the south coast on Sunday, 10th December, although they were not nearly so severe as those experienced 12 months before. 'A big gap was made in the beach near the old tramway station, and water rushed in and flooded the disused building.'[17]

By January 1912 £3,614 had been expended on the new Tramway embankment. Over £1,000 of this expense was due to two washouts that occurred during some extremely rough weather in November, the work having to be carried out in very difficult conditions. A supply of chalk was provided at each end of the new embankment, and ballast was left in various places along its length for immediate use as and when the line settled.

On completion of the restoration works, C. Willes Eborall, M.I.M.E., an expert and well-qualified engineer, hitherto quite unconnected with the Tramway or its Directors, was asked to prepare an entirely independent report on the works. Dated 8th January 1912, under the section entitled 'New Works' he advised

> 'Two schemes were proposed re construction of the bank, and were duly submitted to the Directors. Scheme (a) – that the sea face of the bank should be faced with sods. Scheme (b) – that the facings be made of chalk blocks, handpacked to a height above water level.
>
> 'The Directors decided to adopt the latter scheme which has been carried out.
>
> 'The width of the bank at formation level is about 12ft, the slopes, when settled, will be 1¾ to 1 on the sea side, and 1½ to 1 on the land side.
>
> 'The height to which the bank had to be raised was 8ft above the original level, which raised the formation of the Line throughout to the same level as Sidlesham Mill Dam at its lowest point.
>
> 'The accompanying plan[18] will show the relation of the reconstructed bank to the flooded area. It will be clearly seen from this that the bank is well protected from all storm damage, except from the direct East, and in this case, but a small proportion of the bank is exposed to the direct force of the wind, and that to a great extent, is protected by the outer shingle ridge of the Harbour.
>
> 'The bank has already in its green state, been subjected to a considerable amount of wash and wind pressure, especially during the storm at the beginning of November, 1911, and later storms, to say nothing of the recent heavy rains. So far as I can see, no damage has occurred, and, of course, the bank will become more consolidated as time goes on.
>
> 'During the construction of the bank, which is made principally of clay dug from borrow pits adjacent to the Line, the Directors issued instructions that it would be well to mix land gravel with the filling of the bank, and this was done, somewhat increasing the cost, but no doubt improving the bank.
>
> 'It was also decided locally to leave in the temporary wall of sleepers on the sea side of the bank, with a view of assisting the consolidation of the same. There is no objection to this from an engineering point of view, although, of course, it has considerably increased the cost, though no doubt as long as the sleepers remain, will tend to strengthen the bank.
>
> 'As anticipated, the various leaks through the bank, which were inevitable during the construction, have now practically entirely taken up, as was predicted by the Engineer at the time. The insignificant ones, which still remain, are practically only the result of percolation.
>
> 'Instructions were also given that a fresh Loop or passing place, should be constructed at Sidlesham, making a great improvement in the working capabilities of the Line. At this place a new Goods Siding has been constructed of a more convenient nature than the original one and a more modern platform erected, the Station building having been removed to allow this to be done.[19]
>
> 'The ballast on the bank has had to be exceptionally thick owing to the nature of the material used in the construction, and insomuch as there is now between 18in and 2ft of ballast beneath the sleepers, when the bank becomes consolidated, an exceptionally substantial road should be the result.'

Willes Eborall's report continued by suggesting that the bank should be watched with extra care during the next six months, especially after heavy rains or sudden frosts and that any signs of settlement should at once be put right by platelayers, and concluded 'I am of opinion that if the precautions suggested above are taken, the Directors need have no fear re the stability of the bank which, in my opinion, and also in the opinion of local authorities quite capable of judging, will solidify more year by year.'

Along with a notice that an Extraordinary General Meeting was to be held at the Council Chamber, Chichester at 2.30pm on Friday, 9th February, the above Report and the Directors' Report dated 20th January was circulated to all Shareholders. The latter explained how the greater

HUNDRED OF MANHOOD AND SELSEY TRAMWAYS COMPANY, Ltd.

Statement showing Comparative Receipts and Expenditure

FROM 1906 TO 1911.

Year ending Aug. 31st.	Passenger Receipts	Season Tickets	Carriage of Mails	Goods and Parcels	Rents	Miscellaneous Receipts	TOTAL	Balance of Revenue Account (Profit)	Maint'nce of Way and Works	Locomotive Power, Running	Locomotive Power, Repairs	Reserve for Depreciation	Repairs to Carriages & Wagons	Traffic Expenses	General Charges	Rates and Taxes	Government Duty	Mileage and Demurrage	Claims & Compensation	Sundry Expenses	Balance of Net Revenue Available for Dividends
1906	1,813 2 0	27 17 4	714 6 0	861 12 6	75 12 4	5 17 8	2,708 8	2,559 0 11	506 14 9	677 5 5	157 9 10	100 0 0	58 18 9	294 16 8	203 11 6	88 5 3	11 8 1	104 19 6	1 10 9	79 6 10	125 18 4
1907	1,875 7 9	564 9 3	814 6 0	970 12 4	74 1 0	34 17 1	3,033 13 9	777 0 2	469 9 8	607 18 3	192 17 0	100 0 0	39 8 0	296 3 8	285 1 7	83 7 0	12 19 0	103 8 6	5 9 11	70 11 0	562 9 3
1908	1,861 9 10	817 15 6	418 4 6	1,083 6 1	75 6 0	31 5 11	3,115 10 5	695 16 2	487 11 3	764 11 16	191 16 0	100 0 0	83 3 6	310 0 10	203 4 11	80 3 11	11 7 2	111 7 0	50 9 5	146 0 8	515 7 8
1909	1,880 10 1	1137 2 4	1,026 1 1	1074 19 0	43 8 7	3,080 11 2	771 2 3	474 4 3	723 16 3	156 17 0	150 0 0	20 6 10	327 10 7	304 12 9	85 8 2	10 9 0	113 0 6	2 2 1	146 6	601 1 6
1910	1,966 1 11	35 18 1	520 6 0	1,034 12 6	74 18 0	45 9 6	3,197 6 8	767 10 8	474 16 18	724 2 14	150 14 0	200 0 0	55 15 0	844 19 8	326 18 19	87 1 3	8 14 9	52 17 6	16 2 2	52 0 0	616 9 8
1911	1,903 9 10	57 12 3	822 0 3	1,086 3 6	74 12 6	30 1 6	3,128 19 7	594 18 8	460 18 0	780 17 11	161 3 0	100 0 0	28 7 0	509 5 7	352 10 0	90 14 0	8 14 3	117 5 6	7 11 6	86 3 4	75 2 2

portion of money for the repairs to the embankment had been provided out of the Directors' pockets or by their personal guarantees in the confident expectation that the Shareholders would rally round once the work had been completed. Unfortunately, that expectation had not been realised, and having felt they had done far more than properly should be expected of them, the Directors were now to place the affairs of the line in the shareholders' hands and leave to them the decision whether they, or other persons, should profit by the Directors' labour and expenditure over the past year. The rest of the Report is quoted in full:

> 'It is a significant fact, proving the vitality of your enterprise, that though 20% of the Line was not available for passenger traffic for many months, and consequently 8,250 less passengers were carried than in the previous year, the decrease in receipts for the year was only £73.
>
> 'In spite of these unprecedented difficulties, involving an expenditure of omnibus hire of £167, the year's working showed a profit of £535 of which sum Debenture and Loan Interests with Income Tax absorbed £400, leaving a net profit of £135. This profit, together with the amount of £210 brought forward from the previous year amounted to £345, against which was debited £270 for Flood Account, leaving a balance of £75 which has been absorbed by the subsequent working expenses, which, during the winter months exceed the revenue of the line.
>
> 'The resulting position is that the Board is now confronted by the pressing claims of ordinary creditors amounting to £1,500, by the repayment due in February of a loan from the Bank on the security of Debentures amounting to £800, and by the liability to repay personal loans from the Directors amounting to £400, making £2,700, which sum, or the greater part of it must be immediately forthcoming.
>
> 'To provide this sum the Directors require the support of the shareholders in the form of a contribution equal to 18s 9d per share of each shareholder's holding. As security for these contributions the Directors will issue to the contributors B Debentures of the 1910 issue and the interest on these Debentures will be the usual preferential charge on the Company's Revenue.
>
> 'In order that the Shareholders may be in fullest position of the facts relating to that Revenue a full statement is appended of the Company's working for the last five years, that being the period during which the management of the line has been in its present hands. The working accounts for 1906 are appended for purposes of comparison, prior to which there had been a debit balance in Net Revenue.
>
> 'It will be observed that until the Flood of 1910 your line was in continuously improving condition. The line resumed work uninterrupted by obstacles arising from the reconstruction works in September, 1910[20] and the confidence of the public, which had been severely shaken by all kinds of wild and sensational rumours, began to return. The traffic returns since September last have shown a monthly increase over even the receipts of the corresponding months of 1909, which as will be seen from the working table formed a portion of the most prosperous year in our history.
>
> 'These Traffic Returns are as follows:-

	1909 (Included in year ending Aug. 31st, 1910).	1910 (Included in year ending Aug. 31st, 1911).	1911
	£ s. d.	£ s. d.	£ s. d.
September	344 19 7	391 16 9	424 0 4
October	234 12 6	257 13 8	242 9 1
November	181 0 2	168 10 3	179 14 4
December	180 14 10	186 3 8	197 16 10
	£941 7 1	£1004 4 4	£1044 0 7

MAN MAKES PLANS & GOD LAUGHS (1910–1912)

'In the face of such figures as these, we have no hesitation in asking the Shareholders to provide the necessary funds to tide us over the leaner months, which must ensue before the profitable summer traffic commences.

'Your Directors regret being compelled to point out that they cannot accept the responsibility of carrying on the business of the Company unless they are placed in a position to do so unharassed by pressing Creditors, and they therefore propose not to make use of any contributions unless a sum of at least £2,000 is subscribed within fourteen days of the day fixed herein for the Extraordinary General Meeting.

'If the sum is not subscribed your Directors will have no alternative but that of submitting to the appointment of a Receiver, a step which may involve the realization of the assets of the Company and a division among the shareholders of the surplus (if any), left after paying off the Creditors and Debenture Holders.

'The Shareholders are earnestly requested to make every effort to attend the meeting of the Company called for Friday, the 9th February.

We are, Ladies and Gentlemen,
Your obedient servants,
FOR THE BOARD
Edward Heron-Allen,
Chairman.'

'Liberal facilities are provided by the Tramways Company for Easter', explained the *Chichester Observer* on 3rd April, 'and many extra trams will be run in accordance with the growing popularity of Selsey. On Thursday, Saturday and Monday (Bank Holiday) trams leave Chichester at 10.25, 12.48, 3.20, 4.25, 6.32 and 8.00. Trams leave Selsey for Chichester at 9.15, 11.30, 1.25, 3.05, 5.50 and 7.05. On Good Friday and Sunday trams leave Chichester at 11.20, 2.14 and 5.15 and leave Selsey at 8.50, 1.35 and 7.00.' From 5th June the Thursday and Sunday 9d Cheap Excursion advert appeared regularly in the same newspaper.

A second platform was constructed (like that opposite with second-hand standard-gauge railway sleepers) beside the new passing loop at Sidlesham and the corrugated iron station building was repositioned at the northern end of the main platform, but unusually it faced the road rather than the Tramway so, it was said, to protect passengers from the prevailing southwesterly winds! To cater for the ever-increasing numbers of passengers, the Tramways Company operated a two-train service on weekdays and Saturdays for the first time between 15th July and 14th September, but with only two locomotives available, (their first engine, *Chichester* was now derelict) there was no standby in case of a breakdown. The locomotives *Selsey* and *Sidlesham* must have given a good account of themselves as there was no mention in the local press of any breakdowns, but it must have been with some relief that a second-hand 0–4–2ST locomotive purchased from the Plymouth, Devonport & South West Junction Railway, belatedly joined the fleet at the beginning of September. At long last, the three saloon carriages acquired from the Lambourn Valley Railway two years previously had a proper job to do, but with no signalling, trains crossing at Sidlesham (operating on the 'staff and ticket' system) had to be flagged in and out of the station. Although not marked as such on the original summer 1912 timetable, to show clearly which trams passed at Sidlesham, their timings are given in italics.

	A	A	A	B	B									C
Selsey	7.00	8.30	9.50	7.35	9.18	11.30	12.20	1.15	2.30	3.30	4.30	5.50	7.05	8.55
Ferry Siding	7.04	8.33	9.53	7.39	9.23	11.34	12.24	1.19	2.34	3.34	4.34	5.54	7.09	8.59
Sidlesham	7.10	8.40	10.00	7.43	9.26	11.40	*12.30*	*1.25*	2.40	*3.40*	4.40	6.00	7.15	9.05
Chalder	7.15	8.45	10.05	7.48	9.31	11.45	12.35	1.30	2.45	3.45	–	6.05	7.20	9.10
Hunston	7.15	8.50	10.10	7.53	9.36	11.50	12.40	1.35	2.50	3.50	–	6.10	7.25	9.15
Chichester	7.30	9.00	10.20	8.05	9.48	12.00	12.50	1.45	3.00	4.00	5.00	6.20	7.35	9.25

	A	A	B								C	
Chichester	7.45	9.15	8.38	10.52	12.10	1.05	2.20	3.20	4.20	5.40	6.32	8.15	10.35
Hunston	7.52	9.25	8.45	10.59	12.17	1.12	2.27	–	4.27	5.47	–	8.22	10.42
Chalder	8.00	9.30	8.50	11.04	12.22	1.17	2.32	–	4.32	5.52	–	8.27	10.47
Sidlesham	8.05	9.35	8.55	11.12	*12.30*	*1.25*	2.40	*3.40*	4.40	6.00	6.52	8.32	10.52
Ferry Siding	8.08	9.38	9.00	11.14	12.32	1.27	2.42	–	4.42	6.02	–	8.34	10.54
Selsey	8.15	9.45	9.08	11.22	12.40	1.35	2.50	3.50	4.50	6.10	7.00	8.45	11.05

A Mondays only   B Mondays excepted   C Thursdays only

One might wonder why the 3.20pm tram from Chichester, which only called at Sidlesham, took a similar half hour as the other services that called at all stations, although the 6.32pm 'express' did save passengers a full two minutes! Note that there is no mention of the 'mixed' trams, and that all stopping services were allowed a standard 30 minutes for their journeys. Perhaps a daily goods only service was operated between the passenger trams at some time during the morning. Commenting on the new timetable, the *Chichester Observer* on 31st July suggested that 'the double tram service which was inaugurated a week or two ago is proving a great boon to visitors to Selsey. Trams leave Chichester for Selsey at all times of the day to suit everyone's convenience. A feature of the new service too is that all trams run to time and connexion (*sic*) can be generally relied upon with the Brighton and Portsmouth trains. Next Monday (Bank Holiday) a special late tram will run leaving Selsey at 8.55pm and returning from Chichester calling at all stations at 10.35pm.' An additional late tram was also run in connection with Selsey Carnival on Wednesday, 4th September (no timing given) with the 9d return fare being available to Cicestrians by the 5.40pm and 6.32pm trams from the city. A week later a 'special' left Selsey at 10pm, and on Thursday, 3rd October 'a late tram for Selseyites to see "Faust" at Portsmouth Theatre leaves Chichester at 1150pm connecting with the Theatre Train which arrives at 11.46pm.'[21] It had originally been intended that the full summer timetable was to run until 14th September, after which a slightly reduced service would come into operation, but it had proved so popular that it was continued until the end of that month.[22]

Notes
1. *Chichester Observer*, Wednesday, 16.02.1910.
2. Poole's Myriorama featured local artistes performing humorous and sentimental songs, exhibitions of sleight of hand, table turning, thought reading, shadow harlequinade and India Slave Dances. Proceeds went to the Chichester Infirmary.
3. *Chichester Observers*, Wednesday 6.4.1910, 27.4.1910, 29.6.1910, 13.7.1910 and 5.10.1910.
4. *Going off the Rails – the Country Railway in West Sussex* by Bill Gage, Michael Harris and Tony Sullivan, published by West Sussex County Council, 1997.
5. *A History of Selsey* by Francis Mee, published by Phillimore & Co. Ltd., 1988.
6. *Chichester Observer*, Wednesday, 21.12.1910. Alfred Rusbridge wrote several books, including *Bee Keeping, Plain & Practical, Sussex Old World Bee Lore* and *A Day on a Sussex Marsh*.
7. Vol. 1, *Selseyana*, by E. Heron-Allen, pages 89–93, 'Selsey Tramways', West Sussex Record Office, ref. MP93. No other references to electrifying the Tramway have come to light.
8. *Daily News*, Monday, 19.12.1910. Many sources quote incorrectly that the sea defences were breached at 10.30pm on Thursday, 15.12.1910.
9. When the tide mill lost its natural source of power it had continued to work using steam until milling ceased around 1906.
10. *A History of Selsey* by Frances Mee, as above.
11. The antiquated two-horse single-deck omnibus was operated by J. Mitchell of Selsey, and from around 1900 it had met all trams on arrival at Selsey Town station. A luggage rack on the roof, reached by a ladder at the rear, became a precarious perch for those not wishing to get their feet wet in the saloon!
12. *West Sussex Gazette*, Thursday, 22.12.1910.
13. *Chichester Observer*, Wednesday 28.12.1910.
14. *West Sussex Gazette*, Thursday 14.2.1935.
15. Adverts to this effect were placed in the *Chichester Observer* on Wednesdays 21.6.1911, 9.8.1911, 16.8.1911 and for 3 weeks commencing 29.11.1911.
16. The subject of extending the Tramway at Selsey would be brought up on several future occasions.
17. *Chichester Observer*, Wednesday, 13.12.1911.
18. A copy of this plan has not come to light.
19. Whilst reconstruction work was being carried out, the station building, possibly out of use, was temporarily placed facing Chichester several yards to the south of the new sleeper-built platform beside the main running line.
20. The reconstruction work referred to was probably the replacement of the curved roof of the engine shed at Selsey by a pitched one.
21. *Chichester Observer*, Wednesday, 11.9.1912 and 2.10.1912.
22. *Chichester Observer*, Wednesday, 18.9.1912.

CHAPTER FOUR
THOUGHTS OF EXPANSION
(1913–1919)

Sidlesham with one of the ex-Lambourn Valley Thirds and the Composite carriage, plus one of the low-roof ex-MR vans, heading an 'up' tram northwards across Pagham Harbour towards Sidlesham on the new embankment at low tide. How small the locomotive looks in comparison with the carriages.
COLLECTION PAUL LAMING

IN January 1913 the Tramway operated 6 return trams on weekdays (the 6.32pm down service omitting all stops except for Sidlesham) and four return services on Sundays. Cheap Excursion tickets at 9d return were available on the 2.15pm and 2.20pm trams from Chichester on Sundays and Thursdays respectively. On Maundy Thursday, Easter Saturday and Bank Holiday Monday the service was increased with trams leaving Selsey for Chichester at 8.30am, 10.15am, 11.45am, 1.25pm, 3.05pm, 5.50pm, 7.05pm and 9.00pm, returning from the city at 9.20am, 11.00am, 12.48pm, 2.20pm, 4.20 pm, 6.32pm, 8.15pm and 10.20pm. On Good Friday and Easter Sunday trams left Selsey at 10.00am, 1.35pm, 5.20pm and 7.00pm, returning at 11.20am, 2.15pm, 6.00pm and 8.15pm.[1] A special service was also run over the Whitsun holiday with trams on the Sunday leaving Selsey at 8.50am, 10.40am, 1.35pm, 5.20pm and 7.00pm, and from Chichester at 10.05am, 11.20am, 2.15pm, 6.00pm and 8.15pm. On Whit Monday trams were timed to leave Selsey at 8.30am, 10.15am, 11.35am, 1.25pm, 3.05pm, 4.30pm, 5.55pm, 7.05pm and 8.55pm, returning from the city at 9.20am, 11.00am, 12.48pm, 2.20pm, 3.55pm, 5.20pm, 6.32pm, 8.5pm and 10.40pm.

The first indication to the general public that the Hundred of Manhood & Selsey Tramways Company intended building branch lines from near Hunston to West Wittering and West Itchenor was in this typically unpunctuated notice that appeared in the *Sussex Daily News* dated 23rd May:

PUBLIC NOTICE
LIGHT RAILWAYS ACT, 1896
(WEST SUSSEX LIGHT RAILWAYS).

NOTICE IS HEREBY GIVEN that application will be made during the current month to the Light Railway Commissioners for an Order authorizing the construction, working and maintenance of Light Railways between Hunston, West Wittering, West Itchenor and Chichester and Selsey all in the county of Sussex, and to seek powers for the incorporated Company to acquire or otherwise use the existing undertaking of the Hundred of Manhood & Selsey Tramway (sic) Co. Ltd. (including the lands in which the same is constructed) and to construct reconstruct adapt maintain work and use the same as part of the proposed Light Railway and for other purposes.

RAILWAY No.1 commences in the parish of Hunston by a junction with the Hundred of Manhood and Selsey Tramway at a point 22 yards or thereabouts south of the Tramway Bridge crossing the Chichester Canal and running in a Westerly direction 44 yards or thereabouts North of Bridge Farm in the parish of Donnington thence in a South Westerly direction along the Southern bank of Chichester Canal crossing the public road 22 yards or thereabouts South of Cutfield Bridge in the parish of Appledram thence in a Westerly direction 22 yards or thereabouts South of Courtbarn Cottages 132 yards or thereabouts South of Oldhouse Farm in the Parish of Birdham, thence in a South Westerly direction through the Parish of West Wittering 220 yards or thereabouts North West of Walnut Tree House and running in a South Easterly direction 121 yards or thereabouts South West of The Elms continuing in a South Easterly direction and terminating in the Parish of West Wittering at a point 333 yards or thereabouts on the Western side of the Public Road from West Wittering to West Itchenor measured along the said road in a North Easterly direction from the Rectory East Wittering total length of the above described Railway 7 miles 0 furlongs 0 chains, or thereabouts.

RAILWAY No.2 wholly in the Parish of Hunston commences by a junction with the Hundred of Manhood and Selsey Tramway at a point

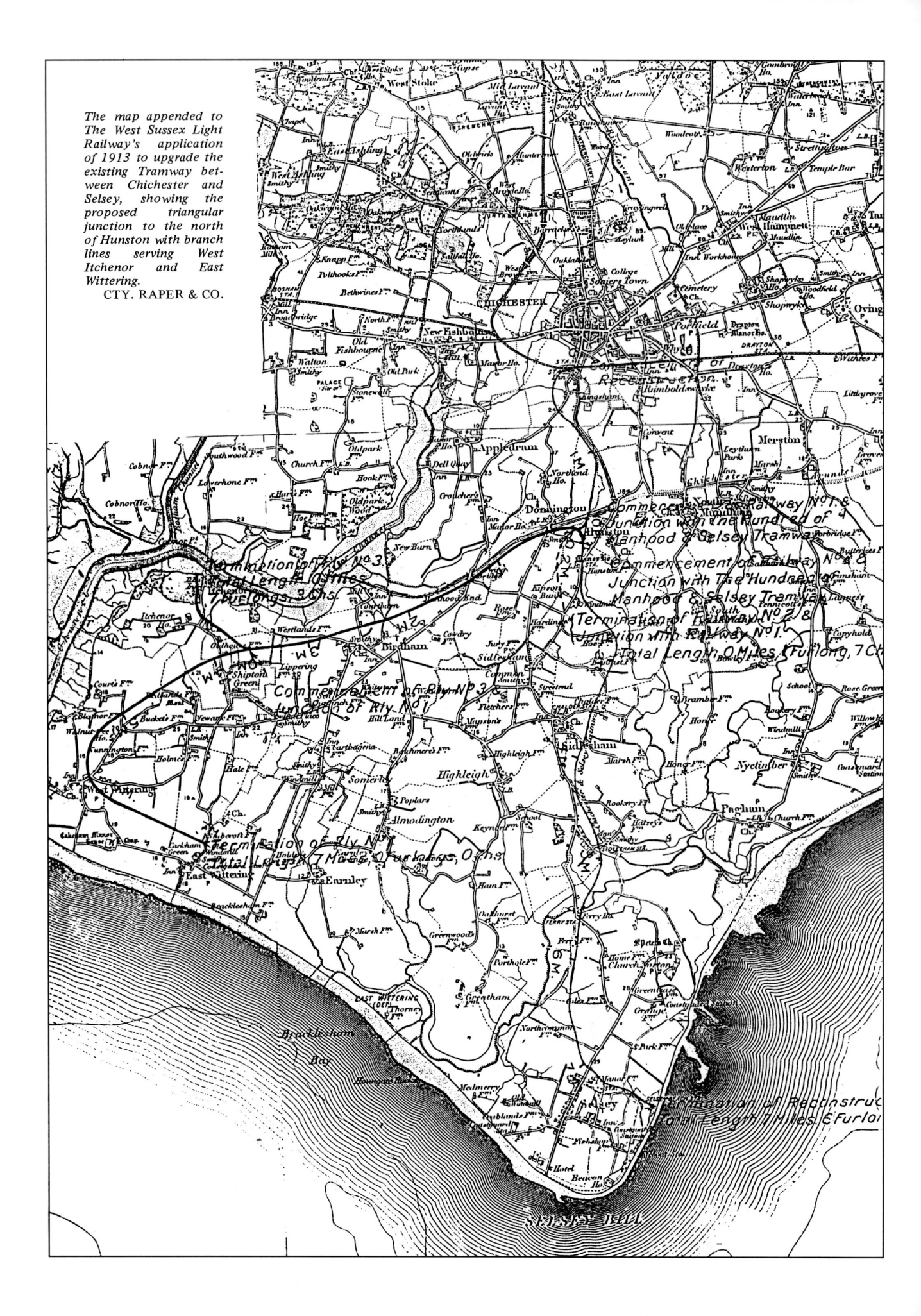

The map appended to The West Sussex Light Railway's application of 1913 to upgrade the existing Tramway between Chichester and Selsey, showing the proposed triangular junction to the north of Hunston with branch lines serving West Itchenor and East Wittering.

CTY. RAPER & CO.

THOUGHTS OF EXPANSION (1913-1919)

242 yards or thereabouts North of Hunston Station and running in a North Westerly direction terminating with Railway No. 1 above described at a point 1 furlong 7½ chains or thereabouts measured from its commencement, total length of described railway 0 miles 1 furlong 7 chains or thereabouts.

RAILWAY No.3 commences in the Parish of Birdham by a junction with Railway No. 1 at a point 493 yards or thereabouts South East of Old House Farm running in a North Westerly direction through the Parish of West Itchenor 44 yards or thereabouts North East of Church Farm thence in a Northerly direction 33 yards or thereabouts West of the Rectory and terminating on the Southern Bank of the Chichester Canal at a point 33 yards or thereabouts West of the Custom House West Itchenor Total Lengths (*sic*) of above described Railway 0 miles 7 furlongs 3 chains or thereabouts.

The area of the land required for the purposes of the Railway is 66 acres or thereabouts.

The gauge of the Railway will be 4 feet 8½ inches and the motive power steam.

On and after the 31st day of May 1913 copies of the plans sections and Book of Reference of the proposed Railways may be seen at all reasonable hours at the Office of the undersigned where copies of the Draft Order may be obtained on payment of one shilling per copy. All persons having objections to the proposed Railways should address the same to the Secretary, Light Railway Commission, Scotland House, New Scotland Yard, Westminster, London, SW, such communications to be on foolscap paper and written on one side only and a copy thereof sent to the undersigned at the address below.

H. F. Stephens,
Salford Terrace,
Tonbridge, Kent.

May, 1913.

Holman Stephens' estimated costs, worked out at £3,292 0s 0d per mile were Railway No.1: £45,626 19s 4d, Railway No.2: £2,906 13s 6d and Railway No.3: £7,413 12s 11d. Reconstruction of the existing Tramway between Chichester and Selsey was expected to cost a further £24,861 7s 6d, making a total of £80,808 13s 3d. The Capital was to be £90,000 in nine thousand shares at £10 each and Messrs. Frank Sanden Street, Edward Heron-Allen, Luther Clayton, Sharp Archibald Garland[2] and Hubert John Powell were to be the first directors of the new enterprise which would be named 'The West Sussex Light Railway Company'.

As the result of a special meeting of West Wittering Parish Council held on Thursday, 12th June to discuss the proposed West Sussex Light Railway Order, it was unanimously agreed that the idea of connecting up the village with the rest of the world would be a great boon to them, provided that sufficient protection was provided for the public at the various level crossings. Mr. W. V. Wray suggested that a railway would bring 'an out-of-the-way village such as West Wittering into the world, and benefit the village educationally'. He continued: 'The place ranks among the most beautiful sea-side resorts in Sussex, but it is little known, and a railway will make it known. A result of the construction of a light railway would be an increase in the number of visitors, more houses would be built and the place would be livelier. It has been stated that it would be better to keep the place select, but I fail to see why our excellent front and fresh sea air should be the monopoly of the select. Let's look forward to seeing our beach in the near future with thousands enjoying the municipal blessings now enjoyed by other resorts in the county, including a "West Wittering Municipal Band". As to the people who state that a railway would drive the motorists away, they are little aware how the motorists tear up the roads which the farmers have to pay for.'[3]

July, August and September saw the most ambitious timetable ever operated by the Tramways Company with 12 return trips on Mondays, 13 on Thursdays and 11 trams Tuesday to Saturday, with 'a double service of trams' in

---

In re—AN APPLICATION MADE IN MAY 1913

UNDER

THE LIGHT RAILWAYS ACT 1896

WEST SUSSEX LIGHT RAILWAY ORDER 1913.

(DRAFT)

Order of the Light Railway Commissioners

[*As*

Authorising the construction of Light Railways in the County of Sussex, and for other purposes.

H. F. STEPHENS,
SALFORD TERRACE,
TONBRIDGE.

PRICE ONE SHILLING.
(*Postage Two pence*).

THE SELSEY TRAMWAY

This time with the sea on either side, Sidlesham *is shown approaching Ferry across the Tramway Embankment with a 'mixed' train comprising a van, an open wagon and two of the ex-Lambourn Valley 4-wheel carriages.*
COLONEL STEPHENS RAILWAY MUSEUM & ARCHIVE

Pictures on a 'down' working near Hunston soon after her arrival on the Tramway in September 1912, the locomotive that would later be named Hesperus *is seen in the condition in which she entered service at Selsey. This is the only known photograph to show her tall, graceful tapered chimney. Although it was winter, the door from the balcony into the saloon of the leading carriage had been left open.*
COLLECTION E. C. GRIFFITH

operation between 12.10pm and 8.15pm each day. One train sufficed on Sundays making six return journeys. For Selsey's annual carnival on Wednesday, 27th August, special excursion tickets were offered at the now familiar 9d return for travel on trams leaving Chichester at 2.20pm, 3.20pm, 4.20pm, 5.20pm, 6.40pm and 7.35pm. A special late tram left Selsey for Chichester at 10.00pm, calling at all stations 'so that Cicestrians and others may stay by the sea during the evening, or attend the entertainments'.[4]

Over the year ending 31st August 1913, the general working of the Hundred of Manhood & Selsey Tramways Company Ltd. was described in the Directors' Report as 'satisfactory' at the Annual General Meeting held on Thursday, 23rd October. A record number of 89,915 passengers had been carried with receipts £83 6s 10d above the previous best. However, there had been a decrease in the goods and parcels receipts of £86 15s 11d, as nearly all the Westhampnett Rural District Council's material for the repair of the public roads had been carried by their steam lorries, rather than the Tram. This resulted in gross receipts over the previous year showing a slight decrease of £12 5s 2d at £3,385 4s 10d. As proposed in the last Report, the embankment through Pagham Harbour had been slightly raised and strengthened for which £42 had been charged to flood account and a further amount of £42 2s 5d for law costs had also been charged to this account, making a total debit of £3,876 16s 11d up to 31st August 1913. Against this, £620 had already been credited in previous years and a further amount of £150 had been credited during the past year, leaving a balance of £3,106 16s 11d. Gross expenses, exclusive of flood account, amounted to £2,603 15s 7d, an increase over the year of £91 16s 2d, leaving a balance of £27 2s 0d which was to be carried forward to the next year's account. The chairman, Edward Heron-Allen remarked

> 'Though it seems an anomaly to say it, evidence that the work, which had been somewhat uphill lately, is now showing an easier gradient, is to be found in the small decrease in our gross receipts on the year. It is seldom that one can point to a decrease, as we can this day, and yet regard it as a healthy sign. With the Westhampnett Rural District's materials going by road, the Company anticipated a loss of £102, instead of which the decrease is only £12 5s 2d. This is due to the normal increase in goods traffic and the larger increase in passenger traffic. We might take this as being consequent on the Board's policy of continually improving the line and rolling stock, and making the conditions more comfortable for passengers; in this respect our endeavours have become common knowledge in the district and is instrumental in getting rid of the impression prevailing that the line is dangerous to travel on. These facts, coupled with the growing prosperity of Selsey, have increased our passenger traffic, and this in spite of the epidemic of diphtheria which broke out at Selsey; this too, though only a small epidemic, was made the most of by the very people I would have thought would want to keep it quiet!'

Selsey had become known all over the country as a place 'reeking with diphtheria', although there had only been around 30 cases, hardly comparable to the great plague of the 17th century! Nevertheless, the Directors found considerable satisfaction in that the increase in passenger traffic was not due to excursionists, but rather to users of the line residing in Selsey and Chichester and places in between. Continuing, the Chairman said that with the heightening and strengthening of the embankment, humanly speaking, there could be no chance of their breaking down again with a recurrence of the disaster of 1910, and 'great credit was reflected on Mr. H. F. Stephens, their engineer, and Mr. Phillips, their manager, for the way the embankments withstood the storms and extraordinarily high tides early this year, when considerable havoc was caused at many other places along the South Coast'. During the year, Horace Charles Mitchell had accepted an invitation to join the Board of Directors.

An Extraordinary Meeting of the Shareholders was held immediately afterwards for the purpose of considering the proposed new extensions, etc., and the following resolution was submitted:

> 'That the shareholders approve the action of the Board in applying for a Light Railway Order for the purpose of reconstructing the existing tramway, and of constructing an extension to East Wittering and Itchenor, and working either or both as a light railway.'

Edward Heron-Allen suggested that the opening of the new routes would be of great benefit to the inhabitants, and would undoubtedly raise the value of the adjoining land, besides developing the Selsey peninsula in a very material way. The Directors felt that the time had come to take the initiative in the matter owing to rumours of others taking it up; they felt it was their duty to be the first in the field. Henry Phillips explained the route and drew attention to the advantages of the line, confirming that the West Wittering terminus[5] would be well within half a mile of the sea. Another great advantage, the Chairman said, would be that whereas at present the Tramways Company was responsible to no one, by placing themselves under Government supervision, as they would do under the proposed Order, they would secure the confidence of the travelling public. He proposed the adoption of the resolution, and after being seconded by E. Harding, it was carried.

On the morning of Tuesday, 4th November a well-attended public enquiry into the West Sussex Light Railway Order was opened at the Chichester Council Chamber before Commissioners The Hon. A. E. Gathorne-Hardy (chairman), Colonel G. F. O. Boughey, RE, CSI and Henry Allan Steward, with Alan D. Erskine as secretary.

First to speak was Holman Stephens on behalf of the promoters, who explained that the application embraced the reconstruction of the existing tramline under the Light Railway Act, and the extension of the existing line to two points, one on the east bank of Chichester Harbour, affording access to the shipping there, and the other at East Wittering, which was expected to develop in the near future as a seaside resort. Proceeding to give a history of the Tramway, he confirmed that the Capital had been entirely raised locally and the takings had been £10 per mile per week which, according to the shortness of the system was very good. So far as the proposed reconstruction was concerned, it consisted of relaying the line, resignalling[6], the erection of swing bridges (sic) with level crossings of a modern nature with or without gates according to the discretion of the Board of Trade. Dealing with the extension, he advised that 'the idea is to run an extension railway parallel with the Chichester Canal for nearly two miles, and then striking south-west past Birdham to a point a quarter of a mile from Shipton Green. There there would be a short junction line of just under a mile in length running down to West Itchenor. At Itchenor the idea is to construct a reinforced concrete jetty, 200ft long at a cost of £2,500 where any vessel coming up the Harbour Channel could unload, and vessels of 700 to 800 tons could get there at certain times of the tide. Another line from Shipton Green would go south-west to West Wittering and East Wittering, which possesses an excellent front of sand, and the proposed railway facilities are calculated to add another seaside resort to the South Coast.' Referring in detail to the attitude of the various owners of land affected by the proposed line, he pointed out that five stations would be erected, but to mention the proposed sites of the intermediate stations would place them too much in the hands of individual landowners.

The Tramways Company's secretary, Henry Phillips, suggested that a considerable amount of sea-borne traffic was expected from West Itchenor, while the agricultural produce from the district would also be considerable, as the traffic on the existing line had increased year by year. He was then cross-examined by J. W. Loader-Cooper (solicitor for the Chichester Corporation) as to complaints of delay to barges coming up the Chichester Canal due to the Tramways Company's failure to open the swing (sic) bridge of the existing railway. 'The agreement with the Chichester Corporation allowed a stoppage of 15 minutes,' Mr. Phillips replied, 'but I admit that barges have been kept waiting three-quarters of an hour, but that was the fault of the barges! Some 10 to 12 trains are run every day on the line during the summer.'[7] Edward Heron-Allen (vice-chairman of the Tramway Company) referred to the finances of the present undertaking, expressing the view that there was 'no insuperable difficulty' and told how money required for the repair of the line after it had been washed away had been raised by the Directors and their friends. In his opinion, the increase in the passenger traffic and in the rateable value of Selsey had been extraordinary in recent years.

In the course of questioning the witness, Mr. Loader-Cooper advised that Chichester Corporation now desired that a new bridge should be erected over the Chichester Canal, and that no one should be kept waiting for more than five minutes, and that the penalty should be reduced to £2, but be made recoverable at a Court of Summary Jurisdiction. After consideration, the Chairman announced that the Commissioners were of the opinion that the clause should specify that 'reasonable time, not exceeding 15 minutes unless there was a train already in the section' should be allowed, action to be taken by the Chichester Corporation or any barge owner. In reply to W. D. Rassel, Henry Phillips confirmed that there would be either a station or a watchman at the crossings on the Chichester to Wittering and Chichester to Selsey roads. Other witnesses called by the Tramways Company were Director Horace Mitchell and land agent and surveyor R. H. Powell of Lewes, who expressed the opinion that there were developments going on in the district which would be accelerated by the new line. Cecil Hogben (surveyor and auctioneer of Chichester) testified to the public benefit accruing from the proposed extensions, mentioning that at East Wittering there were about six miles of sand along the sea shore, and that the railway would tend towards its development. E. G. Arnell (member of West Sussex County Council for Birdham) gave figures showing how Selsey, 'a place of fishermen and agricultural labourers before the opening of the tram-line in 1897', had grown rapidly in population and assessable value until at the present time the former was 1,700 and the latter £11,000, and then spoke of the public convenience and commercial advantages which the line had conferred upon the district.

Among those in opposition to the proposed railway were A. W. Wyatt (on behalf of the Oliver Whitby Trustees) on the grounds of interference of the Trust's land without any compensating advantage, and A. C. Harris who would oppose the application unless there was a station erected at Donnington 'where there are a good many residents'. Mr. Mason, a landowner of Itchenor, objected as the railway would cut up his property 'very considerably', in one instance separating a homestead from its agricultural land, and that it would spoil a good deal of prospective building land.

W. D. Rassel next brought up the matter of public protection, pointing out that while the Westhampnett Rural District Council favoured the extension, certain provision should be made for the safety of the users of the highways. The Council asked for the erection of gates at nine road crossings, four being on the existing line (Stockbridge, Hunston, Sidlesham and Ferry) and five on the proposed extension. Details were laid before the Commissioners who ordered that gates be erected at Stockbridge on the existing line and at Donnington, Birdham and in West Wittering village on the extension, while the question of the remaining five was to be referred to the Board of Trade to deal with.

With respect to the road bridges across the canal at Birdham and Donnington, H. W. Bowen (County Surveyor for West Sussex County Council), expressed opinion that, having regard to the approaches to them, it would be dangerous for the proposed extension tram-line to come within 50 yards of them, but if the bridges were altered and the approaches straightened, the danger would be removed. The Commissioners decided that unless arrangements were made for the alteration of the existing bridges and the improvement of the approaches, the promoters would be required to construct their crossing at Birdham 'not within 50 yards of the canal bridge', and at Donnington 'as far south as the farm buildings would allow', the plans to be submitted to the Commissioners for approval.

THOUGHTS OF EXPANSION (1913–1919)

After a sitting of 2½ hours, and having heard all of the evidence, the Hon. A. E. Gathorne-Hardy announced that the Commissioners were of the opinion that the Light Railway Order should be granted, as there seemed to be no objection which could not be met in the ordinary way of compensation. They were, therefore, prepared to grant the Order, subject to the clauses already agreed upon being inserted in it, and they hoped that the railway would be a benefit to the district.

At a meeting of Chichester Council on Wednesday, 8th April 1914 correspondence was read between Mr. Rogers, a barge owner, and the City Surveyor as to the delays at the Tramway bridge over the canal and it was resolved that the Town Clerk should write to the Tramways Company drawing their attention to the complaint, along with the terms of their agreement, and request that the barge owner should be compensated as he had asked.

These Tramway arrangements for the Whitsun Bank Holiday weekend were advertised in the *Chichester Observer* on 27th May:

Friday, Saturday & Tuesday:
d. Selsey: 8.30, 10.15, 11.45, 1.25, 3.05, 5.50, 7.05 and 9.00 (Friday & Saturday only).
d. Chichester: 9.20, 11.00, 12.48, 2.20, 4.20, 6.32, 8.15 and 10.40 (Friday & Saturday only).

Whit Sunday:
d. Selsey: 9.00, 10.35, 1.20, 5.20 and 7.00.
d. Chichester: 10.05, 11.20, 2.15, 6.00 and 8.15.

Bank Holiday Monday:
d. Selsey: 7.35, 9.00, 10.25, 11.35, 1.25, 3.45, 5.00, 6.35, 8.00 and 9.00.
d. Chichester: 8.20, 9.50, 11.00, 12.48, 2.20, 4.20, 5.45, 7.20, 8.45 and 10.40.

Cheap Day Return Tickets available Chichester – Selsey 1/- return Sunday and Monday

Up to, and including 1913, early to mid-morning tram departures on Mondays in both directions had confusingly varied from the timings for the rest of the week (this had also included Tuesdays between 1905 and 1911 inclusive) but by the summer of 1914, services on all weekdays ran to the same times. With seven return trams, this was to be the most extensive service to be run on a Sunday. Once again, crossing times of trams on the weekday services, although not so marked on the original timetables, are shown in italics here:

Weekdays

Selsey	7.35	8.30	9.18	10.45	12.05	1.15	2.30	3.30	4.30	5.30	6.45	7.45
Ferry Siding	7.39	8.34	9.22	10.48	12.09	1.18	2.34	3.34	4.34	5.34	6.48	7.49
Sidlesham	7.45	*8.39*	9.28	10.55	12.15	1.25	2.40	3.40	4.40	5.40	6.55	7.55
Chalder	7.50	8.43	9.33	11.00	12.20	1.30	2.45	3.45	4.45	5.45	7.00	8.00
Hunston	7.55	8.48	9.38	11.05	12.25	1.35	2.50	3.50	4.50	5.50	7.05	8.05
Chichester	8.05	9.00	9.48	11.15	12.35	1.45	3.00	4.00	5.00	6.00	7.15	8.15
Chichester	8.20	9.08	10.10	11.30	1.05	2.20	3.20	4.20	5.20	6.35	7.35	8.25
Hunston	8.27	9.15	10.17	11.37	1.12	2.27	–	4.27	5.27	–	7.42	8.42
Chalder	8.32	9.20	10.22	11.42	1.17	2.32	–	4.32	5.32	–	7.47	8.47
Sidlesham	8.40	9.28	10.30	11.50	1.25	2.40	*3.30*	4.40	5.40	*6.53*	7.55	8.55
Ferry Siding	8.42	9.30	10.32	11.52	1.27	2.42	–	4.42	5.42	–	7.57	8.57
Selsey	8.50	9.38	10.40	12.00	1.35	2.50	3.50	4.50	5.50	7.03	8.05	9.05

Sundays

Selsey	8.50	10.35	1.00	2.10	5.20	6.50	8.00
Ferry Siding	8.54	10.39	–	2.14	5.24	6.54	8.04
Sidlesham	8.58	10.43	1.08	2.18	5.28	6.58	8.08
Chalder	9.03	10.48	1.13	2.23	5.33	7.03	8.13
Hunston	9.08	10.53	–	2.28	5.38	7.08	8.18
Chichester	9.20	11.05	1.28	2.40	5.50	7.20	8.30
Chichester	10.00	11.20	1.30	2.45	6.00	7.23	8.45
Hunston	10.07	11.27	–	2.52	6.05	–	8.52
Chalder	10.12	11.32	–	2.57	6.10	–	8.57
Sidlesham	10.20	11.40	1.45	3.05	6.15	7.38	9.05
Ferry Siding	10.22	11.42	–	3.07	6.17	–	9.07
Selsey	10.30	11.50	1.55	3.15	6.27	7.50	9.15

Additional Trains (*sic*) Selsey to Chichester Wednesdays and Thursdays: 10pm, Thursdays in August, 11.10pm. Chichester to Selsey Wednesdays and Thursdays 10.40pm, Thursdays in August, 11.50pm.

Looking at this poster headed 'Brighton Railway', which dates from around 1913, a potential traveller to Selsey could be excused for supposing that it was the London, Brighton & South Coast Railway that operated the rail service to the resort. At the bottom of the poster it stated 'For particulars of Train Service and Cheap Ticket facilities apply Superintendent of the Line, LB & SC Rly., London Bridge Terminus'. COLLECTION ROBERT KOSMIDER

Although further away from the Tramway's station, Selsey's West Beach was more popular than the East Beach that was made up mainly of shingle and was also host to the fishing quarter. As at other resorts, children enjoyed riding on donkeys on the glorious golden sands, beyond which bathing and beach huts were positioned slightly above high water mark on this postcard, the original of which was posted on 22nd July 1914.

WSCC LIBRARY SERVICE

THOUGHTS OF EXPANSION (1913–1919)

Whereas Selsey could boast fine beaches, its High Street was nothing out of the ordinary and it looked much the same as any other village street. The 350-seat Pavilion Cinema in the left foreground opened in 1913. The Crown public house features beyond, whilst on the right the shops included a Gentlemen's Tailor, Ellis & Petts, the butcher and a motor garage c.1918.
WSCC LIBRARY SERVICE

Note how the 1.00pm up Sunday tram from Selsey was scheduled to do the single journey in just 28 minutes, stopping at both Sidlesham and Chalder, but with a tight two-minute turn-round at Chichester, the 1.30pm 'express' return trip to the coast (with a record 25 minute running time) must have invariably run late! It will be seen that the late tram now ran on Wednesdays as well as Thursdays. Of course, with the outbreak of the First World War in August, this lavish timetable was suitably reduced and the two-tram weekday service became a thing of the past. The October timetable provided 6 Trams in each direction on weekdays with 4 on Sundays, but strangely, only the 11.30am from Chichester was shown as 'Mixed' with no corresponding up tram.

At the Annual General Meeting on Thursday afternoon, 29th October 1914, Edward Heron-Allen explained that the Directors had hoped to present to the Shareholders an extremely rosy report because the progress that he had alluded to a year ago had been more than maintained until the outbreak of war. Up to July the receipts had shown a large increase, but there was a very serious falling off in August. In spite of this, receipts were in an extraordinary healthy condition. Notwithstanding the war, there had been a considerable increase in passenger tickets, an extra £25 for season tickets, and an additional £140 in merchandise, the receipts for the year once again constituting a record. Building in Selsey had been proceeding by leaps and bounds, and in the ordinary way they were having considerable merchandise traffic, but for the present, the builders were short-handed and the trade was partly suspended. Unhappily, there would be a further decrease in receipts for September and October, but after that he hoped they would return to normal revenue from the residential population of Selsey. The total increase in expenditure amounted to £255, which was considered to be satisfactory and they were holding their own in spite of the circumstances.

With respect to the Light Railway Order, Heron-Allen confirmed that it was being carried through in the most efficient and cheapest way by the Engineer, and if it had not been for the war, which had caused delays in Government departments, the Order would have been issued by now. 'When the Order is sealed', he continued, 'we shall go to the public, and I hope that we would raise sufficient capital to make our line an important railway instead of a small tramway. If the public support the Company as they should, they will find promoted in their midst an extremely valuable and important property. As the shareholders know, the Company has not always been able to see eye to eye with the syndicate, "Selsey on Sea, Ltd." They have often pulled different ways in the past, but the Syndicate, I think have now realized that the interests of the Company are also their own, and they have come to an agreement whereby their differences are adjusted and settled, with the result that there is a scheme to build a new station at Selsey. This station would be suitable for a seaside place and it would be built in conjunction with "Selsey on Sea, Ltd". Within a few years, I hope that the Company will be proud of their line – at least as seen from Selsey.'

Replying later to Mr. Jarman, as to whether the Company had pledged itself to build a new station, the Chairman said that the agreement with 'Selsey on Sea, Ltd.' was a very sound one, and if the Syndicate wanted a new station, it would be built in the middle of their newly developed property. They would give notice to the Company to build, and it would be financed by 'Selsey on Sea, Ltd'.[8]

On Thursday evening, 3rd December at a presentation made to Sydney E. Ray, who was moving away to London, the Rev. C. W. Wilson told how he and his wife would

The oil lamps were probably in the process of being filled by the member of staff on the roof of the carriage while Sidlesham was waiting with her train at Chichester. One of the low height ex-MR vans more often than not accompanied the ex-Lambourn Valley 4-wheel carriages to provide luggage accommodation.

LENS OF SUTTON

never forget the kindness and courtesy shown to them on their first visit to Selsey. It was pouring with rain, blowing a gale and very cold when they had arrived back at Selsey station some considerable time before the Tram was due to leave, and he explained how Mr. Ray had invited them into the inner office where a welcome fire was blazing and they were able to get dry and warm again before leaving on their return journey. The following afternoon, a further presentation of 'a handsome walking stick' was made at Selsey station to Mr. Ray, who had joined the Tramways Company in 1902 and for the past eight years had held the post of Assistant Secretary. He was clearly highly regarded and Henry Phillips, the Secretary and Manager, spoke in terms of high appreciation of the services that he had rendered to the Company, and the complete harmony in which he had worked with each individual member of staff. The walking stick was inscribed 'Presented to Sydney E. Ray by the staff of the Selsey Tramway, December 5th, 1914', the variance of date perhaps referring to his last day of service on the Saturday.[9]

During the second week of January 1915 the Tram had a narrow escape when a large elm tree was blown down across the line in heavy winds just as the last up service of the day was approaching Hoe Farm private siding. After some delay, the Tramway was cleared and the Tram was able to continue on its way, but soon after it had passed, 'another huge elm tree crashed down over the line, smashing a five-bar gate to matchwood and badly damaging the siding. Miss Jupp of Hoe Farm stopped the Tram in time on its return journey to Selsey ... (but) it was not possible, however, to clear the line that night and the passengers, which included a number of soldiers, made the best of their way through the gale to present themselves to the proper quarter, and several other passengers were hospitably put up by Miss Jupp at Hoe Farm ... Those in charge of the tram went on to report the position and in the morning the line was cleared again.'[10]

As Chichester hardware and oil merchant, Mr. Frank Tees, was returning from Selsey one evening early in March with his van of goods, he did not hear the whistle of the engine on approaching Ferry crossing and he drove straight across the Tramway. The horse managed to clear the line in time, but the van was 'smashed to pieces' and much of its contents was also damaged. A lad named Trust, who was accompanying Mr. Tees, did hear the whistle, but it was too late for him to stop the horse and he jumped off the van and escaped injury. Mr. Tees was thrown out and sustained injuries to his arm and head. The Tram was quickly brought to a standstill and one of the passengers, Mr. H. Wilkins of South Street, Chichester, unharnessed the horse 'and released it from its unhappy position'. Extremely lucky to be alive, Mr. Tees was taken to Chichester on the Tram.[11]

'Glorious weather favoured the Whitsuntide Holiday at Chichester, which was celebrated more quietly than usual owing to the war. In the absence of the usual sports in Priory Park, there was no great influx to the city, but many went to Bognor and Selsey in spite of there being no cheap excursions.'[12]

Owing to the absence of the chairman of the Directors (F. Sanden Street), Mr. Edward Heron-Allen once again presided over the Annual General Meeting held at the Council Chambers, Chichester on the afternoon of Thursday, 25th November 1915. In moving the adoption of the report, he stated that it was most deplorable that, with the exception of 'their faithful friends', Messrs. Fogden and Harding, they never met any of their shareholders there. He suggested that it was very complimentary to them (the shareholders) that they should place such absolute confidence in the Directors that they did not want either to criticise what they did, or to hear what they had to say, but the consequence was that they had no opportunity of putting the real position of the Tramway before the shareholders. He recalled the only occasion that it had been necessary to put the position of the Tramway before the shareholders (January, 1911), they were met with 'an attitude of inaction', and the Directors had to pull through the situation. As long as the present Directors were in office, the shareholders knew 'their chestnuts would be pulled out of the fire for them'! He thought he was voicing the opinion of his co-Directors when he said the time had come when the shareholders of the line ought to take a more active interest in the affairs of the Company. Perhaps the shareholders' apathy was due to the fact that a dividend had only been paid for the first four years of the Tramway's existence. Being so entertaining, the rest of Mr. Heron-Allen's speech is quoted in full:

> 'Shareholders are precisely in the same position as a body of gentlemen who owned a gold mine, and had allowed it to be filled with water. If they refused to provide pumps to clear the gold mine, they could not get at the gold, and if they left it to someone else to provide the pumps and get the gold, then the other people would reap the benefit of their action. That was simple an allegory, but it represents our position. Although we work very hard, and have the assistance of an extraordinarily capable and enthusiastic Secretary and Manager, to keep the line in a condition of efficiency, and how we are never now in a state of "hard-up-ness" as has happened in days gone by, still we cannot make money at such a rate as to be able to build up a reserve, out of which we could make the improvements needed. What is required far more than improvements is to be in a position to make the tram line commensurate with the needs of Chichester and Selsey.
>
> 'Selsey certainly seems to grow in attraction every year to people outside it, and it seems to grow too, very much in attraction to the people who were there because commercially there is extraordinary prosperity. The influx of visitors this year has been greater than ever, and there is no doubt that if it were not for the phenomenal conditions existing in the matter of labour and raw materials, building would be going on at Selsey at a very extensive scale. Even in the trying circumstances, building this year has been very substantial. The result is that we have in Selsey real gold at the bottom of the mine, but to take advantage of it and make the best of it, we must have proper machinery and a proper line. I know very well that these observations that I am making will fall stillborn from my lips, and nothing will be done because they did not reach the shareholders, and I wish that some plan might be devised by which the shareholders could be brought to a sense of the tremendous value of their undertaking.
>
> 'There it is. At present we are keeping in a condition of living practically from hand to mouth. If some phenomenal disturbance was to take

THE SELSEY TRAMWAY

Railway enthusiast Ken Nunn visited West Sussex again on Saturday, 12th June 1915 when he took these three pictures. The first shows the driver leaning well out of Selsey's cab to keep a careful lookout as the 3.05 p.m. tram from Selsey slowed to the regulation 6 mph on the sharpest curve on the Tramway at 6 chains radius just short of Chichester station. Above: With the Falcon brake carriage not in the formation, an ex-MR van had been added to the train for the day to cater for any passengers' luggage. The rear carriage was the one supplied by Hurst Nelson in 1900. LCGB/KEN NUNN

Ken Nunn would have had to move quickly to capture the 4.20 p.m. tram to Selsey breasting the 1 in 115 gradient south of Stockbridge Road level crossing a little more than three-quarters of a mile from Chichester station. LCGB (KEN NUNN COLLECTION)

THOUGHTS OF EXPANSION (1913–1919)

place, such as another flood or an earthquake, or something of that kind, we would find ourselves absolutely unable to rebuild our line, and we would be unable to go on; and we have the pleasant reflection always at the back of our minds that there were a great many vultures sitting around on the crags in London, very anxious to buy us up and make a fortune out of our undertaking. It seems a grievous pity that the shareholders do not take their courage into both hands and do something to enable them to make the line worthy of the service which it was expected to provide.'

After the report had been adopted, the Mayor of Chichester and fellow Director, S. A. Garland, JP, thanked Mr. Heron-Allen for giving them such a good resumé of the year's work, and he had no doubt that the shareholders would see, if they had not heard it, because he was sure that the press was represented.

Owing to a change in accounting procedure whereby in future the accounts were to be made up to 31st December, rather than on 31st August each year, the Selsey Tramways next Annual General Meeting was held at 'Ivy Bank', Chichester on Monday, 22nd May 1916. The chairman, Edward Heron-Allen, remarked that 'what is poisonous for many people has proved an advantage to Selsey,' for people had stayed in the town longer, and those who, on account of the Zeppelins,[13] had stayed the winter in Selsey, had realised what a perfectly delightful place it was at that time of the year. Special attention was called by the Chairman to a paragraph in the Report recommending that a sum of 50 guineas be paid annually to each of the directors and, on being put to the vote, this was carried.

On Thursday, 20th July at a Meeting of the Directors held at 48 Broadway, Westminster, London, it was agreed that V.A.D. (Voluntary Aid Detachment) nurses residing at Selsey who, from time to time during the period of the War were on duty at Graylingwill Hospital, should be allowed to travel free between Selsey and Chichester whilst proceeding to and from the hospital. At the following Board Meeting held at the same address on 21st September, authorisation was given to engage more men for permanent way work, if it was possible, and it was suggested that the wages of all staff should be increased 'to meet the extra cost of living' and enable the Company to retain the services of the men employed. A bull straying on the line, belonging to Messrs. Stride & Son, had been killed by the Tram on Tuesday, 12th September, but the Company considered that they weren't responsible for the accident and refused to entertain any claim.

During a severe gale on Sunday, 5th November the locomotive water tank at Selsey was blown down and the engine shed was 'put a little out of plumb'. Being essential for locomotive purposes, the tank was quickly re-erected by a Mr. H. A. Smith, who also repaired the roof and end of the engine shed, the total cost amounting to £26 10 0d.[14]

Earlier in the year, J. L. Belcher, the Company's loyal locomotive foreman/fitter, had left the Tramway to take up a similar post on the 3ft gauge Southwold Railway in Suffolk.[15] His replacement was a Mr. Trueman, but he only stayed until 8th August. It was not until 7th November that another fitter commenced duties, but within a week he too had given notice of his intention to leave![16] This inability to find a competent locomotive fitter was to result in the many motive power problems that were to plague the Tramway throughout the First World War and into the 1920s.

To fall in line with Board of Trade instructions, the Tramway Company increased its passenger fares by 50% commencing on 1st January 1917, the Notice and Table of Fares shown in the accompanying table being displayed at all their stations from 24th December. It will be noted that return fares were still not available between many stations, although where the facility was available, a slight reduction was now made in each case. The special Cheap Return Ticket of 6d between Chichester and Selsey for soldiers and sailors in uniform on active service was not increased,[17] and Cheap Half Day tickets from Selsey to Chichester for all were made available on Wednesdays and Sundays at 1/- return. However, the cheap Thursday and Sunday tickets in the opposite direction were withdrawn. On the basis of a similar number of passengers being carried up to and including 30th November 1916, it was estimated that the increase in receipts (taking into account the increased passenger duty)

INCREASE IN PASSENGER FARES

Notice is hereby given that commencing on Monday January 1st., 1917, in conformity with the Order of the Board of Trade authorizing an increase of 50 per cent in all Railway Fares, the Passenger Fares between stations on the Selsey Tramways will be increased as set out in the following Table of Fares.

Table of Fares (Ordinary Compartment)
Saloon Fares are 5d. above the following.
Ordinary Fares for Single Journey.

Through Bookings to LB & SCR Stations will be temporarily suspended.

Chichester to Hunston	3d	Single	
" " Hoe Farm	6d	"	10d Return
" " Chalder	6d	"	10d Return
" " Sidlesham	7d	"	1/- Return
" " Ferry	9d	"	
" " Golf Links	11d	"	1/9 Return
" " Selsey	11d	"	1/9 Return
Hunston to Hoe Farm	2d	Single	
" " Chalder	3d	"	
" " Sidlesham	6d	"	
" " Ferry	7d	"	
" " Golf Links	9d	"	
" " Selsey	9d	"	
Hoe Farm to Chalder	2d	Single	
" " Sidlesham	4d	"	
" " Ferry	6d	"	
" " Golf Links	8d	"	
" " Selsey	8d	"	
Chalder to Sidlesham	3d	Single	
" " Ferry	6d	"	
" " Golf Links	7d	"	1/- Return
" " Selsey	7d	"	1/- Return
Sidlesham to Ferry	2d	"	
" " Golf Links	6d	"	10d Return
" " Selsey	6d	"	10d Return
Ferry to Golf Links	3d	Single	
" " Selsey	4d	"	
Golf Links to Selsey	2d	Single	

(Taken from Board of Directors Minute Book 23.12.1916, pages 13 and 14.)

This picture headed an article entitled 'The Selsey Tramways' by Rev. V. L. Whitechurch, published in Volume 39 of the Railway Magazine *in 1916. It shows* Sidlesham *in charge of a 'mixed' train heading south across the chalk embankment between Sidlesham and Ferry with two of the original Falcon bogie carriages tagged on at the rear.*
COLLECTION PAUL LAMING

With briefcase in hand, Edward Heron-Allen, the vice chairman of the Tramway Company, was one of the last to leave a busy afternoon arrival at Selsey. Arthur Pennycord, the young lad nearest the camera on the platform ramp, commenced work as a porter with the Company in 1917 at the age of 14, so the photograph can be dated to round about then. He later went on to drive the Wolseley Siddeley and Ford railmotors before leaving the Company in 1926.
COLLECTION PAUL LAMING

THOUGHTS OF EXPANSION (1913–1919)

would amount to approximately £600, although it was appreciated that there would be a falling off in the number of passengers owing to the general increase in all railway fares and the reduced services being run.[18] What was to be the all-time record number of 105,169 passengers travelled on the Tramway during 1916, an increase of 13,361 over the previous year.

Holman Stephens was never a full-time army officer, but as a member of the Volunteer Forces he was able to continue his railway work in parallel with his military career. In 1916 he was promoted to the rank of Lieutenant Colonel in the Royal Engineers, and from then on he became known to the staff on all his railways as 'The Colonel'.

From 1st January 1917, the Tramway timetable was reduced thus:

	Weekdays						Sundays		
	A				B				
Selsey	9.00	11.30	1.25	3.15	5.50	7.05	10.35	5.20	7.20
Ferry Siding	9.04	11.34	1.28	3.18	5.54	7.09	10.38	5.24	7.24
Sidlesham	9.08	11.38	1.33	3.23	5.58	7.13	10.43	5.28	7.28
Chalder	9.13	11.43	1.38	3.28	6.03	7.18	10.48	5.33	7.33
Hunston	9.18	11.48	1.43	3.33	6.08	7.23	10.53	5.38	7.38
Chichester	9.30	12.00	1.55	3.45	6.20	7.35	11.05	5.50	7.50
	A				B				
Chichester	10.10	12.48	2.40	4.20	6.25	8.05	11.20	6.10	8.15
Hunston	1017	12.55	2.47	4.27	–	8.12	11.27	6.17	8.21
Chalder	10.22	1.00	2.52	4.32	–	8.17	11.32	6.22	8.27
Sidlesham	10.30	1.08	2.57	4.40	6.42	8.25	11.40	6.27	8.32
Ferry Siding	10.32	1.10	2.59	4.42	–	8.27	11.42	6.29	8.34
Selsey	10.40	1.18	3.10	4.50	7.53	8.35	11.50	6.40	8.45

A Mixed Train, Saturday only   B Saturday only

During the currency of this timetable, the young Alastair MacLeod[19] travelled from Chichester to Selsey on the Tramway behind *Sidlesham* which was hauling 'two short open bogie coaches and a loaded wagon attached behind'. With a driver and a guard, but no fireman, the train was soon on its way, 'at a very moderate speed, jogging along over the very audible rail joints' until, after passing several stations they pulled up at a facing siding, as far as could be ascertained, away from any station. Here, after getting down from the van portion of the second carriage and uncoupling the wagon, the guard climbed into the carriage where Mr. MacLeod was sitting and asked if any passengers would like to volunteer to help him shunt the van into the siding. 'I got out with some sailors, who were travelling on leave to Selsey, and we waited for the engine and carriages to draw forward. When this had been done, the guard unlocked the points, set them for the siding and we pushed the wagon inside. The points were reset and we climbed back into the train and proceeded to the next station. (I wish I could remember where this incident took place.)' The rest of the journey was made without incident.[20]

At a special meeting of the Directors on 16th February an application form for £500 of 5% War Loan was completed and the relevant cheque was signed. Two months later, at a meeting held at Kings Court, Broadway, Westminster on 26th April, plans that Holman Stephens had prepared for an extra siding at Selsey were passed, subject to obtaining the necessary labour and at a cost not to exceed £25 and it was also agreed that 'a carpenter be engaged to execute the necessary repairs to Coaches and Wagons, and Station Buildings, etc'.

Edward Heron-Allen continued his attack on the non-attending shareholders at the AGM on 21st May, suggesting that he did not think it was worthwhile addressing them as what he had said so often about the line and his financial statements, dry though they might have been, had generally 'fallen upon ground more dry and stony than the statements themselves; they had borne no fruit, and whatever flowers of oratory he had been able to put into his yearly addresses had been withered in the glare of the shareholders' unresponsive silence!' It seemed 'a thousand pities' to him that the shareholders of the Company didn't realise what the position was. Here they were – a little tramline – a tramline· which was deservedly abused as a one-horse affair, but with a most extraordinary virility. This past year they had made gross receipts of £3,802, and £550 had been debited to the Flood Account. The floods of December, 1910 had cost the Company £4,189, and he suggested that it was confidently asserted and hoped in some quarters that that was the end of the line, although he did not know what those pessimists would have done should that have been the case. It was the Directors and not the shareholders, that had kept the line going and they had been rewarded for the anxiety that they went through, and had paid out £2,000 and more of the £4,000. Of course, they ought not to be called upon to pay the flood account out of profits; the money ought to have been subscribed by the shareholders, but the shareholders appeared to him to be either excessively cautious, excessively lacking in foresight, or very, very poor!

It seemed to him that no man who had a certain amount of money in that Company, reading these reports that they sent out every year, could fail to be impressed by the necessity of this tramline. If it were not a necessity, they were told no one would ever travel by their line at all. Why? Simply because they could not afford to make it comfortable. If it were a comfortable line, if the shareholders would give them the money to get new carriages, new engines and a better track, so that they would not be shaken in such a manner as they now were, there was no doubt about it that the traffic between Chichester and Selsey would be enormously increased, and these profits, which they showed year after year, as the result of necessity, would be proportionately increased. The necessity in this case had been the mother of invention. They had invented all kinds of reasons why people should patronise the line, but they looked at their rolling stock and their track and they said 'No, for pleasure, we prefer other means.' A joy-ride on the Selsey tramline was not within the scope of most people's predilections. There was no reason why it should not be, and the time, of course, would come when they would find themselves bound to reconstruct. Whether that reconstruction would be forced upon them, or whether they could do it voluntarily, then the shareholders of the line would find, as he had told them over and over again, that they had got a gold mine. If it was forced upon them, then their shares would not be worth the paper they were written upon; the assets would just about liquidate the debentures and the charges upon the Company.

It was, he thought, a mixture of pessimism and optimism, which was a somewhat similar state of things in the distressing circumstances they were going through, but as applied to the Selsey Tramway Company, it applied with increased force. They had their new Powers – their new Order – and they were prepared the moment they could get the money to extend the line round by Itchenor and Wittering, and make it a really fine going concern. Of course, they knew that the London, Brighton & South Coast Railway were watching them like vultures, with the hope that they would be carrion, and they would try to jump upon them, but if he were chairman of the Company, they would not do it, except at such a price as would satisfy the shareholders. He did not think they would give the price, and the result would be the shareholders would have to reconstruct, but unless they came forward with their share, they would find themselves very badly left behind.

Commencing on 1st June and applying until the end of September, Cheap Return Tickets between Chichester and Selsey were reinstated at the price of 1/- return for travel on Thursdays and Sundays only.

A nasty accident occurred at Hunston station on Monday evening, 2nd July just as the Selsey-bound Tram was leaving the station. On her way home from Chichester High School, 15 years old Mary deCrespigny 'was seen to fall, and being picked up, it was found that the Tram had passed over her leg. A platelayer went to her assistance and Mr. George Harris, farmer of Hunston, rendered First Aid by promptly binding up the injured limb so as to reduce bleeding as much as possible. The poor girl was then taken to the Royal West Sussex Hospital where it was deemed necessary to amputate her leg just below the knee'.[21]

Plans were prepared to erect a porch on Selsey station building at the entrance facing Manor Road, and for fencing to be erected at the western end of the building to prevent passengers joining and leaving the platform in that direction. The cost of the porch was not to exceed £5 and the fencing £2. At Chichester, about 20 yards of the platform from the entrance gate was to be ashphalted.[22]

Another gentleman who made a trip on the Tramway in 1917 also told of the unusual operating procedures employed by the Company. On this occasion the train was headed by *Hesperus*, and again consisted of two of the original bogie carriages, but this time with two LBSCR goods trucks, and the four-wheeled luggage van bringing up the rear. South of Chalder, '...after more prolonged whistling for another crossing, the train slowed down as a permanent way gang was engaged in reballasting the line. As the men had two trucks on the line from which to take the new ballast, the engine pushed these in front of it all the way to Selsey (a truly primitive proceeding); whilst they must have been dropped from the rear of the train on its previous journey to Chichester... On the return journey from Selsey the train was 10 minutes late, owing to the engine taking the two trucks which it had pushed from near Sidlesham to be refilled at the ballast pit in the cutting, and bringing back from there two full trucks which were attached to the rear of the train, and dropped on reaching the scene of action. The passenger vehicles were the same as on the outward journey, and a cattle van full of sheep (attached between the carriages and the ballast trucks) completed the train...'[23]

With no apparent progress being made regarding the West Sussex Light Railway Order that had been authorised early in 1915, Holman Stephens wrote to the Chairman of the Directors, Mr. F. Sanden Street, at his London office, 48 Broadway, Westminster, SW on 7th August:

Dear Mr. Street,
West Sussex Line

I wish you would drop me a note saying it is understood that I am to be employed as Engineer on the West Sussex Line extension to Itchenor and that the ordinary Engineer's Fees and Expenses are to be paid on construction.

It is usual to have this sort of thing. I hope you will be back soon.

Yours faithfully
(signed) H. F. Stephens.

The subject was discussed at the Directors' Board Meeting on 27th September when they confirmed that it was understood that Stephens would be employed as the Engineer on the extension to Itchenor. There had been several incidents of locomotive failure recently and it was reported that the Colonel was looking out for 'a more competent fitter'.

As a 'thankyou' gesture for the way in which the Tramway Company was progressing, in November a gratuity of £25 0s 0d was presented to Henry Phillips, the secretary/manager, and a further sum of £52 0s 0d was split between the members of staff in amounts ranging from £2 to £5.[24]

Suggesting that a certain member of the Selsey Tramway's staff may have got a little muddled up the previous year, on 20th March 1918 the *Chichester Observer* amusingly wrote:

'The *Selsey Parish Magazine* is responsible for the following:
"Our readers are reminded that 'Summer Time' will begin on Sunday, 24th March; clocks should be put BACK one hour during the preceding night." We trust that the Selsey Tramway guard, who doubtless reads this magazine, will not be misled to the extent of causing the 9am tram to leave Selsey at 11am on March 25th.'

It was, however, the *Selsey Parish Magazine* that was 'misled' as clocks should surely be brought FORWARD one hour in the Spring. In further defence of the guard, it is only fair to point out that the Tram always ran to the 'old time' in common with the Selsey village clock which was not changed each spring and autumn!

In the New Year, Tramway Director, Alderman Sharp Archibald Garland[25] received a knighthood and at the Directors' Meeting on 31st January 1918 he was heartily congratulated by the Board on the 'well merited high honour bestowed on him by His Majesty the King'. Letters from Mr. H. A. Smith, (who had repaired the water tank and engine shed at Selsey following gale damage the previous November) offering £35 for the material comprising the 'Beach Extension station building', and Holman Stephens advising the Board not to accept his offer were read out. The secretary explained that since the original offer, Mr. Smith had made an amended offer of the same amount, but to include the extension of a suitable porch at Selsey station from the material. However, the Colonel still did not approve; the disused Beach station building remained where it was and Selsey station building did not receive its porch. Unfortunately for the Tramway Company, Mr. E. Morgan, their station agent at Chichester, had to leave his post as he was refused further exemption from military service, but a further exemption of six months until July 1918 was granted to guard Herbert Barnes.[26]

On 4th April Stephens wrote from his office in Tonbridge to Henry Phillips at Selsey:

'If I am unable to attend the Board on Friday, I wish you would read this letter to the Directors. The Chairman, when he went away, asked me, specially, if I could get anybody who would entrust themselves in the construction of the line to Chichester Harbour and I have, from time to time, made enquiries. I now find some people who are quite capable of doing the work and are inclined to submit a proposal, but, before doing this, they want to see if they can acquire, at a reasonable price, a fair holding in the ordinary stock of the Company, and they have been making enquiries with a view to purchasing some shares.

'I believe they have succeeded in getting some offers, but the prices asked vary so much, and at the present moment they are unable to make any proposal. I have written to Mr. Street several times on this matter, but I think, if the Directors know of any shares that can be sold, it might assist the proposal if they could instruct you to advise me the names of the Sellers and the price they propose for their holdings...'

As he had intimated, the Colonel was unable to attend the Board Meeting in Selsey the following day, but the Directors felt that the subject of shares was not one that they could deal with. A letter to that effect was sent to Stephens which also asked for further information as to what was happening regarding the extension to Chichester Harbour. The details of a claim of £23 for the loss of a heifer, killed by the Tram, were explained by the Secretary, but after discussion, it was decided that the Company could not entertain it. Phillips explained that a strip of meadowland at Hunston had, for several years, been let to Mr. T. Fogden, who had recently sub-let it to a Mr. Harris for the purpose of grazing. Cattle had been turned into this field on several occasions and had strayed onto the line, causing delay to the Trams and being a source of danger. Mr. Fogden was subsequently advised that the Company now required the land (which, of course, they didn't!) and that his tenancy could not continue. Tenders for second-hand sleepers at 10/- and 12/6d each had been obtained and authority was given to purchase 250, no doubt at the lower price.

Following the request from the secretary that an increase to his salary might be considered, it was resolved at the following meeting on 24th May that it should be increased from £250 to £325 per annum. A petition from the platelayers for increased wages was also considered and it was decided that an extra 2/6d per week be given to each member of staff with the exception of Ganger Skinner who would be given an additional 4/6d, and Guard Barnes an extra 3/6d bonus per week. A further £500 in 5% War Bonds was applied for.

A letter had been received from Mrs. deCrespigny of Old Farm House, Selsey asking that a free pass on the Tramway for life be granted to her daughter as a token of sympathy in respect of the accident that befell her at Hunston the previous July. A pass for 1918 was duly sent to her expressing the Directors' sympathy, but explaining that they could not grant a pass for life, but that they would be pleased to consider the renewal of the present issue 'from time to time, subject to the conditions printed on the back of same'.

At a meeting of the Board of Directors immediately prior to the Annual General Meeting on Saturday, 22nd June 'the subject of recent transfers of shares arising from the canvass of the shareholders by a supposed syndicate was discussed. Proxy forms affecting the voting at the Annual General Meeting which had been deposited with the Secretary and since cancelled by persons recently relinquished as shareholders were submitted to the meeting. This subject also was discussed.'

In moving the adoption of the Directors' Report and the accounts as presented at the AGM itself, Edward Heron-Allen said:

'For a great many years now you must have become accustomed to some pungent observations from myself upon the apathy of the shareholders and the difficulty it has been to get them to take any great interest in the proceedings of the Board and the conduct of the Company. But this year I shall not have anything to say upon this subject, because, as presently will appear, that condition of affairs apparently has disappeared.

'The report of the Directors I think I am right in saying, is an extremely satisfactory one. The report is the outcome of a series of traffic returns extending over the year, and from month to month our traffic returns have been satisfactory and more than satisfactory. There is no doubt about it, as I have frequently said from the chair, that this is an extraordinarily necessary Company, and an extraordinarily live Company, though its animation from time to time gives one the impression of being somewhat suspended. At the same time, owing to the very able management of our Manager and Secretary, Mr. H. G. Phillips, to whom the Board this year is even more indebted than usual – for I need hardly say that he has had to run the affairs of the Company in the face of difficulties such as a few years ago we should not for a moment have envisaged – the affairs of the Company have prospered most remarkably. We have been able... to charge a further £605 of the Flood Account to Revenue during the year, and we have to date reduced that terrible load which was on our backs from £4,260 to £1,615. To have been able to do that with the material at our disposal – the rolling stock and so on with which we have to work – shows, I think, that this is a remarkably successful and necessary enterprise. What we should have done if only the shareholders had come forward and enabled us to pay off that flood account it is difficult to say. I think there is no doubt that by this time we should have been paying a very handsome dividend. However, it was their pleasure not to do anything so long as the Directors put their hands in their pockets and did it for them.

'Indeed, the revenue... enable(s) us to carry a small balance forward to next year after paying all our interest on debentures and mortgage, and we are in the proud position today of holding £1000 in War Loan, of which £475 was taken out of the year's receipts. Well, gentlemen, I shall not say anything more about it, as it is quite clear from the progress of the Company that we are, if we are allowed to, capable of doing very well. I don't know whether I'm glad, but I am at any rate interested to find that this is a state of things which has impressed itself upon a certain section of the public at any rate, amongst whom no doubt are some of our shareholders. You are now all of you receiving circulars asking you to part with your shares. The first panic-stricken shareholders, I believe, parted with them at 19s 6d. Shares since then have realised more than double that amount. There is no doubt at all that there is – I hardly know what to call it – a power, a syndicate; at any rate there is somebody to whose interest it is to try and induce you to part with your shares at as low a figure as you can be induced to take. Now, it is the considered advice of the Board that you should look very carefully into the pros and cons of the question before you are induced to part with your shares. I feel some diffidence in saying it, occupying the position that I do, but I think your Board is a strong Board, and I think we have the interest of the shareholders, as apart from any persons who have to found any financial interest upon their shareholders, very much at heart. Of course, it is easy to be an alarmist and to say at any given moment the Company may find itself in difficulties, and that we may be wrecked. As I have said on more than one occasion, there are plenty of people who would be glad to wreck us and buy the salvage. But so long as we sit round this table, if there should be any threat of wrecking, the utmost efforts will be made that the salvage will inure to the benefit of the shareholders and not to the benefit of the wreckers. I think it is only fair that the Board should tell you this because we don't really quite know what the scheme is which is doubtless in the minds of the people who want to get hold of the control of this railway. At present you have the control of an exceedingly lively line.

'There is no doubt about it, and living in Selsey as I have now for twelve years, I am in a position to say that Selsey is going ahead in a manner which we never expected. It is the one good thing perhaps that I have even found has come out of the war. Selsey being free from raids, and we hope free from bombardment from the sea, an enormous number of people have come along since the war began who never came before, people to whom Selsey was only a geographical expression. There is something about Selsey which causes people to come along again and again. They still cherish the fond but mad illusion that land can be bought there very cheap. In the last five years the value of the land has increased considerably, and as soon as building is permitted, Selsey will not only develop itself, but will spread and many of the intervening stations on your line will become the centres of residential population. That being so, let us as the thrush which always sits in the bush when one is gardening says "Stick to it!" (Laughter). It is very funny to hear it when one is gardening, but it is excellent advice, and I don't think I can close the remarks I have to make to you today with better advice than that of the thrush to the gardener, "Stick to it!"'

After the Report and Accounts had been adopted unanimously, H. J. Powell told how he had been interested in the Company since its foundation, and as one of the original promoters, he did not wish to see one of his 'old children' wrecked. He could echo what Mr. Heron-Allen had said in that they had turned the corner and were doing good business now, and he thought the Company had a very good future before it. The traffic returns up to the end of May 1918 were even more satisfactory than they had got in the balance sheet as up to the end of May they showed an increase of over £538 on the previous year. He admitted that it did not show what the outgoings on the other side were, but they were proportionately much smaller than what the increase in the traffic showed.

On 17th July whilst extolling the attractions of Selsey the *Chichester Observer* gave the Tramway an indirect 'plug' when it wrote:

'The casual visitor to Chichester would certainly not think of seaside attractions, and yet with a short train ride lies a lovely stretch of the ocean with its foreshore dotted with bungalows, houses, and two up-to-date hotels. Scores of children revelling in the delights of paddling and castle building and the children of a large growth charmed with the quiet rurality of the surroundings. A great number of people are staying in Selsey just now, and the season promises to be very successful.'

During the early autumn, 10 truck loads of chalk had been placed on the seaside face of the embankment through Pagham Harbour to strengthen it and a further 20 truck loads were approved at the Board Meeting on 7th November to be placed there when it was convenient to traffic.[27] Yet another £1,000 worth of War Bonds were also applied for.

Throughout the summer, when traffic had been the heaviest, there had been frequent delays to the service 'owing to the unsatisfactory condition of the locomotives'. To alleviate these difficulties, drastic action was taken and for the winter the Sunday service of Trams was cancelled completely and only four weekday return trips were operated. Trams were scheduled to leave Selsey at 9.00am, 1.15pm, 3.05pm and 6.30pm, returning from Chichester at 10.15am, 2.20pm, 4.25pm and 7.30pm.[28]

Unfortunately, things went from bad to worse with many of the few Trams scheduled to operate failing to run. Motor cars had been hired for the conveyance of passengers in instances when the Tram had failed to run at all, at considerable expense to the Company, and very serious delay had been occasioned in many instances when the Tram had managed to travel. Several trips from Chichester to Selsey had taken between 1½ and 2 hours and in consequence, the public were very dissatisfied and passenger traffic had fallen off considerably. This serious state of affairs came up for discussion at the Directors' Meeting on 11th December, Edward Heron-Allen stating that he had been unable to use the Tram owing to the uncertainty of being able to reach his destination. At that moment, Holman Stephens joined the meeting and advised that he had obtained several quotations from locomotive builders regarding the supply of a new engine and that he had made enquiries regarding a second-hand one. Around 500 sleepers were required for the permanent way and it was agreed to purchase some from the LBSCR, but in the meantime to use the ex-main line sleepers forming the out-of-use down platform at Sidlesham!

At the next Directors' meeting on Wednesday, 22nd January 1919 the go-ahead was given to purchase a second-hand locomotive, named *Wembley*, from Messrs. Thomas W. Ward, Ltd. of Sheffield, and it was decided that for the year ending 31st December 1918, Directors' travelling expenses would be increased from 18/- to £1 10s 0d. On 8th May the secretary reported to the Directors that the locomotive *Wembley* had entered service and it was resolved to sell the £2,000 worth of the War Loan stock at present held and to place the proceeds of the sale to the credit of the Company's Current Account. From this account, a cheque to the value of £1,250 was to be forwarded to T. W. Ward & Co., representing full payment for the new acquisition.

Back in February, the Company had tried to obtain another 300 sleepers from the LBSCR, but none had yet come to hand. It was decided, therefore, that 600/1,000 sleepers be ordered instead, provided that 'suitable material' could be found.

THOUGHTS OF EXPANSION (1913–1919)

Since the end of the First World War the cost of living had increased dramatically, and Henry Phillips pointed out that the present total wages being paid to the Tramway staff was between £46 and £47 per week, compared to £27 in 1918, an increase to the Company of around £1000 per year. Also, the price of materials showed an increase in many cases and it was decided that the Company's rates and charges should once more be increased from 1st June. The single fare between Chichester and Selsey would now be 1/-, the Saloon Fare being 1/6d, with return fares double the single in all cases. Cheap Excursion Fares would remain applicable on certain Trams on Wednesdays, Thursdays and Sundays, but would now cost 1/6d return. Soldiers and sailors in uniform between Chichester and Selsey would pay 1/- return and bicycles, dogs, etc. would be charged 6d for a single journey. These increased rates and charges for both passengers and goods were estimated to produce £1,000 per year if traffic remained as heavy as it had been in 1918, and an increase of £600 was reasonably to be expected.[29]

With no funds put aside, the problem regarding the repayment of the 7,000 4% Mortgage Debentures due on 1st August 1919, was brought up at the Directors' meeting on

The derelict Sidlesham Tide Mill shortly before it was demolished in 1919.
WSCC LIBRARY SERVICE

Kipson Bank Windmill, close to the Tramway just to the south of Hunston station, had last worked in 1915 and is shown here with its sweeps and fan tail removed prior to being pulled down in 1919. Its unique 10-sided cement-covered brick base remains to this day.
WSCC LIBRARY SERVICE

6th June, the feeling of the Board being that the most convenient policy would be to induce the present holders of the Debentures to continue their holdings by offering them a higher rate of interest. Legal opinion confirmed that the payment could be postponed providing an extraordinary resolution was carried by a three-quarters majority in value of those present in person or by proxy at a meeting of Debenture Holders holding the first Debentures. At the following Board Meeting on Monday, 16th June, Edward Heron-Allen was elected to act on behalf of all the first Debenture Holders and notices and forms explaining the scheme were sent out to them and to those holding 'B' Debentures.

Separate meetings for the First Debenture (£7,000) Holders and the 'B' Debenture Holders were held one after the other at the Council Chamber, Chichester on Friday, 18th July. This was the resolution put to the first meeting:

> 'That this meeting of the first mortgage debenture holders of the Hundred of Manhood and Selsey Tramways Company Limited, hereby assents to certain modifications of the rights of the said holders against the Company whereby the time for payment of the principal moneys is extended from the 1st day of August 1919 to the 1st day of August 1924, and whereby the rate of interest is raised from £4 per cent per annum to £5 per cent per annum and hereby authorises Edward Heron-Allen, the Vice Chairman of the Company, with a view of effectuating such modifications to execute for and on behalf of the whole of the holders of the said debentures and indenture in the terms of the draft which has been submitted to this meeting and has for the purpose of identification been subscribed by the Chairman thereof.'

Mr. W. A. Haines, representing Mr. T. W. Greene (who was unable to attend the meeting), expressed his dissent from the proposal to extend the period covered by the debentures and requested that the principal moneys due to Mr. Greene be paid to him on 1st August 1919. Director and solicitor, Mr. H. C. Mitchell, explained that one of the conditions forming part of the debenture enabled the holders in meeting, by carrying a resolution by a three-quarters majority, to modify the terms of the debenture, and that if the resolution put to the meeting was carried by the requisite majority of the holders present by proxy, or in person, the modification would be binding on the rest of the debenture holders. The resolution was thereupon put to the meeting and carried unanimously. At the meeting of the 'B' Debenture Holders immediately afterwards, the secretary advised that he had received forms of assent, duly signed, from fourteen 'B' Debenture Holders holding in total 133 'B' Debentures of the 168 issued, agreeing to the postponement of payment of the first debentures and the raising of the rate of interest thereon to £5 per cent per annum.

With that important part of the business neatly wrapped up, at least for the next five years, the Annual General Meeting was able to commence, at which the general working of the Company was described as having been 'very satisfactory'. In moving the adoption of the Report and Balance Sheet, Edward Heron-Allen said he hoped that it would be the last time that he would have to do so as their chairman, Frank Sanden Street, had returned from abroad and was that day in their midst. Heron-Allen advised 'We have had very great trouble with the engines, but we have taken the bull by the horns and have got a third engine[30] recently so that we are practically safe, I hope, from any probability of those breakdowns which were so depressing for us at the beginning of the year.' He also reported that they had carried on their concern under the same difficulties as in previous years, but when any new difficulty arose, Mr. Phillips, their able Manager and Secretary, seemed to take a new lease of life and strength and surmounted it. Although self praise was no recommendation, and it was not for the Directors to blow their own trumpets individually, he did think the Directors were to be congratulated on the outcome of the negotiations regarding the repayment of debentures. There was a balance of just £621 outstanding on the Flood Account which he trusted 'would be fully wiped out this following year, and an unhappy chapter in the history of this railway would be closed for ever.'

A Mr. Ernest Gully was extremely lucky to be uninjured when the car he was driving came into collision with the Tram at the Stockbridge Road level crossing on Monday, 18th August. The front of the car was 'completely damaged', but little harm was done to the Tram which was able to continue on its way after a few minutes.[31]

On a lighter note, it was round about this time that a visitor in 'a racing car' made a bet of £1 (a lot of money in those days) with the Tram's driver George Belcher at Sidlesham that he could reach Selsey Town station before him! The young Charles Fidler was on board that Tram and many years later recalled how 'we started off across the ferry while the car had to go round by the road. The train shook so much I thought we would go into the sea, but driver Belcher won his bet, drawing up alongside the platform as the car turned into the yard'.[32] Cyclists would occasionally beat the Tram, but one energetic group of youngsters who tried to race it all the way from Chichester did manage to stay level as far as Ferry, but owing to the winding road, the Tram gained a short lead so as to arrive ahead of them at Selsey.[33]

The peak summer timetable advertised only 7 weekday return trams compared to the prewar two-tram service of twelve, yet no less than 102,292 passengers were to travel on the Tramway during the year. Was it in an attempt to run to time that each single journey had been extended from 30 to 35 minutes, and the non-stop Trams were allowed a full half hour?

	Weekdays							Sundays			
	Mixed										
Selsey	8.30	10.00	12.15	1.35	3.25	5.30	7.00	10.35	1.50	5.30	7.00
Ferry Siding	8.36	–		1.41	3.31	5.36	7.06	10.41	1.56	5.36	7.21
Sidlesham	8.40	–		1.45	3.35	5.40	7.10	10.45	2.00	5.40	7.25
Chalder	8.46	–		1.51	3.41	5.46	7.16	10.51	2.06	5.46	7.31
Hunston	8.52	–		1.57	3.47	5.52	7.22	10.57	2.12	5.52	7.37
Chichester	9.05	10.45	12.45	2.10	4.00	6.05	7.35	11.10	2.25	6.05	7.50
	Mixed										
Chichester	9.15	11.15	1.00	2.35	4.25	6.22	7.45	11.50	2.35	6.20	8.05
Hunston	9.25	–		2.43	4.33	–	7.53	11.58	2.43	6.28	8.13
Chalder	9.29	–		2.49	4.39	–	7.59	12.04	2.49	6.34	8.19
Sidlesham	9.35	–		2.55	4.45	–	8.05	12.10	2.55	6.40	8.25
Ferry Siding	9.39	–		2.59	4.49	–	8.09	12.14	2.59	6.44	8.29
Selsey	9.50	12.00	1.30	3.10	5.00	6.52	8.20	12.25	3.10	6.55	8.40

THOUGHTS OF EXPANSION (1913--1919)

In a letter dated 2nd August, Holman Stephens recommended that the Company purchase 100 tons of rails, but having approached the LBSCR, their Stores Department replied to Henry Phillips on 21st October that it was unlikely that they would be able to supply the material required. Stephens later contacted several other railways for rails and sleepers, but could get no offers.

The subject of raising further Capital to enable the Company to relay and strengthen the permanent way and to improve the rolling stock had been discussed on 23rd October and the subject was brought up again at the meeting on 27th November, by which time Sir Archibald Garland had taken over as the Chairman of the Directors. Fellow Directors, Sanden Street and Mitchell, had interviewed Holman Stephens 'with a view of drawing up a joint scheme' and it was agreed that he 'would see his friends' and report as to what they were disposed to do. However, nothing definite had since been heard from him, and they were under the impression that the Colonel was not interested in the scheme. He had, however, worked out this estimate for the relaying of the existing permanent way which was laid before the meeting:

		£	s.	d.
Rails, 75lb F. B. Rails		13,800	0	0
Plates	£405			
Bolts	£256			
Spikes	£900	1,561	0	0
Laying		2,250	0	0
Points & Crossings	£800			
Laying same	£200	1,000	0	0
Extra Ballast		1,400	0	0
Sleepers		6,000	0	0
		26,011	0	0
Bridge Strengthening & Station Alterations		2,000	0	0
Fences & gates renewals		1,500	0	0
		29,511	0	0
Engineer's Fees 5%		1,475	0	0
Contingencies 10%		2,950	0	0
		33,976	0	0 (sic)
Less Sale of old material		5,250	0	0
		28,726	0	0

Add:
    Rolling Stock as may be s
    Signals if double service required

Note how the calculations do not add up correctly!

After further discussion it was left to Horace Mitchell to write to Stephens asking whether 'he and his friends' would be prepared to buy the Tramway, or, as an alternative, as he appeared to take little interest in the Company, would he be prepared to resign from his post as Engineer?

Notes

1. *Chichester Observer*, Wednesday, 19.3.1913.
2. Sharp Archibald Garland was the son of former director Sharp Garland who had passed away on 9.8.1906.
3. *Chichester Observer*, Wednesday, 18.6.1913.
4. *Chichester Observer*, Wednesdays, 20.8.1913 and 27.8.1913.
5. The proposed terminus was variously described as East or West Wittering.
6. There was no signalling to re-signal!
7. The 10 to 12 trains refers to single journeys, amounting to between 20 and 24 trips across the canal bridge each day.
8. Mainly because of the ongoing war, nothing more was heard of the scheme for a new station at Selsey.
9. *Chichester Observer*, Wednesday, 9.12.1914.
10. *West Sussex Gazette*, Thursday, 14.1.1915.
11. *Chichester Observer*, Wednesday, 10.3.1915.
12. *Chichester Observer*, Wednesday, 26.5.1915.
13. The Selsey district received only the one Zeppelin raid in September 1916, but there were no casualties, or damage to property.
14. Board of Directors' Minute Book, 16.11.1916.
15. *The Southwold Railway* by Alan A. Taylor and Eric S. Tonks, published by Ian Allan Ltd., 1989.
16. Board of Directors' Minute Book, 16.11.1916.
17. This cheap fare was extended to include the men of the 9th Battalion Sussex Volunteer Regiment when travelling in uniform for the purpose of drill, etc. at the Directors' Board Meeting, 26.4.1917.
18. Board of Directors' Minute Book, 23.12.1916.
19. In 1919, Alastair Balmain MacLeod (1900–1990) commenced his railway career in the LBSCR's locomotive works at Brighton and in October 1928 the Southern Railway appointed him as Assistant for the Isle of Wight to take charge of the Locomotive Carriage and Wagon Department. At the beginning of 1930 he also took control of the Traffic and Commercial Departments before being promoted in May, 1934 to the position of the SR's Assistant Western Divisional Locomotive Superintendent, later becoming Store Superintendent. After Nationalisation he moved to the LMR in a similar capacity, retiring at the end of 1964 as Supplies and Contracts Manager.
20. *Yesteryear Transport*, Summer 1981. The shunting operation referred to would have taken place at Church Farm private siding.
21. *Chichester Observer*, Wednesday, 4.7.1917.
22. Board of Directors' Minute Book, 27.7.1917.
23. *Railway & Travel Monthly*, July 1917, article by "P.F.G."
24. Board of Directors' Minute Book, 15.11.1917.
25. On being knighted, Alderman Garland seems to have dropped using his unusual first Christian name of "Sharp".
26. Board of Directors' Minute Book, 5.4.1918.
27. Some of this chalk over the ensuing years, once broken up, would be placed in a locomotive's firebox where it was found that it would disperse clinker which had formed into solid lumps. Former fireman, Ray Apps reminiscing in *The Selsey Tramways*, 3rd edition by Edward C. Griffith, published by the author in 1974.
28. Board of Directors' Minute Book, 7.11.1918.
29. Board of Directors' Minute Book, 8.5.1919.
30. It is not clear why Edward Heron-Allen should regard *Wembley* as a third locomotive when the Company already possessed three, *Selsey*, *Sidlesham* and *Hesperus*.
31. *Chichester Observer*, Wednesday, 20.8.1919.
32. Charles Fidler reminiscing in a series called 'Colourful History of Selsey' published in the *Chichester Observer*, 12.3.1965.
33. *The Selsey Tramways* as above.

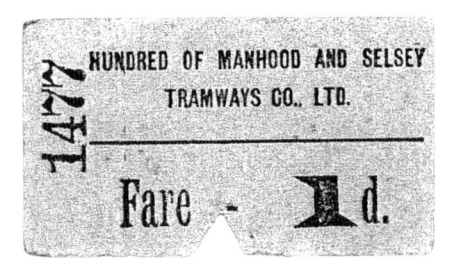

Hunston–Hoe Farm or Chalder to Hoe Farm or vice versa.

Chichester–Hunston or Hoe Farm–Sidlesham or vice versa.

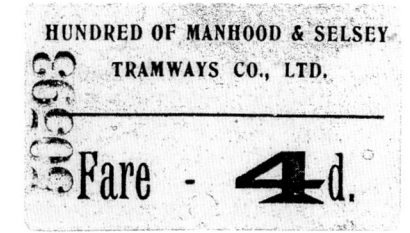

Chichester–Hoe Farm, Chichester to Chalder or Hunston–Sidlesham or vice versa.

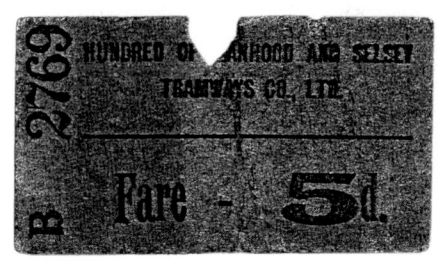

Chichester–Sidlesham or Chalder to Selsey or vice versa.

Hunston–Selsey or vice versa, or Dog, Bicycle or Perambulator (accompanied by passenger) single or return.

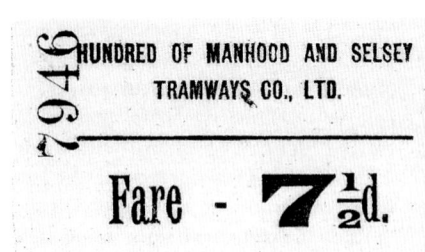

Chichester–Selsey Single.

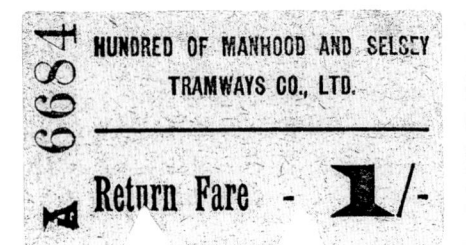

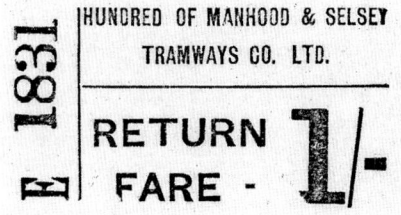

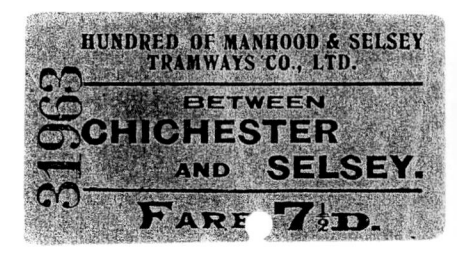

Chichester–Sidlesham or Chalder to Golf Club Halt or Selsey.

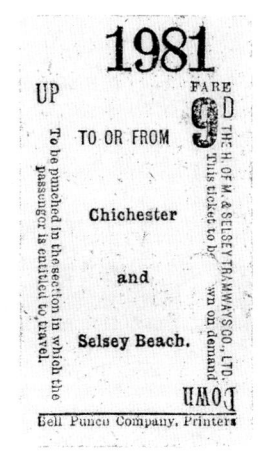

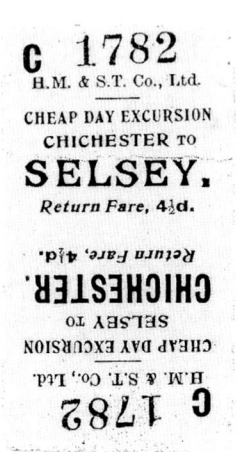

Tickets issued between 1897 and 31st December 1916.   COLLECTION G. R. CROUGHTON

CHAPTER FIVE
COMPLETELY OFF THE RAILS (1920–1923)

HOLMAN Stephens waited until 7th January 1920 before he replied to Mr. H. C. Mitchell's letter when from Tonbridge he wrote:

Dear Mr. Mitchell,

I had an interview with the Solicitors representing my friends yesterday and found that your proposal, that an offer for the shares in the Tramway should be made, has had careful consideration. I was asked to get you to find out from your co-Directors if an offer of £3 per share for the shares, or a reasonable number thereof, was such as they considered themselves justified in submitting to the Proprietors.

Your figures were considered and in view of the sum you report as required to be spent on the original line, coupled with the Capital required for the Chichester Harbour scheme, the figure first herein named appeared to my friends to be a reasonable one. Their idea is to send improved rolling stock to the undertaking, as required, and to make the line suitable for any traffic likely to offer itself.

Perhaps you will be good enough to let me know the views of your co-Directors and if favourable, I could arrange to put you in touch with the Solicitors first mentioned.

I am sorry I am unable to attend the Board, called for Thursday, but I notice no Engineering question appears on the agenda, and the notice was not received in time for me to cancel my previous appointment.

Yours faithfully,
(signed) H. F. Stephens.

At a meeting of the Board the following day, it was agreed to increase the Goods and Parcels Rates to take effect from 15th January. Authorisation was also given for 300 sleepers at 7/6d each[1] to be purchased from the LBSCR, together with a new forge for the engine shed at Selsey from Messrs. Buck & Hickman. Although the roof was described as being in 'bad condition', it was decided not to replace it at present 'in likelihood of the shed being shifted at a later date'![2]

Horace Mitchell subsequently had a meeting with Mr. W. A. Thornton who said that he was disposed to offer £3 10s 0d for each of the Company's £5 shares if it could be arranged for the London, Brighton & South Coast Railway to work the line. Mitchell also wrote to Holman Stephens in reply to his letter of 7th January, eventually receiving the following letter dated 2nd March from Messrs. Davis, Saunders & Swanwick (solicitors) of Chesterfield:

Dear Sir,

Selsey Tramway Co.

We have been instructed in the negotiations which are pending for the purchase of the Shares of this Company at the price of £3 per share.

Our clients, of course, desire to obtain complete control and require that if the purchase goes through, the whole of the shares should be transferred.

The amount issued, we understand, is 2880 and we shall be glad to know whether assents to the Sale have been obtained from all Holders and by what date the purchase could be completed.

We are, Dear Sir,
Yours faithfully,
Davis, Saunders & Co.

To achieve this high vantage point, the photographer must have been standing in an open wagon on the goods loop while passengers kindly posed for him at Selsey station. Prior to the other three ex-LCDR carriages entering service in February 1921, the 4-compartment first class 4-wheeler, purchased two years previously, evidently worked with the original Falcon bogie carriages which formed the rest of this train. The locomotive, also purchased in 1919, and shown here with a home-made wooden cab, carried no name, but it was known by the Tramway staff at that time as Wembley.
COLLECTION E.C. GRIFFITH

Left: These are the four postcards that Mr. Furguson of the Light Railways (Investigation) Committee purchased when he 'happened to be' in Chichester on the weekend of 20th/21st March 1920, none of which are particularly representative of the Company at that time. In the first picture, taken at least 19 years earlier, the new Hurst Nelson carriage was bringing up the rear of Selsey's train in this posed photograph taken between Stockbridge Road level crossing and the canal. The spire of Chichester Cathedral rises majestically above the surrounding countryside. Right: On the same section of line, Sidlesham is seen climbing away from Stockbridge Road level crossing with the 10.35 train to Selsey, c.1907. For many years this departure was advertised as 'mixed' and, as was so often the case, the single carriage had been tagged on at the rear. What with the shunting off of wagons at intermediate stations and sidings, and only chain link couplings on all the rolling stock, any passengers would be in for a very rough and jerky ride.
COLLECTION LES DARBYSHIRE and LENS OF SUTTON

OUR LOCAL EXPRESS.

SELSEY to CHICHESTER and back the same day: if you're lucky.

OUR LOCAL EXPRESS
Chichester to Selsey

The other two postcards were humorous cartoons by the Cynicus Publishing Company entitled 'Our Local Express Chichester to Selsey' and 'Our Local Express, Chichester to Selsey and back the same day. (Perhaps)'. COLLECTION J. WYNNE-TYSON

Following the Board Meeting held in London two days later, Mitchell replied to the above letter to the effect that the Directors were prepared to recommend acceptance of £3 per share, and that he was authorised to enter into a provisional agreement with the purchasers. They also needed to ascertain what was the minimum number of shares they would purchase should any shareholders stand out. It was further proposed that the LBSCR and Mr. Thornton be invited to submit offers for the Company on or before Tuesday, 23rd March.[3]

Immediately after the meeting, Mitchell wrote to Messrs. Davis, Saunders & Co.:

> I am duly in receipt of your letter of 2nd inst. which I brought before the Directors at their meeting today. The position is not quite as you mentioned in your letter. There has been no formal offer to purchase the shares. The Directors, however, are prepared to recommend the Shareholders to sell their shares at the price you name.
>
> I think the best way of carrying the matter would be for a Provisional Contract to be entered into between the Chairman of the Company of the one part, and the Purchasers of the other part, such agreement to be subject to the confirmation of the Shareholders to the number your Clients require.
>
> As each individual Shareholder would have to assent, I do not think it possible to get the whole of the Shareholders into line. Therefore, it seems to me that the Agreement had better be binding with, say Shareholders to the amount of 2,000 approving. If this method of procedure appeals to you and you will let me know the names and addresses of the proposed purchasers, my firm will prepare and send you a draft Contract.
>
> You will understand that the matter has not yet been submitted to the Shareholders.
>
> Yours faithfully,
> (signed) Horace C. Mitchell.

Messrs. Davis & Saunders & Co. sent this reply to Horace Mitchell on 18th March:

> Referring to your letter of the 4th March, if you will send us the draft Agreement you suggest, we should be glad to consider it on behalf of our clients.
>
> The minimum number of Shares they require would be 75% of the issued amount which we understand is 2880. It is understood the purchase price offered to the Shareholders is £3 per share.
>
> We would suggest that while the Agreement is being discussed between us, a circular should be issued to the Shareholders informing them of the provisional offer and recommending acceptance, and ask them to give the Chairman authority to accept the offer to remain in force one month, or say until 30th April as the Easter holidays will intervene.
>
> The names of the parties to whom the shares will be transferred has (sic) not yet been definitely settled, but they will include Colonel H. F. Stephens.

On receipt of the letter the following day, Mitchell wrote back at once explaining that the instructions of the Board were to await the names and addresses of the proposed purchasers before any provisional agreement was entered into, and that the Directors would not sanction any circular to the Shareholders. His letter concluded 'I may mention that we have been approached in other quarters and of course you understand that the Directors are free to deal'.

Over the weekend of Saturday/Sunday, 20th/21st March 1920 Mr. Ferguson of the Light Railways (Investigation) Committee 'happened to be' in west Sussex, where he took the opportunity of having a look at the Selsey Tramway. The Committee had been set up 'to examine and report upon the future policy and possible development of the construction and operation of Light Railways in the United Kingdom', but although outwardly similar to a Light Railway with its minimal facilities, the Selsey Tramway didn't actually come into this category! Ferguson's Report, dated 31st March (somewhat comprehensive for someone who 'just happened to be' in the area) read:

> This Tramway is situated in the County of Sussex, is 8 miles in length (single track) and traverses a flat district which is chiefly agricultural. It has a junction with the LB & SC Rly. at Chichester and terminus at Selsey which is a small seaside resort.
>
> The line is of standard gauge and the ordinary main line trucks are run over it. It was built about 23 years ago, is laid with 40lb flat bottom

rails and has carried and is carrying all the traffic of the district. There is a considerable passenger traffic on which the line is largely dependent for its revenue.

The line is of very light construction, akin to a contractor's service line. It is laid for the greater part of its length practically on the surface of the ground and crosses most of the roads on the level without gates. It appears to have been constructed at small expense in a time of low prices. The standard of maintenance is low. The total cost of construction and equipment as ascertained from the accounts for the year ending 31st December 1918 amounts to £25,339, or £3,167 per mile. The actual cost of working in the year 1918 (including an allowance of £100 for depreciation of rolling stock) was £3,649.

This Company is not included in the Blue Book of Railway Companies for 1913, nor does it appear in Bradshaw's Railway Manual for 1918. It is shewn on the official Railway Map of England as a "Light" Railway. The Report and Accounts for the year 1918 have been examined.

These accounts have not been made up in the form prescribed by the Railway (Accounts and Returns) Act 1911. The Company appears to have taken advantage of Section 6 (2) of that Act and has adhered to the form of Accounts prescribed in the Act of 1868.

It is impossible to form a sound opinion of the financial position of the Company from the Accounts of a single year. For example this Company appears to have suffered considerable damage through flooding prior to the year 1918 and had spent £4,286 10s. 2d. up to 31st December 1918 in repairing the damage. As that expenditure could not be met out of the revenue of the years in which it was incurred it was charged to Suspense Account and liquidated out of the revenue of succeeding years. The undernoted figures show how that Suspense Account was dealt with in the year 1918:-

Amount charged to Suspense Account
up to 31st December 1917 .... £4260:15:0.

Amount liquidated out of Revenue
up to 31st December 1917 .... £2645: 0:0.

Balance to liquidate at 1st Jany. 1918 ....£1615:15:0.

Expenditure incurred in the Year 1918
and charged to Suspense Account .... 25:15:2.

£1641:10:2.
Amount liquidated out of Revenue in 1918......................£1020: 0:0.

Balance to liquidate at 31st December 1918 ....£621:10:2.

It will be seen that although the actual expenditure for 1918 on this apparently abnormal work was only £25 15s 2d, the Revenue for the year had to bear £1020 the bulk of which was in respect of a debt incurred in previous years which may be described as extraordinary maintenance. Evidently this work was not completed at the end of 1918 because the Directors stated they proposed further to strengthen and raise the embankments in 1919 if the necessary labour could be obtained. Having spent £1020 in liquidating this abnormal expenditure, there was no money left at the end of 1918 to pay a dividend on the Company's ordinary stock, nor is there any reserve for renewal of Permanent Way.

If the amount earned in 1918 and appropriated for liquidation of a prior debt had been available for distribution it would appear that a dividend of 6¾% could have been given to the ordinary shareholders.

From the attached Statements prepared from the Published Accounts for the year 1918, the following conclusions may be drawn:-

(1) The Capital position of the Company is very satisfactory.

(2) The Company are paying out of Revenue a large sum on the re-construction of their property due to flooding. So far as that is abnormal expenditure, such a policy is sound and, provided it is not recurrent, the sacrifice of a dividend on the ordinary shares, until it is provided for, presupposes good judgment.

(3) The Company have a reserve fund for renewals of rolling stock of £2,160, the original cost of the vehicles being £3,368. No information is available as to the age of the stock and enhanced prices will have to be faced for renewals in future but the amount of the reserve shows that on a pre-war basis the Company were amply providing for renewals of rolling stock.

(4) The length of the line appears to be 8 miles and the average receipt per passenger is 8.06d. There are 4 intermediate stations and even allowing 1¼d per mile per third class passenger such an average receipt seems to point to a considerable number of First Class passengers.[4] More than two thirds of the gross receipts is obtained from Passenger Traffic.

(5) The receipts per train mile for 1918 was (sic) 4/1.10[5]
The receipts per train mile for the United Kingdom
in 1913 was (sic) 5/8.07
The expenditure per train mile for 1918 was 2/11.12
The expenditure per train mile for the United
Kingdom in 1918 was 3/7.43.

These figures go to show that while the Railway Companies as a whole in 1918 were a burden on the National Exchequer, *this small line*, apart from its abnormal expenditure, *was showing a considerable profit*.

With the Balance Sheet for the year ending 31st December 1918 to hand, the Investigation Committee worked out this Statistical Information, with the figures rounded up or down to the nearest pound:

Total Capital Authorised	£29,800
" " Received	£26,600
" " Expended	£25,339
Further Capital Expenditure	Not known
Capital Powers:-	
Amount unissued £3,200	
" unspent 1,261	
Surplus Lands 155	£4,616
Gross Receipts	£5,210
Traffic Receipts	£5,087
Train Mileage	24,865
Traffic Receipts per train mile	4s/1d.10
Receipts from Passengers	£3,720
No. of Passengers	110,809
Average receipt per passenger	8d.06
Total Expenditure	£3,649
Percentage of Gross Receipts	70.04
Traffic Expenditure	£3,639
Percentage of Traffic Receipts	71.53
Traffic Expenditure per train Mile	2s/11d.12
Total Net Income	£1,562
Expenditure on Maintenance of Way and Works	£686
Miles Maintained	8
Expenditure per mile	£86
Expenditure on Maintenance of Rolling Stock	£567
No. of Vehicles maintained	28
Expenditure per vehicle	£20:5:-
Dividends on Debentures and Mortgages	£540
Dividend on Ordinary Stock	Nil
Appropriation of Suspense Account	£1,020
Brought forward from previous year	£29:17:6.
Carried forward to subsequent year	31:12:5.
Total amount of Reserve Accounts	£2,200
Balance at debit of Flood reconstruction A/c.	£622
Cash at Bank and on hand	£619
Amount invested in War Loans	£1,975
(Nominal Value £2,000).	

On 19th March the Chichester Inspector of Taxes wrote to the Tramways Company advising that its liability for Income Tax for the year 1919–20 had been 're-computed', making the assessable figure £1,522 (instead of £494 which had been agreed back in the previous October), the amount of £1,027 in respect of the Flood Account not now being

CL.4.

2.

MINISTRY OF TRANSPORT.

LIGHT RAILWAYS (INVESTIGATION) COMMITTEE.

STATEMENT of INFORMATION relative to the CONSTRUCTION and WORKING of LIGHT RAILWAYS.

A Light Railways (Investigation) Committee, in the membership of which ~~seven~~ six officers of Light Railways are included, has been appointed by the Minister to examine and report upon the future policy and possible development of the construction and operation of Light Railways in the United Kingdom. For this purpose it is desired to obtain information, under the various heads indicated below, in respect of a number of important representative undertakings, and the Committee request that each Company to whom this form of statement is addressed may be good enough to have it completed, so far as this may be conveniently possible, and returned at an early date.

Apart from the statements of fact desired in respect of the items specified in the form, the Committee would be glad to have the observations or suggestions of the Companies with regard to any matters concerning which their experience may have indicated that modifications of existing practice or the adoption of new methods and devices are desirable, e.g. in respect of such matters as maximum authorised speed, system of signalling, etc.

The views of each Company are particularly desired with regard to (a) the reasonableness or otherwise of any existing regulations or restrictions whether imposed by the Board of Trade or by any Local Authority or other public body or by private individuals or interests, and also (b) the advantages or disadvantages of "through" rates and fares.

The Committee would also be glad to have

(a) a description of the method or methods adopted for the financing of the undertaking;

(b) a statement, in the case of undertakings situated in Great Britain, as to the extent to which the cost of the land acquired has been affected (if at all) by the set-off provided for in Section 13 (1) of the Light Railways Act, 1896; and, generally.

(c) any suggestions which the Company may have to offer as to the means by which the utility of Light Railways might be enhanced, or by which greater economy in their construction and operation might be secured.

In conclusion, the Committee wish it to be clearly understood that the information sought by them is desired, and will be used, solely for the purposes of their investigation and will be treated as confidential.

The object of the investigation is to determine what steps, if any, should be taken to foster and facilitate the operation of existing Light Railways or to encourage the future development of such Railways; and, having this end in view, the Committee will receive with appreciation any suggestions which may be offered by the Companies to whom this form is addressed.

NOTE:- Except where otherwise indicated, the statements of fact desired on each of the subjects enumerated hereafter should be inserted in the adjoining space in the second column of the form. If in any instance this should prove insufficient, use may be made of the "Supplementary Sheets" provided for the purpose.

allowed as an expense against revenue. Although the Company argued that this amount expended on the Flood Account was a genuine expense, the Tax Inspector decided otherwise and the extra amount was eventually paid under protest.[6]

At the Directors' Meeting on 24th March, it was resolved that Horace Mitchell should prepare a form of tender for the various applicants to sign that should be returned by 23rd April. The tenders received would then be considered at the next Board Meeting to be held at Balfour House, 119/125 Finsbury Pavement, London on 29th April.

The *Chichester Observer* dated 31st March advised

Holiday Trams

The Selsey Tramway Company announce a Special Tram Service for Good Friday, Easter Sunday and Monday. The last tram leaves Selsey on Good Friday and Easter Monday at 7.15pm, returning from Chichester at 8.10pm, and on Easter Monday at 9.00pm, returning from Chichester at 10.00pm. The return fare on these days will be 1/6d.

Following the Light Railways (Investigations) Committee's Mr. Ferguson's visit to West Sussex, these notes were typed out by 'C.S.' on 3rd April under the title of 'Hundred of Manhood and Selsey Railway':

Collecting information is difficult owing to Easter holidays. Mr. Phillips, the General Manager and Secretary, was not expected back until some time next week.

The offices of the Company are at Selsey.

The Tramway was constructed over twenty years ago and at that time it was intended to have a branch to Pagham Harbour.[7] Pagham Harbour has since been blocked by accretion of shingle.

The total employees of the tramway, including Mr. Phillips, is 22.

There appears to be only one passenger train. At present this train makes six journeys per day each way – see last page of attached timetable.[8]

The train consists of two or more coaches, see postcards 1, 2, 3 and 4 attached.

There appears to be a spare engine, some coaches etc.

The line is single, about eight miles long, with five or 6 stations. The gauge is 4ft 8½in.

Flat-bottomed, dogged rails are used, of which the annexed is a rubbing.

There is, I believe, some slight variation in the section.

Ballasting consists of gravel and ashes.

The cuttings and backs (*sic*) average about 2ft deep.

This was the Tramway's published timetable for March 1920 as referred to above, where it will be noted that there were 5 return journeys each way on weekdays, and not six:

DOWN	*Every Week Day*					*Sundays*		
Chichester	9.15	11.15	2.20	4.25	7.30	11.50	6.20	8.10
Hunston	9.23		2.28	4.33	7.38	11.58	6.28	8.18
Chalder	9.29	Mixed	2.34	4.39	7.44	12.04	6.34	8.24
Sidlesham	9.35	Train	2.40	4.45	7.50	12.10	6.40	8.30
Ferry Siding	9.39		2.44	4.49	7.54	12.14	6.44	8.34
Selsey Town	9.50	12.00	2.55	5.00	8.05	12.25	6.55	8.45
UP								
Selsey Town	8.30	10.15	1.25	3.05	6.30	10.35	5.30	7.15
Ferry Siding	8.36		1.31	3.11	6.36	10.41	5.36	7.21
Sidlesham	8.40	Mixed	1.35	3.15	6.40	10.45	5.40	7.25
Chalder	8.46	Train	1.41	3.21	6.46	10.51	5.46	7.31
Hunston	8.52		1.47	3.27	6.52	10.57	5.52	7.37
Chichester	9.05	11.00	2.00	3.40	7.05	11.10	6.05	7.50

Only two tenders for the Tramways Company's shares were received at the Directors' Meeting on 29th April, the London, Brighton & South Coast Railway having declined to do so, possibly owing to the pending grouping. W. A. Thornton offered £3 5s 0d for each of no fewer than 2,000 £5 shares and H. Montague Bates (Holman Stephens' 'friend') £3 per share 'plus a deferred share of £2 to carry interest at 3% per annum after the ordinary shares had paid 5% for each ordinary £5 share (not fewer than 2,000 shares) purchased'. The purchasers would have the option to purchase the £2 deferred shares at any time for £1 3s 4d per £2 share. With the tenders, having been carefully considered, the secretary was instructed to write to Mr. Bates, c/o Holman Stephens, explaining that it would be difficult to issue deferred shares unless he purchased all the ordinary shares, and to ask him if he wanted to amend his tender to a total cash offer, or whether to have his tender, as it stood, submitted to the shareholders.

Mr. H. J. Smith, employed as a fireman and occasional guard had, by issuing tickets in advance of his closing numbers, been holding back money belonging to the Tramway Company. The £6 19s 0d outstanding on 27th April had been paid in by Smith, who had since been stood off as guard, and it was resolved that the man should not be allowed to act in that capacity in the future. There had been demands made by several of the Company's employees for an advance of 10/- per week in wages, but the Company could not afford this. However, all the men, excepting H. J. Smith, were given a rise of 5/- per week and Mr. J. Boyling was given a further 5/- per week in consideration of his taking up duties as a spare driver.

The Hundred of Manhood & Selsey Tramways Company had enjoyed a monopoly of carrying passengers between Chichester and Selsey for almost 23 years, but it looked as if this was about to change. On hearing that a local firm was going to commence running a 'bus service between Selsey and Chichester, Southdown Motor Services Ltd. thought that they should 'run a car during the summer',[9] but possibly owing to a shortage of vehicles, luckily for the Tramway, the service did not start.

Montague Bates replied to Henry Phillips' letter on 4th May offering £3 6s 8d cash for each £5 share that was submitted. His amended tender was accompanied by a letter from Holman Stephens suggesting that Bates was prepared to offer the deferred shares as well as the £3 6s 8d cash if necessary. Just prior to the Special Meeting of Shareholders held at the Council Chamber, Chichester on Friday, 21st May a letter was received from W. A. Thornton withdrawing his tender for shares, the Directors, therefore, recommending acceptance of Mr. Montague Bates' tender. The following resolutions were carried unanimously at that meeting:

Resolutions

'It is resolved that the offer made by Mr. Montague Bates dated the 4th May, 1920 for the purchase of shares in the Hundred of Manhood & Selsey Tramways Company Limited for £3 6s. 8d. per share be accepted.

'It is further resolved that in addition to the sum of £3 6s. 8d. to be paid in cash for such shares, the said Mr. Montague Bates is to create and issue to the seller for each share purchased, one deferred share of £2 value upon the terms and conditions set out in Mr. Montague Bates' Tender dated the 22nd day of April 1920.

'It is also further resolved that Messrs. Corbould-Ellis, Mitchell & Mawby Solicitors of Balfour House, Finsbury Pavement, EC do and they are hereby authorised to carry through the purchase and sale of such shares on behalf of the Shareholders.'

Southdown Motor Services Ltd. may have put their plans for the Manhood Peninsula on hold, but as rumoured, in July two Selsey gentlemen, Colonel W. G. Moore and a Captain Fuller, commenced operating two red 'buses between Chichester and Selsey running 4 return trips each weekday. It had often been remarked that the Tram went everywhere but where people lived, and although the 'bus journey took considerably longer, the new service was able to offer passengers a door-to-door service.

Behind the scenes at the Ministry of Transport, enquiries were still being made regarding the Selsey Tramway, F. Soar having written to his colleague J. R. Deans on 6th July stating

'We have no information in "P" Dept. as to when this Tramway was originally authorised, nor have we any details of its construction. Under the West Sussex Light Railway Order, 1915, power was given to the W. Sussex Lt. Rly. for the acquisition or leasing, reconstructing and working of the existing Hundred of Manhood & Selsey Tramway as a light railway.

Communications respecting this line should be addressed to Col. H. F. Stephens, Tonbridge, Kent.'

Nine days later Deans did write to Holman Stephens enclosing questionnaires relating to the East Kent, the Kent & East Sussex, The Shropshire & Montgomeryshire, and the Weston, Clevedon & Portishead Railways, as well as the Selsey Tramway. Work on filling in the questionnaires of the last three railways probably started immediately, but those of the East Kent Railway and the Selsey Tramway were left in abeyance.

A most distressing accident occurred at Stockbridge level crossing on Friday, 27th August while a Mr. J. Durrant was delivering wood to a house close by. Hearing the Tram whistling, he looked out and checked that his pony and green grocer's cart were alright. When he heard the whistle sound again, he went back into the road just in time to see the pony knocked down and run over by the engine, dragging it about 12 feet. The engine driver told PC King that he had released his brakes when he saw that the line was clear, but immediately afterwards, he caught sight of the pony's head and felt a collision. He at once had brought the Tram, which was travelling at a slow speed, to a standstill. The loss of the unfortunate pony and the cart, which was completely wrecked, was estimated at £30.[10]

On 18th September Messrs. Davis, Saunders & Co. wrote to Messrs. Carbould-Ellis, Mitchell & Mawby:

Selsey Deferred Shares

'Referring to your letter of 13th September, Colonel Stephens informs us that Mr. Bates has never agreed to give deferred shares, but he instructs us to say that to settle the question once and for all, he is prepared to give a sum of £225 17s 6d to you for distribution among the Shareholders who have put in Shares through you. These amount altogether to 1807 and the sum of £225 17s 6d will provide 2/6d for each share. Please let us have your early reply to this.

'We find that it will not be possible for any of the new Directors to attend the proposed Board Meeting on the 23rd, but this need not prevent the business being proceeded with. We understand that you will pass the Transfers which are now lodged with the Secretary and that the old Directors will retire one by one appointing with each resignation Mr. Bates, Colonel Stephens and Mr. Jepson in rotation.

'We understand that Mr. Bates and Colonel Stephens are willing that Mr. Clayton should remain on the Board for the present.

'With regard to the Secretary's agreement, we shall be in a position to write you in the course of a few days. In the meantime, will you please let us know what is the salary he is receiving at present.'

Five days later at the Directors' meeting held at Balfour House, the Auditors' Report on the Accounts and the Directors' Report for the year ending 31st December 1919 were left over for the consideration of the new Board. With all the business completed, as requested, Edward Heron-Allen, Sir Archibald Garland and Horace C. Mitchell signed their resignations which were left with Mr. Mitchell (as solicitor to the Company) 'as escrows to await the completion of arrangements entered into by Mr. Bates on behalf of the new Board as to deferred shares and the Secretary, Mr. H. G. Phillips'.

The Light Railways (Investigation) Committee waited patiently for three months until on 6th October J. R. Deans (secretary to the Committee) wrote again to Stephens stating that he was 'desired by Sir Alexander Gibb to say that, before calling a further meeting of the Investigation Committee in order to examine the replies obtained from the Companies to whom questionnaires were addressed, he would like the information to be laid before the Committee to be as complete as possible'. He asked that particulars of the five lines mentioned could be forwarded 'within, say, the next week or two'. He fully realized 'that the completion of the forms must, in each case, involve the expenditure of much time and trouble, and some diffidence is felt in pressing for their early return...and it is hoped that you may be able to supply it soon'.

Acknowledging the Committee's letter on 12th October, Holman Stephens advised that the figures for the Shropshire & Montgomeryshire, Weston, Cleveland & Portishead and Kent & East Sussex Railways were 'well on the way'. With regard to the Selsey line, he was somewhat evasive,[11] as well he might have been, and advised

'I doubt if you will get any figures for the Hundred of Manhood & Selsey Tramways. To begin with, the accounts are not prepared in the manner the Ministry are accustomed to and therefore are not comparable with other accounts. Secondly, it is a very uninteresting private line and I do not think that the figures, if prepared at great trouble, would be of much use to you.

'It belongs, practically, to one Owner and I rather doubt if he would be prepared to go to the expense, re extra staff, to get the figures out, owing to the fact that[12] it is a private line and, therefore, obviously worked on business lines which are not comparable with the present system of working Railways, either so-called "heavy" or so-called "light".

'While we are on the subject, I very much doubt if I shall be able to attend the meetings of the Committee, at any rate, before Christmas.

'However, I shall be very pleased to give you any information which I may have on any point, subject to me being in England.'

Stephens was, of course, referring to Mr. H. Montague Bates as 'practically' the 'one owner'! The Colonel was understandably worried that the dubious legal position of the Selsey Tramway would come to light if the Light Railways (Investigation) Committee pried too much! Two days later J. R. Deans acknowledged Stephens' letter thanking him 'for the trouble which you are kindly taking with regard to the completion of the forms. I quite appreciate,' he continued, 'the difficulty which you mention with regard to the figures for the Hundred of Manhood line, and I am sure that in the circumstances the Committee would not wish the owner to incur the additional expense and trouble which would be involved in completing the financial section of the questionnaire.'

On 18th October Edward Heron-Allen, through his solicitors, advised that on 25th March 1921 he required payment off of the mortgage on the four cottages in Station Road, Selsey dated 8th September 1898 which had been transferred to him by deed dated 19th April 1912. However, Stephens, writing to Henry Phillips on 30th November asked him to point out to Heron-Allen's solicitors that he could not call the mortgages in without the permission of the Court.

It was not until 7th December that the Colonel returned the Selsey Tramways' questionnaire, parts of it completed by himself, and others by Henry Phillips. A typed covering letter accompanied it which read 'I beg to enclose herewith the questionnaire duly completed, in connection with this Company' and then added in pen 'as far as I can complete it'! Some of the more interesting items were:

	ITEM	STATEMENT
1.(a)	Name of Company.	Hundred of Manhood and Selsey (Light) Railway
6.(a)	Date when line authorised	Unknown[13]
11.(b)	Percentages of receipts from passenger and freight traffic respectively.	Passenger traffic 68.4 per cent Freight traffic 29.4 per cent.[14]
12.	Estimated population of the district served by the Line – stating the basis on which the estimate is formed.	Selsey 1,600 West Itchenor 119 Sidlesham 928 Appledram 156 Pagham 762 Donnington 233 Eamley 112 North Mundham 511 E. Wittering 147 Oving 582 W. Wittering 537 New Fishbourne 906 Birdham 411 Hunston 819
13.	Nature and effect of road competition with the Railway, if any such competition exists or is anticipated.	Carriers Chichester to Selsey etc. take small goods and parcels. Omnibus service established July 7, 1920, taking approximately £70 per week during August 1920. Also considerable competition in 1920 from motor lorries carrying heavier goods.

(Note added by the Light Railways (Investigation) Committee referring to the £70 per week taken by the 'bus company: If this rate were maintained through year, total takings would about equal passgr. takings of railway. Trains take 35 minutes for the 8 mile journey – and omnibuses would take about the same.)

18.	Nature of protection provided or precautions taken at public roads, e.g. at level crossings or where the line is laid on or adjacent to a public road.	No gates are provided at Public Road Level Crossing, the usual 'Beware of Train' caution boards are provided on either side of Public Roads. The speed of trains are (sic) reduced to 8 miles per hour over Public Roads and the usual caution is given by long blasts on engine whistles, whilst approaching and crossing roads.
27.	Description of Workshops (if any) and potential capacity thereof, i.e. in respect of output. State whether the Company executes its own heavy repairs – or, if not, by whom these are executed.	Small locomotive Shed at Selsey. All repairs executed with the exception of wheel-tyring, wheelturning, Spring repairs and casting. This work being done by Main Line Railway Companies or other Locomotive Builders.
28.	Description of signalling, if any.	Nil. The facing points are locked with ordinary Padlocks and Key.
41.	Number of vehicles on one train.	Passenger Train Freight Train Max. Average Max. Average 8 3 - - Mixed train Coaches and Coaches and Empty Trucks Full Trucks Max. Average Max. Average - 8 - 8
42.	Maximum gross load hauled by Locomotive.	100 Tons.
46.	Description of any property owned by the Company other than that provided for or use in conjunction with the working of the Line.	Four freehold cottages (six roomed) at Selsey. Two freehold cottages at Chichester Canal Bridge. Total 6.
48.	Engine Mileage.	1913 1919 40,790 27,752
55.	Total quantities of merchandise, mineral and live stock traffic (stated separately) originating on the Company's system – (a) In 1913. (b) In 1919.	(a) Merchandise 3143 tons Minerals 2762 tons (b) Merchandise 5314 tons Minerals 3740 tons Live Stock 40 cattle, 250 sheep.
56.	General description of organisation and management.	General Policy directed by Board of six Directors and Consulting Director. Permanent Way and Rolling Stock in charge of Engineer and Loco. Sup't. General Working in charge of Secretary and Manager.
57.	Total full-time staff (all grades) employed in the working of the Line. (a) Train Staff. (b) Station Staff. (c) Maintenance Staff.	(a) 4 (b) 4 (c) 10[15]
60.	Grades (if any) for whom clothing is provided.	Guard, Assistant Guard and Station Agents.
62.	State whether the Company's Accounts are prepared in the form prescribed by the Railway Companies (Accounts and Returns) Act, 1911.	No. A/cs are prepared in the old statutory form of Railway Accounts.
80.	Basis of fares, rates and charges (with Authority for the same) and the relation of these fares, etc. to those on the main railway systems.	Fares, rates and charges on October 1st, 1920, approximately the same as on L.B. & S.C.R. for similar distance.

(Note added by the Light Railways (Investigation) Committee: The Railway Clearing House classification is not used. A private classification has been arranged which is more suitable for this type of line. Advantage has been taken in this direction of the fact that the line is a private one and not subject to interference from Main Line Companies, as to method of working.)

85. If the Railway is worked as an independent concern – or by another Company which charges the actual cost of working – details of the expenditure under the following heads should be given:-

(a) Maintenance and Renewal of Way and Works -

a) Superintendence — 25 0 0
Maintenance of Roads, Bridges and Works, Permanent Way – Complete Renewals, Permanent Way – Maintenance and Repairs, Maintenance of Signalling and Telegraphs, Maintenance of Stations and Buildings were bracketed to form a grand total of — 903 19 0
Repairs debited to Reserve for Depreciation — 115 15 6
Total: — £1044 14 6

(b) Maintenance and Renewal of Rolling Stock -

(b)   Locomotives   Carriages & Wagons
Complete Renewals, Repairs and partial Renewals, Purchase of New Stock and Workshop Expenses were all bracketed together to form totals of — 661 5 8   152 12 10
Repairs debited to Reserve for Depreciation — 495 5 10   100 0 0
£1156 11 6   £252 12 10

(c) Operating Expenses.

(c) (1) Locomotive Running Expenses:-
Wages — 370 18 10
Fuel — 839 0 8
Other Expenses — 209 9 10
Total — £1419 9 4

(2) Traffic Expenses:-
Wages — 403 0 7
Other Expenses — 190 6 4
Total — £593 6 11

(d) General and Other Charges.

(d) £682 2 11

(e) Balance at Credit or Debit of Reserve and Suspense Accounts (if any) at the end of years 1913 and 1919, in detail.

(e) Reserve Cr.
1913. £2260 18 10
1919. £870 6 11

At the end of the questionnaire, under the final heading of 'General Observations and Suggestions', the Light Railways (Investigation) Committee came to the conclusion that 'The Company being a private undertaking and built on private land, has no useful observations to offer, as the conditions which fortunately govern it, do not govern non-private undertakings.'

Upon the proposition of Sir Archibald Garland and seconded by Mr. H. C. Mitchell, it was resolved to insert on the minutes of the Directors' Meeting on 14th December that, before retiring, the Directors desired 'to convey to Henry Gibson Phillips and all whom it may concern, their high appreciation of his services as the Secretary and Manager of the line for a period of fourteen years. Mr. Phillips has been an assiduous and faithful servant of the Company through times of great difficulty, and has met the responsibilities arising out of adverse circumstances with tact, perseverance, courage and resource, especially when, in 1910, a considerable section of the line was flooded without notice, and required to be reconstructed; and throughout the serious and recurrent difficulties arising out of the War. Mr. Phillips' duties have included not only the Secretariat, but also the General Management of the Line, including Accountancy and the constant supervision of the Undertaking which attained in June last under his management to a condition of prosperity theretofore unequalled in its history, and the Directors desire that this tribute to Mr. Phillips' excellent services should be recorded on the Minutes of the Board.' A written testimonial to this effect under the seal of the Company and signed by the Directors was presented to a no doubt suitably humbled Henry Phillips, who had only just returned to work after recovering from a serious illness.

Horace Mitchell presented to the meeting an account for fees to date of £207 7s 4d due to Messrs. Corbould-Ellis, Mitchell & Mawby, and requested that a cheque be drawn at that meeting. The secretary had to point out that there was only £157 to the credit of the Company's account at the bank, but upon Mr. Mitchell's undertaking not to present the cheque for payment until notified by the secretary to do so, a cheque was drawn for the amount due and handed to him.

One by one, the resignations of the Board, with the exception of Luther Clayton, were accepted and H. Montague Bates, Lt. Col. Holman F. Stephens and William A. Jepson were elected as Directors of the Company in their place. The meeting closed with the retiring Directors reserving their claim for fees and expenses for the year ending 31st December 1920.

The Selsey Tramways Company's AGM took place immediately after the Directors' meeting, when a letter was read out apologising for the non-attendance of Lt. Col. H. F. Stephens, Mr. Bates and Mr. Jepson, namely all but Luther Clayton of the proposed new directorate! Gross receipts for the year ending 31st December, 1919 had totalled £5,848 13s 8d, an increase of £638 4s 0d over the previous year. However, expenses had increased by £1,144 16s 0d to £4,793 9s 2d, accounted for by the increased cost of materials and higher wages to the staff. Since December 1910, no less than £4,387 12s 11d had been expended on the Flood Account, all of which had been charged to Revenue. Mitchell remarked that it was with great regret that he had to announce the retirement from the Board of Frank Sanden Street, Edward Heron-Allen, Hubert J. Powell and Sir Sharp Archibald Garland, after which the proposal that Mr. H. Montague Bates, Lieut. Colonel Holman F. Stephens and Mr. William A. Jepson be elected as Directors of the Company was carried.

Thus an important chapter in the history of the Hundred of Manhood & Selsey Tramways Company Limited came to an end. Through thick and thin for over 23 years the affairs of the Company had been looked after most ably by local gentlemen who had the interests of the people of the Manhood Peninsula very much at heart. Only time would tell what the future might hold for the Tramway.

COMPLETELY OFF THE RAILS (1920–1923)

Soon after the arrival of the three ex-LCDR 4-wheel carriages from Messrs. Vickers of Erith, Kent in 1921, Sidlesham *is seen taking on water at Chichester, suggesting that the watering point at Hunston may have temporarily dried up. Like* Wembley, *the locomotive had a home-made wooden casing built around its minimal cab to provide the crews with better protection from the elements.*
COLLECTION STEPHEN GARRETT

At a meeting of the Southdown Motor Services Board in February 1921, Mr. A. D. Mackenzie (Traffic Manager) announced that Messrs. Moore and Fuller had discontinued their 'bus service between Selsey and Chichester after experiencing repeated breakdowns and he had, therefore, 'put one 'bus on this road on trial'. Operating as Southdown's Route No.32, 5 return journeys were operated on weekdays, with 4 on Sundays, each single trip being scheduled to take some 42 minutes. The trial proved to be a success, and from March 1921 the service was included in the Company's timetables.

Under the heading 'Reduced Tramway Fares', the *Chichester Observer* advised on 23rd March 1921:

> By the revised list of fares which came into operation on Monday, the return fare on the Tramway from Chichester to Selsey has been reduced to 1/9d (III Class). Cheap Excursion Tickets, return fare 1/6d will be issued daily on the 2.20pm tram from Chichester and on Sundays on the 11.25am and 2.20pm trams. These cheap tickets will be issued on all trams on Easter Monday.

Perhaps in an effort to counteract 'bus competition, a month later, the same newspaper advised that the Tramway's special Half Day Cheap Return Tickets were to be reduced to 1/- on Thursdays between Chichester and Selsey, passengers having to travel down on the 2.20pm tram, but they could return by any service on the day of issue only. An advert to this effect became a weekly feature of the periodical throughout the summer commencing on 15th June.

On Saturday, 21st May the 6.15pm tram at the start of its journey to the south had just reached the curve a few hundred yards from Chichester station, when the locomotive left the line. It took around two hours before a relief locomotive arrived from Selsey, and after the stranded engine had been 'forced back onto the track and put on a siding', the beleaguered passengers were eventually carried on to their destination.[16]

From 14th May Southdown Motor Services increased the frequency of their 'bus service between Chichester and Selsey to 6 journeys each way on weekdays, with 5 on Sundays, but the latter were reduced back to 4 journeys from 16th July.

The new Board of Directors held their first meeting in London on Thursday, 30th June where the only business dealt with was to set in motion the opening of an account on behalf of the Tramways Company at Lloyd's Bank, Dover. The bank was instructed that all cheques, bills and promissory notes should be honoured whether the account was in credit or overdrawn, provided they were signed by any two of the directors and countersigned by the secretary! A second meeting was called for at the Council Chamber, Chichester on 30th September, but with only Luther Clayton and the secretary present, it had to be abandoned there being no quorum.[17] At the Annual General Meeting, held immediately afterwards, with only one shareholder, Henry Rowe, present, Luther Clayton was voted to the chair. The Directors' Report revealed that the number of passengers travelling on the Tramway in 1920 had fallen by a massive 22,718 compared to 1919, probably owing to omnibus competition.

On 7th December this oddly set up advertisement appeared in the *Chichester Observer*.

> F. AMEY, 42 The Hornet, Chichester
> Appointed Cartage Agent to the
> SELSEY TRAMWAYS
> will call at addresses in Chichester
> as required for parcels etc. for
> conveyance to Selsey, including collection at
> Chichester and delivery at Selsey
> within the ordinary delivery limits.
> Weights not exceeding
> 7lb 14lb 28lb 42lb 56lb 112lb
> 4d   6d   8d   10d   1/-   1/4d
> Orders received at above address.

Hesperus *was acquired in 1912, and is seen here as rebuilt c.1916 in a spot of bother to the south of Chalder in late summer between the years 1921 and 1923. The rail on the left had given way under the locomotive, but luckily all three of the ex-LCDR 4-wheel carriages remained on the track.*
COLONEL STEPHENS RAILWAY MUSEUM & ARCHIVE

Once again, Hesperus *was the engine in steam and she can be seen in the distance running round the three ex-LCDR 4-wheel carriages at Selsey while a family posed for the photographer.*
COLLECTION ROBERT KOSMIDER

COMPLETELY OFF THE RAILS (1920–1923)

Selsey in the process of taking on water from the tank behind the engine shed at Selsey complete with her train of ex-LCDR 4-wheel carriages c.1922.
LENS OF SUTTON

Whereas up until now, most cheap ticket offers were only made available to passengers originating in Chichester, in July 1922 the Tramways Company issued a leaflet stating that, commencing on the 10th of that month, and until the end of September, the 1/- cheap day return fare could be obtained on weekday services leaving Selsey at 11.50am, 1.25pm, 3.05pm and 5.55pm, returning from the city at 2.20pm, 4.20pm, 6.40pm or 8.25pm. On Sundays, outward travel had to be by the 10.35am, 1.40pm, or 5.30pm services, with return by any tram. The summer timetable was to be the last to feature an 'express' tram, although by now it had been reduced to a semi-fast service omitting just Chalder and Ferry Siding in the 'down' direction only, saving passengers just 3 minutes compared to the stopping trams. The full timetable was shown thus:

	Weekdays						Sundays			
	Mixed									
Selsey	8.15	9.55	11.50	1.25	3.05	5.55	7.20	10.35	1.40	5.30	7.10
Ferry Siding	8.21		11.56	1.31	3.11	6.01	7.26	10.41	1.46	5.36	7.16
Sidlesham	8.25		12.00	1.35	3.15	6.05	7.30	10.45	1.50	5.40	7.20
Chalder	8.31		12.06	1.41	3.21	6.11	7.36	10.51	1.56	5.46	7.26
Hunston	8.37		12.12	1.46	3.27	6.17	7.42	10.57	2.02	5.52	7.32
Chichester	8.50	10.40	12.25	2.00	3.40	6.30	7.55	11.10	2.15	6.05	7.45
	Mixed									
Chichester	9.05	10.55	12.40	2.20	4.20	6.40	8.25	11.25	2.20	6.20	8.10
Hunston	9.15		12.50	2.30	4.30	6.50	8.35	11.35	2.30	6.30	8.20
Chalder	9.21		–	2.36	4.36	6.56	8.41	11.41	2.36	6.36	8.26
Sidlesham	9.27		1.00	2.42	4.42	7.02	8.47	11.47	2.42	6.42	8.32
Ferry Siding	9.31		–	2.46	4.46	7.04	8.51	11.51	2.46	6.46	8.36
Selsey	9.40	11.40	1.12	2.55	4.55	7.15	9.00	12.00	2.55	6.55	8.45

During the year the Pike family was returning to South Africa from Selsey, but a few hundred yards short of Chichester station the Tram that they were travelling on came to a sudden standstill and, despite the driver's best efforts, it refused to move. The family didn't have to worry for long as the driver, fireman and conductor/guard each mucked in to carry all of the family's many possessions, including a large tin bath (!) along the track and on to Chichester main line station so that they were able to make the necessary connections for Southampton Docks and their Union Castle ship home.

Tramway staff weren't always so helpful and in an attempt to guarantee a connection with a London-bound train at Chichester, passengers sometimes felt it necessary to have to bribe the driver with a gratuity! On one occasion things went decidedly wrong when a woman gave William Walker, the conductor/guard, a tip after he had assured her that he would see that she made her connection. Unfortunately for the lady, the driver had overheard and seen what had gone on and deliberately dawdled so that that Tram arrived at Chichester too late. When the lady angrily explained to the driver how she had tipped the conductor/guard to ensure her London connection, he had the audacity to tell her "You've oiled the wrong end, madam!"[18]

In accordance with a decision made some time earlier that locally managed railways could 'opt out', the Hundred of Manhood & Selsey Tramways Company (along with the other lines in Holman Stephens' empire of minor railways) was omitted from the Grouping that took place on 1st January 1923, and so it did not become part of the newly-formed Southern Railway.

Owing mainly to 'bus competition, passenger numbers had plummeted from 102,292 in 1919 to 60,203 in 1922, and as if to reinforce the fact that they were here to stay, in January 1923 Southdown Motor Services Ltd leased land at the New Inn, Selsey from the brewers Henty & Constable, on which they built a small garage for their vehicles. Perhaps in an effort to stem this 'bus competition, from the Spring of 1923 regular advertisements promoting the Tramway were

Wembley approaching Golf Club Halt with the 4.30 p.m. tram from Selsey to Chichester on an overcast Whit Monday, 21st May 1923, with the camera-shy 4-compartment first class carriage next to the locomotive. This is the only known photograph showing all four of the ex-LCDR 4-wheel carriages in service together. Was it to improve drainage that the gravel-like ballast had been scooped out from beneath the centre of the sleepers?
LCGB (KEN NUNN COLLECTION)

COMPLETELY OFF THE RAILS (1920–1923)

3rd September 1923 was the darkest day in the Tramways Company's history, when the first train of the day, with Wembley again in charge, left the rails to the north of Golf Club Halt on its way to Chichester. Thankfully, none of the passengers were injured and, seen here beside the train, they were no doubt thanking their lucky stars for their narrow escape.
COLONEL STEPHENS RAILWAY MUSEUM & ARCHIVE

once again placed in the *Chichester Observer*, the first of which appeared on 16th May:

SELSEY TRAMWAY EXCURSIONS

The Management of the Selsey Tramway are providing special facilities for the Whitsuntide weekend excursionists from Chichester. The return fare has been reduced to 1/- with children under 12 half price, and the following will be the services;

Sun: d. Chichester 11.20 2.25 6.20 8.15
        d. Selsey   1.20 5.30 7.10

Mon: d. Chichester 9.15 11.00 12.40 2.20 5.10 6.35 8.25 10.00
        d. Selsey   10.00 11.50 1.25 4.30 5.55 7.20 9.10

It should be noted that this timetable is incomplete, being aimed only at passengers travelling from Chichester, and the 'up' services to connect with the Chichester departure on Sunday at 11.20am and Monday at 9.15am have been omitted. Commencing with the summer of 1923, the Tramway seemed to take on a new lease of life and weekly adverts appeared in the *Chichester Observer* advertising cheap half-day return tickets between Chichester and Selsey, which would sometimes be accompanied by the current timetable in abbreviated form. This was how it appeared on 18th July:

	Weekdays						Sundays			
Up										
Selsey	8.15	9.45	11.40	1.25	3.05	5.30	7.05	10.35	1.20	5.30	7.15
Chichester	8.50	10.20	12.20	2.00	3.40	6.05	7.40	11.10	1.55	6.05	7.50
Down										
Chichester	9.05	10.48	12.35	2.20	4.15	6.15	8.00	11.20	2.20	6.20	8.10
Selsey	9.40	11.28	1.10	2.55	4.50	6.50	8.35	11.55	2.55	6.55	8.45

Perhaps fearing that prospective passengers might prefer the local Southdown 'bus service, the 10.48am ex-Chichester and the 11.40am trams from Selsey, which must have been 'mixed' trams with their longer journey times, were not now marked as such. This may not have been such a good ploy as with any unsuspecting passengers who had endured one of these slow and uncomfortable journeys it would surely have been a case of 'once bitten, twice shy'! It may be opportune to observe how the rival 'bus service compared with that of the Tramway:

	NS	NS	NS		SO	NS	
Selsey (Marine Hotel)	8.00	9.50	11.15	1.30	3.15	5.15	7.05	7.30
Chichester Station	8.45	10.35	12.00	2.15	4.00	6.00	7.50	8.15

	NS	NS	SO	NS		NS	SO	NS
Chichester Station	9.00	10.35	11.35	12.05	2.25	4.25	6.15	6.40	8.33
Selsey (Marine Hotel)	9.45	11.20	12.20	12.50	3.10	5.10	7.00	7.25	9.25

NS: Not on Sundays   SO: Sundays only
The 7.30pm Selsey to Chichester service only operates on Wednesdays, Fridays and Saturdays.
The 8.35pm Chichester to Selsey service operates on Wednesdays, Fridays, Saturdays and Sundays only.

Only the two usual faithful shareholders, George Harding and Edward Fogden, accompanied the chairman (Luther Clayton) and Henry Phillips (secretary) at the Tramways Company's AGM held in Chichester on 29th August. Harding and Fogden each took turns to propose and second the adoption of the Directors' Report and Accounts and the re-election of the retiring directors and auditors.

On the pleasant late summer evening of Sunday, 2nd September, the young C. E. Green, accompanied by his mother, sister and three brothers, was walking along the footpath beside the Tramway between Selsey and Sidlesham when his mother casually mentioned 'One of these days that tram is coming off the line!'[19] That same evening, Frank Horton had been drinking with friends at the Crab & Lobster public house at Sidlesham, and they caught the last tram back to the coast. He later recalled 'Just as we got on the section between Ferry and Selsey there was a terrific jolt and I thought the engine was derailed, but it must have righted itself. The next morning when the first tram came along, I was working in the fields cutting tares. I told my pal to watch as I thought nothing had been done to the line as no one had been working on it. We did not think there would be a tragedy.'[20]

That day the Hudswell Clarke 0–6–0ST locomotive with three carriages left Selsey with the first train of the day punctually at 8.15am with driver Charles Currie Stewart and fireman Herbert 'Dirg' Barnes in the cab. Midway between Selsey Bridge and Ferry the locomotive suddenly dropped

THE SELSEY TRAMWAY

The derailed tram seen from the opposite side.
COLONEL STEPHENS RAILWAY MUSEUM & ARCHIVE

A closer view of the stricken train on that fateful day.
LENS OF SUTTON

The left-hand buffer of the front carriage pushed the coal bunker forward, trapping the fireman, Herbert 'Dirg' Barnes against the boiler backhead, causing him to lose his life. Much of the splintered wood on and around the locomotive came from its home-made wooden cab. Above the word 'THIRD' on the carriage side, it can be seen how part of the partitions between the compartments had been cut away to provide a narrow corridor to ease the guard/conductor's task of issuing tickets en route.
LENS OF SUTTON

between the rails and ran down the low embankment through a fence to the left, dragging the three carriages behind it. The train came to a halt in marshy ground with the front carriage over the embankment a short way; another two feet and the engine would have been in the rife. Although all three carriages were derailed, they thankfully remained upright, but the left-hand buffer of the first pushed the locomotive's bunker forward, trapping the fireman against the boiler backhead. Driver Stewart, after trying to secure the brake, managed to jump from the engine, slightly injuring one leg in the process. According to one of the twenty or so passengers on board,[21] '... the first indication that something had gone wrong was a series of violent bumps, which threw us out of our seats. Had the engine not been checked from going further down the embankment by the marshy nature of the ground, all the coaches might have been dragged over. It was indeed a merciful escape.'

One of the first on the scene was Mr. Charlie Rusbridge who telephoned for the police and soon PCs Pope and Hampshire from Selsey were in attendance, and they were joined shortly afterwards by Doctor A. A. Humphreys who immediately declared that Herbert Barnes had passed away. The escaping steam made it a difficult task to free the unfortunate fireman and it was not until the carriage's buffer had been sawn through that his body, badly scalded, was removed and taken to Selsey Town station at around 1.00pm. None of the passengers were injured and they had to continue their journeys to Chichester by motor car or 'bus.

Unfortunately for the Tramways Company, the accident was reported in the national press, including *The Times*, and the *Daily Mail* (4th September) and The *Daily Mirror* (5th September). The Tramway was closed while the track was put into good repair, and although some trams ran the following day, public services did not resume until Thursday, 6th September. It was with no little difficulty that the locomotive was recovered, along with the three carriages, two of which would later be returned to service.

The four-hour Inquiry into Herbert Barnes' death took place at the Selsey Hotel, close to Selsey Tramway station, at 11.00am on Wednesday, 5th September under the Chichester coroner, J W. Loader Cooper. He first advised that he had communicated with the Inspector of Factories, but he had replied to the effect that the matter was not his province, but was one for the Board of Trade. Even so, the Board of Trade was not represented at the Inquiry. It was explained to the Jury that so far as the question of alleged negligence was concerned, they would have to trace it directly to some particular individual if they found that it played any part in connection with the fatality.

It was the driver of the fated tram that was first called and he confirmed that he had worked with the deceased, who

With most of the stranded passengers having left the scene to make their way to Chichester by road, this view from the rear shows how the train had fallen between the rails. Note the apparent lack of ballast and the poor condition of the sleepers.

COLLECTION PAUL LAMING

Two of the Tramways Company's servants discussing the tragedy, possibly on the following day. Is it just an optical illusion, or had the area beside and between the rails been raked over? The two rear carriages were to remain in service for a further 8½ years, but it is unlikely that the front vehicle, which had its front left-hand buffer sawn off at the scene, ever ran again in passenger service.
COLLECTION PAUL LAMING

was both a driver and fireman on the Tramway, since Easter.[22] On the day in question, they had left Selsey for Chichester at 8.15am. The engine was in good order. They proceeded at ordinary speed until they got to about 300 yards from the scene of the accident, when he shut off steam, as usual, owing to a slight decline, which was a trifle curved at the top. They ran without steam for 300 yards, and the steam was still off when the engine jumped the rails. He at once turned round to put the brake on, but the engine ran down the bank on the left side, dragging the coaches after it. He was knocked into and pinned in the right-hand side of the cab. When he looked round for the deceased, he found that he had been crushed against the centre of the boiler by the buffer of the first coach, which had crushed the coal bunker over. The witness managed to get clear with a slight scald and then tried to get the deceased out, but he was too tightly wedged in. He also tried to shut off the steam which enveloped Barnes, but was unable to do so as the 'cocks' had been torn off. When the crash came, the deceased never spoke, and he was apparently killed at once. The deceased had been pinned up against the open door of the firebox. There was a number of passengers on the Tram at the time, but none was injured to the witness' knowledge. He had had 25 years' experience of locomotives, and had been driving on the Tramway since July. It was the first accident that he had had.

The Coroner: 'What speed were you travelling?' Witness: '16 miles.'
The Coroner: 'Was that the usual speed for that part of the line?' Witness: 'Yes, sir.'
The Coroner: 'Who employed you?' Witness: 'Mr. Stephens, the engineer.'
The Coroner: 'Did Mr. Stephens warn you that the line was in bad condition?'
Witness: 'No, only what we have seen ourselves.'
The Coroner: 'You yourselves have seen the line was not in a very satisfactory condition?'
Neatly side-stepping the question, Stewart replied 'We have always taken great care in coming along it!'

Questioned by Loader Cooper as to the possible cause of the accident, Stewart said that he had since examined the spot, and it looked as though the rails had spread out and the engine had dropped between them.

The Coroner: 'What about the sleepers there? Were they rotten or sound?'
Witness: 'They were not in a bad condition as a whole. One or two might have been bad,' and he then added 'The rail on the right side was thrust away from the sleepers at the spot where the accident happened.'
The Coroner: 'Do you know whether the line was examined daily?' Witness: 'Yes, sir.'
The Coroner: 'Had it been examined that day?' Witness: 'Yes, sir.'
The Coroner: 'By whom?' Witness: 'The foreman platelayer, William Symes.'

On further questioning, the driver said that about three weeks previously he had spoken to Symes about a bad joint at that point in the line as he had found it bumpy, and that the latter had replied that he would attend to the matter. The previous week, Symes had told him that he had put the gauge on and had found it alright. Witness: 'I was quite satisfied with this. I have not made any complaints regarding any other part of the line.' In reply to the Coroner he added 'I do not think the speed, or the engine itself had anything to do with the accident. It was due, in my opinion, to the rails parting from the sleepers.'

Mr. F. Kemp had been chosen as the Foreman of the Jury and he asked 'After that spot had been examined, did you notice any bumping?' Witness: 'Well, we felt an occasional bump and we thought it was out of gauge a bit.'

The Coroner here interposed that it had been suggested to him that he should give directions that the piece of line concerned should remain in exactly the same state as when the accident happened. He had no power to do so, however, and therefore he did not take upon himself the risk of an action. 'The police,' added Loader Cooper, 'were quite anxious about this and telephoned to the Board of Trade.

They suggested that the Board of Trade should do something, but they said that they had no power to do anything at the moment, anyhow.' Continuing, Stewart said he always took great care when passing the spot to turn off steam.

> The Coroner: 'Did you receive any instructions about that from the Engineer or Secretary?'
> Witness: 'No, sir.'
> A Juryman: 'May I ask whether the employees of the Company are in the habit of making complaints to each other instead of to the responsible officials of the line?'
> Witness 'If we felt any swaying in the line, we spoke to the foreman platelayer.'

William Walker of 2 Station Road, Selsey, employed by the Company as a guard on the trams, was next questioned and he advised that at the time of the accident, he was engaged in issuing tickets in the centre coach. He had felt the carriages bumping and suspected that they were off the line. When the train came to a standstill, he went through the carriages to see if any of the passengers were hurt, but there were no complaints. He then got out of the tram and went to the engine. He found the deceased as described, and 'burst away the framework of the cab' to get near him, but found that he was quite dead. 'I have been guard on the Tram for twenty years,' he said, 'and I can control a hand brake in my compartment at the back of the tram. Even if I had been in a position to manipulate my brake at the time, I could not have stopped the engine from going over the bank.' Asked by the Coroner where he got his instructions from respecting his work, he said he received them from the Secretary at the Selsey office. He had not had cause to complain of the line to anybody. During his connection with the Company, the tram had gone off the line once before on the main track about two years ago.[23] This mishap had been due to platelayers engaged in repairing the track not causing the tram to stop, and he admitted that there had been one or two instances before of 'engines jolting off the line' during shunting operations on side lines.

> The Coroner: 'What do you think of the line yourself?'
> Witness: 'It's not my business to say, sir.'
> The Coroner: 'Do you think the line has been sufficiently sound for use?'
> Witness: 'Well I have travelled on it 20 years,' after which he added this ambiguous gem: 'It is just as good now as when I first travelled on it!'

Walker then advised that the foreman ganger walked the line every morning before the tram started out, but he did not know to whom he made his report. Questioned by Mr. Loader Cooper as to his knowledge of the possible cause of the accident, he understandably stated that he could not express an opinion, and could not corroborate the driver's version. After the accident he had gone for help, but he had not been on the scene of the accident up to the previous evening. Perhaps showing his naivety of the subject, the Coroner said it struck him as funny, and possibly might strike the Jury as funny also, that the guard should be unable to advance any reason from his own observation as to the cause of the accident!

Next it was the turn of William Symes of 25 Jesse Road, Southsea who, at the time, was lodging at Sidlesham, to be interrogated. He confirmed that he had held the position of foreman platelayer with the Tramways Company since 15th August, being engaged by Mr. Stephens, the Engineer, by letter. His employment for the past 20 years had been as a platelayer with the Great Western Railway. He had been told to come to Selsey to examine the line and take over the work, his instructions being to examine the line every morning. He was also told to see the Secretary and to meet the Permanent Way Inspector at Chichester who came down every Wednesday from Tonbridge to inspect the line and they had met every week. The Inspector had instructed him to report to the Secretary if ever he had occasion to do so. Symes confirmed 'Every morning I inspect the line, but I have not noticed anything wrong with that particular spot and I have received no complaints respecting it. The spot that the driver had complained about was a quarter of a mile away, and I put a new sleeper in there.'

> The Coroner: 'I think we all understood that he complained to you about this particular spot.'

Driver Charles Stewart was recalled and he reiterated that it was the place where the accident had happened which formed the subject of his report.[24]

Resuming, William Symes remained adamant that the spot to which his attention had been called was further on, and that on the morning of the accident, prior to its occurrence, he had inspected the line as usual and it appeared to be 'alright'. Returning to where the derailment took place, the Coroner asked 'What was the state of the sleepers? Were they good or bad?'

> Symes: 'I can't say they were good. I have seen worse ones!'
> The Coroner: 'Had they become soft and rotten?' Symes, 'Oh no, sir!'
> The Coroner: 'Did you report these sleepers at that particular spot?'
> Symes: 'Not that particular spot, sir. I did elsewhere, as I am constantly restoring them, on the average of 18 a day.'
> The Coroner: 'Will you tell the Jury why you did not report that these sleepers were bad?'
> Symes: 'I did not think they were bad enough to be reported just yet,' and added 'In my opinion the accident was in no way due to the rails. The engine simply jumped them.'

After putting further questions to the foreman platelayer, the Coroner unfairly suggested 'You give me the impression of trying to cover something up. I don't know whether you give the Jury the same impression' (In all fairness, Symes would have been only too aware that the permanent way on the Tramway was not in as good a condition as it might have been, but he would also wish to be seen to be loyal to his employers.) Resuming the questioning, the Coroner asked 'Did you see any marks of the wheels of the engine inside the rails?'

> Symes: 'No sir, I didn't.'
> The Coroner: 'What have you done with those sleepers?', referring to those at the accident site.
> Symes: 'They are up on the track, sir.'
> The Coroner: 'At the present moment?' Symes: 'Yes, sir.'
> The Coroner: 'Nothing in the accident has been burnt?'
> Symes: 'No sir. If anything has been burnt, it has been unknown to me.'

The Coroner: 'Do you consider the sleepers now throughout the line in a satisfactory condition?'

Symes: 'No sir, but we have some good sleepers in places, and we are putting new ones in.'

In reply to a juryman, the witness said that it was his duty to walk from Chalder to Selsey every morning, starting at six, the rest of the line being covered by another man. Another juryman asked if he would be surprized to learn that at a spot 200 yards away from the scene of the accident, a sleeper could be lifted out. Symes admitted that there might be some spikes which were not fastened tightly, but that whenever he found one loose, he knocked it down. The same juryman commented that the position of the right rail after the accident did not coincide with the witness' opinion of the accident, but with that of the driver. Asked to explain this, Symes answered 'I can't answer that question, sir.' Replying to Mr. R. E. Morris Bew, solicitor of Chichester who was representing the Tramways Company, Symes stated that, in his opinion, the line was safe. He had been on the Tram in question, and if he had thought anything was the matter, he would have reported it.

Doctor A. A. Humphreys of Selsey, who, it will be remembered, had attended the scene of the accident, advised that Herbert Barnes, thankfully, must have been almost instantaneously killed. He was in a terrible state, having sustained a severe blow over the heart, and he had been pierced through the back by some implement in the cab, in addition to having bad scalds.

Holman Stephens told those present that he was a Lieutenant-Colonel in the R.E. Reserves and a member of the Institute of Civil Engineers and, prior to giving evidence, he expressed the deep regret of the Tramways Company at what had transpired, and added that every attention would be shown to the widow in the matter of funeral expenses, etc. Proceeding, he explained how the Company had obtained a Light Railway Order 'some time ago', in connection with a project for extending the line to Itchenor, but that the scheme had not been put into operation and that the Order had expired. 'I am responsible for 12 different lines all over the country,' he said, 'so I have to delegate my duties in different localities to assistants. I have not been down to the Selsey line for about 18 months. Between 1920 and 1923 we have sent down over 4,000 sleepers. We have a limited axle load and also a speed limit of 15 or 16 miles per hour. We do not need a full-sized sleeper for the line, so we use second-hand sleepers as is the usual practice in railways of this sort. The rails are the original ones.'

Questioned by Loader Cooper as to the age of the engine, Stephens said he thought that it was constructed in 1908, but the Coroner said that he had been told that she was 70 years old![25] 'That is absurd!' snapped Stephens, and with regard to the cause of the accident he said 'The only suggestion I can advance is that there might have been an obstruction of some kind on the line. From my own experience – I have driven for 18 months – I am able to say it is not always possible for drivers to see obstructions.'

The last Company employee to be questioned was the Tramway's Secretary and Manager, Henry Phillips of 'Selhurst', Manor Road, Selsey, who advised that the whole of the locomotive etc. department was under the supervision of the Engineer, who was responsible for the permanent way. Phillips said that he had instructed Symes to forward weekly reports in writing and to report to him immediately, personally, or by telephone, in cases of emergency. He had never received any report concerning the piece of line where the fatality occurred. He had also issued instructions to drivers not to exceed 12 miles per hour, to reduce speed at curves, and to proceed at 5 miles per hour over level crossings. (He wasn't passing the buck, was he?) Phillips did, however, confirm that he had found Symes to be efficient.

Finally, PC Pope told of how he had examined the scene of the accident at 9.15am, and found that from the spot where the engine left the rails to where it came to a rest was 126 feet. From the place where it first became derailed to where it left the top of the embankment was 36 feet. Along this 36 feet, the rails on both sides were lying on their sides, and on the left-hand side, three whole lengths of rail were down. The 'nails' which held the sleeper to the rail were sufficiently withdrawn to allow the flange of the rail to come above the 'dog'. He had found marks inside the rails, indicating that the engine had dropped inside, the rails being turned over. The sleepers were bad, and he did not see one completely sound one; they were rotting in one part or another. Replying to a juryman, the policeman said there was a mark indicating where, apparently, the engine had left the rails practically at the juncture of two rails. Two bolts were missing, but it looked as if the engine had torn them out. Answering Mr. Bew, the witness said that the right-hand wheels of the coaches were on the inside of the rail, and the left-hand ones on the outside.

After deliberating in private, the Jury returned the verdict of 'Accidental Death', but with the addition of an expression of opinion to the effect that the Chief Engineer of the Tramways Company (Holman Stephens) was indirectly to blame as there was evidence of neglect in the upkeep of the line.[26] Herbert Barnes' funeral took place the following afternoon.

As a temporary replacement for the late Herbert Barnes, a Mr. E. G. Vine, was taken on for two weeks until a new man was engaged. Normally working for Mr. F. Slade, a threshing contractor of Pound Farm, Chichester, Mr. Vine was well acquainted with steam road locomotives, traction and ploughing engines.[27]

Not being happy with the outcome of the Inquiry into fireman Barnes' death, Selsey Parish Council wrote to the Board of Trade on 17th September demanding a Public Enquiry. They were to be disappointed when the Board's E. W. Rowntree replied '... I am directed by the Minister of Transport to state that the undertaking in question is not authorised by statute and the Minister has no power to hold an enquiry into the causes of the accident...'

COMPLETELY OFF THE RAILS (1920–1923)

Notes

1. Authorisation for 500 sleepers (rather than 300) to be purchased 'as and when required' was given at the Directors' Meeting on 8.1.1920.
2. Two parcels of land on either side of the Tramway to the east of Selsey Bridge had been acquired by the Company on 8.4.1919 with permission to build carriage and/or engine sheds there.
3. R. L. Thornton later verbally expressed himself willing to make an offer, but not if it was a question of bidding.
4. This, of course, was not the case.
5. To get a precise average the pence here, and on the following three lines, have been worked out to two decimal points.
6. Board of Directors' Minute Book 24.3.1920 and 30.9.1921.
7. 'C.S.' is mistaken here. Pagham Harbour had been reclaimed in 1876 and in 1897 when the Tramway opened. the area was pasture land.
8. While in Chichester Mr. Ferguson purchased a copy of the March edition of the City's *ABC Railway Guide* that included the Tramway's timetable for that month.
9. Southdown Motor Services Ltd. Board Meeting 20.5.1920.
10. *Chichester Observer*, Wednesday, 1.9.1920.
11. Holman Stephens was similarly unhappy providing information on the East Kent Light Railways replying that '…they are a non-controlled line with, of course, no money to spend from Public Funds on this sort of thing…It hardly seems fair that non-controlled companies should not be recompensed for obtaining the information desired by your authorities. It seems hardly a "British" proceeding…'
12. Why these words should have been crossed out by hand on the original typed letter is unclear as the sentence does not make grammatical sense without them.
13. As we are well aware, the Tramway was never authorised!
14. The remaining 2.2% would be accounted for by receipts from the rental of the Company's sidings and cottages, etc.
15. Note how the number of staff had fallen from 22 in 1918 to 18, although this figure may have not included the Manager/Secretary, Henry Phillips.
16. *Chichester Observer*, Wednesday, 25.5.1921.
17. The next two Directors' Meetings scheduled for 1.12.1922 and 29.8.1923 in Chichester also had to be abandoned as only Luther Clayton and Henry Phillips attended.
18. *Going off the Rails – the Country Railway in West Sussex* by Bill Gage, Michael Harris and Tony Sullivan, published by West Sussex County Council, 1997.
19. Mr. C. E. Green interviewed by David Bathurst in *The Selsey Tram* published by Phillimore, 1992.
20. *Chichester Post*, Saturday, 23.4.1955.
21. Interviewed by a reporter from the *Chichester Observer*, published on Wednesday, 5.9.1923.
22. Herbert Barnes, a married man aged 41 years, of The Row, Albion Road, Selsey, had worked for the Tramways Company for many years, but had quit their service for a time, rejoining that Spring.
23. Was William Walker referring to the 'only' other derailment as that which occurred outside Chichester station on 21.5.1921? He gives the impression of not telling the truth as a photograph of *Hesperus* exists showing that locomotive (with the same 3 carriages involved in this fatal accident) off the rails on his 'patch' to the south of Chalder station in what must be the summer of 1921, 1922 or 1923. Then there was the derailment at Sidlesham on 12.2.1910…
24. With no mile posts provided on the Tramway at any time, it would have been easy for a genuine mistake to have been made regarding any particular location.
25. The locomotive had been built by Messrs. Hudswell Clarke in 1903 and it had been acquired by the Tramways Company in 1919.
26. Details of the hearing have been compiled from reports in the *Sussex Daily News*, Thursday, 6.9.1923 and the *Chichester Observer*, Wednesday, 12.9.1923.
27. *The Selsey Tramways* by Edward C. Griffith, published by the author, 1974.

This enamel sign was displayed on the side of a building in Selsey village in an attempt to steer prospective passengers away from the competing 'bus service. The Tramways Co. had also boasted that its route was 'the safest', but this claim was in doubt following the tragic events of 3rd September 1923.
COLONEL STEPHENS RAILWAY MUSEUM & ARCHIVE

Ministry of Transport.

RAILWAYS CONSTRUCTION FACILITIES ACT, 1864.

THE WEST SUSSEX RAILWAY CERTIFICATE 1923.

Certificate of the Minister of Transport for the construction of the Railway.

Preamble.

Whereas the Hundred of Manhood and Selsey Tramways Company Limited hereinafter called the Selsey Company have contracted for the purchase of the lands and hereditaments required for the railway and the works connected therewith, and have complied with the requirements of the Railways Construction Facilities Act, 1864, and have constructed the railway, and are desirous that this Certificate should be issued.

Now, therefore, the Minister of Transport does by this Certificate in pursuance of the Railways Construction Facilities Act, 1864, and of the Railways (Powers and Construction) Acts, 1864, Amendment Act, 1870, and by virtue and in exercise of the powers thereby in him vested, and of every other power enabling him in this behalf, certify as follows :—

Short Title.

1. This Certificate may be cited as The West Sussex Railway Certificate, 1923.

Interpretation.

2. In this Certificate " The Railway " shall mean the railway by this Certificate authorised, or any part thereof, and " The Company " shall mean the Company incorporated by this Certificate.

Incorporation of Railways Act, 1867.

3. Section 21 of the Companies Clauses Act, 1863 shall, for the purposes of this Certificate, be read and have effect as provided with respect to a special Act by section 27 of the Railway Companies Act, 1867, and sections 23 to 26 inclusive of the last-mentioned Act, shall be incorporated in this Certificate, and shall apply to Loan Capital in like manner as if this Certificate were a Special Act.

Incorporation of the Company.

4. The persons in this Certificate named as the first Directors of the Company, and all other persons who shall hereafter subscribe to the Company and their respective executors, administrators, successors, and assigns are hereby united into a Company for the purpose of making, working and maintaining the railway and works by this Certificate authorised, and for the purposes of this Certificate, and for those purposes

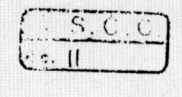

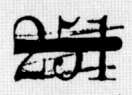

CHAPTER SIX

A CHANGE OF NAME
(1923–1924)

PERHAPS to give the Tramways Company some form of legality, in November 1923 application was made to the Minister of Transport for a Certificate under the Railways Construction Facilities Act of 1864, to incorporate a Company with powers to 'make, repair, maintain and work a Railway, 7 miles 4 furlongs or thereabouts in length, between Chichester and Selsey, all in the County of Sussex on the lands of the Hundred of Manhood and Selsey Tramways Company Limited'. This Act had been passed to cheapen applications for powers where compulsory purchase of land was not necessary, but it had not been used on many occasions.[1] It will be remembered that the Selsey Tramway had been authorised as a light railway under the West Sussex Light Railway Order of 1915, but owing to the War, these powers had been allowed to lapse, and it had been found that the cheapest way of reviving them was to use the little-used Railway Construction Facilities Act. Copies of the Draft Certificate could be obtained from Holman Stephens (as agent for the promoters) at 16 Devonshire Square, London, EC on payment of 6d, plus 2d postage, and any persons desirous of making any representations to the Minister of Transport, or wishing to bring before him any objection to the application, had to do so in writing on or before 1st January 1924. The Capital of the West Sussex Railway Company was to be £45,000 made up of 45,000 shares at £1 each and the first directors were named as Lt. Col. Holman Fred Stephens, William Alban Jepson, Henry Montague Bates and Luther Clayton, each of whom had to be in possession, in his own right, of not less than 50 shares. From time to time, the number of directors could be reduced to two as a minimum. The Act, most importantly, would also enable the West Sussex Railway and the Southern Railway 'from time to time to enter into contracts or arrangements' with each other.

Later that month, the *West Sussex Gazette* explained:

> '... From the point of view of public interest, apart from Company formalities, it is understood that what it is sought to do is to give the present line between Chichester and Selsey the legal standing of a "railway" as distinct from a "tramway". If the application is granted, an effect will be that the line will come under the scope of the Ministry of Transport which as a "tramway" it does not and before the granting of the application, the Ministry would have powers to inspect the line and make such regulations as they thought fit. It is not anticipated, however, that the granting of the application will involve other than minor changes in the working of the line.'

The first to write to the Ministry of Transport was Chichester's Town Clerk on 10th December where he pointed out that

> 1) There is an Agreement existing between the Mayor, Aldermen and Citizens of the city of Chichester and the Hundred of Manhood & Selsey Tramway (*sic*) Company Ltd., dated 22nd July 1897 relating to a moveable bridge across the Chichester Canal which belongs to the Corporation of this City, and it is desired that the proposed certificate should be granted subject to the terms of the said Agreement as regards such bridge.
>
> 2) With respect to the highways of Stockbridge, (in the parish of Donnington) Hunston and Ferry, (in the parish of Selsey) proposed to be crossed on the level, the Corporation are strongly of opinion in the interest not only of the citizens, but of the public at large, that such crossings (especially the one at Stockbridge which is close to the City boundary) should be provided with gates at each side of the road across the Line, and a man in constant attendance to look after such crossings. In view of the increasing passenger traffic on the roads, the Corporation consider these crossings left as they are at present open and to take care of themselves, are a danger to the public and one in which, these days, ought not to be tolerated.
>
> 3) The rights of the Corporation to carry water pipes and sewers along the public roads under the said public level crossings should be reserved and any necessary provisions for the protection of the pipes at present laid under the crossings should be made.
>
> 4) There is at the present time a public footpath which is crossed by the existing Tramway on the level through private grounds at the end of Terminus Road near the railway station. It is understood that eventually this road will be carried through into Westgate and in the event of this being done, the Corporation ask that provisions should be made for the Company erecting and maintaining gates and a man to look after them at this point and that no opposition or objection be allowed to be taken when the time comes for such improvement.'

That same day, some 48 property owners and residents sent a petition to the Westhampnett Rural District Council in which they urged very strongly that representation should be made to the Minister that measures should be insisted on for the protection and preservation of Stockbridge level crossing, in view of the constantly increasing traffic. They claimed that the state of the crossing constituted a public danger, which should long ago have stopped, and they also hoped that such measures would do away with 'the present intolerable nuisance' of the long whistling of the engines. Upon receipt of the petition, W. D. Rassell, the Clerk of the Council, wrote to the Ministry of Transport on 20th December, embracing not only Stockbridge crossing, but those at Hunston and Ferry as well. It was also asked that the Company should 'maintain and repair the portions of road for which they are responsible at each of the level crossings within the Rural District of Westhampnett with a similar class of material to that used by the Local Authority in maintaining and repairing the roads adjoining the said level crossings' and 'that all work erected or executed by the Company in connection with the level crossings or superstructure of bridges affecting public roads under the control of the Rural District of Westhampnett should be carried out to the reasonable satisfaction of the Surveyor of Highways for the time being of the said Council'.

A copy of this last letter had been sent to Holman Stephens who replied from his Tonbridge office four days later that they hoped that they should 'be able to satisfy your Council'. He explained that the Certificate gave the Ministry of Transport power to order gates at any time, and he was sure that it would be 'much better for all concerned if

113

this position is regularised, and instead of being a Tramway the line becomes a Railway, or Light Railway. It seems to me to be better for the public and better for the Company'.

At an Extraordinary General Meeting of the Hundred of Manhood & Selsey Tramways Company held in the Committee Room, Council House, Chichester on 17th December, the secretary submitted to the meeting proxy forms duly completed by the non-attending directors Henry Montague Bates and William Alban Jepson along with W. H. Austen from the Salford Terrace office, Tonbridge, each appointing Lt. Col. H. F. Stephens (the chairman) as his proxy to act at the meeting. Following a brief explanation by the Colonel as to the purposes of the West Sussex Railway Certificate, it was resolved 'That the West Sussex Railway Certificate, 1923, be approved by the Hundred of Manhood & Selsey Tramways Company Limited, and that the Directors of the Company be hereby empowered to make such arrangements for carrying out the Powers, if granted by the Certificate, as they may think fit.' It was also unanimously resolved 'That the following Article be substituted for Article 78 of the Articles of Association that is to say 78. The General Meetings of the Company shall be held in such place in the City of Chichester or in London as may from time to time be determined by the Directors'.[2]

Sidlesham Parish Council were the next to write to the Ministry of Transport when, on 29th December, they requested that it enforced the conditions of the agreement which the Tramway Company made as to the maintenance of the accommodation road leading to Chalder station under which the Company agreed to provide and carry to the station the materials for the purpose of keeping the road in repair that had not been done for several years.

With the Draft Certificate from the Ministry of Transport in front of them, the Highway Committee of the Rural District Council met on Friday, 4th January 1924. The chairman, Rev. W. J. H. Newman, pointed out that there had always been a danger, particularly at the Stockbridge level crossing, that there was no means of signalling the approach of trains. He believed that gates had originally been provided, but that they had rotted away and had not been replaced.[3] He would also like to see gates provided at Mill Pond Road, and suggested that the driver could get out and open them! (Laughter!) W. D. Rassell explained that under the terms originally granted to the Hundred of Manhood & Selsey Tramways Company, they were responsible for the repair of the highway within their metals and for 7ft on either side. They had been repaired from time to time under the instruction of the local manager, but they had not given satisfaction and the Westhampnett Rural District Council's surveyor had been in communication with the Company, and they had asked him to undertake the work and charge it to them. At present he wondered whether anything positive would be done with the passing of the Act, beyond the passing of resolutions! A. C. Harris referred to the proposal in the Surveyor's monthly report that the consideration of the repair of the crossings should be deferred in view of the formation of the new Company, but suggested that this should be deleted. He added 'People coming along there not knowing of the state of the crossing were almost jumped out of their cars', and he moved that the Highway Surveyor be instructed to see that the repairs at the crossings were done forthwith, at the expense of the Tramways Company. On being put to the vote, the motion was carried.

Eventually, on 12th February Holman Stephens wrote to the Town Clerk at Chichester advising that the promoters of the West Sussex Railway Certificate 1923 were desired by the Minister of Transport, in order to avoid, if possible, the necessity of an enquiry in London, in this case, to enter into communication with the objecting Local Authorities with a view to a settlement of their objections if it could be arranged. With regard to the moveable bridge across the Chichester Canal, Stephens advised that the promoters believed that 'it is intended to fill in, and pipe (in fact, the work is at present in progress) at least one of the road bridges between the moveable bridge and the sea, in which case, it is submitted, that the moveable bridge at present, is not required. Should this not be so, there will be no objection, however, to the agreement of the 22nd July 1897 being referred to in the Certificate.' He did, however, confirm that the Company would undertake to make the bridge moveable again, should the filled-in bridge be restored to its present moveable condition, at any time.[4]

Regarding the level crossing at Stockbridge, the Colonel suggested that it 'appears to be outside the jurisdiction of the Corporation of Chichester, but their observations are, obviously, entitled to respect in nearness of the crossing to the city Boundary'. He continued 'It should be pointed out that the crossing will be inspected by an Inspecting Officer of Railways, who will decide whether the proposed cattle guards should be replaced by gates and will also decide the speed at which trains are to be allowed to cross the road. In some cases a speed as low as 4mph is enforced in certain parts of the country. It should also be pointed out that if the traffic increases, the Ministry of Transport, on the representation of a Local Authority, or otherwise can, at any time, cause the substitution of gates for cattle guards or even open crossings.' Stephens confirmed that the right for the Corporation to carry water pipes and sewers under the crossings would certainly be preserved, but in regard to paragraph(4), the matter would be for future consideration as the work in question was not already in being.

Two days later, Stephens sent similar letters to Sidlesham Parish Council and the Westhampnett Rural District Council. In the former's letter, referring to the road at Chalder station, he advised that the promoters were of the opinion that the Agreement was between the Dean and Chapter of Chichester, the Ecclesiastical Commissioners and the Tramway Company, and that it did not appear to be within the purview of the Sidlesham Parish Council. He confirmed that the £2 per annum, payable to Nash's charity for the right of way over the private road, had been and would be duly paid. In his letter to the Westhampnett Rural District Council he further explained that the repair of the level crossings was under consideration, and it was suggested

A CHANGE OF NAME (1923–1924)

that the repairs should be sub-let to the Council at a reasonable price, thus following the practices carried out by many other Light Railway Companies. As regards Mill Pond Road in the parish of Sidlesham, he understood that it might well be 'stopped up and dis-mained' with the traffic being diverted to the road at present crossing the Tramway at Sidlesham station, thus saving considerable expense to the Council. Hardly allaying the fears of the councillors, in conclusion the Colonel wrote '... In reference to the general observations, I am desired to say it is within the knowledge of the Promoters, and to the Ministry of Transport, that no more accidents have occurred at any crossings on this line, than have occurred at crossings in other parts of the country worked by similar undertakings.'

On Tuesday, 11th March 1924 a new era dawned for the Selsey Tramway when a single 'rail motor' entered service working the afternoon timetable. The *Daily Mail & Evening News* dated 13th March entertainingly (if not completely accurately) reported:

MOTOR CARS TO RUN ON COUNTRY LINE

Chichester, Wednesday

The 'Clicketty Click' or the 'Bumpity Bump', as the old fashioned tramway between Chichester and Selsey has been described is, if its proprietors have their way, to blossom forth as the West Sussex Railway, dropping its title of 'The Hundred of Manhood & Selsey Tramway'.

Yesterday the officials successfully experimented with a new type of railway carriage, the ubiquitous Ford car, provided with wheels to run on rails.[5] Orders have been placed for additional cars.

It is really a hedgerow railway, for the promoters had to place their line wherever the farmers would permit, and they were driven to the sides of the meadows through which they wished to pass. This railway of 8 miles has 8 stations, but only two station masters, one at each end. The other six stations look after themselves. 'We do the 8 miles in 35 minutes, and with our new motor vehicles, expect to do it in 9 minutes less.

During March and April an advertisement appeared in the *Chichester Observer* promoting weekday Cheap Half Day Tickets from Chichester to Selsey at 1/- return on the 2.20pm tram, with the return journey available by any service. In May, June and July the offer was extended to the trams leaving at 11.10am, 12.40pm and 2.20pm on weekdays, on Sundays at 10.00am, 11.30am and 2.20pm. It was further amended in July, August and September to weekday departures from Chichester at 9.50am, 11.45am, 1.40pm and 3.10pm, together with the 9.50am, 11.25am and 2.00pm trams on Sundays. Finally, during October and November the advert only mentioned the 11.50am and 2.00pm trams from Chichester, with no mention of Sundays.

As if to reinforce the concerns of the local Councils that the road crossings should be protected by gates, on Saturday, 20th April 'the motor tram from Chichester was passing over

It wasn't a Ford railmotor that entered service on the Selsey Tramway eventually in March 1924, but a single Wolseley Siddeley unit, but the experiment proved successful enough for a 40-seat Ford to enter service in the autumn of that year. The Chichester Observer *published this photograph on Wednesday, 5th September, showing the brand new railmotor posing beside* Ringing Rock *with her train of ex-LCDR 4-wheel carriages at Selsey station.*
COLONEL STEPHENS RAILWAY MUSEUM & ARCHIVE

Ferry crossing when a motor car...came into collision with it. The back part of the motor car was badly smashed, and the motor tram and a goods coach (sic) were derailed and the axle of the motor tram was bent. A considerable time elapsed before a new axle could be substituted and the tram could be put on the rails again, and was able to proceed to Selsey.'[6]

Much correspondence regarding the West Sussex Railway Certificate passed between the local authorities concerned, Holman Stephens and the Ministry of Transport, but to no avail, and a Public Enquiry was held at the Council Chamber, Chichester on Wednesday, 30th April which was conducted by Major C. Hall of the Ministry of Transport and Mr. A. D. Erskine, an officer of the Ministry. The Tramways Company was represented by Holman Stephens with W. D. Rassell and J. W. Loader Cooper for the Westhampnett and Chichester Councils respectively. Stating that road traffic over the Tramway crossings had more than doubled 'in recent years', reference was made by Rassell to a census of traffic taken during seven days the previous August which showed that the total number of vehicles travelling backwards and forwards between Chichester and Selsey was 3,840 motors of various sorts, 365 horse-drawn vehicles and 2,337 'push' bicycles. Twenty 'buses were running daily on the Selsey road, with a similar number serving The Witterings. As to the former gates at Stockbridge having 'been allowed to disappear' without objection from the local authorities, there was no comparison between the traffic then and the present day traffic. The Inspector pointed out that the Ministry would make an inspection before the Certificate was granted, and that care would be taken to impose such conditions as they considered essential for the safety of the public, without necessarily embodying them in the Certificate. Local authorities could be asked to be represented at the inspection. Called for the Company, M. T. Hughes expressed the opinion that the difficulty would best be met by the trams or railmotors using the line pulling up just before they reached the crossings and making sure that it was safe to go over before they did so, which the Inspector confirmed was a good deal employed in America. After the meeting had closed, the two Ministry of Transport representatives visited the Tramway crossings in question.[7]

That same day, at a Special Meeting of Directors in Chichester, it was resolved to issue the remaining unissued £800 of the £5,000 'B' Debenture issue to Lt. Col. H. F. Stephens, against £800 cash already received from him. 'B' Debentures nos. 169–200 inclusive, each for £25, were thereupon sealed and signed and handed to the secretary for registration.

At the Westhampnett Rural District Council's meeting on Friday, 23rd May the Clerk reminded those present that in the draft of the West Sussex Railway Certificate, whilst there was a Clause providing for the repair of the roadway by the Tramways Company at the level crossings, it did not include 'the provision of gates and competent attendance' which the Council had asked for. 'The Ministry,' the clerk admitted, 'do not seem disposed to vary their decision on the question raised by the Council as to compulsory gates at level crossings,' and this proved to be the case. The Certificate specified that

(A) Where a railway or road is fenced such cattle-guards or other suitable contrivances shall be constructed at the sides of the road and so maintained as to prevent cattle or horses on the road from entering the railway;

(B) At each of two points one two hundred yards along the railway in one direction from the level crossing and the other two hundred yards along the railway in the other direction from the level crossing there shalt be erected and maintained a white post standing five feet above the ground and bearing upon it and so as to be plainly legible by the driver of an engine approaching a figure indicating the number of miles per hour which is fixed under the provision of this Order as the maximum rate of speed of a train or engine approaching and within a distance of two hundred yards from the level crossing;

(C) At points fifty yards or thereabouts along the road from the point of crossing it in each direction and such other points instead thereof or in addition thereto as the Minister of Transport may direct there shall be erected and maintained by the Company a notice board cautioning the public to beware of the trains.

Section 17 of the Certificate, however, did state that 'At any time after the completion of the railway, the Ministry may require the Company to maintain and erect gates across the railway at each side of the road'. One cannot help wondering why the onus to provide gates should fall on the Railway Company – it was hardly its fault that road traffic had increased – and if the local authorities thought that gates were that necessary, couldn't they have erected and manned them at their own expense? In due course 10mph restriction posts were placed alongside the Tramway either side of the level crossings at Stockbridge, Hunston and Ferry, along with new 'BEWARE OF THE TRAIN' signs beside the relevant roads. As an extra safeguard after dark, steam locomotive crews would open the firebox door, thus making a glow across the road.

Concerned about the number of debts owed to the Tramways Company for an unreasonable amount of time, Holman Stephens wrote from his Tonbridge office to Messrs. Raper & Co. (solicitors) at 55 South Street, Chichester on 26th May asking 'Could you kindly give me the name of someone in Chichester who could collect small outstandings for this Company? The outstandings have been allowed to go to a greater extent than is reasonable.' Court action was later taken to clear some of these debts in a few cases.

Following the resolution of 17th December 1923 the Company's Ordinary Annual General Meeting was held in London at the Charing Cross Hotel on Wednesday, 11th June with Holman Stephens (Chairman), Luther Clayton, Colonel A. Hacking and F. Montague Bates in attendance. Needless to say, being so far from west Sussex it was impossible for the two loyal shareholders, George Harding and Edward Fogden, to attend the meeting, and they would not be present at any other meetings in the future. Another link with the past was severed when Mr. E. M. Worsford of Dover replaced Messrs. Edmonds, Clover and Ackery as auditor, his fee being reduced from their current 30 guineas plus out-of-pocket expenses to just 5 guineas per annum.

A CHANGE OF NAME (1923–1924)

By the beginning of July 1924 a new Ford rail motor had entered service and the Tramway's timetables from that month onwards were headed 'Motor Cars – One class only'. Although not advertised as such, there was still one steam-hauled morning 'mixed' trip from Selsey to Chichester and return every weekday and, with the railmotor being somewhat temperamental and only having 40 seats available, in practice conventional locomotives and carriages would have still worked a good deal of the services. All journey times had been reduced by 5 minutes to half an hour and a further note advised 'All trains call at Selsey Golf Links Platform when required for passengers using the links'. This was the complete timetable:

	Weekdays									*Sundays*				
Selsey	7.50	9.10	10.40	1.00	2.25	3.50	5.15	6.35	7.55	9.00	10.35	1.20	5.45	7.15
Ferry	7.56	9.16		1.06	2.31	3.56	5.21	6.41	8.01	9.06	10.41	1.26	5.51	7.21
Sidlesham	8.00	9.20		1.10	2.35	4.00	5.25	6.45	8.05	9.10	10.45	1.30	5.55	7.25
Chalder	8.05	9.25		1.15	2.40	4.05	5.30	6.50	8.10	9.15	10.50	1.35	6.00	7.30
Hunston	8.10	9.30		1.20	2.45	4.10	5.35	6.55	8.15	9.20	10.55	1.40	6.05	7.35
Chichester	8.20	9.40	11.20	1.30	2.55	4.20	5.45	7.05	8.25	9.30	11.05	1.50	6.15	7.45
Chichester	8.30	9.50	11.45	1.40	3.10	4.35	5.55	7.15	8.35	9.50	11.25	2.00	6.25	8.10
Hunston	8.38	9.58		1.48	3.18	4.43	6.03	7.23	8.43	9.58	11.33	2.08	6.33	8.18
Chalder	8.43	10.03		1.53	3.23	4.48	6.08	7.28	8.48	10.03	11.38	2.13	6.38	8.23
Sidlesham	8.48	10.08		1.58	3.28	4.53	6.13	7.33	8.53	10.08	11.43	2.18	6.43	8.28
Ferry	8.52	10.12		2.02	3.32	4.57	6.17	7.37	8.57	10.12	11.47	2.22	6.47	8.32
Selsey	9.00	10.20	12.25	2.10	3.40	5.05	6.25	7.45	9.05	10.20	11.55	2.30	6.55	8.40

'New Tram Selsey'. Shortly after entering service, and looking very smart, the Ford railmotor is seen here heading south across the Tramway embankment towards Ferry.
LENS OF SUTTON

The West Sussex Railway Company wasted no time in producing this enamel 'Public not to Trespass' sign dated July 1924 as the WSR Certificate was only issued on the 15th of that month.
COLONEL STEPHENS RAILWAY MUSEUM & ARCHIVE

In contrast, commencing on 10th July, Southdown Motor Services ran no less than 12 return weekday services on the Selsey road and from the beginning of August the frequency was increased from 9 to 10 each way on Sundays, although since the previous October the single journey time had been increased to 50 minutes.

On 1st August, the 'A' Debentures that had been extended five years previously became due for repayment, but only some of these were repaid. However, the holders of 'B' Debentures were not informed that some of the 'A' Debentures were being held as still in existence. Later that month a Post Office telephone was installed at Selsey station, its number being Selsey 59.[8]

It was during August that Holman Stephens persuaded one of the Tramway's gangers, Edward ('Teddy') Skinner, to move north to Clay Cross in Derbyshire, his job being to ensure that the Colonel's latest venture, the Ashover Light Railway, was in order for its official inspection that eventually took place on 31st March 1925. He was appointed foreman ganger and remained with the Ashover Company until he retired in December 1945.[9]

Apparently unaware that the West Railway Certificate (Statutory Rule and Order 1924, No. 935) had been issued by the Ministry of Transport on 15th July, after having a 'dig' at the Southern Railway's unpopular current timetable, the *Chichester Observer* wrote on 5th September:

> 'If Chichester station ought to be made more up-to-date,[10] what can be said with regard to the Tramway from Chichester to Selsey? For years it has been the subject of humorous comment by local residents and visitors alike and Press referees have given it such undignified names as "the Clicketty-Clack", "the blackberry line" and so on. To start on a journey from either end was by no means to feel sure that you would reach your destination and "little mishaps" sometimes happened which made the timetable far less reliable than anything which could be complained of in connection with the new "service" on the Southern Railway. Yet it cannot be denied that the line has fulfilled a decidedly useful purpose for a good many years, and still does so, particularly now that Ford motors have been introduced in place of the old system of travel.
>
> 'But what are the possibilities? It is common knowledge that the Selsey Tramways Co. have been seeking new powers from Parliament under the title of the "West Sussex Railway". A local authority through whose district the line passes recently received notification from the Ministry of Transport of the terms of the order which they proposed to authorise. The effect of the order will be to give the undertaking the full status of a railway, and the question which is interesting many people is what use the Company propose making of the order. There are plenty of possibilities. Perhaps an extension of the line such as was contemplated in pre-war days! Perhaps the disposal of the undertaking to the Southern Railway, with the possible establishment of a direct service between London and Selsey! A glance at a map makes it all look extremely simple to effect an extension of the Brighton line to the Selsey line at Hunston.
>
> 'But these things are purely conjectural! We gather that the Company's new powers have not yet been fully sanctioned by Parliament, and the use which may be made of them is therefore very much in the air. It is certain, however, that the time is ripe for railway development in the Hundred and Manhood of Selsey, where there is considerable growth everywhere, more especially in coastal places. The 'bus services are not losing their opportunity, and a step forward on the part of the rail services in the direction of improving the grass-grown track and giving it something approaching the status of a railway, would undoubtedly be an aid to the development which is otherwise going on in every direction.'

Although shown here outside Chichester Cathedral on the long coastal service to Brighton via Littlehampton and Worthing, this was the type of 'bus that Southdown Motor Services Ltd. were operating between Chichester and Selsey in 1924. Rather than a standard gearbox, the Tilling-Stevens TS3A chassis featured a petrol-electric transmission, controlled by two levers on each side of the steering column, but whereas it was claimed that they were easier to drive, the extra weight of the dynamo and electric motor made their performance somewhat sluggish. The Tilling bodies carried 27 passengers on the open top deck, with a further 24 in the lower saloon (O27/24R) and, with their solid tyres, they can have hardly been any more comfortable to travel in than the newly introduced Ford railmotor on the Tramway.
COLLECTION ALAN LAMBERT

The *Chichester Observer* may have thought that the time was ripe for railway development in the Hundred of Manhood of Selsey, but reality suggested otherwise. With so many prospective passengers deserting the Tramway for the ever-conquering Southdown 'bus, Sunday services were discontinued from the end of September.

In some ways quite understandably, Holman Stephens felt bitter at having to take the indirect blame for the death of fireman Herbert ('Dirg') Barnes in the tragic derailment near Golf Club Halt back in September 1923, being of the opinion that the upkeep of the permanent way was the responsibility of the Company's manager and secretary, Henry Phillips. As long ago as 9th March the Colonel had informed Phillips that they should have to reconsider his appointment in view of the Company's decreasing receipts, but the secretary claimed that he was entitled to 6 months' notice. Failing to receive a satisfactory reply from Phillips as to his conditions of service, commencing on 15th October Stephens entered into correspondence with Messrs. Raper & Co., the Tramways Company's solicitor, to find out exactly what the secretary's position was. Despite Edward Heron-Allen's regular praises for the secretary at so many AGMs during and after the War, and the glowing testimonial presented to him in December 1920, Stephens admitted finding him to be 'a very difficult man to deal with' and that he was 'tired of writing letters on the subject'.

In response to a letter from Messrs. Raper & Company dated 17th October, Phillips replied to them on 21st October:

> '…I do not agree to your interpretation of the Agreement dated 20th September, 1906, as modified by the Board during the past 18 years and

recorded in the Minutes of the Company. Moreover, when Colonel Stephens and his friends tendered for purchase of the Company's shares in 1920, the tender contained a stipulated clause that they should enter into an agreement respecting my terms of office. A draft was subsequently submitted to Colonel Stephens by my late Directors. I suggest you ascertain that you are in possession of full particulars before giving what will probably be considered responsible opinion.'

Two days later, Stephens wrote again to Messrs. Raper & Co.:

'You may not be aware of the fact that Mr. Phillips' Salary is £37 10s 0d per Month, and one of my complaints is, in October 1919, when the late Board knew very well about my negotiations for the purchase of the Line, without referring to the new possible Purchasers, this Salary was increased from £325 to £450 per annum, or about 40%. We say we should have been consulted in this matter. I enclose a table of the salary paid to Mr. Phillips since 1916, you will see in the last 5 years he has drawn £2,250 out of this unfortunate undertaking, and that under decreased working receipts.

'The job could have been sufficiently done by a retired Station Master who would have jumped at the job at £150 per annum, say about £750 for the same period.

'This information is to enable you to form your own opinion re the position, if one exists, we should like to see it.

'If you think we should give Mr. Phillips six months' notice, please say so, but I am bound to say it seems an unreasonable proposal. We can find nothing in the Minute books of the Company herein which you are welcome to see if you choose.'

TABLE OF SALARY PAID TO HENRY PHILLIPS

August 17th	1906:	£120 0s 0d per annum
September	1907:	£132 0s 0d per annum
October 22nd	1908:	£144 0s 0d per annum
October 28th	1909:	£155 0s 0d per annum
October 20th	1910:	£168 0s 0d per annum
June 18th	1914:	£200 0s 0d per annum
June 22nd	1916:	£250 0s 0d per annum
May 24th	1918:	£325 0s 0d per annum
October 14th	1919:	£450 0s 0d per annum

Upon checking the records, it was revealed that the Draft Agreement compiled in 1920 would have extended Phillips' services until August 1923, but it was never executed. Ironically, if this had been adhered to Phillips might have left a month before the fatal derailment! Always a considerate man, Stephens confirmed 'I have no wish whatever to quibble, or do anything which can be considered directly, or indirectly an unfair action, but you will see that we have kept Mr. Phillips on for over 14 months beyond the three years suggested'. No wonder the unfortunate manager and secretary was reluctant to forward details of his appointment as per the records because his insistence on being given six months' notice turned out to be not a legal one, but purely sentimental!

Notes

1. Other applications had been for the Van Railway in Central Wales, an extension of the Wirral Railway in Cheshire, what was irreverently known as the 'Lunatic Railway' which connected mental hospitals in the Epsom district with the London & South Eastern Railway at Ewell and the Lee on the Solent Railway in Hampshire.
2. These resolutions were confirmed at a further Extraordinary General Meeting held at the same venue on 2.1.1924.
3. Henry Phillips, the Tramways Company's secretary, suggested at the Public Enquiry held at Chichester on 30.4.1924, that the Stockbridge crossing gates had been removed in 1906. However, the crossing was ungated prior to this as witnessed by a cyclist's narrow escape there on 29.6.1904 when it was revealed that the roadside warning sign was partly obscured by a hedge. See Chapter 2.
4. The Tramways Company's bridge, already out of use, was, in the event, never to be raised again.
5. This first railmotor was built onto a Wolseley Siddeley chassis, not a Ford, although vehicles of this latter marque were operating quite successfully on two of Holman Stephens' other lines, the Kent & East Sussex Railway and The Shropshire & Montgomeryshire Railway.
6. *Sussex Daily News*, 22.4.1924. The 'goods coach' would refer to the Ford flat-bed lorry that had recently entered service which was arranged to run back-to-back with the Wolseley Siddeley railmotor.
7. *Chichester Observer*, Wednesday, 7.5.1924.
8. *Chichester Observer*, Wednesday, 13.8.1924.
9. Edward Skinner's young son, Harold, who had moved north with the family, left school in 1925 and on Whit Monday the following year, he commenced working as a fireman on the Ashover Light Railway. Ten years later, he was promoted to driver. *The Ashover Light Railway* by Robert Gratton & Stuart R. Band, published by Wild Swan Publications Ltd.,1989.
10. Chichester's mainline station had recently been described as the worst on the Brighton system.

This is the result of the Ford railmotor colliding with a lorry owned by Messrs. Sadler & Co. of Westhampnett at Stockbridge level crossing on the afternoon of 10th June 1925. With no sign of the other half of the unit, does it mean that it was operating between Chichester and Selsey by itself? Already the curly spoked wheels had been replaced by solid disc ones following previous collisions with motor vehicles on the ungated level crossings.
COLLECTION ROBERT KOSMIDER

CHAPTER SEVEN
THE SLIPPERY DOWNWARD SLIDE (1925–1934)

A copy of this postcard showing Morous *with a 'mixed' train approaching Ferry was sent to Alastair B. MacLeod (of the Southern Railway) in London on 20th August 1926. Describing Selsey, the writer advised 'Bar one or two hideous bungalows, the place is as before'. As a teenager, MacLeod had twice travelled on the Tramway to Selsey in 1917.* COLLECTION PAUL LAMING

AT the Directors' Meeting held in London on Monday, 2nd February 1925 it was decided not to entertain Henry Phillips' offer that he should receive £500 on the determination of his office. Instead it was resolved that he be given one month's notice, 'as from a date to be settled by the Chairman, but without prejudice, and in order to give him an opportunity of finding another employment, he be permitted to continue in office, from month to month hereafter, for a period not exceeding six months, at a Salary at the rate of £200 per annum, subject always to his duties being satisfactorily carried out to the satisfaction of the Board'. In accepting this offer, Phillips was to receive less than half of his then current salary, the new rate being equal to that paid to him until 21st June 1916.

While leaving Chichester on the afternoon of Wednesday, 10th June 1925, a lorry owned by Messrs. Sadler & Co., corn merchants of Westhampnett, was in collision with the Ford railmotor at the Stockbridge Road level crossing owing to what was thought to have been a misunderstanding between the driver and the flag man waving the train across the crossing. The railmotor was knocked completely off the line, but, as luck would have it, the three passengers on board were not injured.[1]

Ignoring the fact that a good number of visitors must have travelled down to the coast on the Tramway, under the heading 'Increase of Visitors', the *Chichester Observer* that same day wrote:

'Selsey is making rapid progress as a seaside resort, for visitors are besieging the pretty little village in large numbers daily. The motor traffic is astonishing and it is estimated that, during weekends latterly, the average number of incoming cars has exceeded all previous years by nearly 50%. There was a record crowd on Whit Sunday, and then over 500 cars lined the sea front. Whit Monday was quieter, but nevertheless, better than other years…'

Mr. E. S. Johnson, the tobacconist of High Street, Selsey, showed an interest in purchasing No. 4 Tramway Cottages (just around the corner from Selsey station in Station Road) and wrote to the Tramways Company on 21st June asking for full particulars. The property was in poor condition and, having seen inside, negotiations were dropped. One might wonder why a property only 27 years old should be in such a bad state!

Ringing Rock at the same location with a down train consisting of two of the ex-LCDR 4-wheel carriages and seven goods vehicles.
COLLECTION PAUL LAMING

In an attempt to encourage passengers back onto the Tramway, the *Chichester Observer* printed the following rather complicated timetable arrangements in their edition dated 15th July:

> 'A considerably extended service on the Selsey Tramway came into operation on Sunday. The weekday "up" service has been augmented by the addition of "trams" at 11.30, 2.10, 4.25 and 7.40 and the "down" service by the corresponding "trams" of 12.20, 3, 5.20 and 8.25. It should be noted that the last "tram" in each case does not run on Mondays and Tuesdays. The Sunday service, which was discontinued last September will be resumed until September 27th, with the following service:- "Up," 8.55, 10.30, 1.20, 5.10 7.5; "Down," 9.50, 11.30, 2.10, 6, 8.5. During the present month and August and September, cheap day return tickets (1s) will be issued from Chichester to Selsey on weekdays on the 9.10, 11.15, 2, 3 and 4.15 "trams" and on Sundays on the 9.50, 11.30 and 2.10 "trams" and from Selsey to Chichester on weekdays on the 10, 11.30, 1.10, 2.10 and 3.10 "trams" (and also the 4.25 and 6 "trams" on Wednesdays and Saturdays) and on Sundays by all "trams".'

During the summer, the millionaire, Captain John ('Jack') E. P. Howey, was giving serious thought to where he could build a 'main line in miniature', his first idea being to purchase the Ravenglass & Eskdale Railway in Cumbria, but although Henry Greenly had carried out a preliminary survey on his behalf, Sir Aubrey Brocklebank (who had just taken over the 15in gauge line) was not prepared to sell it. Howey wanted a line at least as long as the R & ER, and it was left to Greenly to find a suitable site, the original intention being to re-gauge an existing standard-gauge railway to 15in. Already engineered and with minimal gradients, the West Sussex Railway fitted in with their scheme to satisfy a local demand for public transport, and an advantage would be that tourists might be attracted to it owing to its proximity to the coast. Greenly duly travelled down to Chichester and inspected the line to Selsey, but the six level crossings with their speed restrictions would have made reproducing main-line running almost impossible and with the fear that if the grouping went any further the line might be lost to the Southern Railway, he moved on elsewhere.[2]

The unfortunate Henry Phillips continued his duties as manager/secretary at Selsey until at the Directors' Meeting held at the Charing Cross Hotel in London on 23rd September it was resolved that one month's notice be given to him to terminate his employment and that it be left to the chairman (Holman Stephens) to make the necessary arrangements for carrying on his work. Thus Henry Gibson Phillips left the Company after what can only be described as 19 years' loyal service, his post, newly renamed as Superintendent, being taken by Mr. G. Eckford.

Under the heading of 'Some Places Worth Visiting – Selsey, in Sussex' in the September 1925 edition of *The MORRIS Owner Magazine,* Galway Power provided this

THE SLIPPERY DOWNWARD SLIDE (1925–1934)

delightful description of the Tramway and the Ford railmotor that had entered service on the line twelve months previously:

'Since the parish boundary is formed on all sides by water, the only method of reaching Selsey is by road, or the curious little railway which must be seen to be believed. From Chichester, the nearest main line station, one enters an antiquated wooden carriage with straight-up back to back seats.

'For twenty years a steam tram served the district faithfully and well, but such an antiquated method of conveyance was considered too slow for these hectic days, and Henry Ford came to the rescue. The result is an almost ludicrous, but none the less effective combination of ancient body and up-to-date machinery, and by means of this strange conveyance one bumps merrily along to Chichester or Selsey as the case may be. Two Ford standard one-ton trucks, engines facing opposite ways, rear axle to rear axle, compose this exceedingly strange outfit; the chassis and special four forward and reverse gear box of which were

As related by Dick Cash in Volume Two, the Ford railmotors did operate singly on occasions. Smartly dressed in the Company's uniform, the driver is seen unlocking his door on the southward facing portion of the unit at a neat and tidy Chichester station. The fact that this railmotor must have been driven in reverse all the way from Selsey over the Tramway's rickety track with the driver looking over his shoulder, does not bear thinking about!
LENS OF SUTTON

With the door open, it would appear that the photographer had (wisely) been travelling in the rear saloon, but the obliging driver had stopped the Ford railmotor soon after leaving Sidlesham en route for Selsey to enable him to take this picture.
COLLECTION E. C. GRIFFITH

Other than the inevitable litter, all appears to have been quite spick and span at Selsey station on 10th April 1926. The two ex-LCDR 4-wheel carriages at the eastern end of the goods loop would form part of the daily 'mixed' train. Two of the ex-Lambourn Valley carriages and the Company's cattle wagon may be glimpsed behind the goods shed. H. C. CASSERLEY

built to order. When the train arrives at a terminus the driver descends, lever in hand, as do the tram men, and proceeds to the other driving seat ready to start off again, thus obviating the necessity of shunting and turning round. He performs his driving duties reclining in a chair similar to those seen in London parks, turning round now and then to talk to the passengers. The fact that there is a steering column but no wheel adds to the impression of comic opera transport. If the wind is not too strong, one or two open luggage vans are interposed between the two passenger coaches.'[3]

From 1st October the 1/- Day Return Fare was extended to cover all six return services every weekday between Chichester and Selsey, but what had been Wednesday and Saturdays only services were cut back to Saturdays only. The Sunday service had not proved to be commercially viable and it was destined not to be repeated in the future.

On 3rd December Stephens wrote to Messrs. Raper & Co. stating that he should like to sell all four of the cottages belonging to the Tramway Company in Station Road, five days later adding in another letter: 'Is it necessary to give the mortgage notice? I do not want to find £1,000 at a few hours' notice. I have already about £16,000 locked up in the concern'.

From 1st. March 1926 the following reduced timetable came into operation:

	m	*	m	m	m	m	m.so
Selsey	8.15	10.00	1.10	3.10	5.00	6.20	7.45
Ferry Siding	8.20	10.05	1.15	3.15	5.05	6.25	7.50
Sidlesham	8.27	10.12	1.22	3.22	5.12	6.32	7.57
Chalder	8.32	10.20	1.27	3.27	5.17	6.37	8.02
Hunston	8.37	10.27	1.32	3.32	5.22	6.42	8.07
Chichester	8.50	10.40	1.45	3.45	5.35	6.55	8.20
	m	*	m	m	m	m	m.so
Chichester	9.10	11.15	2.00	4.05	5.40	7.05	8.50
Hunston	9.22	11.28	2.12	4.17	5.52	7.17	9.02
Chalder	9.27	11.35	2.17	4.22	5.57	7.22	9.07
Sidlesham	9.32	11.42	2.22	4.27	6.02	7.27	9.12
Ferry Siding	9.36	11.46	2.26	4.31	6.06	7.31	9.16
Selsey	9.45	11.55	2.35	4.40	6.15	7.40	9.25

m rail motor, 3rd. class only * mixed train so Saturdays only

Because of its irregular timings owing to the likelihood of goods wagons being shunted on and off the train at intermediate stations, the Company did its best to put passengers off travelling on the one and only daily 'mixed' (steam) train in each direction, this notice appearing below the timetable:

'The Company herewith give Public Notice that they are desirous that Passengers visiting the line do not travel by the Mixed Train, but by ordinary passenger trains shown on the time bill. If, however, passengers elect to travel by this train it must be on the distinct understanding that they will hold the Company free from all liability in respect of any injury, loss, delay or inconvenience that may happen by accident or otherwise to their person or property whilst travelling in the mixed train, or in joining or leaving the same.'

With there being no carpenter or painter on the Tramway, Holman Stephens sent Jim Smith, the East Kent Railways' carpenter/painter, down to Selsey to work on some carriages and a week later, 16 year old Dick Cash was sent down to join him. The young lad was not at all impressed when Jim Smith was sent back to Kent almost straight away, leaving him on his own 'to scrape and paint the inside of the carriages. They had hard wooden seats and had been varnished. We had to scrape the old varnish off and revarnish them. They were grained under the varnish…I wasn't interested in the job, nor very happy while I was there; it seemed a boring, endless job and I felt I was getting nowhere with the coaches…The job was done at the Selsey engine shed.' Although the Tramway Company had paid him, on his return to Kent the Colonel gave him an extra 'fiver' which Cash considered 'was very generous'.[4] Owing to the General Strike, his journey to and from Kent had been difficult with so few trains being run, but as the Tramway staff did not take any industrial action, for most of the day the complete timetable was operated, other than the last tram left Selsey for Chichester at 5.00pm every evening.[5]

The *Chichester Observer* explained on 12th May:

'The poor old Selsey "tram" (that is the old steam driven system) is never out of trouble for very long. Some time ago the invitation of residents in Stockbridge at the ear-piercing blasts on the whistle with which the locomotive signified its approach to the level crossing, vented itself in public complaints. Now has come a protest at the disagreeable sooty smoke the funnel has been in the habit of emitting while the engine is at or in the vicinity of the station. The Council wrote to the Tramway Company…suggesting that hard steam coal should be used, and that stoking should not be indulged while the "tram" is in the station! It was intimated at last week's Council meeting that the matter was being looked into. The steam "trams" are, of course, supplemented by coaches driven by ordinary "Ford" motor engines.'

In June Messrs. Arnell Brothers of Banff House, East Street, Selsey enquired as to what the lowest price might be that the owner would accept for the four cottages in Station Road that Stephens wished to sell, bearing in mind that 'they are in a very bad state of repair'! The Colonel, in a letter to Raper & Co. dated 24th of the month said he 'would take £400 per cottage, and as much *more* as I could get. At any rate, I shall not sell them for less than four hundred pounds each.' The solicitor tried to get £1,700 for all four, but on the 30th June the Arnell brothers pulled out, replying that 'considering the state of the cottages and the rents paid for them, this price is about £600 too high!' Once again the properties remained unsold!

The Ford railmotor unit might have been less than two years old, but it had already earned itself a reputation for regularly breaking down to the detriment of the published timetable. The *Chichester Observer*'s correspondent, A. Cooing, gave this entertaining account of such a journey that he made on the evening of Friday, 30th July 1926:

'I seem to remember once reading of a Ford that, being somewhat erratic in its habits, and inclined to be "stand-offish", was named by its owner "Ebenezer". When travelling down to Selsey last Friday, the idea somehow came to me that the Selsey Tram must be a close relative to "Ebenezer". It had all the characteristics. It was certainly erratic, and on Friday, anyway, emphatically "stand-offish". This week, however, I do not entirely blame the car. I think it had a good deal of reason on its side, but let me start at the beginning.

'I first suspected something wrong when the tram came in just over half an hour late. It came with a rush which at the time made me feel uneasy. There seemed to be a lot of suppressed indignation on the engine at the other end that was shortly to be used for the return journey. One felt that it was already determined to "proceed with caution" and so it proved.

Stroudley 'Gladstone' B Class 0-4-2 locomotive No. B176 (named Pevensey until c.1906) running into Chichester with an early afternoon train from Portsmouth to Brighton on a misty Saturday, 16th July 1927. Built in November 1890, the engine was scrapped in February 1929. The running-in board displayed the legend 'CHANGE FOR SELSEY ON SEA' but, had plans in 1934 come into fruition to run the Selsey line into the main-line station, it would have utilised the bay platform on the far left.
H.C. CASSERLEY

On that same day, H. C. Casserley travelled down to Selsey and persuaded Selsey's driver to pull the 'dead' Ringing Rock, Sidlesham and Chichester (II) out of the engine shed and into the daylight. With the rear of Morous visible on the other shed road, this unique photograph shows five Tramway locomotives at once.
H. C. CASSERLEY

THE SLIPPERY DOWNWARD SLIDE (1925–1934)

'We had only got about two miles out (bowling along at a high turn of speed), when just as I was wondering if I dare hope for a clear passage, there came a snort from the engine. At last I knew it had come. All was quiet for the next quarter of a mile, and then came a series of snorts, such that only an engine worked up to the highest pitch of indignation could give, at least that was my opinion, but the driver said he didn't think it could be, he described it as "blowing back through the carburettor". However, I noticed that three times between Chichester and Ferry he got to argue with it, he even called for pliers, and tried to reason with it, but the engine always maintained a dignified silence until it was started. Then being so "wound up" that it couldn't keep silent any longer, it would answer with another snort, expressive on these occasions of a lofty and noble contempt. At Ferry, however, our driver began to think that there was something more than obstinacy wrong. My private opinion is that he was seriously alarmed, and feared apoplexy; so seeing a garage close by he decided to call in a "specialist".

'First of all they revived it with some water supplied out of a red petrol can. I thought at first that they might be trying to persuade "Ebenezer" that it was genuine "spirit", but I hastily discarded that idea, for I knew even our driver, who, up to now, had personally shown great personal courage, would never risk facing "Ebenezer's" indignation if a dirty trick like that were played on her. Finding the water did no good, the "specialist" got down to things. Lying flat on his back he proceeded to undo all the nuts and bolts within his reach. I once discussed the peculiarities of motor mechanics with a man I knew, who had been stranded in the middle of Dartmoor. He said he had had the opportunity of studying the specie for approximately three hours. He gave it as his opinion that motor mechanics must either have a little pouch somewhere conveniently placed just inside the glottis[6] or else they were possessed of a sort of double part to their abdomen that has, up to now, been attributed solely to the cow. I came to the conclusion that there certainly seemed to be a good deal to be said for my friend's theory. This man seemed to have a special "passion" for nuts and bolts. He gave one the impression that he throve on them; indeed, one might have been excused for thinking they were the sole means of his existence. He undid nut after nut, shoved them in his mouth and without any mastication whatever, simply "bolted" 'em. Bolts, rods, etc. all followed, 'til I began to wonder seriously if he could "put away" both compartments or only one. Our conductor, who is still quite young, gazed at him much as St. Peter must have gazed on his first vision. He seemed to be wondering whether that second helping of lobster mayonnaise he'd had for supper wasn't making him see things.

'But to return to the business in hand. The way the man produced each article out of his inside in the correct order, each one as he wanted it, was perhaps the most marvellous of all.

'I must admit, however, that by this time, the proceedings had begun to become a little tedious. All I wanted to do before I left was to satisfy a natural curiosity as to what was really wrong. After a most serious consultation between the "specialist", the driver and conductor as to what could be the malady, seeing that they did not seem to be coming to any definitive conclusion, I strolled nonchalantly to the other side of the hedge, from which, before making a hasty departure, I suggested it might be "hay fever". I immediately resumed my journey – I hate scenes.'[7]

Still operating 12 return journeys between Chichester and Selsey on Wednesdays, Fridays and Saturdays (reduced to 11 on Mondays, Tuesdays and Thursdays) and 7 each way on Sundays, from 20th September 1926 Southdown Motor Services renumbered their service from 32 to 52. Since February the timings had been amended to take 45 minutes from the city to the coast and 50 minutes for the return trip.

Despite the use (when it was available) of the Ford railmotor on all but the busiest services and on the 'mixed' trains, which remained steam hauled, expenditure exceeded receipts on the Tramway by £550 over the year, the number of passengers having fallen by 4,591 to 17,171.

Since 1904, the Selsey Tramways Company had received much adverse publicity following numerous collisions with motor vehicles on the several ungated level crossings along its route. However, it was the Tramway's competitor, Southdown Motor Services, Ltd's Tilling Stephens TS3 open-top double-decker No. 80 (registration No. CD4880) that made the headlines in the local newspaper after colliding with a car and running into a barn at Upper Norton near Selsey, late in the evening of 25th April 1927. This was the scene the following day, prior to the 'bus being recovered. COLLECTION ALAN LAMBERT

On 28th February 1927 the *Chichester Observer* published this rather odd paragraph:

'Visitors making their first trip to Selsey by the trans-peninsular tramway must receive many amusing impressions of the Stations *en route*, and imagine for a moment that they are being conveyed into the back of beyond. After being bumped over a track red with rust, they eventually cross a bleak and desolate stretch of moorland and arrive at the Ferry where a dilapidated structure like a cross between a cow shed and a kennel is perched jauntily on an antiquated platform and does duty as a waiting room. If it wasn't for the honour of the thing, I would prefer to wait in the rain...'

Collisions continued to take place between motor vehicles and trains on the ungated level crossings, but it was the Tramway's competitor, Southdown Motor Services Ltd., that made the headlines in the local paper following an accident on 25th April. It was at about 10.45pm, as the last 'bus of the day from Chichester reached Upper Norton on its way to Selsey, when the offside wheel of open-top double-decker, Tilling Stevens T53, CD8280 came into contact with the offside wheel of a Humber car travelling in the opposite direction, causing both drivers to lose control of their steering. The 'bus slewed across the road and into the brick wall of a barn, damaging the bonnet and driver's cab whilst, amongst other things, both axles of the car were broken. No one was seriously injured.[8]

As a Statutory Requirement, an advertisement was placed in the *Morning Advertiser* dated 15th July stating that the Company's Annual General Meeting was to be held at 23 Salford Terrace, Tonbridge on Wednesday, 10th August, but no one attended. Strangely, there is no reference in the Directors' Minute Book amending Article 78 to include Tonbridge as a venue for the General Meetings of the Company.[9]

On 7th December an advertisement appeared in the *Chichester Observer* advising that Third Class cheap tickets

What a difference two years make; Chichester station had become very shabby and run down. The 'Home & Colonial Teas' advert of 1926 had been replaced by a ubiquitous 'Petter Oil Engine' sign. The driver is seen here topping up the radiator of the Ford railmotor with water c.1928.
LENS OF SUTTON

were still available on all trams for 8d single and 1/- Day Return. Timings, identical to those of October 1925 and omitting the first up service, were confusingly shown thus:

    d Chichester: 9.10, 11.15, 2.00, 4.05, 6.50 (Sats. excepted) 5.40 and 7.25 Sats. only.
    d Selsey: 10.00, 1.10, 3.10, 8.00 (Sats. excepted) 5.00 and 6.30 Sats. only.[10]

After only two years' service, Mr. G. Eckford left the Company to be replaced by the beginning of December by Mr. A. W. Smith as Superintendent at Selsey station. Known by his colleagues as 'Smudger', he had come from the Colonel's East Kent Railway, where he had been employed as the stationmaster at what must surely have been one of the most unusual termini in the country, Wingham (Canterbury Road).[11]

Having suffered a steady decrease over eight years, passenger numbers showed a welcome increase in 1927 with 5,304 more travelling on the Tramway than in 1926, a total of 22,475 being carried over the year. Perhaps it was the lower fares that had enticed people back onto the line, but despite the increase in passengers, receipts had fallen by £44 1s 11d to £685 4s 2d.

As previously noted, the Ford railmotor was not the most reliable of machines, but, more important to the Selsey Tramway, it was much cheaper to run than a conventional steam train and, early in 1928, a second rail motor entered service. It cost nothing to the hard-up Railway Company as it was paid for in full by Holman Stephens. Suitably impressed, the *Chichester Observer*'s correspondent, A. Cooing, writing in that newspaper under the regular heading of 'Selsey Billings', on 29th February advised:

> 'For the first time in many months, I had the pleasure of travelling down to Selsey once more by the Selsey Tramway – I say it in no spirit of levity – it was a real pleasure. Since "Ebenezer" has been super-annuated, she has been replaced by a most up-to-date vehicle, a Shefflex, which has already done much to restore the fair name of the Company for punctuality and well maintains their boast of being the quickest, cheapest and safest route to Selsey.'

Although the Tramway had long since been managed from Tonbridge, the local staff were still proud of providing a personal service to their passengers. Having obtained permission from the conductor/guard to travel in the open baggage truck between one of the railmotor units, a young lad lost his new felt hat when a strong gust of wind blew it into a field beside the Tramway on the way to Chichester. Needless to say, the boy was very worried as to what his parents might say when he arrived home! At Chichester the situation was explained to the driver and on the return journey the Tram was stopped and staff and passengers joined in the search until the errant hat was found.[12]

In May, Westhampnett Rural District Council resolved to make up Manor and Church Roads in Selsey, with the West Sussex Railway to be charged the sum of £75 towards the cost of improving each of them. The Railway

THE SLIPPERY DOWNWARD SLIDE (1925–1934)

Company's objection came before a special sitting of the Chichester County Bench on Monday, 23rd July where Mr. C. W. Cutts, representing the Company, complained that the apportionments were 'too heavy having regard to the circumstances of the case'. On the other hand, a number of ratepayers urged that the sum being paid by the Selsey Tramways should be increased. Mr. G. E. Barker, representing Westhampnett District Council, explained that the roads had remained good for the first ten years until the railway came into existence, when all goods had to be hauled over one or other of them. During the previous twelve months, Mr. A. W. Shorland (surveyor to the Westhampnett District Council) had estimated that the goods traffic had contributed about 75% towards the destruction of the original gravel roads. Over the past 30 years, 180 tons of material had been placed in Church Road, but, unlike other frontagers, the railway had not paid any proportion of the costs. An objection, signed by fourteen residents to the effect that the sum to be levied on the Selsey Light Railway Company (*sic*) was 'ridiculously inadequate' suggested that it should be increased to at least £500 having regard to the fact that 'this railway would have ceased to function and could not have functioned without the use of the two roads as an outlet and inlet for their goods traffic'. Another objection was that had the roads not been used for access to the railway to remove freight, they could have been made up for 'quite one half' of the present cost. One resident of Manor Road said that only two people in that street owned cars, but during the day there was a constant stream of traffic coming from the Tramway station, whilst another said that for 20 years the roads had been nothing but dust in summer and mud in winter, mainly owing to traffic from the Tramway.

The main objection raised by Mr. Cutts on behalf of the West Sussex Railway Company was that 'the allegation that the apportionment of the expenses amongst the several landowners on the principle upon which the same had been based were unfair, incorrect, unequal and erroneous.' He suggested that £40 should be the total contribution to the making up of both roads, arguing that the benefit to the Company's premises had been over-estimated and that the private street works in contemplation would attract competitive road services to a district now served by the Tramway with the result that the loss on working sustained by the Company would be considerably increased.[13] Referring to the Company's finances, Mr. Cutts asked if the witness was aware that the receipts in 1927 were £2,184?

Witness: 'I'm very sorry to hear it!'

Concluding his address, Mr. Cutts urged that the destruction of the roads in question was due to the lorries of outside contractors who had to take their goods from the station

Spot the lone female amongst the scouts in the baggage truck attached to the rear of the six-month-old Shefflex railmotor on an 'up' service at Sidlesham on August Bank Holiday, 1928. Although long since out of use, the northern ramp of the 'down' platform beside the passing loop is just visible on the right.
COLONEL STEPHENS RAILWAY MUSEUM & ARCHIVE

Left: The 11.20 a.m. 'mixed' tram to Selsey on 5th November 1928 with one of the ex-Lambourn Valley third class carriages pressed into service, a covered goods van marshalled next to the engine, and the rest of the goods wagons bringing up the rear. Right: Selsey at the head of the train, now numbered No. 1 on her front buffer beam. H. C. CASSERLEY

Having been in service for just over eight months, the Shefflex railmotor is seen here over the outside maintenance pit at Selsey engine shed prior to running the passenger services for the rest of the day once Selsey and her 'mixed' train had arrived back from Chichester. Just visible to the right, the two units of the Ford railmotor had been separated for maintenance purposes. 5th November 1928.
H. C. CASSERLEY

THE SLIPPERY DOWNWARD SLIDE (1925–1934)

It wasn't only the Tramway that was affected by flooding at Sidlesham in the winter of 1928, as related by fireman Ray Apps, but the lower-lying parts of the village were under water as well. WSCC LIBRARY SERVICE

yard and it was not fair to charge the Company with that. The magistrates decided that the Railway Company had no access to Church Road within the meaning of the Private Street Works Act of 1892 and could, therefore, not be considered liable. As to Manor Road, they increased the Company's proportionment from £75 to £100, thus reducing the original sum by £50.[14]

A Directors' Meeting was called for 17th September 'for the purpose of considering the Agreement proposed to be entered into between the Company and the West Sussex Railway Company', but, with no attendance, it had to be rearranged for 10th October. The typically unpunctuated document read:

> AN AGREEMENT made the tenth day of October 1928 BETWEEN THE WEST SUSSEX RAILWAY COMPANY (hereinafter called "the Railway Company") by the hand of John Elcombe its secretary pro tem of the one part and THE HUNDRED OF MANHOOD AND SELSEY TRAMWAYS COMPANY LIMITED (hereinafter called "The Tramway Company" by the hand of Holman F. Stephens its Secretary pro tem of the other part.
>
> WHEREAS the Tramway Company have constructed and for many years operated a tramway from the City of Chichester in the County of sussex (sic) to Selsey in the same County AND WHEREAS the Railway Company was incorporated by the West Sussex Railway Certificate 1924 under the Railway Construction Facilities Act 1864 and the Railways (Powers and Construction) Acts 1864 Amendment Act 1870 AND WHEREAS the Railway Company have powers by agreement with the Tramway Company to purchase and take over and procure a conveyance and assignment of the railway and undertaking of the Tramway Company together with all or any of the lands tenements hereditaments plant works rolling stock and other property and things whatsoever of the Tramway Company AND WHEREAS the Railway Company have powers by agreement to take upon themselves all or any of the debts and liabilities of the Tramway Company against all or any of such debts and liabilities and may execute any agreement covenant or other instrument requisite for the purpose NOW IT IS HEREBY AGREED between the Railway Company and the Tramway Company as follows:-
>
> (1) The Railway Company shall take over reconstruct work and maintain the undertaking of the Tramway Company and they shall undertake to pay the interest on the Debentures of the Tramway Company as and when demanded by the Debenture Holders of the Tramway Company and/or any other interest for which the Tramway Company is liable and shall either purchase or arrange to issue Debentures of the Railway Company in exchange for Debentures of the Tramway Company if and when the Debentures of the Tramway Company become redeemable.
>
> (2) The Railway Company shall if requested by the Shareholders of the Tramway Company create and exchange twenty-five shares of One Pound each in the Railway Company for every two shares of Five Pounds each in the Tramway Company.
>
> (3) The Railway Company shall take over all debts and liabilities of the Tramway Company and shall indemnify the Tramway Company against all or any of such debts and liabilities.
>
> (4) In consideration the Railway Company shall hold Two thousand seven hundred and seventeen Shares of Five Pounds each of the Tramway Company standing in the names of Holman Fred Stephens Henry Montague Bates Alfred Hacking and William Henry Austen.
>
> (5) Any profit on the working of the undertaking after payment of the interest as provided in Clause 1 of this Agreement shall be paid to the holders of the Shares herein referred to and to any other Shareholders in the Tramway Company and divided according to the amount of their respective holdings.
>
> THIS AGREEMENT shall be perpetuity unless determined by the mutual consent of both parties.
>
> AS WITNESS THE HANDS OF THE PARTIES HERETO THIS TENTH DAY OF OCTOBER 1928.
>
> FOR AND ON BEHALF OF THE WEST SUSSEX RAILWAY COMPANY.
>
> (Signed) John Elcombe.
> Secretary (pro tem)
>
> FOR AND ON BEHALF OF THE HUNDRED OF MANHOOD AND SELSEY TRAMWAYS COMPANY LIMITED.
> (Signed) H. F. Stephens.
> Secretary (pro tem)

Although built up on its embankment, Sidlesham station was still regularly flooded in winter months, now by land water, rather than the sea. Concerned about this, Holman Stephens had asked the Tramway's solicitors to take up with Messrs. Wyatt & Sons to see what was being done to prevent it back in January, September and October 1926, but apparently to no avail. Fireman, Ray Apps recalled that on a steam Tram's journey from Selsey to Chichester one afternoon in 1928, water covered the permanent way to rail height, but on the return trip, aggravated by high tides and gales, the line near Sidlesham was completely submerged. He and his driver decided to 'make a dash for it', but this extinguished the fire. However, with quick thinking and the aid of some lineside fencing that they ripped up, the fire was re-lit and they were able to complete their journey! On another occasion round about this time, driver H. Davies leaned out of the cab of his locomotive to be struck under the chin by the badly sagging lineside telephone line which almost encircled his throat. The (typically rotten) telegraph pole broke, but prompt action by fireman Apps saved the day when he applied the brakes and brought the train to a rapid standstill.[16]

There was yet another serious accident at Stockbridge level crossing on Monday afternoon, 10th December when the Tram collided with a car driven by a Mrs. Cover of East Beach, Selsey, turning it over and smashing the rear completely. Incredibly, Mrs. Cover was not hurt, although she was severely shaken and covered in petrol, and 'she must have escaped death by a matter of inches only'.[17]

Director Henry Montague Bates passed away on 30th December, and Mr. Jeremiah MacVeagh of 5 Woburn Place, Russell Square, London, WC[18] was voted in as a Director in his place at a meeting of the Directors on 4th January 1929. Perhaps it was owing to the introduction of the more reliable and slightly more comfortable Shefflex railmotor at the beginning of 1928 that passenger numbers increased for the second year running with 35,493 being carried during the year, which brought in increased receipts of £749 16s 8d.

On 30th January, 50 West Sussex Railway Shares each were allotted in order to the Company's Directors Holman Stephens, Luther Clayton and Jeremiah Macveagh 'fully paid for services rendered'. According to the Company's 'Register of Members & Share Ledger', these were the only shares to be issued. By this time, Holman Stephens would have become the major shareholder in the Hundred of Manhood & Selsey Tramways Company Ltd.[19]

At a meeting of the Westhampnett Rural District Council on Friday, 1st February 1929 Mr. E. G. Arnell spoke up on 'the danger at present existing at certain points of the Chichester to Selsey road where the Selsey Tram track crosses it. There has been more than one collision there and another one occurred the previous Thursday when a Southdown omnibus came into collision with the Tram',[20] and he hoped that something would be done in the matter in the near future. The body of the Shefflex railmotor involved in this latest accident was so badly distorted that when an attempt was made to move the vehicle, the stress on the crank shaft was so great that it fractured! Having obtained all the spares he thought necessary from the manufacturer, it took the Tramways Company's fitter, John Bratley, no less than 6 weeks to rebuild the railmotor.[21]

The timetable for March showed five return trips on weekdays, with seven on Saturdays and the daily mixed train now had its intermediate timings at all stations shown. Its down schedule was identical to that of the railmotors except that a full 13 minutes were allowed for the minute's run between Selsey Bridge and Selsey Town!

Week days only

Up					S	E	S	S
Selsey Town	8.10	9.50	1.10	3.20	5.00	5.40	6.20	8.00
Selsey Bridge	8.11	9.52	1.11	3.21	5.01	5.41	6.21	8.01
Ferry	8.16	9.58	1.16	3.23	5.06	5.46	6.26	8.06
Sidlesham	8.21	10.03	1.21	3.28	5.11	5.51	6.31	8.11
Mill Pond Halt	8.23	10.05	1.23	3.33	5.13	5.53	6.33	8.13
Chalder	8.26	10.08	1.26	3.36	5.16	5.56	6.36	8.16
Hunston	8.31	10.17	1.31	3.41	5.21	6.01	6.41	8.21
Chichester	8.40	10.30	1.40	3.50	5.30	6.10	6.50	8.30
Down					S	E	S	S
Chichester	9.10	11.20	2.00	4.10	5.40	6.50	7.15	8.40
Hunston	9.19	11.29	2.09	4.19	5.49	6.59	7.24	8.49
Chalder	9.24	11.34	2.14	4.24	5.54	7.04	7.29	8.54
Mill Pond Halt	9.27	11.37	2.17	4.27	5.57	7.07	7.32	8.57
Sidlesham	9.29	11.39	2.19	4.29	5.59	7.09	7.34	8.59
Ferry	9.34	11.44	2.24	4.34	6.04	7.14	7.39	9.04
Selsey Bridge	9.39	11.49	2.29	4.39	6.09	7.19	7.44	9.09
Selsey Town	9.40	12.02	2.30	4.40	6.10	7.20	7.45	9.10

E Except Saturdays S Saturdays only

Concern was growing over the many collisions taking place with such regular monotony on the level crossings and the *Chichester Post* had this to say on 29th June:

'Quite a number of accidents have occurred in recent years on parts of the Selsey–Chichester Road crossed by the Selsey Tramway. The Tramway is now known by the important title of The West Sussex Railway. But, although its name has been brought up to date, the methods employed at the level crossings are still sadly antiquated. True, "Beware of the Trains" notices are displayed on either side of the crossings, but a visiting motorist, unfamiliar with the surroundings, is liable to overlook them. Anyway, I should imagine that the onus is on the engine drivers to ascertain whether the road is clear before proceeding over the crossing. There are always two men on the train, and it is advocated, quite rightly, that one should alight and give the "all clear" signal before the engine crosses the main road. It may be argued that the drivers always give warning of their approach by blowing the whistle, but this is not enough in these days of fast moving cars.[22]

'As recently as Friday of last week an accident occurred at the Stockbridge level crossing which might easily have been attended with fatal results. The view of the Stockbridge Crossing is obscured by a high hedge, and Doctor M. B. Hay, who was driving at a very moderate speed towards Selsey, had the misfortune to arrive at the crossing at the same moment as the train. He escaped personal injury, but the car was badly damaged. After the train came to a standstill, the driver alighted and blandly enquired whether the doctor had heard his whistle. I should like to know the nature of his reply. Should a doctor tell?'

According to the West Sussex Railway's Return forwarded to the Ministry of Transport, receipts in 1929 totalled £2,806 16s 10d, but expenses had risen to £3,295 3s 5d, resulting in a deficit of £488 6s 7d. Not accounted for in these figures was £246 14s 7d which had been earned in rent. Passenger trains ran a total of 22,542 miles, carrying 22,676 passengers, an alarming decrease of 12,817 compared to the previous year, with receipts down by £183 5s 3d. Goods (mixed) trains ran just 1,785 miles with shunting

THE SLIPPERY DOWNWARD SLIDE (1925–1934)

With the conductor/guard sitting behind and to the right of the driver, the Shefflex railmotor is seen here creeping gingerly across the main road into Ferry station with a Selsey-bound service in the late 1920s.
COLLECTION PAUL LAMING

This was the alternative way of travelling between Chichester and Selsey in 1929. Although Leyland were already producing their closed-top Titan TD1 double-decker by this time, Southdown Motor Services Ltd. bought 23 of their chassis and had them fitted with open-top O27/24R bodies by Messrs. Brush of Loughborough in that year. No. 810 (UF4810) is pictured competing with the Tramway in Chichester's West Street on Southdown's Route No. 52 to Selsey. Compared to a rough and noisy journey in one of the Tramways Company's railmotors, the prospect of a ride on the open top deck through the Sussex countryside on a warm summer's day must have appealed to many locals and visitors alike.
THE OMNIBUS SOCIETY

The Shefflex railmotor running into Selsey station c.1930. Followed by a gentleman with a pipe, one passenger looks to have been in such a hurry to get out of the noisy, rough-riding and fume-ridden vehicle that he was already about to open the door behind the driver. The SR open and two private owner wagons on the goods loop had brought in supplies of coal whilst somewhere over to the right, the run-round loop was hidden beneath the ever-encroaching weeds.

LENS OF SUTTON

THE SLIPPERY DOWNWARD SLIDE (1925–1934)

adding a further 845 miles. Wages for rail motor and steam train working amounted to £174 and £100 respectively.

The new year got off to a bad start when two more accidents occurred at Stockbridge crossing in quick succession. The first was on Tuesday morning, 7th January 1930 when an Essex car driven by a Mr. L. R. Snook of Portsmouth, came into collision with the Tram and the whole of the rear part of his car was completely smashed. The driver and his passenger, a Mr. Porter of Chichester, escaped unhurt. Two days later the Tram collided with a lorry belonging to Messrs. Davy's of Hove, which was 'knocked' onto a private car driven by none other than the same Mrs. Cover who had been hit by the Tram on the same crossing only a month before. The lorry was damaged and the windscreen and radiator of Mrs. Cover's car were smashed, but in both accidents there were no personal injuries.[23] The story is told that the fireman went to check that the car driver was alright, but on finding to his horror that it was the same woman who had given him a piece of her mind on the previous occasion, he made a hasty retreat to the train.[24]

These last two incidents must have been the last straw because, later that month, the 'owner-drivers' of Selsey decided that it was time to take some immediate action in an attempt to safeguard their lives and property. After discussing their grievances, they decided that the best way forward would be to write a personal letter to Mr. Herbert Morrison, the Minister of Transport. The letter, which carried over 200 signatures, read:

'We, the undersigned, motor owners and drivers of Selsey and district, have the honour to call attention to the dangerous condition prevailing at the level crossings of the West Sussex Railway, Selsey Tramway Section. Two types of transport vehicles are used on this line. One is a motor driven tram, about which we make no complaint. The other is a light steam engine[25] which draws main line trucks between Chichester and Selsey. The level crossings are not protected by gates and the only warning given of the approach of the engine is its own whistle which, under certain conditions, cannot be heard. The engine habitually crosses the road at a dangerous speed from blind corners. There have been several accidents, particularly at the Stockbridge Road Crossing. Up to the present there have been no fatalities, though cars have been wrecked. We ask that one of your inspectors may be sent to see the conditions, and that steps be taken to render the main road from Chichester to Selsey reasonably safe for all road traffic.'

The *Chichester Post* suggested on 25th January that they hoped that the ultimate outcome would not be the introduction of crossing gates, adding that

'In these days of fast moving traffic and congested roads, gates at the level crossings on our main roads only aggravate the congestion and cause irritating delays. As I have said before in these notes, there is a simple and inexpensive solution to the Selsey problem.

'The train, which only runs about twice daily, should be compelled to stop before reaching the crossings and the guard should alight and wave a red flag in the middle of the road before allowing the train to proceed. Rather a laborious procedure, no doubt, but infinitely preferable to the fatality which is bound to occur if some precautions are not taken at these danger spots. Providence cannot be tempted for too long.'

The letter had the desired effect and a Ministry of Transport official soon came to inspect Stockbridge Road level crossing but when he enquired as to why the line had never been inspected, he appeared to be quite happy to accept the explanation that the line was a Tramway and not a railway! Whether it was on the insistence of the Ministry of Transport, or that Holman Stephens decided to take matters into his own hands is not clear, but the following instructions were issued to Tramway staff on 9th April encompassing both goods and passenger trains:

A DEAD Stop must be made by all trains on either side of the Public Road Level Crossings at Stockbridge Road, Chichester, and Ferry Road, Selsey.

A DEAD Stop must be made by all trains travelling in the direction Chichester to Selsey, at HUNSTON Public Road Level Crossing, on the CHICHESTER side of the crossing.

FURTHER, the following Rule is to be strictly observed, BEFORE an attempt is made to cross such roads, viz:-

RULE.

The FIREMAN, in the case of a Steam Train, and the CONDUCTOR, in the case of a PETROL RAIL CAR TRAIN will, upon such train being brought to a standstill, proceed to the centre of each of the above-mentioned Public Road Level Crossings, with a red hand signal flag, by day, and a red hand signal lamp, by night, and with such, will prevent any movement being made by users of the Public Road across the said crossings.

When it is assured that the roads are free for the passage of such trains, the FIREMAN, in the case of the STEAM TRAIN, or the CONDUCTOR, in the case of the PETROL RAIL CAR TRAIN, will signal the Drivers of such trains to cross the said Roads, and on the Trains having passed over the said roads, the FIREMAN or CONDUCTOR will rejoin his train and proceed.

At a meeting of the Directors at the Charing Cross Hotel, London on 7th November, it was decided to invite Mr. James Ramsay and Mr. John Pike onto the Board, but it was revealed at the following meeting on Tuesday, 3rd March at The Grosvenor Hotel, Buckingham Palace Road, London, SW1, that they had intimated that 'in view of the fact that they could not be of service to the Company, they were regretfully unable to accept such invitation'. On the 27th of the month, Luther Clayton and Jeremiah MacVeagh signed a letter from 23 Salford Terrace addressed to the Selsey Tramways Company advising that '…owing to the much regretted continued disability of Colonel H. F. Stephens, our present Secretary pro tem, that Mr. J. Elcombe, should take over his duties, in that capacity and that he is hereby appointed Secretary pro tem, as from this date'.[26]

Yet another enquiry had been made regarding the purchase of No.4 Tramway Cottages in Selsey, but on 31st January 1931 Stephens advised through the Company's solicitors that he 'should not be inclined to consider the sale of a single house'. Two months later, a Mr. C. Fowler of 'Lakeham', Selsey did show an interest in all four cottages, but he was not prepared to pay the £1700 asking price either. Negotiations on the purchase of the Tramway Cottages came to an end on 20th March when it was announced that 'owing to Col. Stephens' absence from the office in a Nursing Home, this matter must stand over.'

The Company found itself unable to pay the interest due on the 'B' Debentures due on 31st March and the Secretary had written to the Debenture Holders asking it they would agree to their redemption being held over 'until the Managing Director, Colonel Stephens, was restored to health and able to attend to the matter'. Replies were received from Edward Heron-Allen and Miss E. Moore

Here are two photographs from 1930 of the fine beach at East Wittering which the Selsey Tramways Company had hoped to have reached with a branch line from near Hunston in 1913. Even though the all-conquering motor car had now invaded the scene, the pebble beach and sands remained unspoilt, the only development being a few bungalows to the south-east of the village.
WSCC LIBRARY SERVICE

THE SLIPPERY DOWNWARD SLIDE (1925–1934)

With very little development around it, the Marine Hotel at Selsey stood out on the horizon as it looked out over the sands and sea from its advantageous position above the West Beach in 1930. In June 1928 Selsey's first public car park had opened to keep the sea front free of cars, a fee of 1/- being charged for the whole day. One car owner had decided to ignore the rules! WSCC LIBRARY SERVICE

Another motorist had decided to park on the sea front at the West Beach, Selsey, behind which a row of beach huts extend north-westwards towards the Marine Hotel. It must have been early or late in the season with so few visitors. WSCC LIBRARY SERVICE

saying that they desired their stock to be redeemed on the due date, but Mr. F. Grafton was more sympathetic and in his letter stated that, in the circumstances, he was willing to leave the matter in abeyance.[27]

It was not only the redemption of the Debentures that was causing concern, and on 20th March Luther Clayton (Chairman of the Directors) and Jeremiah MacVeagh (Director) made the following resolutions:

(a) The Secretary having presented a bill from Colonel Stephens for £600, being Salary as Engineer to the Company for the years 1925–1930 inclusive, it was resolved that Colonel Stephens be informed that whilst admitting the Company's liability, the Directors regretted that in the present state of the Company's finances, they could only carry forward the debt.

(b) It was resolved for the same reason the Directors' Fees during the same period at the rate of Fifty guineas each, a year, be also carried forward, and

(c) Mr. J. Elcombe having offered to accept £26, in full discharge of Salary as Assistant to the Managing Director as from January 1st 1930, and as Secretary to the Company from November 1930, to this date, it was decided to accept the offer.

One of the debenture holders who had refused to part with his holdings, fearing the purchase of the fully secured debentures at a heavy discount, issued a writ in the High Court to enforce the payment of the overdue interest and the redemption of the debentures. Shortly afterwards a second writ was issued by Lieut. Col. Holman Stephens claiming, as a holder of 'A' debentures, to enforce payment of the moneys secured by the debentures and for the appointment of a Receiver, to be nominated by him. This second writ was immediately opposed by Edward Heron-Allen 'on behalf of himself and the other holders of "B" debentures (if any), other than a lady joined with him as co-

With the conductor hanging on to the rear handrail of Southdown Motor Services' Leyland Titan TD1 No. 844 (UF5644), this picture shows it ploughing through flood water on Route 52 between Sidlesham and Ferry on its way to Selsey from Chichester in 1931.
COLLECTION J. WYNNE-TYSON

In 1930, Southdown Motor Services Ltd. at last took delivery of a fleet of closed-top Leyland Titan TD1 double-deckers, some of which were soon to be found working between Chichester and Selsey on their Route 52. This Publicity Department photograph shows No. 863 (UF5663) when new in apple green and primrose livery. To keep the height down, the 24 seats on the upper deck were inconveniently arranged in rows of four, with a sunken gangway along the offside that intruded into the lower saloon, which also had a capacity of 24 passengers.
COLLECTION ALAN LAMBERT

THE SLIPPERY DOWNWARD SLIDE (1925–1934)

defendant in Lieut. Col Stephens' writ', and put forward as Receiver Mr. Owen Walker, FSAA of 103 Cannon Street, London, EC4. This gentleman was described as being 'an Incorporated Accountant of London, whose knowledge of local conditions and land values as director and some time secretary of the Selsey Gas & Water Companies, is probably unequalled, and who, moreover, is not in any way connected with any person having large financial interests in the Tramway Company'. On 8th April Justice Eve in the Chancery Division, without hesitation, accepted the nomination of Owen Walker, who was thus appointed Manager and Receiver of the Tramways Company.

At the Company's Annual General Meeting held at The Charing Cross Hotel, London, WC2 on Thursday, 14th May it was disclosed that although expenses had been reduced by £424 9s 9d to £2,870 11s 8d, receipts had fallen by a massive £439 14s 2d to £2,347 2s 8d, which resulted in a loss of £523 9s 0d. The Secretary reported that the Directors had not received their fees for some years and that at the rate of fifty guineas per year, the sum now owing to Luther Clayton would be £300 and to Jeremiah MacVeagh £100. It was resolved to carry forward these amounts.

Commenting on the Tramways Company going into receivership, two days later under the heading 'Passing of the Selsey Tramway', and sub-titled 'The True Facts', the *Chichester Post* wrote:

> 'Unwept, unhonoured and unsung, "The Hundred of Manhood and Selsey Tramway" – rechristened in its decrepit old age "The West Sussex Light Railway" (sic) – passes out of existence, crushed by the Juggernaut of Progress, after being etiolated[28] by the Paralysis of Neglect. Those who have watched it staggering to its inglorious end will be neither shocked or surprised...
>
> '...It may be said at once that there is small probability of the shareholders and unsecured creditors getting much, if anything, the line having been allowed to fall into a very grievous condition, and the passenger traffic having practically disappeared...Under the Receivership and management of Mr. Owen Walker the debenture holders may, in our opinion, rest easy. There are only £7,000 "A" debentures partly paid off in 1924, and £5,000 "B" debentures, and beyond this a mortgage of the entire undertaking for £1000, making a total of £13,000.
>
> 'Against this amount, as realizable assets, there is the entire rolling stock and other working property of the line (the value of which is problematical), a large plot of freehold land adjoining the line, and fronting upon Stockbridge Road, Chichester, a row of houses in Station Road, Selsey, and eight miles of freehold railway line, with its stations, water tanks and associated property complete.
>
> 'Though the passenger traffic between Selsey and Chichester has been reduced to a negligible quantity, there is a considerable amount of traffic in goods, coals, building materials and other commodities, and it would now be well while of the Southern Railway to acquire the whole concern at the small price which would satisfy all claims of secured creditors, and which, in view of the ever-increasing development of Selsey as a seaside resort, should be a remunerative present asset to the Southern Railway, with great potentialities for future development, both as regards goods and passenger traffic.
>
> 'It may therefore be confidently asserted that a new era has dawned for Selsey, and that increased prosperity may be anticipated when the improved facilities for communication with the outer world are considered...'

On 5th October, Luther Clayton and Jeremiah Macveagh, as Directors of the Hundred of Manhood & Selsey Tramways Company Ltd., (rather than the West Sussex Railway) gave notice that the registered office of the Company would, in future, be at 23 Salford Terrace, Tonbridge. It will be noted that whereas the West Sussex Railway Company had taken over the Tramways Company, official business was still carrying on under the original title.

Having spent the last months of his life at the Lord Warden Hotel, Dover, Lt. Col. Holman Stephens passed away following a heart attack there in the early hours of Friday, 23rd October 1931, eight days short of his 63rd birthday. With no surviving family, four members of his staff at Salford Terrace, Tonbridge (William H. Austen, secretary Arthur Iggulden and brothers Fred and George Willard) shared equally in his estate of around £30,000 as per Stephens' will dated 19th January 1931. Since the Colonel's incapacitation, Austen had assumed responsibility of the office, and he was duly appointed acting Manager, Engineer and Locomotive Superintendent on 7th November.

On 29th April 1932 William Austin found it necessary to renew the instructions originally issued on 9th April 1930 that ordered all trains to stop at the three main road level crossings, but even this did not prevent a collision with a lorry at Ferry four months later on 20th August when both parts of the Shefflex unit ended up on the road at right-angles to the Tramway! As a last resort, Chichester Corporation proposed that colour light signals should be provided at the Stockbridge Road level crossing, but the impoverished Tramways Company could not afford Messrs. Tyers & Co. Ltd's estimate of £39 10s 0d and the trams continued to be guided over the level crossings by the conductor/guards. If the Corporation was so worried about the situation, couldn't they have provided the lights themselves?

Back in the previous May, the Sanitary Engineer for Westhampnett Rural District Council was in the process of issuing a demolition order on the Company's cottage close to the canal at Hunston, unless repairs were carried out. Under the authority of Mr. Owen Walker (the Receiver and Manager of the Company) these repairs had been completed and the cottage let. However, early in 1932 the WRDC demanded further repairs and as 'no rent had been obtainable from the tenant for some considerable time', it was not considered economic to keep the cottage open and it was closed on 31st March and put into the hands of Messrs. Wyatt & Sons for the purpose of Sale.[30]

The Accounts for the year ending 31st December 1931 presented at the AGM held in Chichester on Tuesday, 31st May showed just how bad things were getting. With only 13,416 passengers having been carried (a reduction of 2,488 on 1930) receipts amounted to a paltry £279 15s 2d. Total receipts came to £2,299 13s 3d, but these were completely outweighed by expenses which had risen to an all-time high of £3,922 10s 10d. The deficit of £1,622 17s 7d did not include income earned from rents, etc., which provided an additional £241 4s 0d. At the meeting, Luther Clayton reported that Messrs. William Henry Austen (and more recently) James Arthur Iggulden, Alfred Willard and George Henry Willard (all on the staff at Salford Terrace, Tonbridge) had been co-opted by him as Directors of the

Morous and the ex-SR 6-wheeled 4-compartment Brake Third No. 3639 (which had been acquired in 1932) with a mixed train for Selsey.
LENS OF SUTTON

A charming photograph of a calf in a sack being carefully carried from the Shefflex railmotor's baggage truck at Selsey. The wagon was used for all manner of goods including churns of milk and, in this instance, a shrub.
COLLECTION LES DARBYSHIRE

THE SLIPPERY DOWNWARD SLIDE (1925–1934)

Company as, owing to the deaths of Holman Stephens and Jeremiah Macveagh (17.4.1932), he had been the sole remaining Director. The first 50 West Sussex Railway Shares numbers, 1–50, which had been issued to Holman Stephens in 1929 were transferred to William Henry Austen.

Doctor Hugh Nicol travelled on what would have been the 11.10am Tram from Chichester to Selsey in September 1932 and he later wrote of his experience which was published in the April 1935 edition of the *Railway Magazine*:

'Though unaware that most of the passenger trains were in fact Ford motor cars on flanged wheels, I was lucky enough on the journey from Chichester (South Street) terminus to Selsey Town terminus to catch a steam train. Headed by the ex-Shropshire & Montgomeryshire engine, *Morous*, this train consisted otherwise of a six-wheeled Southern Railway five-compartment third class coach and some goods trucks, mostly loaded with coal, picked up in the adjacent Southern Railway sidings. The motor car trains were timed to do the whole journey in 30 min., but the up and down steam trains were allowed 12 min. extra[31] for attaching and detaching wagons at intermediate points. Although the day return fare between the termini was only a shilling, I was the only passenger when the train left Chichester five minutes late, but we pulled up again for some belated person – possibly a railway official. Hardly were we out of the station before there was another stop; this time the guard got down and stood in a road the train was to cross. Having flagged it across the train proceeded. This flagging operation was repeated several times at level crossings, none of which had gates. There were two stops at Hunston, the next station, then some wagons were dropped and one picked up at Chalder. The empty wagon thus picked up had to be incorporated in the train between the locomotive and the coach.

On 20th August 1932 the Chichester-bound Shefflex railmotor was in collision with a lorry at Ferry level crossing. There must have been some considerable force to knock the front unit into the middle of the road at right-angles to its track! The front bumper had been smashed and the front wheels look as though they might have been slightly buckled.
COLONEL STEPHENS RAILWAY MUSEUM & ARCHIVE

Understandably, the rear portion of the railmotor did not sustain any damage and it was only dragged off the rails and onto the road. Bearing in mind that there were few houses in the vicinity of Ferry station and that it was high summer, might the onlookers, other than those with bicycles, have been passengers in the Shefflex?
COLONEL STEPHENS RAILWAY MUSEUM & ARCHIVE

NOTICE.

Passenger Train Parcels Traffic.

PARCELS, etc.,

From or to London, Brighton, Portsmouth, and intermediate places, are now conveyed from and to Selsey and Sidlesham at the same rate as from and to Chichester (S.R.).

A. W. SMITH,
Superintendent.

West Sussex Railway
(SELSEY TRAMWAY SECTION)

TIME TABLE

July 3rd, 1933, and until further notice.

PASSENGER FARES.
CHEAP DAY TICKETS.

Stonestreet & Sons, Tonbridge. 250/4977.

WEST SUSSEX RAILWAY.
Table of Single Fares.

THIRD CLASS. CHILDREN UNDER 14 YEARS (HALF FARES.)

	Selsey Town	Selsey Bridge	Golf Links	Ferry	Sidlesham	Mill Pond Halt	Chalder	Hoe Farm Halt	Hunston
Selsey Bridge	1 2								
Golf Links	2 2	1 2							
Ferry	3 3	3 3	1 2						
Sidlesham	4 4	4 4	3 3	2 2					
Mill Pond Halt	4 4	4 4	3 3	3 3	1 2				
Chalder	6 6	6 4	4 3	3 3	3 3	3 3			
Hoe Farm Halt	6 6	6 6	6 3	6 3	3 3	3 3	3 3		
Hunston	8 8	6 6	6 3	6 3	6 3	6 3	3 3	3 3	
Chichester	8 8	8 8	8 6	8 6	6 3	6 3	6 3	6 3	3 3

Return Fares.
Chichester & Hunston, Selsey & Sidlesham 6d.
For Cheap Day Tickets see next Panel.

CHEAP DAY RETURN TICKETS BETWEEN
CHICHESTER
AND
SELSEY
(In either direction)

WILL BE ISSUED DAILY ON ALL TRAINS

RETURN FARE 1/- (THIRD CLASS)

(Children under 14 years half-fare, 6d.)

Available for return by any Train on day of issue only.

Return Fare 8d. Third Class.

Also between
Chichester and Sidlesham
Chichester and Chalder
Selsey and Hunston.

Children under 14 years half-fare, 4d.

WEST SUSSEX RAILWAY.
(SELSEY TRAMWAY SECTION).
OFFICIAL TIME TABLE.

From MONDAY, JULY 3rd, 1933, until further notice.

DOWN. — WEEK DAYS.

	a.m.	a.m.	a.m.	a.m.	a.m.	p.m.	p.m.	p.m.	p.m.	p.m.	p.m.	Wed. and Sat. only p.m.
Victoria ...dep.	6 15	—	—	11ns18	—	1s32	—	4 15	—	5 NO	—	—
London Br. ,"	6 28	—	—	11ne43	—	1 40	—	4s52	—	5 s	—	7 20
Brighton ,"	7 50	8 46	9 36	11 28	12 0	2 45	3 20	5 15	5 50	6s50	—	9 15
Bognor ,"	8 30	10 13	10 25	12 0	1 3	3 20	3s05	5 50	6 45	7 5	—	9 56
Portsmouth ,"	8 30	10 52	10 0	1 19	1 19	3s05	4 10	5 53	6 55	7 45	—	9 45
Chichester ...dep.	9 15	11 5	11 40	1 19	2 10	4 10	4 19	6 45	6 55	7 45	—	10 30
Hunston ...arr.	9 24	11 14	11 50	1 50	2 19	4 19	4 24	6 55	7 4	7 54	—	10 39
Chalder ,"	9 29	11 19	11 56	11 56	2 24	4 24	4 29	7 4	7 59	—	—	10 44
Mill Pond Halt ,"	9 32	11 22	12 4	12 4	2 27	4 27	4 29	7 4	8 2	10 49	—	10 47
Sidlesham ,"	9 34	11 24	12 10	12 10	2 29	4 29	4 34	7 11	8 4	8 9	—	10 49
Ferry ,"	9 39	11 29	12 16	12 16	2 34	4 34	4 39	7 16	8 9	8 14	—	10 54
Selsey Bridge ,"	9 44	11 34	12 24	12 24	2 39	4 39	4 40	7 24	8 14	8 14	—	10 59
Selsey Town ...,"	9 45	11 35	12 25	12 25	2 40	4 40	4 40	7 25	8 15	8 15	—	11 0

NS — Not on Saturdays.   **SO** — Saturdays only.

UP. — WEEK DAYS.

	a.m.	a.m.	a.m.	a.m.	a.m.	p.m.	p.m.	p.m.	p.m.	p.m.	p.m.	Wed. and Sat. only p.m.
Selsey Town ...dep.	8 10	10 10	11 0	10 15	1 10	2 50	5 35	7 0	—	—	9 45
Selsey Bridge ,"	8 11	10 11	11 1	10 17	1 11	2 51	5 38	7 2	—	—	9 46
Ferry ,"	8 16	10 6	11 6	10 23	1 16	2 56	5 44	7 8	—	—	9 51
Sidlesham ,"	8 21	10 11	11 21	10 28	1 21	3 1	5 49	7 13	—	—	9 56
Mill Pond Halt ,"	8 23	10 13	11 23	10 30	1 23	3 3	5 51	7 15	—	—	9 58
Chalder ,"	8 26	10 16	11 26	10 33	1 26	3 6	5 54	7 18	—	—	10 1
Hunston ,"	8 31	10 21	11 31	10 42	1 31	3 11	6 3	7 27	—	—	10 6
Chichester ...arr.	8 40	10 30	11 40	10 55	1 40	3 20	6 15	7 30	8 30	10 53	10 15
Portsmouth ,"	9 26	11 21	11 48	11 35	2 36	4 9	6 59	8 7	11 7	—	—
Bognor ,"	9 30	11 21	11 35	1 20	3 27	3 50	7 39	9 6	—	—	—
Brighton ,"	10 34	1 31	—	4 14	4 18	7 14	9 6	—	—	—	—
London Br. ,"	10 55	1 31	1 17	4 15	4 42	9s11	10 7	—	—	—	—
Victoria ,"	11 13	—	1 17	—	5 33	8s25	9 53	—	—	—	—

NO SUNDAY SERVICES.

s — Via Brighton.

NOTE. — The Company will not be responsible for (i) loss, damage, inconvenience or expense by delay or detention of or to a passenger unless occasioned by the wilful misconduct of the Company or their servants; or (ii) any omission or inaccuracy in these tables; or (iii) any special, indirect, or consequential damages.

Every effort will be made to ensure the connections with the trains of the Southern Railway, as shown, but the same cannot be guaranteed.

Notice is hereby given that the Company reserve the right to cancel any or all the Trains herein scheduled at any time without giving further Notice.

Selsey Town, July, 1933.   A. W. SMITH, Superintendent.

THE SLIPPERY DOWNWARD SLIDE (1925–1934)

After Mill Pond halt (no stop) came Sidlesham, the only intermediate station with a loop line. This station was notable for the fact that its little waiting room was detached from, and not upon the platform.

'The train then ran over the "Tramway Bank" through Pagham Harbour and across the only underbridge on the line...[32] The train was then flagged into Ferry station, and ran through Golf Links halt, and Selsey Bridge station, after passing a locked siding into an apparently disused brickworks. The road bridge which gave the station its name was the only overbridge. Selsey Town terminus was a very short distance further. This was the principal station on the line, and the only one with a booking office. With its loco sheds, sidings, office and parcel goods on the platform, Selsey Town presented a cheerful appearance after the sight of the rotting, deserted platforms elsewhere...'

The Receiver and Manager purchased bulk storage petrol equipment on a three-year term in December 1932 so that the Company might benefit by the lower price of bulk petrol purchases. With a saving of 2½d per gallon, the equipment was installed at Selsey later that month.[33]

At a branch meeting of the National Farmers' Union held in Chichester on Wednesday, 11th January 1933 it was revealed that the Sussex Sugar Company had been incorporated on the 12th of the previous month to carry out the initial steps for the erection of a factory near the city at a cost of some £250,000 that would be capable of handling at least 10,000 tons of beet per annum.[34] The West Sussex Railway's hopes were soon raised when it was learnt that the Sugar Company had acquired a 45 acre plot of land adjacent to their line at Stockbridge level crossing and it was hoped that this would bring a considerable amount of goods traffic to the Tramway. As it was, around 1,000 tons of sugar beet were conveyed over the Tramway from Ferry Siding each year.

Selsey received some publicity from an unusual source when the *Southern Railway Magazine* dated May 1933 published an article by J. Elcombe, FCIS, entitled 'Selsey Bill as a Holiday Resort'. Following a description of 'this charming old-world seaside town' he had this to say about the Tramway:

'The town of Selsey is well served, as regards transport facilities, by the West Sussex Railway. The incoming visitor can obtain through tickets to Selsey from any Southern Railway station. Similar facilities from Selsey to any S.R. station are provided for the outgoing traveller. Southern Railway trains convey the visitor to and from Chichester, from which point the West Sussex Railway (or "The Tramways" as it is known locally, owing to the fact that, until 1924, it was called "The Hundred of Manhood and Selsey Tramways Company") transports him to Selsey.

'As regards luggage, the visitor can obviate all fears of trouble, by sending it on in advance from his home station, whence it is conveyed by the Southern Railway and the West Sussex Railway direct to Selsey.

'Cheap day return tickets are issued between Chichester and Selsey and vice versa, on all trains, the cost for the return journey of 16 miles, being one shilling only. Cheap day return tickets are similarly issued between other stations on the railway.

'In addition to the ordinary steam trains, variation in the method of conveyance of passengers is afforded by the use of two petrol-driven rail car sets, which are popular owing to the fact that the visitor is able to view the surrounding country on all sides.

'The value of the West Sussex Railway to this growing holiday resort is evidenced by the fact that in the holiday season of 1932, the number of passengers who travelled over the line increased to the extent of over 50 per cent, as compared with 1931.[35]

'Every effort is made for the convenience of visitors, trains connecting with those of the S.R. being run from Chichester to Selsey, whilst the S.R. Company assists in every possible way by means of close co-operation with the West Sussex Railway. To ensure that all goods from London and elsewhere are delivered to Selsey with expedition, a daily goods service on the West Sussex Railway is provided.

'...In conclusion it is suggested that the following quatrain is worth memorising:-

'VISIT SELSEY for quiet enjoyment and rest,
Bring the children, happy with spade and pail,
Holidays spent there prove to be of the best,
And remember – TRAVEL THROUGHOUT BY RAIL.'

The writer (none other than the Tramways Company's secretary) did well to come up with something positive to say about the railmotors, but note how he carefully omitted to mention how fume-ridden, noisy and rough-riding they were to travel in! Connections at Chichester between the two Companies' lines were, more often than not, nowhere near as convenient as the article suggested either, but on those Saturday trips that were, the luggage truck of the railmotors would often be filled to capacity with passengers' accompanied baggage.

At the Directors' Meeting held in Chichester on 1st June, it was reported that Mr. J. Elcombe had taken up a business appointment in Brighton, but that he was continuing to act in his capacity as Secretary to the Tramways Company. The Board discussed whether Selsey Bridge Halt could be better advertised as it was felt that many local residents did not realise that trains stopped there. A suitable notice board was subsequently erected beside the road at the top of the footpath that served the halt. The Annual General Meeting immediately followed at which it was announced that receipts had fallen in 1932 to their lowest level ever at £2,248 7s 6d. Expenses had been reduced to £3174 11s 2d, resulting in a lesser, but still most unsatisfactory loss of £936 3s 8d.

For the duration of the summer timetable, timings were changed yet again and, extravagantly, two trains were in operation with what must have been the 10.15am steam-hauled 'mixed' train from Selsey (although not shown as such) following just 15 minutes behind the railmotor service. The 'mixed' train was now allowed 40 minutes in the up direction and a full three-quarters of an hour on the down journey. Might the 6.45pm down Tram have been 'mixed' as well with its 40 minute schedule? The passing loop at Sidlesham saw some action when this service crossed the 7.00pm from Selsey there. It would certainly have been interesting to witness the latter tram attempting to run the two miles between Hunston and Chichester in just 3 minutes – surely a misprint in the timetable:

		a.m.	a.m.	a.m.	p.m.	p.m.	p.m.	p.m.	Wed. and Sat. only. p.m.
Selsey Town	dep.	8.10	10.00	10.15	1.10	2.50	5.35	7.00	9.45
Selsey Bridge	"	8.11	10.01	10.17	1.11	2.51	5.38	7.02	9.46
Ferry	"	8.16	10.06	10.23	1.16	2.56	5.44	7.08	9.51
Sidlesham	"	8.21	10.11	10.28	1.21	3.01	5.49	7.13	9.56
Mill Pond Halt.	"	8.23	10.13	10.30	1.23	3.03	5.51	7.15	9.58
Chalder	"	8.26	10.16	10.33	1.26	3.06	5.54	7.18	10.01
Hunston	"	8.31	10.21	10.42	1.31	3.11	6.03	7.27	10.06
Chichester	arr.	8.40	10.30	10.55	1.40	3.20	6.15	7.30	10.15

Morus taking on water opposite the station building at Chichester on 26th September 1933. The original fencing had recently been replaced with a crude post and rail one, and the station nameboard had yet to be returned to its position near the station building. A narrow gap in the fence provided access to the Tramways Company's land behind the platform.
COLLECTION TOM MIDDLEMASS

This photograph, taken later the same day, shows the Shefflex unit awaiting passengers at Chichester, more in hope than certainty. The left-hand portion of the buffer bar at the Selsey end had been broken off, no doubt the result of another collision at a level crossing. The pile of sleepers behind the railmotor served as a buffer stop.
COLLECTION TOM MIDDLEMASS

THE SLIPPERY DOWNWARD SLIDE (1925–1934)

We might well wonder what the solitary prospective traveller was thinking as he stood by the Shefflex railmotor at Chichester in 1934. The driver's door appears to have been painted black, probably after another accident repair, and it is now the right-hand section of the buffer bar that had been broken off. At least the station nameboard was back in position.
J. W. SPARROWE
Cty. R. S. CARPENTER

								Wed. and Sat. only.	
Chichester	dep.	9.15	11.05	11.40	2.10	4.10	6.45	7.45	10.30
Hunston	"	9.24	11.14	11.50	2.19	4.19	6.55	7.54	10.39
Chalder	"	9.29	11.19	11.56	2.24	4.24	7.01	7.59	10.44
Mill Pond Halt.	"	9.32	11.22	12.04	2.27	4.27	7.04	8.02	10.47
Sidlesham	"	9.34	11.24	12.10	2.29	4.29	7.11	8.04	10.49
Ferry	"	9.39	11.29	12.16	2.34	4.34	7.16	8.09	10.54
Selsey Bridge	"	9.44	11.34	12.24	2.39	4.39	7.24	8.14	10.59
Selsey	arr.	9.45	11.35	12.25	2.40	4.40	7.25	8.15	11.00

Having worked for the Company for a very short time in 1927, Mr. A. W. Smith had returned to the Tramway to resume his position of Superintendent earlier in the year, replacing Mr. G. A. Mansfield who had previously been employed by the Southern Railway, latterly at Hither Green. The passenger records for two Saturdays in August 1933, traditionally the busier days, make disappointing reading:

TRAIN EX-CHICHESTER			TRAIN EX-SELSEY		
	No. of passengers			No. of passengers	
Time	5th	12th	Time	5th	12th
9.15	7	5	8.10	11	2
11.05	53	31	10.00	8	18
11.40	24	Nil	10.15	5	4
2.10	48	44	1.10	34	63
4.10	28	26	2.50	21	29
6.45	25	24	5.35	20	33
7.45	5	9	7.00	8	5
10.35	4	4	9.45	Nil	2

Note how the 10.35pm Saturdays only Tram ran 5 minutes later than advertised in the timetable above. Three of the trains were locomotive hauled, and it will be seen how passengers (wisely) tended to steer clear of what must have been the mixed train from Selsey at 10.15am that returned from Chichester at 11.40am, its average speed being recorded as only 10mph, compared with the railmotors' 14.7mph. Why on earth did the Company continue to run the late Saturday service when it received such poor patronage? On another (unspecified) day the same month, a total of 33 passengers originated at Selsey, 19 at Sidlesham and 10 at Hunston.

In October, Mr. W. Bishop and his future wife made a journey over the Tramway, the locomotive being *Morous* in charge of the two ex-LCDR 6-wheel carriages acquired from the Southern Railway around 18 months previously. They were the only passengers, and while waiting at Chichester, Mr. Bishop asked the conductor/guard what time the train would be leaving, but he didn't know, explaining that the regular locomotive was out of service (*Ringing Rock*, surrounded by weeds, was parked in the siding beyond the platform) and that the one they had was short of steam owing to leaking tubes in the firebox. Eventually they were ready to leave, but when Mr. Bishop asked for two return tickets to Selsey, the conductor/guard said he would collect their fares on arrival as they would probably want to return by 'bus! After being flagged across Stockbridge Road and passing over the canal, the train came to a sudden halt. Although within sight of Hunston station, *Morous* had been uncoupled from her train and was heading down the line to take water there.[36] With her tanks replenished she returned and the train was able to continue on its way. After leaving Hunston, the train came to another halt in open country, this time for the fireman and conductor/guard to round up a horse that had strayed onto the track! There were no other incidents, but the scheduled half-hour's journey had taken well over an hour. The conduc-

With the wagons and carriage pushed back beyond the platform, this picture shows Morous running round her 'mixed' train at Chichester. The hedges and fences at the bottom of the rear gardens of the houses fronting Terminus Road look very neat and tidy, which is more than can be said for the Company's allotment beyond the platform!
COLONEL STEPHENS RAILWAY MUSEUM & ARCHIVE

Morous appears to have done more than her fair share of the work latterly, and she is seen here again with another 'mixed' train arriving at Selsey.
COLONEL STEPHENS RAILWAY MUSEUM & ARCHIVE

tor/guard could hardly believe it when Mr. Bishop again asked for return tickets, but their reason for going to Selsey was to travel on the Tramway. After a quick visit to the beach, the couple returned to the station to find *Morous* in the shed and, with no staff around, they feared they would have to return to Chichester by 'bus after all. Suddenly, to their surprise, the Ford railmotor with the baggage truck in the middle, arrived at the station, once again with no passengers. The timetable appeared to have been scrapped, and the railmotor left on its return trip when the crew were ready. Our travellers (the only passengers once again) soon regretted taking their seats in the front unit 'as the fumes and noise from the engine were terrific. I think it must have been running on paraffin oil. Owing to the uneven track and bad joints, one had to hold onto the seats, and conversation was impossible'. The return journey was no quicker than the outward one, and apart from having to be flagged laboriously across each of the main roads, the guard went off at several farms along the way to see if there were to be any parcels or produce to pick up the following day. Beside the driver was a pile of stones which he would throw at any rabbit or game bird that was foolish enough to come close enough to the tram, but luckily for them, on this journey, they didn't.[37]

With the area's sugar crop being lifted towards the end of October, work on the proposed beet factory at Stockbridge had yet to begin. Unfortunately for the West Sussex Railway and the local economy, the Government subsidies turned out not to be guaranteed for 1934 and the five succeeding years as had been hoped, and the scheme was not proceeded with.

After so many years of decline, at last passenger numbers showed a slight improvement and some 21,088 (excluding season ticket holders) travelled over the Selsey line during the year, an increase of 121 over 1932. Of these, only 1,725 passengers had through tickets, the remaining 19,363 having originated on the Tramway. Gross receipts had risen to £2,369 18s 10d and expenses had been reduced by £196 1s 11d to £2,978 9s 3d, resulting in a lesser deficit of £608 10s 5d. The reduction in expenses was probably achieved with a similar reduction in the maintenance of the rolling stock and the permanent way, weeds at this time allegedly being several feet tall between the four foot in places! Steam-hauled trains accounted for only 5,410 miles out of the 20,861 total.

At the Board meeting held at 23 Salford Terrace, Tonbridge on Saturday, 14th April 1934, owing to a transfer of debentures and shares, George Henry Willard and Alfred Willard stood down as Directors to be replaced by James Ramsay, OBE of 15 Florida Street, Mount Florida, Glasgow and William Holman Austen of 29 Douglas Road, Tonbridge, Kent.[38]

On 31st May a meeting was held at the Receiver and Manager's Office, 103 Cannon Street, London, those present being Owen Walker (receiver and manager) William Austen, Mr. Pitt of Pontifex Pitt & Co. (Plaintiff Debenture Holders' Solicitor) and the Company's secretary, J. Elcombe.

It was decided that 'the only course open, subject to approval by all parties interested, was to offer the West Sussex Railway to the Southern Railway at a figure of £15,000 and should no sale materialise, then to close the line and sell it at the best price'.

Another Directors' meeting took place, this time in Chichester on Wednesday, 27th June, at which J. Elcombe read a letter he had received from Owen Walker dated 20th June wherein he stated that he had interviewed Sir Herbert Walker, General Manager of the Southern Railway, who confirmed that his staff were already preparing estimates for the rebuilding of the Tramway and that the latter would arrange a further interview as soon as the Southern Railway investigations were completed. William Austen raised the point as to whether Elcombe might accept a reduction in his salary which related purely to the secretarial work, as distinct from the balance of his work which was performed as the Receiver and Manager's Assistant, but after discussion, and in view of 'the peculiar circumstances', it was resolved 'to leave the secretary's remuneration as at present'.

Leslie Harrington (the assistant to Edwin C. Cox, the Traffic Manager of the Southern Railway) accompanied by William Austen, made a detailed and thorough inspection of the Tramway, but the subsequent 14 page report[39] was damning to say the very least and it dramatically emphasised the difference between the standards that the Southern Railway considered acceptable, compared with the so much lesser ones of the West Sussex Railway.

The Report noted:

> The Company's rolling stock appears to have little value beyond scrap judged by S.R. standards and brief details are set out hereunder. It should be specially noted that the stock marked thus * does not belong to the Tramway Company but to the executors of Col. Stephens. It is on loan, but no recompense is received. At the present time the locomotive and rail car are working the traffic and if withdrawn the line could not carry on without further acquisitions.

Locomotives:

Name	Type	Approx. date	Remarks
Selsey	2–4–2T	1897	Beyond repair
Maraus (?) (sic)	0–6–0T	1883 (40)	
Ringing Rock	0–6–0T	1883	*

Rail Motors (converted 'Bus Chassis and Body type):
(a) Ford Twin (in poor condition).
* (b) Shefflex Twin.

Carriages:

No. -	Type	Remarks
4	Bogie Tram (original)	Hopeless condition
3	4-wheeled	
3*	4-wheeled	Bad condition
2	6-wheeled	Recently purchased from S.R.

Wagons:
4 open and 4 covered.
* 1 special truck for Shefflex unit.

The village of Selsey was described as

> '...isolated to a great extent to the east and west, and the main road from Chichester runs right to the coast at Selsey, serving en route the villages of Hunston and Sidlesham. Selsey itself has many attractions as a holiday resort; the sands are very good and well suited for bathing, and boating, fishing and golf are available. Up to the present, the best class of development has taken place on the West Beach which is farthest from the Selsey Tram Station. Schemes have been considered from time to time to divert the line so as to adequately serve the West Beach. On the east side, however, development is now proceeding. Adjacent to the station Mr. W. Hobbs of Sutton is opening an estate of small houses and, in addition, Messrs. Selsey Estates Ltd. and Messrs. Duncan Gray and Partners are offering land for sale. A Holiday Camp consisting of brick buildings to house 300 people is being erected on the Bill at Selsey.

> 'The occupants of the property on the West Beach appear mostly those of the classes owning private cars, but the development on the east side appears to cater for a less wealthy clientele. It therefore seems that the station as at present positioned will be suitable for serving that part of Selsey to which most traffic will go.

> 'The lobster pot fishery at Selsey is not unimportant and most of the traffic emanating therefrom is at present conveyed by rail.

> 'It must not be overlooked that Selsey is the nearest seaside town to Chichester which has a population of 13,912, and beside being a cathedral city has certain industrial activities, including a sausage and potted meat factory of Messrs. Shippams, a tannery and dye works, and an ice and cold storage works. Moreover, the huge population of 249,000 centred at Portsmouth is only 23 miles away from Selsey by rail.'

The report went on to suggest that if an 'up-to-date rail car' was provided that had good acceleration and braking power, it might be possible, whilst observing the present restrictions, to perform the journey between Chichester and Selsey, calling at the stations, but not the halts, in 23 minutes, with the possibility of being able to run an hourly service with such adjustments as were necessary to make connections with the main-line services at Chichester. If colour light signals were provided at the public road crossings and the track put into a good state of repair, it was believed that there would be more reason that the Ministry might sanction a speed of 40 miles an hour over the public road crossings. It was admitted, however, that there might be difficulties if a Sentinel Rail Car was employed seating 44 passengers with its very limited luggage capacity.

Attached to the report was a copy of Statutory Order No. 148 in which the Court of the Railway Rates Tribunal stated that they were satisfied that the West Sussex Railway was a railway company rather than an amalgamated company, a light railway company or a company whose powers of charging had since 14th August 1919 been increased by special Act and had applied the schedule of standard charges of the Southern Railway Company to the West Sussex Railway. The Report suggested '...it appears that the Tribunal have applied a scale of charges to a Railway Company which has but little more than a fictitious existence'! Passenger fares, in many cases, were on a very low scale. For the 7 mile 27 chain single journey between Chichester and Selsey the Company charged just 8d, whereas the standard scale for the journey should have been 11½d, and even on through fares the West Sussex Railway received only 8d single and 11d on third class summer tickets. The cheap day return ticket remained at just 1/- whereas the Southern Railway would have probably charged 1/3d.

It was blatantly obvious that the fall in the number of passengers was largely attributable to the competing Southdown Motor Services 'bus service which, although more expensive (11d single and 1/6d return) provided an hourly service

THE SLIPPERY DOWNWARD SLIDE (1925–1934)

throughout the day, including Sundays. It had been found that many rail passengers only booked as far as Chichester, completing their journey to Selsey by 'bus, although their luggage in advance would have been sent over the Tramway. Contrary to Mr. Elcombe's article of May 1933, the Report revealed that 'only very limited through booking facilities exist to Selsey'! Passenger business was the least profitable of the Company's undertaking.

In contrast to the passenger fares, standard charges were observed with regards to freight traffic, receipts for 1933 being as per the following table:

Description	Local	Through	Total
Goods	£78 11s 4d	£638 1s 3d	£716 12s 7d
Minerals	–	£166 17s 9d	£166 17s 9d
Coal & Coke	–	£692 3s 6d	£692 3s 6d
Parcels	£16 4s 0d	£241 1s 9d	£257 5s 9d
Miscellaneous traffic	£11 1s 9d	£45 9s 9d	£56 11s 6d
Live stock	–	15s 2d	15s 2d
Mails and Parcel Post			£41 7s 9d
Miscellaneous Receipts			£3 17s 1d

The revenue from merchandise, minerals and parcels amounted to £1,931 over the year and receipts had been fairly well maintained, i.e. £2,019 in 1931 and £1,818 in

Morous had again worked the daily 'mixed' train to Chichester and back and, having been coaled in readiness for the next day's trip, was still in steam as she stood over the inspection pit outside the decrepit engine shed. The Ford railmotor unit had once again been separated from its twin.
H. F. WHEELLER
CTY. R. S. CARPENTER

Standing clear of the main platform road, Morous looks somewhat lost amongst the weeds on the run-round loop at Selsey. On the extreme left of the picture, the Shefflex railmotor can be glimpsed running into the station. 6th August 1934.
H. F. WHEELLER
CTY. R. S. CARPENTER

West Sussex Railway
(SELSEY TRAMWAY SECTION).

OFFICIAL TIME TABLE.
MONDAY, OCT. 1st, 1934, and until further Notice.

DOWN — WEEK DAYS.

		a.m.	a.m.	a.m.	p.m.	p.m.	Sat. only p.m.	
Southern Railway	Victoria ....dep.	6 15	8 46	11ᴬ20	1ᴮ25	4 15	5ᴮ28	
	London Br..... ,,	6 28	8 35	11ᴬ8	1 40	4ᴮ50	5ᴮ16	
	Brighton .... ,,	7 50	10ᴮ13	12 0	2 45	5 15	7 4	SUNDAYS
	Bognor.......... ,,	8 30	10 52	1ᴺ3	3 20	5 58	7 42	No
	Portsmouth ... ,,	8 30	10 22	1 19	2 59	5 50	7 30	Service
West Sussex Railway	Chichester .... ,,	9 15	11 30	2 10	4 10	6 45	8 30	
	Hunston ...... arr.	9 24	11 39	2 19	4 19	6 54	8 39	
	Chalder ,,	9 29	11 46	2 24	4 24	6 59	8 44	
	Mill Pond Halt ,,	9 32	11 49	2 27	4 27	7 2	8 47	
	Sidlesham ...... ,,	9 34	11 55	2 29	4 29	7 4	8 49	
	Ferry .... ,,	9 39	12 1	2 34	4 34	7 9	8 54	
	Selsey Bridge ,,	9 44	12 10	2 39	4 39	7 14	8 59	
	Selsey Town ,,	9 45	12 12	2 40	4 40	7 15	9 0	

UP — WEEK DAYS.

		a.m.	a.m.	p.m.	p.m.	p.m.	Sat. only p.m.	
West Sussex Railway	Selsey Town dep.	8 10	10 0	1 10	2 50	5 30	7 20	
	Selsey Bridge ,,	8 11	10 2	1 11	2 51	5 31	7 21	
	Ferry .... ,,	8 16	10 8	1 16	2 56	5 36	7 26	
	Sidlesham ...... ,,	8 21	10 13	1 21	3 1	5 41	7 31	SUNDAYS
	Mill Pond Halt ,,	8 23	10 15	1 23	3 3	5 43	7 33	No
	Chalder ,,	8 26	10 18	1 26	3 6	5 46	7 36	Service
	Hunston .... ,,	8 31	10 27	1 31	3 11	5 51	7 41	
	Chichester ....arr.	8 40	10 40	1 40	3 20	6 0	7 50	
Southern Railway	Portsmouth.... ,,	9 26	11 17	2 34	4 10	6 59	8 30	
	Bognor........... ,,	9 30	11 35	2 26	3 50	6ᴮ36	8 27	
	Brighton .... ,,	10 36	1 17	3 25	5 10	7 14	9 6	
	London Br..... ,,	10 55	1 31	4 14	5 42	9ᴬ11	10ᴮ32	
	Victoria .... ,,	11 13	1 17	4 15	5 33	8ᴮ25	10ᴮ23	

A—Change at Worthing.　　**B**—Via Brighton.　　**S.O.**—Saturdays only.　　**NS**—Not Saturdays.

Every effort will be made to ensure the connections with the trains of the Southern Railway, as shown, but the same cannot be guaranteed.

NOTE.—The Company will not be responsible for (i) loss, damage, inconvenience or expense by delay or detention of or to a passenger unless occasioned by the wilful misconduct of the Company or their servants; or (ii) any omission or inaccuracy in these tables; or (iii) any special, indirect, or consequential damages.

Notice is hereby given that the Company reserve the right to cancel any or all of the Trains herein scheduled at any time without giving further Notice.　　A. W. SMITH, Superintendent.

Through rates for Goods, Cattle, and Mineral Traffic on ordinary scales now in force between all Stations on the W.S.R. and all other Railway Stations and Ports in Great Britain and Ireland.

Passenger Parcels Traffic.

PARCELS, ETC, from or to London, Brighton, Portsmouth, and intermediate places, are conveyed from and to W.S.R. Stations at the same rate as from and to Chichester Station (S.R.) saving all road charges.

WEST SUSSEX RAILWAY.
Table of Single Fares.

THIRD CLASS. — CHILDREN UNDER 14 YEARS (HALF FARE).

	Selsey Town	Selsey Bridge						
Selsey Bridge	-	2						
Golf Links	-	2	2	Golf Links				
Ferry	-	-	3	3	3	Ferry		
Sidlesham	-	-	4	4	4	3	Sidlesham	
Mill Pond Halt	-	4	4	4	3	2	Mill Pond Halt	
Chalder	-	-	6	6	6	4	3	3
Hoe Farm Halt	6	6	6	4	3	3	2	Hoe Farm Halt
Hunston	-	-	8	8	8	6	6	3	3	Hunston
Chichester	-	8	8	8	8	8	6	6	3

Return Fares.
Chichester & Hunston. Selsey & Sidlesham 6d.
For Cheap Day Tickets see next Panel.

CHEAP DAY RETURN TICKETS
BETWEEN

CHICHESTER
AND
SELSEY

(In either direction)

WILL BE ISSUED DAILY ON ALL TRAINS

RETURN FARE 1/- (THIRD CLASS)

(Children under 14 years half-fare, 6d.)

Available for return by any Train on day of issue only.

Also between Chichester and Sidlesham Chichester and Chalder Selsey and Hunston.

Children under 14 years half fare, 4d.

Return Fare 8d. Third Class.

September, 1934.

Stonestreet & Sons, Printers, Tonbridge.—Phone 15.　100/6421.

THE SLIPPERY DOWNWARD SLIDE (1925–1934)

1932. The total of 11,948 tons conveyed over the line during the year was made up of 4,464 in goods, 2,260 minerals and 5,224 tons of coal and coke, but of this, only 704 tons of goods and 1,117 tons of minerals originated on the Tramway. Sidings on the West Sussex Railway's premises at Chichester served the Anglo American (rent per annum £8 8s 0d) and Shell Mex Oil Companies (£94 0s 0d), Sadler's Mill (£12 12s 0d) and Botrill's coal wharf (£4 4s 0d) and a good proportion of the Company's goods revenue came from this traffic, although it was only shunted into position by the Tram engine and did not go down the line to Selsey at all. 3,417 tons of traffic were dealt with in this way at Chichester Tram Station in 1933, with receipts amounting to £399, the small amount of goods traffic local to the Tramway providing a revenue of only £7!

Apart from Chichester, the most important station for freight traffic was (as would be expected) Selsey, although there was some coal traffic to Charlton's coal wharf at Chalder (rent £5 0s 0d) and a small tonnage of general goods to Sidlesham. Traffic to Selsey gas works amounted to more than 500 tons per year, but it had to be taken by road from the station. The Company received annual rents of £10 0s 0d from Arnell & Son and £7 0s 0d from H. Prior for coal wharves at Selsey, plus £3 0s 0d from the Trojan Brick Company for its siding and land at Selsey Bridge. Over 1,000 tons of beet sugar was carried by the Tramway, this being only 117 tons short of the total minerals carried during the year which, for the most part, was loaded at Ferry station. Further income came from the rents of the Company's properties at Selsey, amounting to £132 10s 0d per annum, the total rents received by the Company in 1933 being £293 0s 0d. As far as goods traffic was concerned, the Report thought that it was probable that 'provided the road was in good condition', a Southern Railway engine could be found to work a trip from Chichester to Selsey, although additional staff expenditure would be incurred.

There was an amount shown as a balance debit of net revenue account of £13,216 whilst the sundry accounts due to the Company amounted to £17,693 2s 7d, the latter figure including accounts incurred before and after the appointment of the Receiver. Details were set out in the following statement:

	£	s	d
Suspense account	47	5	0
Mileage and Demurrage	8	0	0
Commissioners of Inland Revenue	336	15	9
Advertising	111	6	0
Directors' Fees	463	4	10
Debenture interest	5,274	1	11
Cartage	13	1	11
Southern Railway Co	1,961	11	7
Painter Mayne & Walker (per Mr Owen Walker)	598	4	10
Pontifex Pitt & Co. (Solicitors to Receiver)	32	0	0
Southern Railway Co	430	9	8
The Executors of Lt. Col. H. F. Stephens	7,467	13	7

It was understood that the Executors of Holman Stephens would be prepared to waive the amount of £7,467 upon a reasonable offer being accepted for their holdings in the Company.

The Report concluded that there was no doubt that the resuscitation of the line would involve substantial expenditure being incurred, apart from the necessary attention being given to the track to bring it into a condition to allow the line to be worked at speeds to enable it to compete with the 'bus service. These were the features that were regarded as being important:-

(a) The general appearance of dilapidation must be removed, suitable direction notices provided and some improvement made to the buildings at Selsey. In this connection it may be remarked that apart from the derelict rolling stock standing in the yard, a casual visitor would have no idea of the presence of the station.

(b) The layout at Chichester should be altered so as to provide for the line either running into the bay platform or into another line at the back of the platform, the Selsey tram premises being used to compensate for loss of certain room in the Southern Railway coal yard.

(c) Comfortable and attractive rolling stock must be obtained.

From the particulars previously set out it will be observed that the Southdown Bus Company is providing some 750 passenger seats each way daily between Chichester and Selsey. No particulars of the loading of these 'buses have been obtained, but assuming that only 25 per cent load were secured, it means that 68,000 passengers travel each way on the route in the course of a year. If only half of these were secured to the Selsey line at the present low fares, the additional revenue would amount at least to £1,700 per annum.

'Selsey is developing and even though the line itself may not be a financial success, it must not be overlooked that there is the contributory value of the traffic to the Southern Railway to be considered. The Southern Railway cannot expect to share to the full in the developments at Selsey unless there is a rail connection available.

'In view of the relatively heavy expenditure which will have to be incurred in improving the line, I am of opinion that any investment that the Southern Railway might make will initially have to be regarded in this light. Doubtless also some increase in staff costs will arise, even if the adoption of standard conditions is avoided. It may be, however, that financial assistance could be obtained from those interested in developments at Selsey.

'It is of course very difficult to give a considered opinion on these matters until an estimate is obtained from the Technical Department of the costs involved and possibly the first step would be for the appropriate Departmental representatives to confer with Mr. Austen and the opinion of the Solicitor obtained respecting the legal position of the line.'

Other information gleaned from the Report showed that only 12 members of staff were employed on the Tramway in 1934, each of whom worked a nominal 54 hour week. Included in their weekly wages (shown below) were small items of overtime in some instances to cover Saturday working between 8.00am and 9.00pm, and on Wednesdays when the line was open until 11.00pm.

Traffic			
Superintendent	£3	1s	6d [41]
Selsey – Part-time temporary Clerk	£1	1s	0d
Hunston-Sidlesham. Lad Porter (also performs parcel Delivery)	£-	13s	0d
Chichester – Station Agent	£2	10s	0d
Guard-Conductor	£1	0s	0d
Locomotive Running			
Fitter Driver	£3	3s	0d
Fireman Labourer	£2	0s	0d
Rail-car Driver	£2	12s	1d
Engineers			
Ganger	£2	3s	6d
Undermen (3)	£1	13s	0d
	£1	10s	0d
	£1	10s	0d
Total	£22	17s	1d

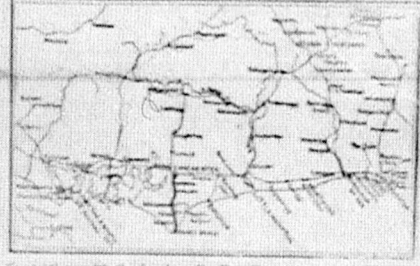

Despite the Tramway being in decline, no expense was spared with this timetable poster introduced on 1st October 1934. One photograph shows Sidlesham heading across the Tramway embankment with a 'mixed' train, another shows Selsey's fishing quarter at the turn of the century, whilst the two lower ones depict scenes on the resort's sands.
COLONEL STEPHENS RAILWAY MUSEUM & ARCHIVE

THE SLIPPERY DOWNWARD SLIDE (1925–1934)

Taken during the currency of that timetable, this view shows the Shefflex railmotor waiting for custom at a very shabby Chichester station.
COLONEL STEPHENS RAILWAY MUSEUM & ARCHIVE

In addition to these wages, other expenditure included the not inconsiderable amount of part rent of £48 for 23 Salford Terrace, Tonbridge, part salaries of £209 of that office's staff and £31 towards office expenses.

Coming into effect on Monday, 1st October, this timetable was issued:

							Sat only
Selsey Town	dep.	8.10	10.00	1.10	2.50	5.30	7.20
Selsey Bridge	"	8.11	10.02	1.11	2.51	5.31	7.21
Ferry	"	8.16	10.08	1.16	2.56	5.36	7.26
Sidlesham	"	8.21	10.13	1.21	3.01	5.41	7.31
Mill Pond Halt	"	8.23	10.15	1.23	3.03	5.43	7.33
Chalder	"	8.26	10.18	1.26	3.06	5.46	7.36
Hunston	"	8.31	10.27	1.31	3.11	5.51	7.41
Chichester	arr.	8.40	10.40	1.40	3.20	6.00	7.50
							Sat only
Chichester	dep.	9.15	11.30	2.10	4.10	6.45	8.30
Hunston	"	9.24	11.39	2.19	4.19	6.54	8.39
Chalder	"	9.29	11.46	2.24	4.24	6.59	8.44
Mill Pond Halt	"	9.32	11.49	2.27	4.27	7.02	8.47
Sidlesham	"	9.34	11.55	2.29	4.29	7.04	8.49
Ferry	"	9.39	12.01	2.34	4.34	7.09	8.54
Selsey Bridge	"	9.44	12.10	2.39	4.39	7.14	8.59
Selsey Town	arr.	9.45	12.12	2.40	4.40	7.15	9.00

This timetable was short lived and on 16th November it was announced that 'until further notice, one train only for the conveyance of passengers will be run each day as follows: Leaving Selsey at 10.00am (approx.), arrive Chichester 11.00am (approx.): leave Chichester 11.30am (approx.), arrive Selsey 12.15pm (approx.).' A note advised that it was operated by motor cars – 3rd class only), so why were the journeys scheduled to take so long? Despite the note, this service was surely steam hauled and was run more for the carriage of goods, rather than passengers. As can be seen, anyone from Selsey would have had to complete their business in the city within half an hour, and a return trip by rail from Chichester to Selsey would take two days!

Notes

1. *Chichester Observer*, Wednesday, 17.6.1925.
2. The next site surveyed at Burnham on Sea, Somerset was also unsuitable and the 15in gauge main line was eventually built in Kent in 1927, despite the many level crossings, where it became the world-famous Romney, Hythe & Dymchurch Railway. Details from *The Marshlander*, Summer 1985, journal of the RH & DR, and correspondence with the Company's Marketing Manager, Derek Smith.
3. Only one open baggage truck was ever run at one time with the railmotors.
4. The description of these carriages suggests that they were the original bogie stock and/or the ex-Lambourn Valley vehicles, all of which were rarely used by this date. From an undated interview that John Miller (honorary curator of the Colonel Stephens Railway Museum) had with Dick Cash.
5. *Chichester Observer*, Wednesday, 12.5.1926.
6. The opening of the upper end of the windpipe between the vocal chords.
7. Rather than try to fix the defective engine *en route*, couldn't the driver have driven the rear unit (each car was fitted with two reverse gears) under the guidance of the conductor who could have kept a careful lookout from the front?
8. *Chichester Observer*, Wednesday, 27.4.1927. The 'bus, fleet No. 80, had been delivered new to Southdown Motor Services Ltd. on 19.7.1920 with a Brush single deck B29F body. Its chassis survived a serious fire at the Company's Bognor garage on 9.7.1923 to be rebodied by Tilling as

an O27/24R double decker in March 1924. This body was removed on 20.10.1928 and fitted to 'bus No. 97, the chassis being scrapped at Portslade that same month. Details from correspondence with John Allpress, Honorary Chairman of the Southdown Enthusiasts' Club, 11.5.2003.
9. The AGMs for 1928, 1929 and 1930 were similarly advertised in the *Morning Advertiser*, but there was no attendance at any of them.
10. Identical details were advertised in the *Chichester Observer* on Wednesday, 29.2.1928.
11. With no run-round loop at Wingham (Canterbury Road) the locomotive would be run into the single goods siding whilst its train ran past down the 1 in 50 gradient over an ungated level crossing and alongside the platform by gravity.
12. *Going off the Rails – the Country Railway in West Sussex* by Bill Gage, Michael Harris and Tony Sullivan, published by West Sussex County Council, 1997.
13. Southdown Motor Services' route 32 on its return to Chichester had originally served East Street, Manor Road and Station Road, but from 1.2.1926 their 'buses operated into and out of the village via High Street. This may have been owing to the poor condition of the roads, but after they had been improved, Southdown's route remained as amended.
14. *Chichester Post*, Saturday, 28.7.1928.
15. According to the Southern Railway Report published in 1934, the expenditure in obtaining the West Sussex Railway Certificate was borne by Holman Stephens out of his private resources.
16. *The Selsey Tramways* by Edward C. Griffith, third edition published by the author, 1974.
17. *Chichester Observer*, 12.12.1928.
18. Jeremiah ('Jerry') MacVeagh was born in Belfast in 1870. He became involved in several of Holman Stephens' later activities, serving as a director on the East Kent, North Devon & Cornwall Junction, Shropshire & Montgomeryshire and Kent & East Sussex Railways, as well as being a promoter of the ill-fated Southern Heights Light Railway.
19. Holman Stephens held only the one share in the Hundred of Manhood & Selsey Tramways Co. Ltd. from 1896 until some time after 1915. By 1925 he held 221 shares and by 1930 he had no less than 2,621 of the 2,880 shares issued.
20. The Southdown Enthusiasts' Club has been unable to find any reference to this collision in the surviving 'Bus Company's records. Mr. Arnell's comments suggest that it occurred at Ferry crossing, rather than at Stockbridge Road.
21. *Old Motor*, Volume 9, No. 5.
22. The speed of trains was limited to 5mph for 200 yards on the approach to each level crossing, but although it was suggested that trains pulled up just before they crossed each main road, this was not specified in the West Sussex Railway Certificate.
23. *Chichester Post*, Saturday, 11.1.1930 and the *Chichester Observer*, Wednesday, 15.1.1930
24. *The Selsey Tramways* as above. Edward Griffith erroneously quotes the year as 1933.
25. 'Light engine' would not refer to a locomotive running by itself, but a 'small engine'.
26. Holman Stephens had suffered a stroke back in January, followed by a more serious one in April which left him partially paralysed and unable to speak or write.
27. Board of Directors' Minute Book, 3.3.1931.
28. Etiolate: make pale by excluding light; give sickly hue to.
29. William Henry Austen was born on 8th May 1878 and commencing with the construction of the Rye Camber Tramway in 1895, he was employed as Holman Stephens' assistant.
30. Board of Directors' Minute Book, 31.5.1932.
31. For the past few years the extra timings of the 'mixed' steam trams had been reduced from 12 minutes to just 5 minutes in each direction.
32. Doctor Nicol had somehow missed the (albeit non-operational) drawbridge across the Chichester Canal north of Hunston.
33. Board of Directors' Minute Book, 1.6.1933.
34. *Chichester Observer*, Wednesday, 18.1.1933.
35. Excluding Season Tickets Holders, just 13,416 passengers travelled on the Tramway in 1931 – an all-time low – compared with 20,967 passengers in 1932.
36. Staff had always been discouraged from using the water supply at Chichester as, being connected to the mains, it had to be paid for.
37. *Branch Line to Selsey* by Vic Mitchell and Keith Smith, published by Middleton Press, 1983 and the video *The Selsey Tramway 1897–1935*, by Magic Box Productions, 1997.
38. Also employed at 23 Salford Terrace, Tonbridge, William Holman Austen was William Henry Austen's son and Holman Stephens' Godson.
39. For an edited version of the 1934 Report see *The Tenterden Terrier*, Numbers 79 and 80 Summer and Winter 1999, the Journal of the Kent & East Sussex Railway.
40. *Morous* was built in 1866.
41. Note the great reduction in wage compared to Henry Phillips' £8 13s 0d per week in 1924.

CHAPTER EIGHT
CLOSURE, SALE & WINDING UP (1935–1947)

AT the Directors Meeting held at Luther Clayton's residence, 'Nortonlea', Selsey on Wednesday, 2nd January 1935 it was decided that as negotiations for the sale of the undertaking to the Southern Railway Company were being continued, the matter should be left in abeyance pending a definite decision being known. It was also reported that 'certain documents were missed (sic) from the Registered Office of the Company, and on the Secretary being approached on the matter, it was admitted that they were in his possession. These documents were removed without the authority of the Directors, and a satisfactory explanation not being forth-coming from the Secretary, it was decided to recommend to the Receiver that his services be dispensed with one-month from the present date'.[1] Not that any of this mattered as within days it was confirmed that the Southern Railway's chief engineer, George Ellson, considered the estimate to bring the Tramway into a bay adjoining the down mainline platform at Chichester, along with upgrading the permanent way to an acceptable standard, was unrealistic,[2] so the hoped for sale did not go ahead. All too soon, this dreaded fateful notice appeared on the Company's notice boards:

**ON AND FROM
14TH JANUARY 1935
UNTIL FURTHER NOTICE
PASSENGER
&
FREIGHT
TRAFFIC WILL BE
ENTIRELY CLOSED**

According to newspaper reports, the Tramway continued to work until Saturday, 19th January, the *Hampshire Telegraph & Post* advising the day before that '...inquiries reveal that no passengers have been carried this week, and no goods accepted for transport other than those for which invoices had previously been received...' It was hardly surprising that there had been no passengers when the public had been advised that the line was closed! The last train to run was steam hauled, as they probably all had been during the last week and there was much mournful whistling from the locomotive (it had to be *Morous*) on the final trip down to Selsey. Many believed that the closure was only temporary and the same newspaper optimistically suggested that 'the rapid development of the Witterings and the steady growth of Selsey seem to suggest that there is a good cause for railway development along the coast, perhaps from Bognor Regis.' Some hopes! In its 'obituary' to the Tramway, The *West Sussex Gazette* wrote on 17th January:

'...This quaint little light railway between Chichester and Selsey has seen many changes in its long life, and in its prime was practically the only serviceable means of communication between the villages of the Selsey peninsula and the rest of the world. Its single track, wandering across roads and through fields to curious and isolated little stations, has carried thousands of holiday-makers to and from Selsey in the days long before Selsey began to aspire towards urban status, and its oddities have been the subject of many good-humoured jokes, verbal and pictorial. Among the regulations of the line was one that, whenever the trains crossed the main road, a man with a red flag had to stand in the road and give warning to traffic before the engine slowly emerged from the adjacent fields. The prolonged warning scream of the Selsey engine is among the memories of local old-timers, who may be permitted a sentimental sigh over the closure of the line. In recent years the railway business has been materially affected by the 'bus services and the general growth of the motor traffic of all kinds...One serious disadvantage which the closure, whether temporary or permanent, of the line will probably involve for Selsey people is a considerable addition to their coal bills to cover the cost of haulage, and there are other demands for heavy transport which will lead to a hope that this service, which has been available for so long, may be found restorable to the community it catered for for so long.'

As Mr. Stuart Arnell supervised the unloading of the last wagon to deliver coal to his wharf in Selsey goods yard on Saturday, 19th January he echoed the thoughts of the *West Sussex Gazette* when he admitted 'It's going to be pretty awkward for us and it will mean going back to the ships for the heavy traffic and for coal for the gas works unless the line is developed.'[3] Prior to the arrival of the Tramway in 1897, approximately 50 tons of coal at a time would be brought to Selsey by small colliers. They were beached at low tide, and would have to be unloaded by the next high tide.

News of the closure of the Tramway even reached the national press, the 'Special Correspondent' of the *Daily Express* writing from 'Selsey-on-Sea' on Sunday, 20th January for publication the following day:

END OF THE 'SELSEY BUMPER'
PAST GLORIES OF A MINIATURE LINE

The whole staff of a railway line, from superintendent to messenger boy, received their last week's wages and became out of work yesterday. They were the twelve employees of the 'Selsey Bumper' or the West Sussex Railway – which ceased to operate today after thirty-eight hectic years of life on the nine-mile-run between Chichester and Selsey.

The railway was formed 'without parliamentary assistance or interference' in 1897, at a cost of £21,000. Four years ago it went into the hands of a receiver. A few weeks ago, negotiations for its sale to the Southern Railway broke down. A week ago the staff received notice.

Tonight, with ex-engine driver George White, I toured the sheds and saw about the strangest collection of railway stock in the world. In a huge corrugated iron shed, with half the roof off – it was blown away in a gale last year – were three old engines. One bore, in brass lettering, the words 'Shropshire and Montgomeryshire Railway', another was called The *Ringing Rock* and was dated 1883, and the third (which burst its boiler six months ago)[4] bore the letters '*Selsey*, 1897'.

Outside were some more 'engines' – old motor coaches of the famous 'tin lizzie' type, fitted with steel wheels. Selsey station is a corrugated iron shed. Further along the line is the Ferry station – a few sleepers piled together for a platform, a small wooden shed for shelter. There are nine stations along the line. Not one of them has a porter or a booking office.

As we toured round George said: "We've had some strange things happen on this old line in the past two years. Being a single track meant that if there was a breakdown the service was finished for the day. We

PLAN Nº 1

CHICHESTER

Southern Railway

Chichester Terminus Level Crossing

Terminus Road

Basin

Level Crossing

Chichester Canal

SCALE
6 Inches to

Donnington

Drawbridge
Cottages

CLOSURE, SALE & WINDING UP (1935–1947)

used to send a boy on a bicycle instead of the train, just to tell anyone waiting at the stations that we wouldn't be along that day. There was a day... but come with me..."

We went to a little house over-looking the 'station', and there I met Tim Johnson, sixty-four years old, first driver on the line in 1897... holder of the speed record for the trip... "So it's finished... eh?" he mused... "Pity... Smart line it was. Once I did the trip in a real engine,[5] the old *Sidlesham*, in eighteen minutes... Go like a deer she would... That's a record no one ever broke. We used to take 300 passengers at a time some trips. So the old *Selsey*'s got a boiler bust... Ah! That's sad. Wonderful little engine she was... go like a hare. Strangest thing I ever remember about the line was in 1910, when the sea flooded a great deal of it and they had to use a stage coach... Well, I'm sorry it's ended..."

Next week the old engines and 'motor trams' will stand silent. And the epitaph of the old 'Selsey Bumper' will be... 'Railway for Sale'.

Not all staff were made redundant on 19th January and driver Harry Davies and fireman Ray Apps were employed transferring the remaining main-line wagons back to Chichester, along with *Ringing Rock* and the chassis of the Shefflex railmotor unit and its baggage truck which were the property of the late Holman Stephens. With the transfer of rolling stock completed, *Morous* was steamed for the last time on Thursday, 24th January.

Under the heading 'EXIT "SELSEY BILLY"' the *Chichester Post* had the last say when it wrote of the Tram on 26th January:

'Puffing, bumping, Selsey Billy is no more. He has served his purpose, and, like the old horses he superseded, he has become worn out and out of date. During the last few years the Billy has been the subject of many a quip in Chichester, but it must be admitted that he has made his contribution to the history of this corner of West Sussex. Not only did he establish a newer, quicker and more regular means of communication between the little fishing village called Selsey, and starting then (to) become quite fashionable because of its bracing air and glorious sunshine, but he opened up the rich agricultural land between Chichester and the Bill. The years wore on, and Billy wore with them, and now the line has been closed. People are already talking of a successor: an ordinary gauge track, (sic) with fast engines and modern railway carriages. We shall soon know if this is true or not.'

It wasn't true, of course, and with the Tramway having been closed with such indecent haste, the February edition of *Bradshaw* still showed the one train per day service as being in operation! Over the next twelve months the weed-ridden track began to disappear under the ever-encroaching undergrowth as nature began to reclaim her own, but at least motorists were now able to speed over the level crossings without the fear of being hit by a train! Southdown Motor Services Ltd. didn't increase the hourly frequency of their 'bus service between Chichester and Selsey; there was no need to as hardly anyone used the Tramway by the end.

The Official Receiver put the complete railway up for sale through George Thatcher & Son, (solicitors) of 32 Essex Street, London WC2, these being the Special Stipulations and Conditions of Sale:

PARTICULARS OF THE HUNDRED OF MANHOOD and SELSEY TRAMWAY

TO BE SOLD BY TENDER in one lot pursuant to the Order of the Chancery Division of the High Court of Justice dated the 7th February 1934 (sic).[6]

The Railway (which is no longer working having been closed down on the 19th January 1935 the staff having been dismissed) operated over a total length of about eight miles between Chichester and Selsey, which in recent years has rapidly developed as a seaside resort.

STATIONS AND HALTS

<u>Chichester Terminus</u> Area about 1½ acres, adjoins the Southern Railway Station on the South.

The buildings consist of a waiting room and office of timber and corrugated iron on brick foundations, and other buildings of corrugated iron, let to the Shell-Mex Company. The agreement of 1935 between Owen Walker on behalf of this Company and the Southern Railway the latter has the non-exclusive right to work its traffic to and from certain premises therein mentioned for a period over part of the Company's track free of charge but this right ceases on the Conveyance to the present Purchaser.[7]

<u>Hunston</u> Timber and corrugated iron waiting room.

<u>Hoe Farm</u> No buildings.

<u>Chalder</u> Timber and corrugated iron Waiting room on cement rendered brick base.

<u>Mill Pond</u> Timber and felt covered waiting room.[8]

<u>Sidlesham</u> Timber and corrugated iron Waiting room on concrete piers.

<u>Ferry</u> Timber Waiting room.

<u>Golf Links</u> No buildings.

<u>Selsey Bridge</u> Timber Waiting room.

<u>Selsey Terminus</u> Area about 2½ acres. The buildings of timber and corrugated iron consist of waiting room, booking office, superintendent's office, ladies' lavatory, oil store, engine shed, goods shed and fitters' shop.

THE PERMANENT WAY
is laid for single track of standard gauge.

LEVEL CROSSINGS
The line crosses the public highway by level crossings at seven points as shown on the plan. Agricultural accommodation crossings are provided at Bridge, Hoe, Brinfast and Church Farms.

COTTAGES

Station Cottages <u>Selsey</u> (Coloured blue on Plans).	A terrace of four cottages built of brick and roofed with slates each containing:
	<u>On the first floor.</u> Three rooms and a W.C.
	<u>On the ground floor.</u> Two rooms, scullery and larder; with a W.C. outside and a small garden. Water and gas are laid on.
Drawbridge Cottage, <u>Hunston.</u> (Coloured green on Plan No.1)	A cottage built of brick and roofed with slates, containing:
	<u>On the first floor.</u> Three rooms
	<u>On the ground floor.</u> Two rooms, kitchen and scullery. Water is supplied from a well. This cottage is vacant and has been condemned for want of drainage.

RENTS RECEIVABLE
RENTS are receivable in respect of cottages, sidings etc. as follows.

Description of Premises	Tenant		Annual Rent	Term
1 Station Cottages Selsey	Mansfield G. A.	(13/- weekly)	£33.16.0.	Weekly
2 do. do.	Outram	(13/- weekly)	33.16.0.	do.
3 do. do.	Lee B.	(12/- weekly)	31.4.0.	do.
4 do. do.	Thorogood Mrs.	(13/- weekly)	33.16.0.	do.
Siding, Chichester.	Anglo-American Oil Co. Ltd.	(Temporarily suspended)	8.8.0.	Quarterly
Siding and Wharf, Selsey	Arnell E.G. & Sons	(ditto.)	10.0.0.	do.
Siding, Chichester	Bottrill R.	(ditto.)	4.4.0.	do.
Siding & wharf, Chalder	Charlton C. E.	(ditto.)	5.0.0.	do.
Cable under line	Chichester Corporation		1.1.0.	Yearly
Rubbish Dump, Sidlesham	Parris P.S.		1.0.	do.
Siding & Ground at Chichester	Shell-Mex & B.P. Ltd.		93.18.5.	21 years from Sept. 1922 determinable at 7th or 14th year.

HUNSTON

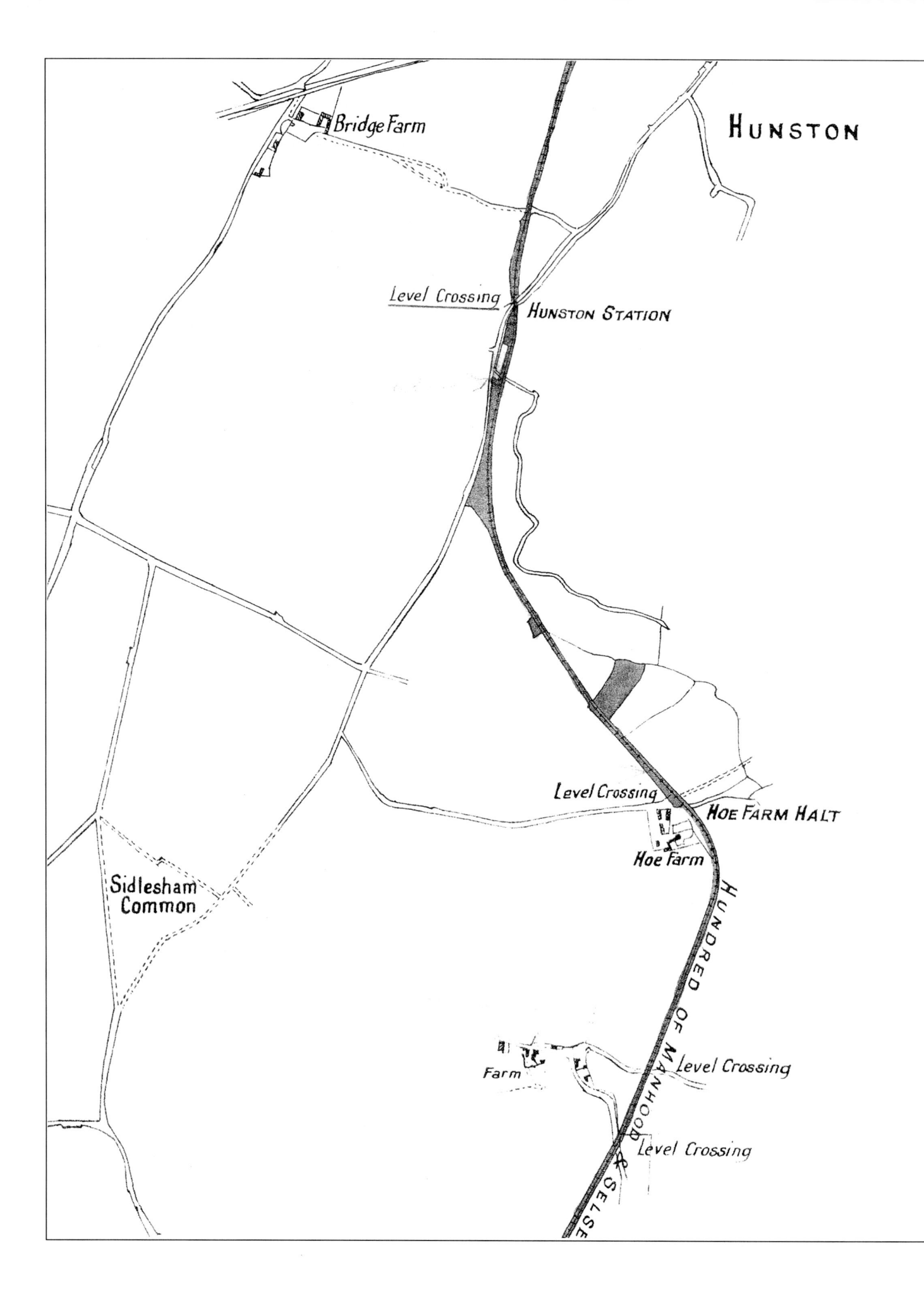

Bridge Farm

Level Crossing — Hunston Station

Level Crossing — Hoe Farm Halt
Hoe Farm

Sidlesham Common

Farm — Level Crossing

HUNDRED OF MANHOOD & SELSE

Level Crossing

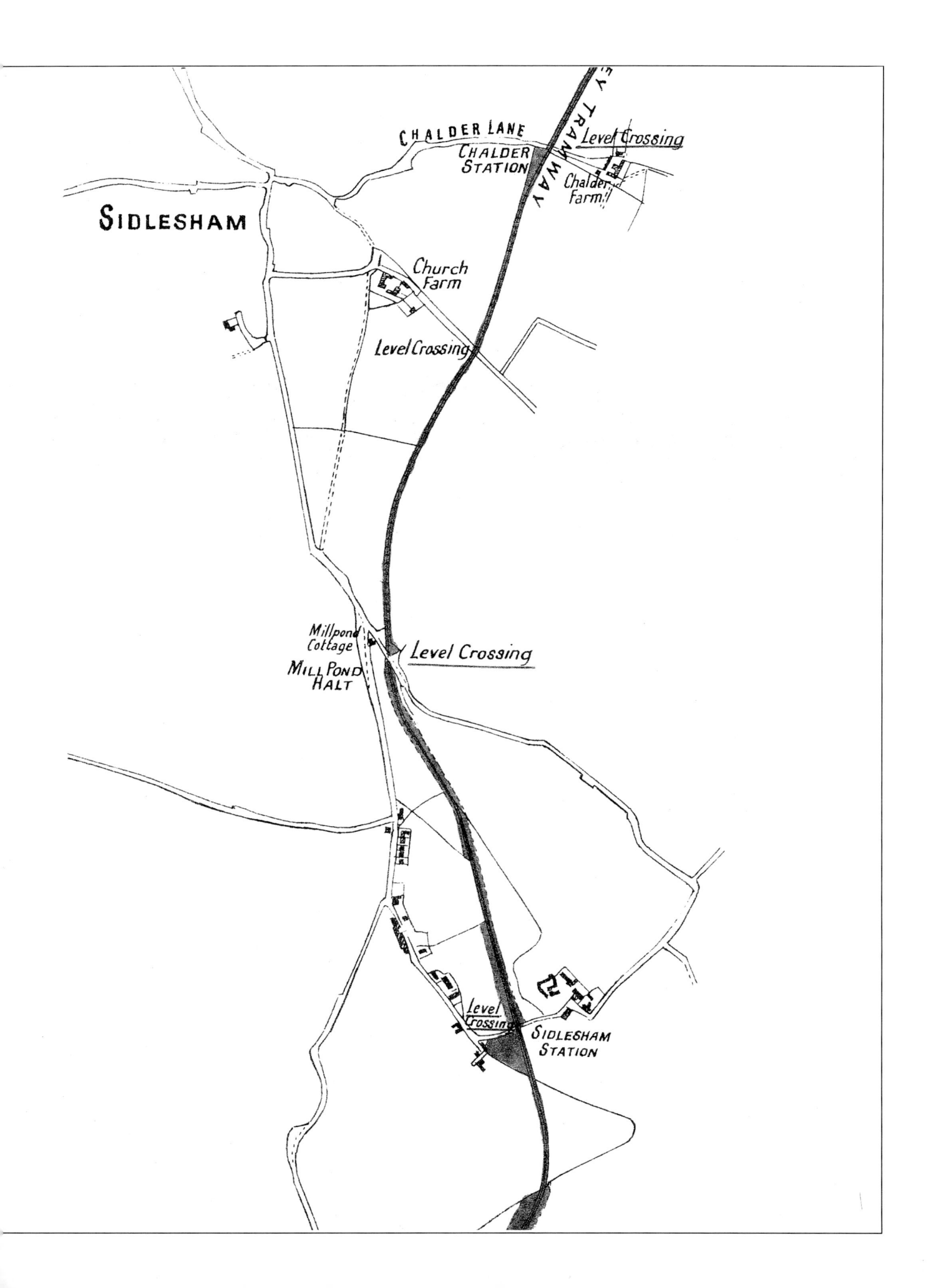

SIDLESHAM

CHALDER LANE
Level Crossing
CHALDER STATION
Chalder Farm
Y TRAMWAY

Church Farm

Level Crossing

Millpond Cottage
MILL POND HALT
Level Crossing

Level Crossing
SIDLESHAM STATION

FERRY BANK

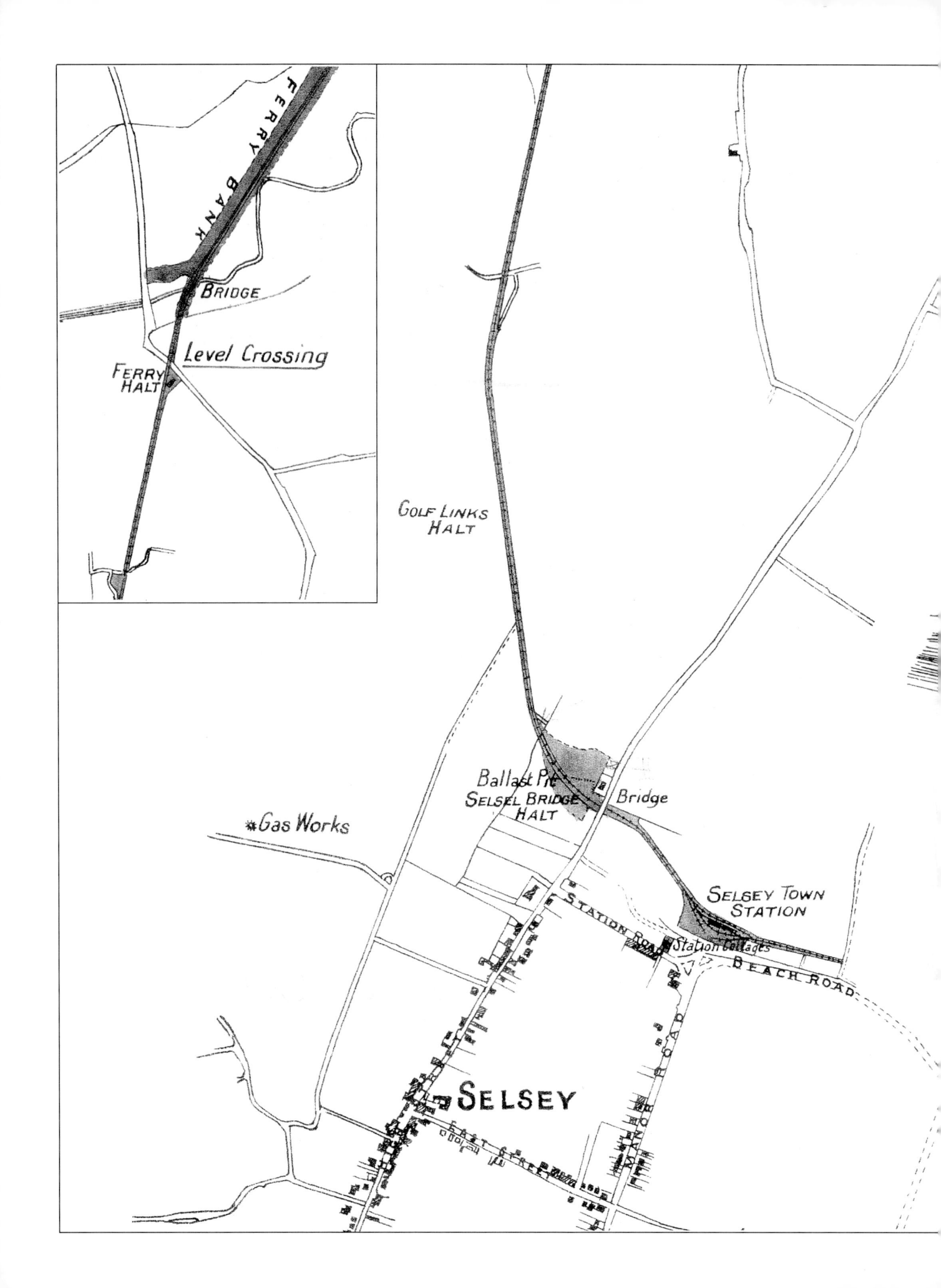

BRIDGE

Level Crossing

FERRY HALT

GOLF LINKS HALT

Ballast Pit
SELSEL BRIDGE HALT
Bridge

*Gas Works

SELSEY TOWN STATION

STATION ROAD
Station Cottages
BEACH ROAD

SELSEY

Taken soon after closure, this picture shows the three horizontal wooden bars (by the man in the dark coat) fixed to prevent access to Chichester Tramway station.
PHOTOMATIC

Plan No 2.

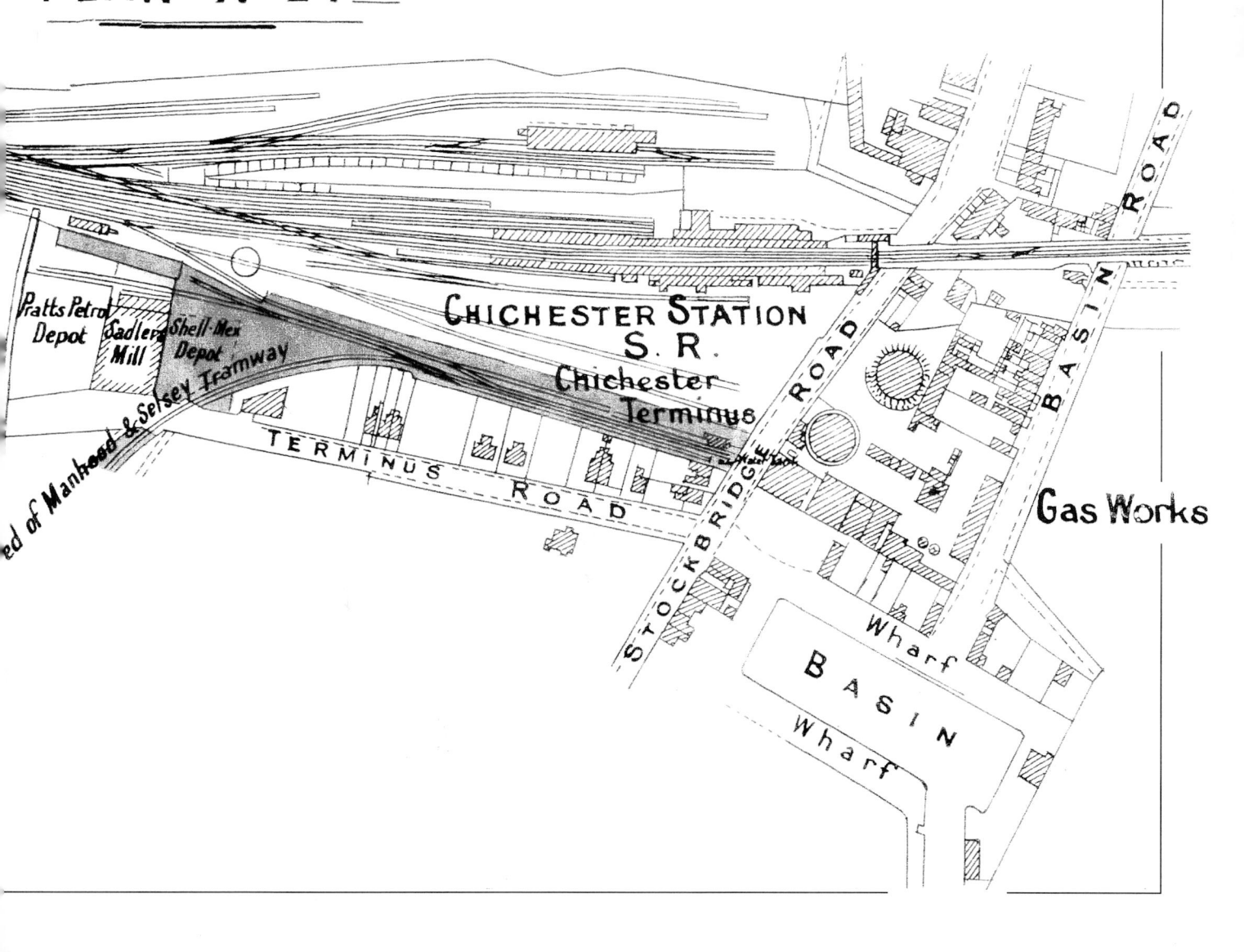

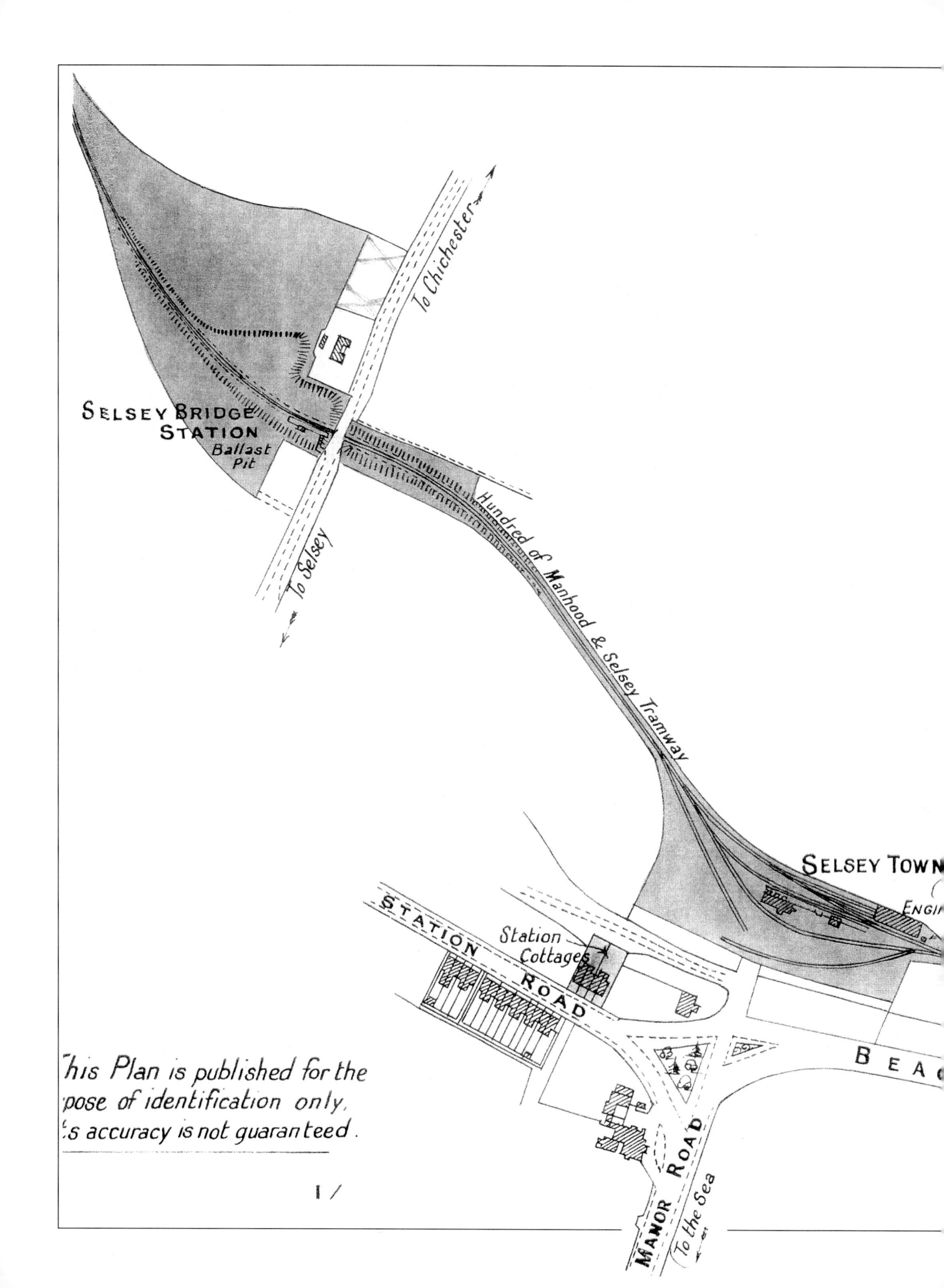

SELSEY BRIDGE STATION
Ballast Pit

To Chichester

To Selsey

Hundred of Manhood & Selsey Tramway

SELSEY TOWN
Engi[ne]

Station Cottages

STATION ROAD

MANOR ROAD

To the Sea

BEA[CH]

This Plan is published for the purpose of identification only. Its accuracy is not guaranteed.

Probably on the same day as the photo of Chichester, it looks like 'business as usual' at Selsey with what could have been merchandise on the platform, and wagons and carriages awaiting their next turn of duty in the yard. PHOTOMATIC

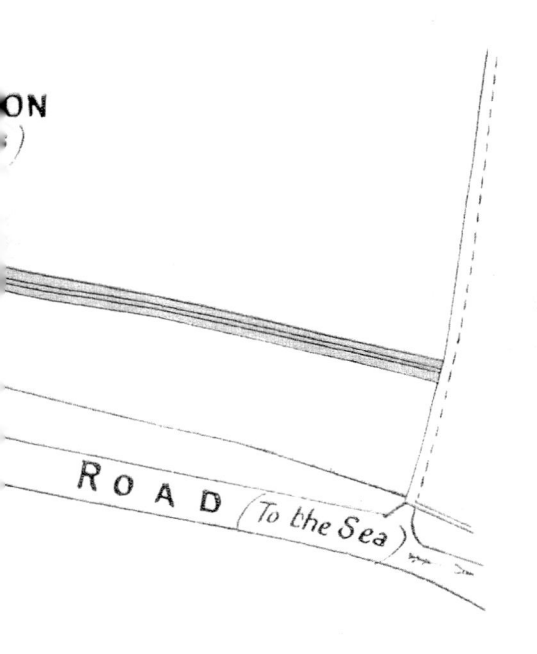

Description of Premises	Tenant	Annual Rent	Term
Siding, Selsey	Trojan Brick Co.	3.0.0.	Quarterly
Garden ground, Chichester	Hollingdale	1.0.	Yearly
	Carried forward	258.5.5.	
	Brought forward	258.5.5.	
Plot of land, Selsey Bridge	Lawrence E.	4.0.	Yearly
Garden Ground, Chichester	Linfield E.	3.6.	do.
do. do.	Lingfield C. A.	1.0.	do.
do. do.	Jeffries	2.0.	do.
do. do.	Tyler	2.0.	do.
do. do.	West	1.0.	do.
do. do.	Wilkinson	1.0.	do.
do. do.	Harper W. T.	4.0.	do.
Coal Wharf, Selsey	Prior H. (Temporarily suspended)	7.0.0.	do.
Land in Chichester Station Yard	Sadler & Co.	12.12.0.	do.
Wayleave for Water Pipe	Selsey Water Co.	1.0.0.	do.
Advertisement Plates	Smith, W. H. & Sons	4.5.5.	do.
Garden Ground, Selsey	Lee T. B.	2.6.	do.
do. do.	Pratt	1.0.	do.
do. do.	Burbridge N. T.	9.	do.
do. Stockbridge	Eames, F.	2.0.	do.
do. do.	Lingfield C. A.	4.0.	do.
do. do.	Pick E. E.	5.0.	do.
do. do.	Tadd L.	2.0.	do.
Wayleave for Pipe	City of Chichester Gas Co.	10.6.	do.
do.	Stockbridge Estate	10.6.	do.
Wayleave for Gas Main	Petersfield & Selsey Gas Co.	1.0.0.	do.
Field adjoining Tramway Selsey	Selsey Utilities Co. Ltd.	6.0.0.	Monthly
		£292 19.7.	

By 17th March 1935 the three wooden horizontal bars across the station entrance at Chichester had been removed and one might (unofficially?) expect the Ford railmotor to arrive at any moment with a handful of passengers from Selsey. One of Morous's last duties was to bring the chassis and baggage trailer of the Shefflex unit up from Selsey and leave them on the headshunt of the transfer siding.
H. C. CASSERLEY

By 30th June 1935, Ringing Rock, the chassis of the Shefflex railmotor unit and its baggage truck were knee deep in weeds, silently awaiting their fate.
LENS OF SUTTON

CLOSURE, SALE & WINDING UP (1935–1947)

ROLLING STOCK AND PLANT
TO BE INCLUDED IN THE SALE

Locomotives.

'Morous'	by Manning Wardle & Co. Leeds.
'Selsey'	by Peckett & Sons, Ltd., Bristol.
Pair of 'Ford' Rail Cars.	Seating capacity 14 passengers in each coach,[9] Third Class only.

Coaches

One six wheel Southern coach, standard rolling stock type, with four Third class compartments, guard and luggage compartment.
One similar coach, but having five Third class compartments only.
Also the following obsolete rolling stock in Selsey Station Yard:-
1. Four Wheel 32 seater coach.
1.   do.   do.
3. Saloon type coaches
4. Four wheel coach under-carriages.

Trucks.

4 Eight Ton trucks
6 Box vans.
3 Box van bodies without undercarriages.[10]

SCHEDULE OF PLANT AND MACHINERY

In the Engine Shed at Selsey Town Station.
  1 Hand operated grind stone.
  1 do.   do.   vertical drill.
  1 Treadle lathe, 4" centres.
  1 do.   do. 6" centres.
  1 Power driven vertical drill.
  1 Anvil.
  1 Swage block
  1 Portable smithy hearth
  1 Single cylinder vertical steam engine.
     About 20'0' of 1½" diam. overhead shafting
  3 Jacks.
  1 Small two ton do.
  1 4 Wheel plate layers trolley.

In the Fitters workshop at the rear of the Engine Shed
  Wood Bench.
  Screw Vice.
  Hand operated drill on Bench.
  Sundry Stores, tubes, etc.

The engine shed would not provide cover for the Tramways Company's faithful old servants Morous (Lot 323) and Selsey (Lot 324) for much longer as it was soon to be pulled down around them before they were cut up where they stood in the autumn of 1936.
ROGER KIDNER

H. C. Casserley made another trip to Chichester on 26th October 1935. The hedge on the right appears to have been trimmed but the elevated locomotives' water tank had lost its ladder, the gutter on the end wall of the station building had come adrift and weeds were rapidly taking over the site.
H. C. CASSERLEY

Another view of Chichester station taken after closure, showing the auctioneers lot number painted on the end of the building.
R. W. KIDNER

In Goods Yard.

- 1 Timber gantry with lifting blocks.
- 1 Petrol pump and tank containing about 80 gallons of petrol.
- 1 Steel water tank on timber framework, size 10'0" x 7'4" supplied from mains
- 1 Two Wheel luggage trolley.
- 1 5 cwt. weighing machine in booking office.
- 2 Gas standards on platform.
- 4 tons engine coal.

In Superintendent's Office.

- 1 large mahogany table
- 1 small wooden table
- 4 arm chairs (wood)
- 1 chest with 6 drawers
- 1 do. 5 do.
- 1 Roll top desk and cupboard
- 1 Steel safe with 2 shelves and 2 drawers Makers S. Withers & Co. West Bromwich.
- 1 Press on Stand

At Hunston Halt.

Two steel water tanks each 4'0" x 4'0" x 4'6" on timber frames fed by small hand pump at base.

At Chichester station

- A steel water tank on a timber framework about 5' x 3' x 3'
- 2 wood platform seats
- 1 small four wheel milk trolley
- 1 5 cwt. weighing machine.

At Mill Pond Halt.

1 Carriage body without wheels.

An annual payment of £2 is made to the Chichester Corporation in respect of the bridge over the canal at Hunston.

SPECIAL STIPULATIONS

(1) Where it is stated in these Stipulations that inspection of any document either specifically or generally referred to is offered that document or a copy thereof may be inspected by persons proposing to tender at any time on working days in office hours during the period of 4 weeks next prior to the 12th December 1935 (the date by which tenders must be sent in) at the office of Messrs. Geo. Thatcher & Son of No.32 Essex Street, Strand, London WC2 the Vendors Solicitors And notwithstanding mis-statement error or omission in or from the particulars plans these stipulations or the conditions the Purchaser whether inspecting or not shall be deemed to take with full notice of and subject to all the contents of such documents

(2) The Agreement of the " 1935 with the Southern Railway mentioned on page 1 of the Particulars may be inspected. Such of the Tenants Agreements and Leases as are in writing may be inspected, but the majority are verbal and the purchaser if he thinks fit should enquire of the Tenants as to their version of their respective tenancies, but in case of difference between the Tenant's version and the Vendors version the latter shall be conclusively accepted as correct. Notwithstanding as stated in paragraph 1 the Purchaser shall be deemed to take with full notice of and subject to the terms of all tenancies and the tenants rights statutory or otherwise whether arising during the continuance or at the expiration of the tenancy.

(3) Station Cottages, Selsey are sold subject to certain covenants affirmative and restrictive including restrictions on user for any other purpose than as private dwellinghouses lodging houses or professional residences or offices contained in a Conveyance to the Company of 1898 July 14th. The parcels coloured pink on the plan each side of the line at Selsey Bridge Halt are sold subject to certain covenants affirmative and restrictive of erections except car or engine sheds or other buildings in connection with the Undertaking of the Company contained respectively in two Conveyances to the Company of 8th April 1919. The three Conveyances in this clause mentioned may be inspected.

(4) Persons proposing to tender may by arrangement inspect all the property hereby offered for sale (and also the Bridge referred to in Special Stipulation 8), for the period of the fortnight prior to the said 12th day of December 1935 and the Purchaser whether inspecting or not and not withstanding any error misdescription or omission in or from the Particulars plans these stipulations or conditions shall be deemed to purchase or take with full knowledge of the physical state and condition as regards want of repair or otherwise howsoever of all such property sold and of the said Bridge and its appliances.

(5) Almost all the numerous Conveyances of different parcels to the Hundred of Manhood and Selsey Tramways Company Limited (hereinafter called 'the Company') (the Majority of which were executed in the years 1897 and 1898 though some parcels were only acquired in the years 1912 and 1919) contain covenants or obligations on or by the Company in respect of accommodation works and crossings and other matters and some of their reservations of easements and of mines and minerals and rights of working the same.

The purchaser takes subject to all such reservations covenants and obligations and shall covenant to perform and observe the same in so far as the same are validly and specifically enforceable and shall in every or any event covenant to indemnify the Company against all actions proceedings claims and demands on or in respect of such reservations covenants and obligations. And all the Conveyances mentioned in paragraph 1 of these Special Stipulations.

In especial without in any way prejudicing the generality of the foregoing are specially here mentioned.

(A) The reservation to the Ecclesiastical Commissioners of the minerals and substrata below a depth of 200 feet from the surface of the parcels of land containing about 3 acres 2 roods and 2 perches[12] with the rights of working reserved to the Commissioners contained in a Conveyance by them to the Company of 1897 June 3rd.

(B) The covenant therein contained for reconveyance free of cost to such Commissioners of certain of the parcels thereby conveyed in the event of the Company or its assigns discontinuing working as a Tramway or Railway for a year

(C) The covenant therein contained giving a right of preemption of the Commissioners of a small parcel thereby conveyed.

(D) A reservation to the Dean and Chapter of the Cathedral church of Chichester of minerals and substrata below a depth of 200 feet from the surface of land containing 2 acres 2 roods and 35 perches or thereabouts with rights of working same and a covenant by the Company for reconveyance to that Dean and Chapter at its agricultural value to be ascertained as there provided of the major part of that land on the Company or its assigns discontinuing working as a Tramway or Railway for a year and the ancillary covenants for removal of buildings and other things on the land so to be reconveyed contained in a Covenance to the Company of the 3rd May 1897 made between the said Dean and Chapter of the first part the Ecclesiastical Commissioners of the second part and the Company of the third part.

(6) The Purchaser shall conclusively assume that certain life annuities against which and the duties arising on cesser[13] whereof a Vendor to the Company in a Conveyance of 5th June 1897 covenanted to indemnify the Company have long since expired and been fully paid and that such duties have been paid.

(7) It is believed that Conveyances to the Company of every parcel of the land hereby sold can be produced to the Purchaser, but should it be discovered that the Company have no such conveyance of any parcel or parcels the Purchaser shall accept a Statutory Declaration to be furnished at his expense that the Company has been in undisputed possession of the parcel for the last 20 years as conclusively evidencing the title thereto of the Company in fee simple free from all incumbrances other than those created by the Company.

(8) The Company does not own the Bridge or Towing path carrying the line over the Canal and Towing Path at Hunston but has and sells only a right to use such bridge and towing path for the portion of the line for so long as the Company's undertaking exists and subject to the agreements and conditions contained in a certain Agreement dated the 22nd July 1897 between the Mayor Aldermen and Citizens of the City of Chichester of the one part and the Company of the other part (which agreement may be inspected) paying yearly to the said Corporation the sum of £2. The purchaser shall covenant to perform and observe all the obligations of the Company contained in such Agreement and to

indemnify the Company there-against and shall raise no objection whatsoever on the ground of the present state or condition of the said Bridge or in the appliances or of inability to raise the said Bridge in its present state.

(9) The Drawbridge cottage has been condemned for want of drainage. The Purchaser must indemnify the Company against all liability on this account and reimburse to the Company any expenses to which it may be put subsequent to the date of contract on this account.

(10) The respective parcels sold are respectively sold subject to all existing rights of way (public or private) light and other easements affecting the same and to all liability to repair or contribute to the repair of roads bridges banks fences walls ditches streams or other like matters or the Chancel of any Parish Church.

Tenders in a sealed envelope (marked 'Selsey Tramway Company') were to be addressed to M. G. Willmott Esq., Master of the Supreme Court, Room 237, Royal Courts of Justice, Strand, London, WC, to arrive on or before Thursday, 12th December 1935. A crossed cheque marked 'Good' (or a Banker's Draft) payable to the Order of the Bank of England Pay Office Account had to be enclosed representing by way of deposit an amount equal to 10% of the amount of the Tender. It was understood that there was no obligation to accept the highest, or any Tender. Within the week, notice of the acceptance would be given to the person whose tender was accepted, and the deposits of those tenders not accepted would be returned.

On 14th January 1936 at 12 noon, the Master of the Supreme Court certified that it was Mr. F. Watkins' tender for the paltry sum of £3,610 that had been accepted. Described as a contractor of Sling, Gloucestershire, Watkins became the legal owner of the Tramway on 3rd March 1936. Such a small amount, a little less than a quarter of what it was hoped to have realised by sale to the Southern Railway, resulted in the mortgage and debenture holders receiving only a very small percentage of their holdings.

As the only surviving locomotive in working order, *Morous* worked the demolition train, commencing at the Chichester end and working southwards. At each station, the rails were heaped in large stacks with the sleepers bundled together 50 at a time according to their condition. The chart below gives an idea of just how many of the original rails and half-round sleepers remained in service right to the end:

Station	Sleepers fit for contractors	Sleepers fit for fences/roadways	Sleepers fit for firewood	56lb rail	40lb rail
Chichester:	–	70	un-specified quantity	–	–
Hunston:	–	25 standard 50 half round	–	–	–
Sidlesham:	150 standard 150 half round	350 standard 200 half round	–	1200yds (400 fishplates)	800yds
Ferry:	300 standard	680 standard 358 half round	162 (partly burnt)	1000yds (800 fishplates)	300yds
Golf Club Halt:	–	295 standard 114 half round	–	800yds (200 fishplates)	1200yds
Selsey Bridge:	–	76 standard 140 half round	–	–	350yds
Selsey:	–	200 standard	–	300yds (1000 fishplates)	–

With the (not so) permanent way lifted, little time was wasted in setting up the date for the sale and in the 17th and 24th June editions of the *Chichester Observer*, Messrs. Wyatt & Son, the local auctioneers, placed the following advertisement:

SELSEY ON SEA.
At the Terminus Station of the Selsey Tramway, about 8½ miles from Chichester
WYATT & SON
are favoured with instructions to Sell by Auction, at Selsey Station, on TUESDAY, JUNE 30TH. 1936, commencing at one o'clock sharp the greater portion of the RAILWAY PLANT lately used in conjunction with the Hundred of Manhood and Selsey Tramway Co. Ltd. including:

Quantities of useful timber, firewood, telegraph poles, engineers' tools, water tanks, grindstones, fencing, sack truck galvanised and barbed wire, 9,000 YARDS OF STEEL CONTRACTORS RAILS,[14] two-screw traversing jacks, vertical drill, 4in and 6in treadle lathes, drilling machines, two blacksmith's forges, stocks and dies, Well's flairlight plant, 18 new oak gate posts, CORRUGATED IRON and TIMBER BUILDINGS, forming the various stations along the line from Chichester to Selsey, coach tops and waggons, five tons of coal, petrol pump with tank complete, weighing machine and weights by DOYLES, OFFICE FURNITURE, mahogany table, four office arm chairs, American oak roll-top desk, fire proof safe by WITHERS, cabinets and cupboards and miscellaneous items.

The Lots will be on view three days before the Sale, and Catalogues may be obtained from the Auctioneers, 59, East Street, Chichester; and at High Street, Selsey-on-Sea; and 10 West Street, Havant.

The two steam locomotives, *Selsey* and *Morous* were not mentioned in the advertisement, but they were featured in large print on the front of the sale catalogue. Surprisingly, the auction was not reported by the local press.

SELSEY-ON-SEA

At the Terminus Station of the Selsey Tramway, about 8¼ miles from Chichester.

CATALOGUE OF THE SURPLUS

RAILWAY PLANT

including

5,000 SLEEPERS

9,000 Yards of Contractors Steel Rails

TWO LOCOMOTIVES

Station Buildings, Engineers Tools
Fishplates & Bolts, Weighing Machines

AND NUMEROUS OTHER EFFECTS :

Which Messrs.

WYATT AND SON

Will sell by Auction

At The Selsey Terminus Station
On Tuesday, June 30th, 1936

At 1 p.m. sharp.

On View three days prior to the Sale.

Catalogues may be obtained at the Auctioneers' Offices, 59, East Street, Chichester and at High Street, Selsey-on-Sea and 10, West Street, Havant.

CLOSURE, SALE & WINDING UP (1935–1947)

SELSEY-ON-SEA.
At the Terminus Station of the Selsey Tramway, about 8¼ miles from Chichester.
WYATT & SON
are favoured with instructions to Sell by Auction, at Selsey Station, on TUESDAY, JUNE 30th, 1936, commencing at one o'clock sharp, the greater portion of the
RAILWAY PLANT
lately used in connection with the Hundred of Manhood and Selsey Tramway Co. Ltd. including:
Quantities of useful timber, firewood, telegraph poles, engineers' tools, water tanks, grindstone, fencing, sack truck, galvanised and barbed wire, 9,000 YARDS OF STEEL CONTRACTORS RAILS, two-screw traversing jacks, vertical drill, 6in. and 4in. treadle lathes, drilling machines, two blacksmith's forges, stocks and dies, Wells flarelight plant, 18 new oak gate posts, CORRUGATED IRON and TIMBER BUILDINGS, forming the various stations along the line from Chichester to Selsey, coach tops and waggons, five tons of coal, petrol pump with tank complete, weighing machine and weights by DOYLES, OFFICE FURNITURE, mahogany table, four office arm chairs, American oak roll-top desk, fire proof safe by WITHERS, cabinets and cupboards and miscellaneous items.

The lots will be on view three days before the Sale, and Catalogues may be obtained from the Auctioneers, 59, East Street, Chichester; and at High-Street, Selsey-on-Sea; and 10, West Street, Havant.

Advertisement for the sale of the Tramway as featured in the Chichester Observer *dated Wednesday, 17th June 1936.*

The main running line and run-round loop now had been lifted at Selsey station, but shortly after the auction on 30th June 1936, some items of rolling stock still stood in the goods yard behind the station building.
COLONEL STEPHENS RAILWAY MUSEUM & ARCHIVE

The once proud and smart Selsey *awaiting the cutter's torch at Selsey. The engine shed had been demolished around her and, with her name plate removed, she suffered the indignity of carrying the auction's legend 'Lot 324'.*
COLONEL STEPHENS RAILWAY MUSEUM & ARCHIVE

One final look at the last two of the Selsey Tramway's steam locomotives to survive; Selsey and Morous just weeks before they were both cut up for scrap in the autumn of 1936.
COLONEL STEPHENS RAILWAY MUSEUM & ARCHIVE

CLOSURE, SALE & WINDING UP (1935–1947)

Mr. Frank S. White walked the length of the Tramway in December 1936 and found that all the station buildings (with the exception of Sidlesham and Selsey) had been removed, although the platforms at Selsey, Hunston and Chalder were still *in situ*. The stacks of sleepers and rails remained beside the level crossings along the route and in one or two places the ground on which the line had run had been bought and enclosed by local residents, including the Tramway embankment across Pagham Harbour.[15]

Despite the closure of the Tramway, the various level crossings were still causing problems for the local authority, admittedly for a different reason, and on 27th April 1937 West Sussex County Council wrote to Messrs. George Thatcher & Son at 32 Essex Street, Strand, London, WC2:

Dear Sirs,

re Hundred of Manhood and Selsey Tramways Co. Ltd.

In January of last year I wrote you regarding the position which had arisen in connection with the crossings where the line of the above Company crosses the public highway leading from Chichester to Selsey and you may remember that you kindly gave me some very useful information concerning the matter.

I have since been in communication with the purchaser from the Debenture Holders and the persons to whom he subsequently sold his interest and I have been informed that when the undertaking was originally sold the rails etc. at the crossings and one bridge were by the omission to colour the same on the plan on the Conveyance not included in the Conveyance, so that they would appear to be still vested in the Company.

When my Assistant Solicitor saw Mr. Walker, the Receiver for the Debenture Holders before the completion of the sale of the Company's undertaking, he was informed that the proceeds would in all probability fail to satisfy the claims of the first Debenture Holders, let alone the Second Debenture Holders.

I should be much obliged if you would kindly let me know the position which actually arose when the sale was eventually completed, as the bridge, which was constructed to take the railway under the road near Selsey Station, is in a dangerous condition, which needs immediate attention.

Inasmuch as the crossings would still appear to be vested in the Company, it would seem that the Company is liable for the reinstatement of the road and repair of the bridge.

Yours faithfully,
(signed) J. EDWARD SEAGER,
Clerk of the County Council.

Messrs. George Thatcher & Son wrote to Messrs. Walker Freer & Brown (solicitors) of 130 High Street, Tonbridge, Kent the following day explaining that 'all the level crossings were coloured in the plan on the Particulars of Sale, but the bridge was not, presumably because the road is a public highway, and we imagine the Company was responsible for the upkeep only; the Surveyors Report states that there is a board there set up by the Company limiting the weight of vehicles to ten tons'. J. A. Iggulden from the Salford Terrace, Tonbridge office discussed the problem with Owen Walker in London on 10th May, after which the matter seemed to be quietly dropped, at least for the time being.'

Perhaps as a result of the above correspondence, it must have become apparent that the relevant authorities had not been notified of the closing of the Tramway in January 1935. This letter was eventually sent to The Secretary (or Manager), The Hundred of Manhood and Selsey Tramways Company, Ltd., per Holman F. Stephens Esq., 23 Salford Terrace, Tonbridge on 23rd October 1937:

Companies Registration Office,
Bush House,
South-west Wing,
Strand,
London, WC2.

Sir,

PURSUANT to section 285 (1) of the Companies Act, 1929, I have to inquire whether your Company is carrying on in business or in operation.

If the Company is not carrying on business or in operation, it will be my duty, on receiving a letter to that effect to publish in the London Gazette and send to the Company a Notice that at the expiration of three months from the date of that Notice the name of the Company will be struck off the Register and the Company will be DISSOLVED.

It will, however, be seen on reference to Sub-section 5 of Section 295 of the Act above-mentioned, that this Dissolution is subject to the proviso that the *liability (if any) of every Director, Managing Officer, and Member of the Company shall continue and may be enforced as if the Company had not been dissolved.*

I shall be glad to receive a reply to this inquiry as early as possible.

(Signed) Registrar.

Two days later, this reply was sent:

Sir,

The Hundred of Manhood and Selsey Tramways Company Limited.

I am desired to refer to your letter – 47717 – of the 23rd instant, in connection with the above-mentioned Company, and to state that this Company no longer carries on business, having ceased to operate during the year 1935, that being so, the name of the Company should be struck off the Register.

I am, Sir,
Your obedient servant.
(Signed) (late) Director.[16]

Although the Company had changed its name to The West Sussex Railway, that was all that was achieved under the West Sussex Railway Certificate of 1924, the other Powers being allowed to lapse. It was, therefore, the Hundred of Manhood & Selsey Tramways Company Ltd. that was struck off the Register and finally dissolved following an announcement (under Section 295 (5) of the Companies Act of 1929) in the *London Gazette*, dated 23rd September 1938.

Negotiations were still continuing regarding Selsey Bridge and on 20th April 1939 the Clerk of the West Sussex County Council, T. C. Hayward, wrote to Messrs. Walker, Freer & Brown, 130 High Street, Tonbridge:

Hundred of Manhood and Selsey Tramways Co. Ltd. Selsey Bridge

I thank you for your letter of yesterday's date returning the draft Agreement relating to the above mentioned bridge and note the information which the Secretary of the Company has given you upon the matter. My point in joining the Company in the deed however was purely a technical one inasmuch as I understand that the Company had not been formally wound up and therefore being still in existence, so far as the Register of Companies is concerned, was technically in a position to carry on its undertaking and thereby prevent the space underneath the existing bridge being filled up.

I should be much obliged if you would kindly let me have the Secretary's view having regard to this position.

Messrs. Walker, Freer & Brown forwarded copies of the letter dated 23rd October 1937 from the Companies Registration Office together with a copy of the reply dated

This was how Selsey Town station's goods yard looked on 22nd August 1947. Only the grounded body of ex-LCDR 4-compartment first class carriage No. 2410 behind the road cart in the centre background suggests that this was once the Tramway's main station.
PETER J. WALKER, CTY. THE COLONEL STEPHENS RAILWAY MUSEUM & ARCHIVE

The wooden platforms at Sidlesham were soon dismantled, but the station building remained in situ until the autumn of 1947 when it was sold and removed to North Mundham to become part of a bungalow.
COLLECTION TOM MIDDLEMASS

CLOSURE, SALE & WINDING UP (1935–1947)

25th October, adding 'In view of this Correspondence, I fail to understand the point that has been raised by the Clerk of the WSC Council As you know, the Company has long since ceased to exist, the whole of the assets being disposed of, by the Receiver some two years ago'!

It has been suggested that the canal bridge near Hunston was destroyed by the army early in the Second World War as a defence against an imminent German invasion,[17] but it had previously been carefully dismantled and taken to the Council's depot in Chichester. Here it remained until, following an air raid on 17th September 1942, the track-bearing girders were taken by road to replace a bomb-damaged bridge over the Rife in Shripney Road, Bognor where the bridge took on a new lease of life supporting three water pipes.[18] It was to spend more years in this capacity than it did on the Tramway until it was removed at some time in the 1990s. The bridge over the Bremere Rife to the north of Ferry was not so lucky and it was apparently needlessly destroyed at some time during the war. Selsey station building remained in situ until it was dismantled by German prisoners of war in December 1946 and Sidlesham station building remained isolated beside the Tramway that it had served for 37½ years until it was removed to become part of a bungalow at North Mundham in the autumn of 1947.

With the station building and platform having been demolished and the dividing fence removed, the Southern Railway had laid in new sidings by May 1937 to extend its coal yard on the site of what had been the Tramway's Chichester terminus. It was probably in 1940 that the 6 chain radius curve leading away from the Tramway station was re-laid for approximately a quarter of a mile, for what was believed to be the use of a rail-mounted gun, the purpose of which would have been to fire at Selsey Bill should the Germans have invaded the country.[19] Without the gun firing a single shot, the siding was removed in 1947.

After the line had closed, Chichester Corporation removed their Tramway bridge across the canal to the north of Hunston for storage at their depot in the city. Following an air raid in Bognor on 17th September 1942, the two track-bearing girders gained a new lease of life carrying three pipes across the rife at Shripney Road in the town. They were to be used in this capacity until they were removed at some time in the 1990s. 14th July 1989.
E. W. J. CRAWFORTH

Notes

1. This was the last minute to be entered into the Directors' Minute Book.
2. *The Railway Magazine*, March 1984, letter from Leslie Harrington.
3. *Sidlesham* by the Rev. W. H. Haynes, published in 1946.
4. *Selsey* had not suffered a burst boiler, but had failed the Boiler Insurance Company's hydraulic test late in 1933.
5. By a "real engine", Tim Johnson would be referring to a steam locomotive as opposed to a railmotor.
6. The year should surely read 1935.
7. The space for the actual date was left blank.
8. I have found no previous evidence of there being a waiting room at this halt. However, listed under Mill Pond Halt in the 1936 Auction Itinerary, clearly referring to the same building, Lot No. 29 is described as a 'Timber-built span roof shed about 7ft 6in x 4ft'. To add even more to the confusion, at the end of the 1935 Particulars of Sale it will be seen that under the section headed 'Schedule of Plant and Machinery', '1 carriage body without wheels' is listed under Mill Pond Halt. This could well be the ex-LCDR 4-wheel 5-compartment carriage damaged in the fatal derailment near Golf Club Halt on 3rd September 1923, but it may have been grounded away from the platform.
9. Seating capacity was 20 passengers per coach.
10. Note how this list of rolling stock differs to that recorded in the Southern Railway's Report of 1934.
11. The space for the date was again left blank.
12. 1 Rood = quarter of an acre, 1 Perch = 5½ yds, 1 (square) Perch = 30¼ sq yds.
13. Cesser = coming to an end.
14. The catalogue only listed 5,950 yards of contractors' flat-bottom rails.
15. *The Railway Magazine*, September 1937.
16. This (late) director would undoubtedly be William Henry Austen writing from 23 Salford Terrace, Tonbridge.
17. 'Raising the Drawbridge', by George Smith, published in *Waterways World*, December, 1996.
18. Letter from Ted Crawforth dated 16.2.2004. Following the closure of the Rye & Camber Tramway, its bridge across the Broadwater Stream, near Rye, has also carried a pipe which it continues to do to this day.
19. There were other similar sidings for this type of gun laid in southern England, all of which were on a sharp curve owing to the weapons' limited deflection of only one or two degrees. Details from a telephone conversation with Alan Blackburn, 19.2.1999.

Having removed the dividing fence along with its adjoining allotment and demolished the station building and platform at Chichester, the Southern Railway used what had been the Tramway's main running line into the station as an extension to its goods yard, access still being via the erstwhile transfer siding. In this photograph dated 3rd September 1952, it will be seen that the run-round loop and the transfer siding's headshunt were not required and had been lifted.
H. C. CASSERLEY

This is the scene today from a similar, but closer, viewpoint. The gas works beyond Stockbridge Road have long since been demolished and a modern office block with its car park occupies the site of the former Southern Railway's goods yard.
AUTHOR

CHAPTER NINE

GONE BUT NOT FORGOTTEN

A new licensed house and restaurant was opened by Messrs. Brickwoods Brewery of Portsmouth in February 1968 which they named 'The Selsey Tram'. Ray Apps, the Tramway's former fireman, was brought out of retirement and invited along as guest of honour and to pull the first pint! Situated on the main A286 road in Donnington on the outskirts of Chichester, the public house can be found a few hundred yards south of where the Tramway's notorious Stockbridge Road level crossing used to be. The artist responsible for the pub's first sign outside must have been erroneously briefed as it depicted an electric double-deck tramcar! This sign has now been replaced with one which does, at least, show a steam train, although it bears little resemblance to anything that ever ran on the Tramway! Inside, some photographs of the Tram in its heyday grace the walls of the bars.

Today, only the houses in Terminus Road that backed on to the Selsey Tramway's terminus at Chichester remain to show where the Company's station used to be situated, some 50 yards south of the main-line station. The actual site is now a neatly landscaped private footpath serving the large office block that has been built on the main-line company's former goods yard. All other traces of the existence of the Tramway in Chichester have been lost under housing, industrial developments and the A27 ring road that skirts the southern side of the city.

However, all is not lost and, with the assistance of West Sussex County Council, the centenary of the opening of the Selsey Tramway was commemorated in 1997 by the creation of a way-marked footpath known as the Selsey Tram Way that follows the original route as closely as possible. Small brass plates depicting the locomotive *Selsey* were attached to each of the many sign posts, although a good number of these have since been removed (possibly for souvenirs), making progress somewhat difficult at times.

Lost to the north beneath a parade of shops, the footpath commences on the south side of the now much wider Stockbridge Road, the scene of so many collisions between the Tram and road vehicles. Taking a rather crooked course to skirt modern housing development, the path soon arrives at the Chichester Canal, the Tramway formation being carried on an embankment some six feet above the towpath to the right. Although covered in trees and undergrowth, the more agile may walk this section of trackbed quite easily until it bears gently away to the right to pass through a waterlogged section after which it is lost under meadows. By following the towpath for a few hundred yards to the outskirts of Hunston village and then turning westwards, now

The site of Stockbridge Road level crossing looking south, the Tramway's former right of way more or less following the footpath to the right of the house that had looked out on so many collisions between the Tram and road vehicles during the 1920s and early 1930s.

AUTHOR

(A) *Only the northern abutment of the lifting bridge over the canal to the north of Hunston remains, the other having been removed when the bridge was dismantled and the canal reverted to its full width at this point.* (B) *Beside the Tramway's former trackbed immediately to the south of the canal, the house provided for the platelayer responsible for lifting the bridge, and described by the local authority in the 1930s as insanitary, is today a picturesque cottage.* (C) *Looking south from the site of the drawbridge, the former trackbed is now a rough track providing access from the main road at Hunston to the Tramway's cottage. Had it been built, the triangular junction for the line to East Wittering would have branched off immediately to the right, whilst the double-ended siding that served the West Sussex Brick Company's premises in the early 1900s was a little further down on the left. This was the view on 18th October 1989.* (D) *At Hunston, the concrete face of the former platform can still be found hidden under a hedge in the corner of a field on the outskirts of the village.* (E) *Chalder's platform is complete below the undergrowth, and the concrete base on which the station building stood is still in situ.* (F) *From the foot of the platform, the Tramway headed northwards in a straight line across the flat landscape beyond the modern 5-bar gate. Chalder Farm, after which the station was named, is about ¼ mile along the now made-up lane to the right, whilst the main road and the northern end of the straggling village of Sidlesham are half a mile to the left.* (G) *Sidlesham station occupied the area left to right in the centre of this picture, and it is now the beginning of a popular footpath along the former Tramway embankment to Ferry. The road curves right in the distance to climb up to the main Chichester to Selsey road.* (H) *With the tide out, it is possible to see how the Tramway's embankment across Pagham Harbour was built with blocks of chalk following the floods of December 1910. The rotting remains of sleepers used to strengthen the formation are still visible in places.*

(C) E. W. J. CRAWFORTH, OTHERS AUTHOR

GONE BUT NOT FORGOTTEN

along the southern side of the Portsmouth – Arun canal, the site of the former lifting bridge is soon reached, but only the northern concrete abutment remains *in situ*. To the southwest of the Tramway's former trackbed the cottage provided for the staff responsible for lifting the bridge is still inhabited: it was not demolished back in the 1930s owing to its insanitary condition after all!

The footpath now more or less follows the original formation southwards past a modern housing estate to the east, prior to crossing the main road at the west end of Hunston village at Oak View. Sited immediately to the south of the road, a part of the concrete facing of the platform is just visible in the hedge, but owing to the widening of the road, the Bremere Rife is much closer to the platform than it was hitherto. Beyond Hunston no trace of the Tramway remains, much of it having disappeared under a golf course that was constructed in the 1990s, although one short section of a tarmac footpath is said to follow the original trackbed. Almost hidden from view beneath brambles, Chalder station platform is more or less intact and it formed the subject of a detailed investigation back in March 1990 which provided much useful information as to the construction of the Tramway's station buildings.

Beyond Chalder, no trace of the Tramway can be found across the flat landscape until the trackbed can be taken up once again at the site of Sidlesham station. Small bushes occupy the area, but the Tramway's 1911 chalk embankment heading south is now a much used public footpath. There is a slight diversion where the line used to cross the Broad Rife, but parts of the original crumbling concrete abutments of the Tramway's bridge can be clearly seen behind the more modern replacements that carry a pipe across the river at the same spot. A hundred yards or so beyond the bridge, the position of the level crossing at Ferry is easily found, but all traces of Ferry station, including its inclined siding, and the course of the line beyond have disappeared. Green Lawns Caravan Park occupies the site of Selsey Bridge station but the bridge has long since been filled

Top left: The Tramway's crumbling original abutments are still visible behind the modern replacements of the bridge that now carry a pipe across the Broad Rife rather than the permanent way. Top right: Immediately in front of the 'bus stop and 40mph sign was where the Tramway crossed the main Chichester to Selsey Road by an ungated level crossing to enter Ferry station on the left. Right: Looking south, nothing whatsoever remains of Ferry station; even the site of the inclined siding to the left has been levelled. AUTHOR

Left: *Following the closure of the Tramway, Station Road reverted to its original name, Nos. 1-4 Tramway Cottages being renumbered as 27-33 Church Road.* Above: *The road layout near Selsey Town station remains much as it did in the days of the Tramway, except that Manor Road (with the Selsey Hotel boarded up on the left) has been extended through the Company's yard and where the station building had once stood, to serve a modern housing development.*
AUTHOR

in. However, beyond the main road to the east a public footpath runs along the top of the cutting which is still extant, though now mainly hidden beneath undergrowth and mature trees. Manor Road has been extended northwards across where Selsey's station building once stood and Mount Wood Road and Allandale Close occupy the site of the Tramway's former 2½ acre terminus site. Around the corner, the four houses previously known as 1–4 Tramway Cottages have been renumbered 27-33 Church Road. It will come as no surprise that the short-lived extension to Selsey Beach is completely lost under further housing development and a children's play area.

Today the erstwhile Tramway's route is more than adequately served by Stagecoach 'bus service 51 which operates a half-hourly headway on weekdays and Saturdays for the greater part of the day throughout the year between Chichester and Selsey, via Hunston, and Sidlesham. On Sundays and public holidays, an hourly service suffices. The single journey is scheduled to take 35 minutes, 5 minutes longer than the tram took in its latter days, although the 'buses do serve the north and east of the city prior to paralleling the course of the Tramway south of Hunston.

That the Tramway served the inhabitants of the Manhood Peninsula very well is beyond doubt, particularly in the first twenty years or so of its existence, and without it the village of Selsey would not have developed into the charming seaside resort that it is today. Perhaps if the line had not been built so cheaply, funds wouldn't have had to be drained continually from the hard-earned revenue to upgrade it right from the start, and if only the shareholders had put their hands into their pockets following the floods of December 1910, they might have earned a handsome annual dividend thereafter. One commentator[1] many years later eloquently summed up the Hundred of Manhood & Selsey Tramways Company to perfection:

'...Everything about the West Sussex Railway, as the Selsey line later styled itself, was of the most ephemeral nature. Take the track, for instance; the flimsiest excuse for permanent way, almost negligible in its rail section, attached but indeterminately to shoddy sleepers, kept in questionable alignment by a ballasting of assorted dross, much improved when the inevitable invasion of herbage actually bound it together. The buildings, too, were the meanest of tin shacks, and survived but shortly the seasalted air, while the skimpy fences proved but little obstacle to wildlife and grazing beasts alike. The level crossings were ungated and the bridges comprised no more than timber baulks on crudely-cast abutments in sea shingle concrete, crumbling and corroding from the day the shuttering came down. To be brutally frank about it, the West Sussex was a cheapskate railway, thrown together as meanly as possible. It was, however, a prudent railway; it lasted just long enough to carry what traffic the district offered, before the motor-bus and lorry took it all away – and not a day longer!'

You might be long gone, Selsey Tramway, but you will never be forgotten!

Notes
1. Iain Rice in *Light Railway Layout Designs*, published by Wild Swan Publications, Ltd., 1991.

APPENDIX ONE
PASSENGER TOTALS & PASSENGER RECEIPTS

Year	No. of Passengers Carried	Passenger Receipts	Year	No. of Passengers Carried	Passenger Receipts
1897	–	–	1924	31,352	£949 8s 2d
1898	'over 89,000'[1]	?	1925	21,762	£799 6s 1d
1899	?	£1,616 14s 6d	1926	17,171	£685 4s 2d
1900	?	£1,829 4s 7d	1927	22,475	£514 15s 11d
1901	?	£1,908 19s 11d	1928	35,493	£749 16s 8d
1902	?	?	1929	22,676	£556 11s 5d
1903	?	?	1930	15,904	£354 4s 11d
1904	?	?	1931	13,416	£279 15s 2d
1905	?	?	1932	20,967	£427 17s 9d
1906	?	£1,813 2s 0d	1933	21,088	£427 9s 11d
1907	?	£1,875 7s 5d	1934	?	?
1908	?	£1,861 9s 10d			
1909	?	£1,880 10s 11d			
1910	?	£1,986 1s 11d			
1911	?	£1,903 9s 10d			
1912	?	?			
1913	89,915	approx. £2,069 0s 0d[2]			
1914	?	approx. £2,159 0s 0d[3]			
1915	91,808	?[4]			
1916	105,169	?			
1917	?	?			
1918	?	?			
1919	102,292	£3,912 13s 0d			
1920	79,574[5]	£3,272 1s 9d			
1921	66,349	£2,406 14s 0d			
1922	60,203	£1,910 16s 8d			
1923	44,977[6]	£1,404 6s 4d			

Notes

1. This was the figure quoted at the AGM on 22.9.1898.
2. The figure quoted at the AGM on 23.10.1913 was '£83 more than the previous record'.
3. The figure quoted at the AGM on 30.10.1914 was '£90 1s 10d over the previous year'.
4. Up to and including 1914, the Company's accounts had been made up to the 31st August, but from 1915 they were made up to 31st December.
5. The dramatic drop in the number of passengers carried is, without doubt, due to the rival 'bus service operated by Messrs. Moore & Fuller that began operations between Selsey and Chichester in 1920.
6. This further 25% reduction in the number of passengers carried could well be attributed to the fatal derailment near Golf Club Halt in September 1923 and the resulting bad publicity that the Tramway received.

APPENDIX 1A – TABLE OF FARES – 1897

Saloon Fares are 3d above Ordinary Fares as below for Single Journey.

Chichester to Hunston	3d	Single	
" " Hoe Farm (Private Station)	4d	"	
" " Chalder	4d	"	
" " Sidlesham	5d	"	10d Return
" " Selsey	7½d	"	1/3d Return
Hunston to Chichester	3d	"	
" " Hoe Farm (Private Station)	1d	"	
" " Chalder	2d	"	
" " Sidlesham	4d	"	
" " Selsey	6d	"	
Hoe Farm (Private Station) to Chichester	4d	"	
" " " Hunston	1d	"	
" " " Chalder	1d	"	
" " " Sidlesham	3d	"	
" " " Selsey	5d	"	
Chalder to Chichester	4d	"	
" " Hunston	2d	"	
" " Hoe Farm (Private Station)	1d	"	
" " Sidlesham	2d	"	
" " Selsey	5d	"	
Sidlesham to Chichester	5d	"	10d Return
" " Hunston	4d	"	
" " Hoe Farm (Private Station)	3d	"	
" " Chalder	2d	"	
" " Selsey	4d	"	6d Return

Children under 12 years of age Half-Price. Under 3 years of age free.
All Return Tickets are available for return within one month including day of issue.
Tickets from and to Hoe Farm Station will be issued only to persons entitled to use this Station.

Dogs (accompanied by Passenger)	6d each Single or Return
Bicycles & Perambulators (accompanied by Passenger)	6d each Single or Return
Tricycles & Tandem Bicycles	9d each Single or Return

APPENDIX TWO
BALANCE SHEET FOR YEAR ENDING 31st DECEMBER, 1918

CAPITAL AUTHORISED RECEIVED AND UNISSUED

	Amount Authorised	Amount Received	Amount Unissued
Ordinary Capital			
3360 Shares © £5 ea.	£16,800	£14,400	£2,400
Loans & Debentures.			
4% Mortgage Debenture repayable on 1st August 1919.	7,000	7,000	
Mortgage of Selsey Cottages and other property	1,000	1,000	
5% B Mortgage Debentures	5,000	4,200	800
	£29,800	£26,600	£3,200

EXPENDITURE ON CAPITAL ACCOUNT

On Lines open for Traffic	£19,826: 8: 6
" Working Stock	3,368: 7: 3
" Special Items	1,643: 4: 8
" Preliminary Expenses	501: 4: 6
	£25,339: 4: 11
Balance on Hand	£1260: 15: 1
	£26,600: 0: 0

CAPITAL ASSETS:

8 Miles, Single Track, Standard Gauge laid with 40lb. F.B. Rails at a cost of £19286: 8: 6. (excluding preliminary expenses)

3 Locos: 3 Composite Carriages, 4 3rd. Class Carriages

6 Covered Vans, 13 Open Wagons, 2 Ballast Wagons

Total 28 at a cost of £3368: 7: 3 (excluding preliminary expenses)

Cottages Surplus Lands and other property = £1643: 4: 8 (excluding preliminary expenses).

NET REVENUE ACCOUNT

Dr.   Cr.

To Interest on Debentures and Mortgages:-		By Balance from last Account	29: 17: 6
£7000 4% Debentures £280			
£5000 4% " 250		" Net Revenue Account	1561: 16: 6
£1000 Mortgage 10 £540: 0: 0			
" Dividend on Ordinary Shares Nil			
" Income Tax			
Amount Paid £146: 0: 9			
Less collected from Shareholders 145:19: 2	1: 7		
" Flood Account	1020: 0: 0		
By Balance carried forward	31:12: 5		
	£1591:14: 0		£1591:14: 0

GENERAL BALANCE SHEET

To Capital Account		By Cash at Bank and	
Balance at Credit	1260:15: 1	in hand	618: 19: 0
" Net Revenue Account		" General Stores.	
Balance at Credit	31:12: 5	Materials on hand	533: 10: 1
" Sundry Accounts due		" Sundry Accounts due	
by the Co.	804:17: 4	to the Co.	512: 17: 5
" Proportion of season		" Proportion of Insurance	
Tickets Unexpired	1:11: 3	Premium and Rates paid in advance	37: 0: 7
" Reserve Account	2160: 1: 2	" Flood Reconstruction Account	621: 10: 2
" Reserve for Bad Debts	40: 0: 0	" £500 of 5% War Loan 1929-1947	475: 0: 0
		" £1500 of 5% War Loan 1923	1500: 0: 0
	£4298:17: 3		£4298: 17: 3

REVENUE ACCOUNT

Dr.   Cr.

EXPENDITURE		RECEIPTS	
To Maintenance of Way & Stations	686: 3: 9	By Passengers	3720: 3: 10
" Locomotives	406: 7: 2	" Season Tickets	70: 13: 3
" Carriages & Wagons	60:11: 4	" Mails	43: 14: 9
" Depreciation of Rolling Stock	100: 0: 0	" Merchandise, Minerals Parcels etc.	1252: 2: 10
" Locomotive Running Expenses	1154: 6: 0	" Rent of Cottages &c.	78: 12: 4
" Traffic Expenses	412:18: 5	" Miscellaneous	43: 2: 8
" General Charges	526:18: 5	" Transfer Fees	2: 0: 0
" Rates & Tithes	101:11: 6		
" Government Duty	183:10: 1		
" Rents Payable	4: 0: 0		
" Mileage & Demurrage	2:10: 0		
" Repairs of Cottages	9:16: 6		
" Claims	—		
	3648:13: 2		
" Balance of Net Revenue A/c	1561:16: 6		
	£5210: 9: 8		£5210: 9: 8

APPENDIX THREE
GOODS TONNAGES FOR YEARS 1913 & 1919

Goods Traffic in tons-cwts.

	1913 In	1913 Out	1919 In	1919 Out
Coal & Coke:	2170–9	–	3048–5	328–1
Granite for road repair:	461–0	–	–	–
Chalk:	130–1	–	194–11	–
Flint, ash, sand, clay:	–	–	169–13	–
Bricks, tiles:	794–2	16–16	721–6	–
Building materials, timber:	501–6	2–0	669–0	–
Tar:	–	–	93–10	66–10
Hay & straw:	16–0	431–2	–	498–9
Corn, roots, cake, manure:	258–17	412–5	–	–
Corn, cake, feedstuff:	–	–	266–17	1476–2
Manures:	–	–	173–15	–
Greens (Turnip tops, etc.):	–	–	–	151–4
Miscellaneous	631–13	78–12	695–4	137–6
Pit props, etc.:	–	–	–	171–0
Totals:	4963–15	940–15	6032–1	3022–3

Locomotive coal excluded.

APPENDIX FOUR
CATALOGUE OF SURPLUS RAILWAY PLANT
SOLD BY AUCTION AT SELSEY STATION
30th JUNE, 1936[1]
CONDITIONS OF SALE

1. The highest bidder to be the buyer, and if any dispute arise between two or more bidders, the Lot so disputed shall (if the Auctioneer be also in doubt) be put up again and resold; but the decision of the Auctioneer shall, in all cases, be final. The seller reserves the right to bid by himself or his Agent, and the Auctioneer reserves the right of withdrawing and altering any Lot or Lots, and of refusing the bidding of any person he please.

2. No person to advance less than 1s. under One Pound; above One Pound 2s.; and so on in proportion, or such bidding as the Auctioneer shall regulate who is to be the sole arbiter in any matter in dispute. No lot to be delivered DURING THE TIME OF SALE. No allowance will be made for any deficiencies or imperfections.

3. The Purchasers to give in their names and places of abode, and pay down 5s. in the Pound at the fall of the hammer if required, in part payment of the purchase-money, in default of which the lots so purchased to be put up again and re-sold. No cheques will be taken from persons unknown to the Auctioneers, without a satisfactory reference or Banker's guarantee.

4. The lots are at the risk of the Purchaser at the fall of the hammer, and shall be taken away (with all defects, faults and errors of description) at the buyer's expense within three weeks of the Sale and the Purchase-money must be paid on or before delivery. As the whole is on view, the Purchaser is presumed to have examined and have full knowledge of the Lots, therefore no warranty is given or to be implied by the description in this Catalogue

5. To avoid mistakes, No Lot must on any account whatever be taken away, unless delivered by the person appointed for that purpose; and on no account, will the transferring of any Lot or Lots be allowed; and no Purchaser shall be entitled to remove one or a portion of a Lot until the whole of his lots are paid for in cash.

Lastly. Upon failure of complying with the above conditions the money so deposited in part payment shall be forfeited, and if not cleared within the time specified shall be re-sold by public or private sale, and the deficiency (if any) together with all charges attending the same, shall be made good by the original defaulter at this auction. The Auctioneers, while taking every reasonable care to respect the respective lots after they are sold, do not hold themselves responsible for any loss or damage that may arise to any such lot or lots after the fall of the hammer, the purchaser taking all risk.

SPECIAL CONDITIONS OF SALE

1. **Sleepers** – The sleepers will be sold in lots as catalogued at per sleeper and will be graded as follows:-

    Grade 2, fit for contractors.
    Grade 3, fit for fences, roadways etc.

Some stacks of sleepers contain more than 50 but they will be sold as lotted and delivered as they arise from the stack.

2. **Rails** – The rails are heaped in large stacks and will be sold in lots as catalogued by the yard run. They will be delivered by the vendor's employees as they arise from the various stacks.

3. All lots must be cleared away within three weeks from the day of the sale.

4. The lots are on view for 3 days prior to the sale, at the various halts and stations.

As the whole of the sale will take place at the Selsey-on-Sea Terminus station, **intending purchasers must view the goods prior to the sale** and the Auctioneers cannot entertain any dispute which may arise owing to the failure of purchasers to do so.

CATALOGUE
AT CHICHESTER STATION

Lot:
1. Galvanised water tank, about 250 gallons, together with timber framing supporting same and galvanised barrel pipe
2. A notice board, 12ft 3ins by 1ft 10ins on 4 in. by 4in posts
3. About 150ft run of post and rail fencing as fixed to platform
4. The brick supporting wall to platform with blue Stafford brick coping, about 3 ft deep, about 59 yards run
5. Two old iron-frame platform seats
6. The corrugated iron and timber **Station Building**, with canopy in 2 compartments, lined match-boarding, fitted with seats and cupboard. Size 26ft by 10ft 9in, plus corrugated screen to urinal
7. Fifty sleepers (grade 3)
8. Twenty ditto (ditto)
9. Quantity of sleepers (firewood)
10. Ditto   (ditto)
11. Ditto   (ditto)
12. The telegraph poles and wire as standing in the station yard
13.
14.
15.

AT HUNSTON STATION
16. Two iron water tanks, each 4ft by 4ft by 4ft 6ins, with timber framing and galvanized water barrel and part of water pump
17. About 32 yards of timber lattice fencing and sign board
18. The galvanized iron and timber station building, lined matchboarding, in 2 compartments, fitted cupboard, shelves and seats, with canopy. Size 20ft by 9ft 9ins.
19. The Stafford blue brick platform coping, about 40 yards run
20. Twenty-five sleepers (grade 3)
21. Fifty ditto (ditto ½ round)
22. Firewood (written by hand)
23. 38 sleepers forming shed (written by hand)

AT CHALDER STATION
24. About 33 yards of timber lattice fencing and sign board
25. The Staffordshire blue brick platform coping, about 38 yards
26. The corrugated iron and timber station building of 2 compartments, lined matchboarding, with canopy, fitted cupboards and seats, about 20ft by 9ft 6ins
27.

AT MILL POND HALT
28. The timber platform staging and supports, about 16yds by 2yds, 7 sleepers and the Timber rail fencing
29. Timber-built span roof shed about 7ft 6ins by 4ft and a 9ft iron frame platform seat[2]
30.

AT SIDLESHAM STATION
31. Three telegraph poles, about 8ft long by 8in diameter
32. Four ditto, about 8ft long by 5in diameter
33. Five ditto, about 8ft long by 4in diameter
34. Fifty sleepers (grade 3)
35. Fifty ditto   (ditto)
36. Fifty ditto   (ditto)
37. Fifty ditto   (ditto)
38. Fifty ditto   (ditto)
39. Fifty ditto   (ditto)
40. Fifty ditto   (ditto)
41. Fifty sleepers (grade 3, ½ round)
42. Fifty sleepers (ditto)
43. Fifty ditto (grade 2)
44. Fifty ditto (ditto)
45. Fifty ditto (ditto)
46. Quantity of firewood
47. Ditto
48. Ditto
49. 50 Sleepers Half Round (Grade 3) (written by hand)
50. Ditto (written by hand)
51. 200yds of contractor's F. B. Rails, about 56lbs per yard section[3]
52. Ditto
53. Ditto
54. Ditto
55. Ditto
56. Ditto
57. 200yds of contractor's F.B. Rail, about 40lbs per yard section[4]
58. Ditto
59. Ditto

60. Ditto
61. 100 fish plates, at each
62. 100 ditto
63. 100 ditto
64. 100 ditto
65. The corrugated iron and timber station building, lined matchboarding, 2 compartments with canopy and fitted shelving, cupboard and seats. Size 20ft by 9ft 9ins
66. 50 sleepers (grade 3) (written by hand)
67. Ditto   (ditto)   (ditto)
68. Ditto   (ditto)   (ditto)
68A. 16 sleepers & supports for platform and fencing as fixed (written by hand)

AT FERRY STATION

69. Stack of useful timber
70. Three telegraph poles, about 18ft by 10in diameter
71. Three ditto, about 18ft by 8in diameter
72. Three ditto, about 18ft long by 6in diameter
73. Three ditto, about 18ft by 5in diameter
74. Corrugated iron and timber hut on timber supports
75. 50 sleepers (grade 2)
76. 50 ditto   (ditto)
77. Fifty ditto   (ditto)
78. Fifty ditto   (ditto)
79. Fifty ditto   (ditto)
80. Fifty ditto   (ditto)
81. Fifty ditto (grade 3)
82. Fifty ditto   (ditto)
83. Fifty ditto   (ditto)
84. Fifty ditto   (ditto)
85. Fifty ditto   (ditto)
86. Fifty ditto   (ditto)
87. Fifty ditto   (ditto)
88. Fifty ditto   (ditto)
89. Fifty ditto   (ditto)
90. Fifty ditto   (ditto)
91. Fifty ditto   (ditto, ½ round)
92. Fifty ditto   (ditto)
93. Fifty ditto   (ditto)
94. Fifty ditto   (ditto)
95. Fifty ditto   (ditto)
96. Fifty ditto   (ditto)
97. Fifty ditto   (ditto)
98. Fifty ditto   (ditto)
99. Quantity of partly burnt sleepers (written by hand: 190)
100. Ditto (written by hand: 32)
101. 100 sleepers (grade 3) (written by hand)
102. Ditto   (ditto)   (written by hand)
103. 200yds of contractor's F. B. rails, about 56lbs per yard section
104. Ditto
105. Ditto
106. Ditto
107. Ditto
108. 200yds of Contractor's F. B. rails, about 40lbs per yard section
109. Ditto
110. Ditto
111. Ditto
112. Ditto
113. Ditto
114. Ditto
115. Ditto
116. Ditto
117. Ditto
118. Ditto
119. Ditto
120. Ditto
121. Ditto
122. 100 fish plates, at each
123. Ditto
124. Ditto
125. Ditto
126. Ditto
127. Ditto
128. Ditto
129. Ditto (written by hand)
130.
131.
132.
133.
134.

AT GOLF CLUB HALT

135. Fifty sleepers (grade 3)
136. Fifty ditto   (ditto)
137. Fifty ditto   (ditto)
138. Fifty sleepers (Grade 3)
139. Fifty ditto   (ditto)
140. Forty-five ditto (ditto)
141. Fifty-seven ditto (ditto, ½ round)
142. Fifty-seven ditto (ditto)
143. Quantity of firewood
144. Four telegraph poles, various
145. 200yds of contractor's F. B. Rails, about 50lbs per yard section
146. Ditto
147. Ditto
148. Ditto
149. 200yds ditto, about 40lbs per yard section
150. Ditto
151. Ditto
152. Ditto
153. Ditto
154. Ditto
155.
156.
157. 100 fishplates at each
158. Ditto
159.
160
161.

AT SELSEY BRIDGE HALT AND BRICKWORKS

162. A framed notice board, 12ft by 3ft
163. Heap of firewood
164. Ditto
165. Two telegraph poles, various
166. Fifty sleepers (grade 3)
167. Twenty-six ditto (ditto)
168. Fifty ditto (ditto ½ round)
169. Fifty ditto (ditto)
170. Forty ditto (ditto)
171. 200yds of F. B. contractor's rails, about 40lbs per yard section
172. 150yds   (ditto)
173. Four lengths of 3in shafting and couplings (about 70ft run)
174. **Twin cylinder portable engine**, by *Clayton and Shuttleworth*, cylinders about 14in, with heavy flywheel, pulley and fire bars
175. Iron feed tank, 4ft by 3ft by 3ft
176. Horse roller
177. (something illegible written by hand)
178.
179.
180.

AT SELSEY STATION

181. Corrugated iron and timber **Station Building**, comprising General and Ladies' Waiting Rooms, with W.C., and inner and outer offices, lined matchboarding with canopy and fitted fireplace, range of cupboards and shelves and seats; size 42ft by 16ft and the lean-to corrugated store shed and urinal adjoining

Contents of above:-

182. Mahogany extending table with 2 extra leaves, 5ft 9ins by 5ft 9ins
183. Small deal kitchen table
184. Two birch office chairs

185. Two ditto
186. Painted nest of 5 drawers with cupboard under, 3ft 3ins wide
187. Painted nest of 6 drawers, 2ft 3ins wide
188. **4ft oak roll-top desk**, fitted 8 drawers
189. Iron letter press and stand, 4 stationery packs and 6 letter baskets
190. **Iron fireproof safe** by *G. Withers*, 22ins by 21ins by 30ins
191. Linoleum as laid, spark guard, iron kerb and sundries
192. Quantity of sundries
193. Salters' 56lb spring balance
194. Ditto
195. Three railway engine lanterns
196. Three ditto
196A. (Written by hand: Sundry Office supplies)
197. Three porters' hand lamps
198. Deck chair, stationery rack, letter basket and sundries
199. **Doyle's platform weighing machine**, for 4-cwts and weights
200. **Avery's ditto**, for 4-cwts and weights
201. 10ft iron-frame platform seat and another, and timber and lattice fencing as fixed to platform.
202. Earthenware water sluice by Doulton
203. Ditto
204. Ditto
205. Two telephone sets and a 16 cell battery
206. Two fire extinguishers
207. Sundry gas fittings
208. (something illegible, written by hand)
209. (something illegible, written by hand)
210. (something illegible, written by hand)
211. Corrugated iron and timber **stores building**, about 20ft by 12ft

   Contents of above:

212. New 25in 'Interwoven' range with fittings
213. Pair of iron rope blocks
214. New 5in iron pulley and wheel, 15in diameter
215. Quantity of bolts and fittings
216. Set of smith's bellows
217. Three new 8ft galvanised iron sheets
218. Sixteen lengths of 4ft asbestos guttering
219. Ten hair-stuffed carriage cushions
220. Quantity of galvanized nails
221. Coil of galvanized wire and 2 parts ditto
222. Two rolls of barbed wire and part roll ditto
223. Sundry tools (shovels, picks, etc.)
224. Ditto
225. Ditto
226. Two iron rail benders
227. **Well's flair light plant**, No.3 and fittings
228. Six new 4in by 4in oak gate posts
229. Ditto
230. Ditto
231. About 50ft by 1½in piping, new
232. Sundry notice boards
233. Case of earthenware jars
234. Gas cooking stove
235. Sack truck
236. Ditto
237. Wagon sheet (written by hand)
238. Staffordshire blue brick coping to platform, about 70 yards run
239. Corrugated iron and timber watchman's hut
240. **'Bowser' petrol pump** and storage tank, with about 80 gallons of petrol
241. Quantity boiler nuts (written by hand)
242. Quantity boiler washers (written by hand)
243. Corrugated iron and timber frame span roof **engine shed**, about 90ft by 30ft

   Contents of same:-

244. About 20ft of 1½in shafting with 4 pulleys, and 3 brackets and short length of shafting with fast and loose pulleys and five ballata belts, various lengths.
245. **6in centre treadle lathe**, 5ft gap bed
246. **4ft centre ditto**, 4ft bed
247. **Power drilling machine**, by Eliza Tinsley
249. (*sic*) Smith's anvil and block
249. Smith's hearth and fan
250. Portable ditto by *Linley, Linacre and Co.*
251. Bench drilling machine
252. Iron stocks and dies
253. Screw traversing jack, about 10 tons capacity
254. Ditto, 4 tons[5]
255. Ratchet brace and drill post
256. Ditto and tube expander
257. Useful bolts and nuts
258. Ditto
259. Ditto
260. Hand grindstone in iron frame
261. Bench drilling machine
262. Quantity of armoured hose pipe
263. Quantity of waste
264. Small emery wheel in iron frame
265. Two coils of engine packing
266. Quantity of asbestos and sheet ditto
267. Salters' 200lb spring balance
268. Useful spanners
269. Engineer's fittings and tools
270. Rotary pump No.0
271. Three balks of timber and door
272. Quantity of 2in piping
273. Iron stocks and dies
274. Ditto
275. Sundries (written by hand)
276. Iron water tank, about 10ft by 7ft by 3ft, about gallons capacity, on timber framing with overflow pipe.[6]
277. Railway van body
278. Ditto
279. Ditto
280. Ditto
281. Ditto (damaged)
282. Two glass and timber saloon carriage tops
283. Three old van bodies and a passenger ditto[7]
284. Heap of steam coal, about 5 tons
285. A timber erection forming a lifting gantry
286. Stack of firewood
287. Ditto
288. Ditto
289. Ditto
290. Ditto
291. Ditto
292. Useful timber
293. Ditto
294. Ditto
295. Ditto
296. Ditto
297. Ditto
298. Fifty sleepers (grade 3)
299. Fifty ditto   (ditto)
300. Fifty ditto   (ditto)
301. Fifty ditto   (ditto)
302. Quantity of spares (written by hand)
303. Force Pump (written by hand)
304. Quantity of various pumps (written by hand)
305. 200yds of contractors' rails, about 40lbs per yard section
306. Ditto
307. Ditto
308. Ditto
309. Ditto
310. 100 fish plate bolts ⅞in by 4½in
311. 100 ditto
312. 100 ditto
313. 100 ditto
314. 100 ditto
315. 100 ditto
316. 100 ditto
317. 100 ditto

183

318. 100 ditto
319. 100 ditto
320. Quantity Iron sheets (written by hand)
321. (something illegible, written by hand)
322. (something illegible, written by hand)

LOCOMOTIVES
323. 'Morous', 3-wheel coupled, approx. 12in cylinders
324. 'Selsey', 2-wheel coupled, approx. 10in cylinders with copper firebox by *Peckers* (*sic*)

END OF SALE
Added in handwriting on a further sheet of paper were the following:

325. Quantity of seats (Damaged)
326. 3 Doors
327. 2 Benches
328. Sundry oak
329. Ditto Tools
330. Pr. Heavy Spring (new)
331. Qty. firewood
332. Qty. Sundries
333. Qty. Fencing Wire
334. Ditto
335. length 1½in pipe
336. Luggage Bogey (*sic*)

Notes
1. The descriptions of the Lots has been reproduced here as per the original catalogue.
2. In the several descriptions of the Tramway, there has been no mention of a building at Mill Pond Halt.
3. A programme of installing 56lb rails, mainly on curves, began within a year of the opening of the Tramway.
4. The rails described here as about 40lbs per yard section are the originals which weighed 41¼lbs in 1897. The Southern Railway in its Report of 1934 doubted whether the rails would weigh 36lbs as they were so worn.
5. One of these jacks is now on display at the Colonel Stephens' Museum, Tenterden.
6. The actual tank capacity was left blank.
7. On the original catalogue, 'Three' has been crossed out and replaced with '1'.

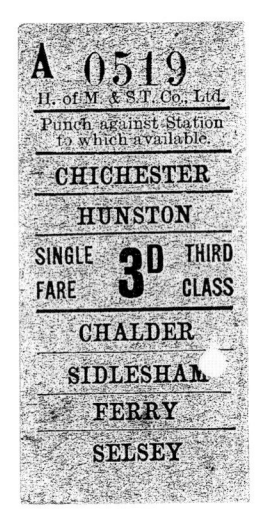

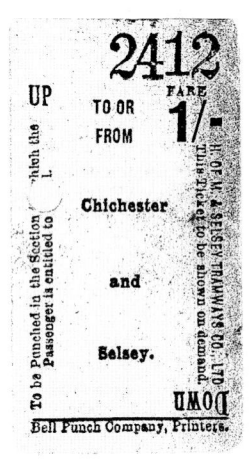

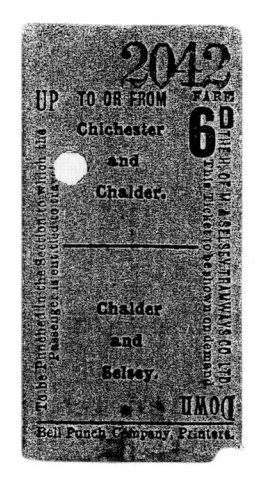

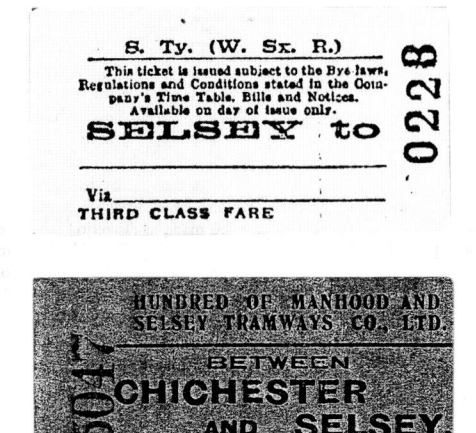

Tickets issued after 1st January 1917.   COLLECTION G. R. CROUGHTON

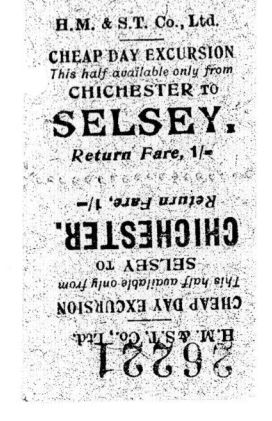

APPENDIX FIVE
GOODS & PARCELS RATES

It wasn't until mid-November 1897 that goods facilities were made available on the Selsey Tramway, the charges being as hereunder

FROM	To CHICHESTER Station			To HUNSTON Station			To CHALDER Station, Church Lane & Hoe Farm			To SIDLESHAM Station			To SELSEY Station		
	1 per ton s.d.	2 per ton s.d.	3 per ton s.d.	1 per ton s.d.	2 per ton s.d.	3 per ton s.d.	1 per ton s.d.	2 per ton s.d.	3 per ton s.d.	1 per ton s.d.	2 per ton s.d.	3 per ton s.d.	1 per ton s.d.	2 per ton s.d.	3 per ton s.d.
CHICHESTER	...	...	...	10	13	16	13	16	20	19	20	26	26	29	30
HUNSTON	10	13	16	...	...	...	10	13	16	13	16	20	19	20	26
CHALDER Church Lane Hoe Farm	13	16	20	10	13	16	...	...	...	10	13	16	16	19	23
SIDLESHAM	19	20	26	13	16	20	10	13	16	...	...	...	13	16	20
FERRY	20	23	29	16	19	23	13	16	19	10	13	16	10	13	16
SELSEY	26	29	30	19	20	26	16	19	23	13	16	20	...	...	...

Special Scale of Minimum Charges applicable to Consignment of Goods in Class 3, in less than 1 ton Lots. Charges are Station to Station.

RATE NOT EXCEEDING	WEIGHT NOT EXCEEDING							
	1 qr.	2qrs.	3qrs.	1 cwt.	2cwt.	3cwt.	5cwt.	10cwt.	15cwt.
1s.9d. PER TON	2d.	3d.	3d.	4d.	6d.	7d.	8d.	1s.	1s.6d.
2s. 6d. PER TON	3d.	4d.	4d.	5d.	7d.	8d.	10d.	1s.	2s.
3s. 0d. PER TON	4d.	5d.	6d.	7d.	9d.	1d.	1s.	2s.	2s. 6d.

Class 1. Applicable to consignments of Mineral Traffic, Coal, Bricks, Chalk, Cement, Lime, Ashes, Stone, Oil Cake, Corn, Manure, Roots, and other Articles classified as 'A', 'B', or 'C' traffic in the General Railway Classification of Goods by Merchandise Trains, excepting articles especially mentioned below in Class 3, in quantities of not less than four tons per truck.

Class 2. Applicable to consignments of the description set forth under Class 1 in less quantities than four tons per truck but not less than two tons per truck.

Class 3. Applicable to consignments in not less than 1 ton lots of Timber, Vegetables, Chaff, Hay, Straw, and all other traffic (including Class 2 Traffic in lots less than 2 tons per truck), excepting as mentioned in Regulations Nos. 13 & 14 of the General Railway Classification of Goods, which articles will be carried by special arrangement only. See special scale of minimum charges for Class 3 Traffic in less than 1 ton lots.

NOTE:- 400 Common Bricks will be charged as 1 ton
10 Sacks of Wheat will be charged as 1 ton
10 Sacks of Barley will be charged as 1 ton
15 Sacks of Oats will be charged as 1ton

Cattle, per head 1/-. Eight or more in one truck, 7/6d. per truck, Minimum Charge 4/- per truck.
Sheep and **Pigs**, per head 3d. thirty or more in one truck, 7/6d. per truck. Minimum charge 3/6d. per truck.
Returned Empty Cases, Crates etc. 2d. each.
Returned Empty Beer Casks, Kilderkins, and larger barrels, 2d. each. Firkins and smaller barrels 1d. each.
Empty Grain Sacks or Bags (sent to be filled for conveyance by the Tramway Coy, or returned empty after conveyance) Free.

All rates are for haulage only, and do not include labour.

The Selsey Tramways Company will upon due notice being given, procure from the L.B. & S.C. Railway and place at the most suitable Station or Siding along their line, any Trucks required for traffic in quantities of not less than one ton intended for transit over the L.B. & S.C. Rly's system; and Truck loads of goods put on at any of the L.B. & S.C. Rly. Company's Stations and consigned to Stations or Sidings on the Selsey Tramway will be hauled from Chichester to their destination.

PARCELS RATES

The Rates for conveyance of parcels between any pair of Stations on the Selsey Tramways are as follows:

Under 14lbs.	Under 28lbs.	Under 56lbs.	Under 112lbs.
2d. each	4d. each	6d. each	8d. each

Rates are exclusive of collection and delivery.

Senders are requested to insert under the address of parcels sent to Selsey, either 'Wait till called for' or 'To be delivered.' In the absence of any instructions the parcels will be sent out for delivery in the usual way.

Rates for Collection or Delivery at Selsey.
Within the ordinary limits.

Parcels up to 28lbs .... 2d. each
Parcels from 28lbs. to 56lbs .... 3d. each
Parcels from 56lbs.to 112lbs .... 4d. each
Parcels from 112lbs. to 224lbs .... 6d. each

Consignments from 2 cwts. to 1 ton (inclusive) .... 3/- per ton.
Truck loads from 1 ton to 2 tons (inclusive) .... 2/6 per ton.
Truck loads from 2 tons to 4 tons (inclusive) .... 2/3 per ton.
Truck loads above 4 tons (inclusive) .... 2/- per ton.

Minimum charge above 1 cwt., 6d.

When Ferry Siding opened on 1st August 1898 the goods rates to and from there were set as per the following table:

FROM	To CHICHESTER Station			To HUNSTON Station			To CHALDER Station, Church Lane & Hoe Farm			To SIDLESHAM Station			To SELSEY Station		
	1 per ton s.d.	2 per ton s.d.	3 per ton s.d.	1 per ton s.d.	2 per ton s.d.	3 per ton s.d.	1 per ton s.d.	2 per ton s.d.	3 per ton s.d.	1 per ton s.d.	2 per ton s.d.	3 per ton s.d.	1 per ton s.d.	2 per ton s.d.	3 per ton s.d.
FERRY SIDING	20	23	29	16	19	23	13	16	19	10	13	16	10	13	16

These rates remained in force until the subject came up for discussion at the Board Meeting held at 1 Church Court, Clement's Lane, London, EC4 on Thursday, 8th May 1919. After discussion, it was decided that 'as the expenses of the Company were rising so rapidly, the Rates and charges must be advanced to meet a proportion of the increased costs', and it was resolved that the new Rates and Charges would come into effect on 1st. June 1919. Henry Phillips estimated that these increases would produce £1,000 per year if traffic remained as heavy as it had done in 1918, and an increase of £600 per annum could reasonably be expected. The Minutes recorded:

Parcels Rates: Parcels Rates to be 4d. for each parcel under 14lbs.
8d. for each parcel under 28lbs.
1/- for each parcel under 56lbs.
1/4 for each parcel under 112lbs.

Goods Traffic Rates: the Goods Rates to be in four classes, and between Selsey and Chichester to be:

Class 1   2/9d. per ton
Class 2   3/4d. per ton
Class 3   5/- per ton
Class 4   7/6d. per ton

The rates between other pairs of stations to be proportionately increased.

Class 1: Applicable to Coal and Minerals generally classified as Class 'A' in the Railway Classification of Goods, 4 ton loads.

Class 2: Applicable to Bricks, Cement, Corn and goods classified as 'B' or 'C' in the Railway Classification of Goods in loads of not less than 2 tons per truck.

Class 3: Applicable to goods classified as Class 1, 2, or 3 in the Railway Classification of Goods in loads of not less than 1 ton per truck.

Class 4: Applicable to goods classified as Class 4 or 5 in the Railway Classification of Goods in loads of not less than 1 ton per truck.

These rates were quickly to prove inadequate to cover the ever-increasing running costs, and the Minute Book at a Board Meeting held at the same venue on 8th January 1920 recorded:

'It was agreed to increase the Goods Rates and the Parcels Rates in accordance with a scale of rates submitted by the Secretary, adjustments to be made at discretion, the rates for goods traffic between Chichester and Selsey being Class 'A' 3/- per ton, Class 'B' 3/4d per ton, Class 'C' 4/6d per ton, Hay and Straw in 2 ton loads 7/- per ton, Class 'D' 9/- per ton, Class 'E' 13/8d per ton, classes 'D' and 'E' being subject to special scale of minimum charges. The rates for parcels by passenger train between any pair of stations to be: Under 7lbs 4d each, 14lbs 6d each, 28lbs 8d each, 42lbs 1/- each, 56lbs 1/4d each, 84lbs 1/8d each, 112lbs 2/- each.

The increased rates came into effect one week later on Thursday, 15th January 1920, but perhaps too much business was being lost as the secretary suggested at a meeting of the Board seven weeks later on 4th March that 'it would likely be policy at a little later date to slightly modify by a reduction of the new figures affecting the small goods scale.' With no further mentions on the subject in the Directors' Minute Book, it is not clear whether this reduction was made or not.

APPENDIX SIX
PULLMAN CARS KNOWN TO HAVE TRAVELLED OVER THE SELSEY TRAMWAY

This advertisement appeared in the 30th May 1923 edition of the *Chichester Observer*:

PREPARE FOR THE SUMMER

RAIL COACHES

SUITABLE FOR BUNGALOWS

5 COMPARTMENT 3RD CLASS...... £25 EACH
4 COMPARTMENT COMPOSITE ....£27 EACH

DELIVERED ON SITE
PLOTS OF LAND SUITABLE FOR ABOVE FOR SALE
APPLY 4 WESTGATE, CHICHESTER

Over the following 11½ years, a good number of these carriages would be hauled by the Tramways Company's locomotives in special trains down to Selsey. On the goods loop a timber gantry was erected where, under the supervision of a Southern Railway carriage and wagon examiner, the bodies would be separated from their underframes and with their wheels, would be returned to the Southern Railway at Chichester. The bodies were hauled by Mr. H. Prior's horse-drawn vehicles to their final resting places to become inexpensive housing, or holiday accommodation near the beach. Along with less glamorous rolling stock, at least eleven Pullman carriages made the single journey south down the Tramway and, in varying condition, several of these remain in use to this day.

Date Built	S.E.R. no.	Sold to Pullman	Rebuilt	Name (After rebuild)	Withdrawn
-.8.1876	-	-	-	Ariel	31.12.1929[1]
-.12.1888	-	-	-.-.1915	Albert Victor	31.12.1929[2]
31.12.1891	35	-	-	Dolphin	-
31.12.1891	47	4.1.1919	28.4.1920	Figaro	1.6.1930
29.9.1897	201	4.1.1919	5.12.1919	Hilda	1.6.1930
29.9.1897	202	4.1.1919	5.12.1919	Dora	1.6.1930
29.9.1897	203	4.1.1919	5.12.1919	Mabel	1.6.1930
29.9.1897	205	4.1.1919	27.3.1919	Dorothy	1.6.1930[3]
29.9.1897	206	4.1.1919	18.11.1919	Venus (11)	-.11.1929
11.10.1897	171	4.1.1919	27.3.1919	Tulip	1.6.1930
-.8.1906	-	-	-	Princess Ena	-.6.1932

Notes
1. Originally named *Louise* in 1881.
2. Lost to redevelopment in the 1960s.
3. Lost to redevelopment in the 1980s.

APPENDIX SEVEN
MANUAL STAFF KNOWN TO HAVE WORKED ON THE SELSEY TRAMWAY

Ray Apps was a locomotive fireman by 1920 and he remained in this position until the Tramway closed in 1935, having the distinction of firing on the last Tram. He later went on to work as a signalman at Chichester with the Southern Railway.

Herbert Barnes, known as 'Dirg', was working for the Tramway by 1908 as a conductor/guard, but he left the Company at some time during the early 1920s. He returned in the Spring of 1923 as a fireman, only to lose his life in the derailment near Golf Club Halt on 3.9.1923.

George Belcher – locomotive driver in the 1920s.

J. L. Belcher probably took up his position as a fitter when the Tramway opened in 1897. After 19 years' loyal service, he left to take up a similar post with the Southwold Railway in Suffolk which, unfortunately for him, was to be one of the first independent railways to surrender to road competition in April 1929. Mr. Belcher was instrumental in trying to reopen that line by converting it to standard gauge, but with a rival attempt to retain its 3ft gauge by Mr. Ronald Shepherd only dividing support, by October 1930 both schemes had come to nought.[1]

J. Boyling was a locomotive fireman who was promoted to spare driver in 1920.

John Bratley was employed as a fitter from the late 1920s.

S. Colins – position unknown.

Mr. Cosens – a lengthsman in the 1920s.

William (Bill) Crees joined the Company in 1927 straight from school at the age of 14, where he was employed as assistant to the superintendent at Selsey station, Mr. A. W. Smith. Later he became a conductor/guard on the railmotors where there was a chance of being able to supplement his meagre wage of ten shillings per week with tips from some of the wealthier passengers. He left the Company in 1929.[2]

Harry Davies was employed as a locomotive driver and fitter from the 1920s and with Ray Apps as fireman, he drove the last steam train on 24th January 1935.

Charlie Fullick was a conductor/guard in the early 1930s who was known as 'Constantinople' as he was always singing that song. It was said that he didn't need a warning flag to wave a railmotor across the level crossings as his face was so red with embarrassment![3]

A. Gilbert – locomotive fireman in the early 1900s.

Henry Albert Goff – probably employed by the Tramway Company from the opening of the Tramway in August 1897. His position is unknown.

George Gray, an ex-Tank Corps driver and mechanic, was responsible for keeping the railmotors operational during the Tramway's last years. With the closure of the line, he was transferred to the Kent & East Sussex Railway where he completely stripped down and repaired both engines of their Shefflex railmotor thus enabling the unit to remain in service until the Spring of 1938.[4]

Mr. Hellyer – a lengthsman in the 1920s.

Tim Johnson drove the first train on Opening Day, 27.8.1897 and worked for the Company for over 20 years. He held the speed record for the Tramway, having allegedly driven from Chichester to Selsey on *Sidlesham* in 18 minutes.

Donald W. Jones, known as 'Poor Don', to his colleagues, possibly started working as a conductor/guard in 1897. He died suddenly while still employed by the Company in October 1903, aged just 32.

Edward Leech was working for the Tramway Company in January 1898, but his occupation is unknown.

J. Norris – position unknown.

Arthur Pennycord commenced working for the Tramway Company in 1917 as a boy porter at Selsey and between 1924 and 1926 he drove the Railmotors.

Stanley Richards was employed first as an office boy at Selsey and then as a locomotive fireman during the First World War.

Alf Robinson spent two years on the Tramway in the early 1930s, for the first twelve months looking after passengers' luggage, and then as a conductor/guard on the railmotors where, like Bill Creese before him, he could earn extra money from passengers' gratuities. On one occasion, when there was no stoker available, he spent the day as a fireman on one of the steam locomotives.[5]

Edward 'Teddy' Skinner worked as a ganger from the cutting of the first sod until Holman Stephens persuaded him to transfer to The Ashover Light Railway in August 1924. He remained with that Light Railway until retirement in December 1945, but he passed away just eleven months later.[6] The Colonel seems to have had a soft spot for Mr. Skinner because, on hearing that he was about to have a new set of dentures fitted, he wrote to him on 8th June 1920 saying: 'I enclose cheque £2/0/0 for teeth as promised. I hope they will be a success.'

H. J. Smith commenced his employment as a locomotive fireman, but by 1920 he occasionally worked as a conductor/guard. In May of that year he returned to his previous post of fireman.

Mr Sprouce – a lengthsman in the 1920s.

Charles Currie Stewart was the driver of the train that was derailed near Golf Club Halt on 3.9.1923. He had joined the Company in July that year, but it is not known how long he stayed after the accident.

William Symes had joined the Company as the Foreman Platelayer on the southern section of Tramway between Chalder and Selsey on 15.8.1923, having previously worked for the Great Western Railway for 20 years. Again, it is not known if he continued to work for the Tramway following the fatal derailment on 3.9.1923.

Jack Terry – locomotive fireman in the first decade of the 1900s.

Mr Wackford – a lengthsman in the 1920s.

William Walker was a Conductor/guard employed by the Tramway Company from 1903 until 1924.

Mr Warwick (senior) – employed to maintain the newly introduced Wolseley Siddeley and Ford railmotors, no easy task with instructions being given to keep expenses down to a minimum. Herbert, his son said that the only time he heard his father swear was whilst he was underneath the temperamental machines attempting to carry out running repairs.

Herbert ('Herby') Warwick followed his father onto the Tramway as a railmotor driver, commencing in 1924 at the age of 16. He had been hurriedly taken on after Mr. Eckford (the Superintendent) had sacked the previous driver in a fit of temper. On the last trip from Chichester on a Tuesday and Thursday evening, Mr. Warwick and his conductor/guard would make all the passengers get into the rear unit so that they could each in turn change their clothes in readiness to go to the dance hall in Selsey. He was later able to boast that he was the only railmotor driver who never came off the rails. When asked how he managed it, he replied that he went so fast that the railmotor never had time to come off![7] Mr. Warwick left the Company in 1926 to start his own taxi business in competition with the Tram. Holman Stephens had visited the family's home in Manor Road, Selsey on several occasions and considered Mr. Warwick's action to be one of betrayal, so was it just coincidence that one day he found his taxi jacked up off its wheels? He did not run his taxi for long, and from 1930 until the 1970s he drove 'buses for the Tramway Company's main competitor, Southdown Motor Services Ltd.

George White – locomotive driver, but his dates of service are not known.

Ted Withall was a Platelayer on the northern section of the Tramway between Chalder and Chichester from 1920 until 1935. His responsibilities included the raising and lowering of the bridge over the canal north of Hunston while it was operable.

Sometimes, Holman Stephens moved staff between his several railways, **Jim Smith** and **Dick Cash** having come down to the Selsey Tramway from the East Kent Light Railways in 1926 to work on the carriages. Surprisingly only classed as 'a temporary staff member', despite working for the Company for no less than 15 years, **Charlie Turner** was similarly sent down to Selsey from The Kent & East Sussex Railway for a short while in 1928 'to help out with repairs to their steam stock'.[8]

Notes
1. *The Southwold Railway* by Alan Taylor and Eric S. Tonks, published by Ian Allan, Ltd, 1989.
2. Taken from an interview with Bill Crees, featured in *The Selsey Tramway, 1897–1935* video, released by Magic Box Productions, 1997.
3. *Going off the Rails, the Country Railway in West Sussex* by Bill Gage, Michael Harris and Tony Sullivan, published by West Sussex County Council, 1997.
4. From an article in *The Tenterden Terrier* No. 68, Winter 1995, by Monty Baker entitled 'The Shefflex Set'.
5. From the video *The Selsey Tramway, 1897-1935* as above.
6. *The Ashover Light Railway* by Robert Gratton and Stuart R. Band, published by Wild Swan Publications Ltd., 1989.
7. From a letter sent by Herbert Warwick to Philip Shaw (editor of *The Tenterden Terrier*) in 1976.
8. From a letter published in *The Tenterden Terrier* No. 69, Spring 1996 from M. C. Turner, Charlie Turner's son.

BIBLIOGRAPHY

BOOKS:

The Ashover Light Railway by Robert Gratton and Stuart R. Band, published by Wild Swan Publications Ltd., 1989. ISBN 0 906867 72 X.

Branch Line to Selsey by Vic Mitchell & Keith Smith, published by Middleton Press, 1983, ISBN 0 906520 04 5.

Callington Railways by Roger Crombleholme, Brian Gibson, Douglas Stuckley and C. F. D. Whetmath, published by Forge Books, 1985.

Colonel Stephens Railmotors by Stephen Garratt & John Scott-Morgan, published by Irwell Press, 1995. ISBN 1-871608-46-5.

The Colonel Stephens Railways – A Pictorial Survey by John Scott-Morgan, published by Book Club Associates by arrangement with David & Charles Publishers plc, 1978.

The Colonel Stephens Railways – A View from the Past by John Scott-Morgan, published by Ian Allan Publishing, 1999. ISBN 0 7110 2628 9.

A History of Selsey by Frances Mee, published by Phillimore & Co. Ltd., 1988. ISBN 0 85033 672 4.

Going off the Rails – the Country Railway in West Sussex by Bill Gage, Michael Harris & Tony Sullivan, published by West Sussex County Council, 1997. ISBN 0 8626 0400 1.

A History of Sussex by J. R. Armstrong, published by Phillimore & Co. Ltd., 1974. ISBN 0 85033 316 4.

The Hundred of Manhood & Selsey Tramway, later known as the West Sussex Railway, 1897–1935 by Edward C. Griffith, 1st & 2nd editions, published by the author 1948 and 1968.

The Kent & East Sussex Railway by Stephen Garrett, third edition, published by the Oakwood Press, 1999. ISBN 0 85361 516 0.

The King's England – Sussex by Arthur Mee, first published by Hodder and Stoughton 1937.

The Lambourn Branch by Kevin Robertson & Roger Simmonds, published by Wild Swan Publications Ltd., 1984. ISBN 0 906867 24 X.

Light Railway Layout Designs by Iain Rice, published by Wild Swan Publications Ltd., 1991. ISBN 0 906867 94 0.

Minor Railways of England & their Locomotives 1900–1939 by George Woodcock, published by Goose & Sons, Norwich. ISBN 900404 06 X.

Railways of Arcadia by John Scott-Morgan, published by P. E. Waters & Associates, 1989, ISBN 0 948904 50 X.

The Railways of Southern England; Independent and Light Railways by Edwin Course, published by B. T. Batsford Ltd., 1976. ISBN 0 7134 3196 2.

The Rye & Camber Tramway – A Centenary History by Laurie A. Cooksey, published by Plateway Press, 1995. ISBN 1-871980-26-7.

The Selsey Tram by David Bathurst, published by Phillimore & Co. Ltd., 1992. ISBN 0 85033 839 5.

The Selsey Tramways by Edward C. Griffith, published by the author, 1974.

The Shropshire & Montgomeryshire Railway by Eric S. Tonks, published by The Industrial Railway Society, 1972.

Southdown, Volume 2 – The Details by Colin Morris, published by Venture Publications, December 1994. ISBN 1 898432 10 4.

The Southdown Story 1915–1965 published by Southdown Motor Services, Ltd., 1965.

The Southwold Railway by Alan R. Taylor and Eric S. Tonks, published by Ian Allan Ltd., 1979. ISBN 0 7110 0952 X.

MAGAZINES:

The Colonel, (various editions) the journal of The Colonel Stephens' Society.

Industrial Railway Record, No. 176, March 2004, 'Railway Foundry Ramblings' by Trevor Lodge.

The Locomotive, 15th February 1909 and 15th March 1909, 'The Selsey Tramway' and 15th February 1928, 'Shefflex Railcar, West Sussex Railway'.

The Marshlander, summer 1985, journal of the Romney, Hythe & Dymchurch Railway, 'The Search for a Site'.

Model Railway Journal, No. 12, 1987, 'Morous and Friends' by Don Townsley.

The Morris Owner, September 1925, 'Selsey in Sussex' by Galway Power.

Old Motor, Volume 9, No. 5.

The Railway Magazine, April 1898, 'A Trip on the H. of M. and S.T.' by Victor L. Whitechurch, April 1935, 'The West Sussex Railway' by R. W. Rush, and 'A recent Trip on the West Sussex Railway' by Dr. Hugh Nicol.

Southern Railway Magazine, May 1933, 'Selsey Bill as a Holiday Resort' by J. Elcombe, F.C.I.S., and February 1935, 'Selsey Light Railway Closed'.

Steam World, June 1997, 'The Blackberry Line', by Bill Gage.

The Tenterden Terrier, (various editions) the house journal of the Tenterden Railway Company.

Waterways World, December 1996, 'Raising the Drawbridge' by George Smith.

Yesterday Transport, Summer 1981, 'To Selsey in 1917' by A. B. MacLeod.

ACKNOWLEDGEMENTS

With special thanks (in alphabetical order) to: John Allpress (The Southdown Enthusiasts Club), J. Armstone, Julian Aubanel, Alan Blackburn, Richard Casserley, the staff of Chichester Reference Library (in particular Mrs. J. Peters), Jack Clarke, Leon Coast, Terry Corder, Phil Coutanche, E. W. J. (Ted) Crawforth, Godfrey W. Croughton (for Selsey Tramway tickets), Leslie Darbyshire, Greg Dodsworth, Jeremy Engert (Family History Society), Robin Fielding, Sue Fullwood and Simon Kitchen (Chichester District Museum), Stephen Hannington (past Editor of *The Colonel*, journal of the Colonel Stephens Society), Peter A. Harding, Ralph Hoult, Industrial Railway Society (in particular Cliff Shepherd and Trevor Lodge), Roger Kidner, Robert Kosmider, Alan Lambert (The Southdown Enthusiasts Club), the late Ian Lyle, Frances Mee, Tom Middlemass, E. John R. Miller (Colonel Stephens' Railway Museum and Keeper of Archives, The Kent & East Sussex Railway, Tenterden), the staff of the National Railway Museum, York, Andrew Neale, Richard Newman (Isle of Wight Bus Museum), Malcolm Parker (South Eastern Railway Society), the staff of the Public Record Office, Kew, Kevin Robertson, R. Schofield, Chrissy Sewett, Philip Shaw (Editor of *The Tenterden Terrier*, journal of the Kent & East Sussex Railway), Ross Shimmon (Editor of *The Colonel*, journal of The Colonel Stephens Society), Roger Silsbury, Derek Smith (Marketing Director of The Romney, Hythe & Dymchurch Railway), Graham Stacey (The Locomotive Club of Great Britain), the staff of the West Sussex Record Office, Chichester (in particular Bill Gage, Assistant County Archivist), John Watling, David Woodcock, the staff at Worthing Library (in particular Martin Hayes, Morwenna Peters and Gill Tucker) and Jon Wynne-Tyson.

Stephen Garrett has been most helpful, particularly by putting me onto the right trail to obtain several important documents from the Public Record Office, Kew and David Churchill has been invaluable in sorting out details of the goods rolling stock. Many thanks also go to Brian Janes for reading through and checking my draft for me and coming up with so many useful suggestions and comments. Words are completely inadequate to explain what a great debt I owe to Ron Mann who has not only prepared all of the superb drawings for this book, but has done so much detective work in helping to solve the many idiosyncrasies that come to light when attempting to unravel the true facts behind any of Holman Stephens' small empire of railways.

Lastly, very special thanks must go to my wife, Carol, for putting up with my collection of railway books and magazines, not to mention my model railways, that constantly litter our small flat and to Paul Karau of Wild Swan Publications for having the faith to publish my work for me.

Throughout this book you will see numerous references to *The Colonel* (the Journal of the Colonel Stephens' Society) and without the expert knowledge of several of the members of this Society, this work would never have seen the light of day. The fact that you are reading this suggests that you have an interest in the railways of Holman Fred Stephens and I strongly recommend that you join the Society. Please contact

David Powell (Membership Secretary),
'Gateways',
Bledlow Road,
Saunderton,
PRINCES RISBOROUGH,
Bucks. HP27 9NG,

or The Colonel Stephens Society Website on
www.colonelstephenssociety.org.uk.